THE DUKES OF DURHAM, 1865-1929

THE DUKES OF DURHAM,
1865-1929

Robert F. Durden

1975

DUKE UNIVERSITY PRESS

Durham, N.C.

© 1975, Duke University Press
Sept. 25, 1975
L.C.C. card number 74–83785
I.S.B.N. 0–8223–0330–2

PRINTED IN THE UNITED STATES OF
AMERICA BY HERITAGE PRINTERS, INC.

This book is dedicated to
W. B. H., M. S., and R. L. W.,
three who have loved and
nobly served an institution
that the Dukes befriended.

CONTENTS

ILLUSTRATIONS

PREFACE

This is the history of Washington Duke and two of his sons, Benjamin Newton Duke and James Buchanan Duke. Although numerous other members of the family play their parts in the story, it focuses primarily on the three men who were at the center of the economic and philanthropic activities which made the Dukes of Durham one of America's famous families.

Several years ago my friend and colleague, Frank deVyver, who was then chairman of the committee for the Duke University Press, suggested that the time had come for a scholarly biography of James B. Duke and asked if I would be interested in tackling the project. My immediate reaction was that I would not. Why? Because I suspected then, as I now know, that the Dukes operated closely and constantly as a family and that only in that context could their full story be told fairly and effectively.

In the years after the Civil War, Washington Duke proved to be an unusually able industrialist and a conscientious Methodist philanthropist. He was, in fact, a major Tarheel, even Southern, pioneer in both industry and philanthropy. Because of circumstances explained later in this book, his two sons by a second marriage were remarkably devoted to each other as well as to their father. Both sons also reflected traits of their father. While Benjamin N. Duke and James B. Duke had lifelong involvement with the business world—first in tobacco, then textiles, and finally electric power—as well as with philanthropy, they actually developed complementary specializations. That is, Benjamin N. Duke, the older of the two, served as the family's primary agent for philanthropy from his early manhood in the late 1880's until he gradually became a semi-invalid after 1915. James B. Duke, on the other hand, early displayed a marked talent, even a genius, for business. Toward the end of his life, with the establishment of The Duke Endowment late in 1924, he emerged as one of the nation's major philanthropists, ranking alongside Andrew Carnegie and John D. Rockefeller. A central theme of this book is, however, that The Duke Endowment, despite its magnitude and far-reaching scope, was essentially the institutionalization and culmination of a pattern of family philanthropy that emerged in the 1890's and for which the older brother had always been the primary agent. In other words, the story of James B. Duke, who was and has remained the more well known of the two brothers, cannot be told properly out of the family context from which he emerged and in which occurred most of the important phases of his life.

There are already two biographies of James B. Duke, one by John Wilber Jenkins published in 1927 and the other by John K. Winkler published in 1942. Jenkins' portrait tends toward adulation and Winkler's toward melodrama, and neither study is documented. Vast amounts of rich manuscript materials, largely in the William R. Perkins Library of Duke University and much of which has never been used by historians, are now available. These bibliographical matters are discussed more fully in the note on sources at the end of this volume. Suffice it to say here that ten letterbooks of James B. Duke that have only recently been "rediscovered"; the massive collection of Benjamin N. Duke Papers (which, in part, are really the family's papers); the voluminous papers of Richard H. Wright, an early partner of the Dukes and then their business rival; the papers of John F. Crowell, John C. Kilgo, William P. Few, and Robert L. Flowers—successive presidents of Trinity College and Duke University—all these plus other manuscript sources cast important new light on the Dukes.

The source materials are not complete, however. Because there are too few records for the period prior to the Civil War, I have had to settle for a hasty survey of Washington Duke's life between his birth in 1820 and his return from the war in 1865. Yet, as a small, landowning, yeoman farmer, he was typical of the great majority class not only in antebellum North Carolina but in the South as a whole. Only after the war, when he and his sons emerged as large-scale industrialists and philanthropists, did the Dukes become atypical. Their story is, then, both agricultural and industrial, both Southern and national. Born Tarheels, they moved on to a national, even global, stage. Yet all the while they kept deep roots, as well as vast investments of capital, in the Old North State, and they poured many millions into philanthropy, largely in the two Carolinas.

This book is neither authorized nor in any sense an official study. As a student of American history in the nineteenth and early-twentieth centuries, I undertook to write the book because I was attracted by this family as a subject, because the materials were here and had not been tapped, and because I knew that the academic climate of Duke University, not to mention my professorial tenure, made the writing of valid history, as I saw it, quite feasible—even essential.

This is not to say that innumerable persons, both in and out of Duke University, have not assisted me in many different ways. Frank deVyver not only triggered the whole thing but continued to encourage and aid me at various stages. Paul H. Clyde has helped from an early phase, and the late Thomas L. Perkins facilitated several aspects of my work, as did John Day, John Spuches, and Richard Henney. I am especially grateful to my colleague and longtime office neighbor, William T. Laprade, who came to Trinity College to teach history in 1909 and who has taught me a good many things during the past twenty-two years.

Two friends of mine and well known experts in the history of tobacco, Nannie M. Tilley and Joseph C. Robert, have been generous with their time and most helpful with their suggestions about my manuscript. For assistance of various kinds, including in some cases a close reading of my manuscript, I am also grateful to Jean Anderson, James Gifford, Craufurd Goodwin, Hugh Hall, I. B. Holley, William Jennings, Richard Knapp, Richard Leach, Harold Lewis, Stuart Noblin, Patricia O'Connor, Richard Pierce, Earl Porter, David Ross, and Thomas Terrill.

Jeffrey Crow, Paul Escott, and Larry Nelson, three of my students who have been writing their doctoral dissertations as I labored on this book, have been good library companions as well as sharp-eyed critics. I owe a special thanks to Larry Nelson for his capable research assistance on matters related to the Duke Power Company. Other former students who have assisted me at one time or another over the past several years and whom I thank are Mary Louise Briscoe, Edward Burgess, Bruce Clayton, Patricia Hummer, Heather Low, Linda McCarter, Anne Trotter, and Edie Wolfeskill. Dorothy Sapp typed most of the manuscript and did it with great efficiency and speed that were matched by good humor and kindness.

The library of Duke University has always been a fine place to work, partly because of its extensive holdings but more especially because of the invariable helpfulness and kindness of its staff. Aside from my friends in Reference, I am especially indebted to the director of the Manuscript Department and my good friend, Mattie Russell, and to the members of her staff, David Brown, Paul Chestnut, William

Erwin, and Sharon Knapp. A carrel in the Manuscript Department has been my second home for many months now, and I greatly appreciate the constant courtesy shown me by the entire staff of the Manuscript Department.

William E. King, the Archivist of Duke University, has gone far out of his way to befriend me and this project in various fashions, and I thank him as well as two members of his staff, Marjorie James and Mark Stauter.

William Baxter, a senior in Duke University, skillfully reproduced the photographs and prepared them for the printer. Ashbel Brice and John Menapace of the Duke University Press are old friends from earlier projects, and I appreciate their contributions to this book as well as the editorial talents of William Hicks and Joanne Ferguson.

Outside of my debt of gratitude to Anne Oller Durden and other close friends who have been generous with their interest and encouragement, I am most obliged to the Mary Duke Biddle Foundation for enabling me to stretch a sabbatical semester into a full year's leave, a year during which I finally had the freedom to write this book.

The research for it began more years ago than I care to admit (although there were several unavoidable interruptions), but the Research Council of Duke University stood behind and encouraged the work with great patience. Next to the library, the Research Council is scholarship's best friend at Duke University, and I thank all the members of the Council, especially its chairman, Charles Bradsher, and its secretary, George Williams.

ROBERT F. DURDEN

Perkins Library
Duke University
June, 1974

THE DUKES OF DURHAM, 1865-1929

CHAPTER 1. YEOMAN FARMER HOME FROM THE WAR

Footsore veterans of the Confederate army dotted the Southern landscape in the early summer of 1865. Thus Washington Duke's trek of some 130 miles from New Bern, North Carolina, to his inland home in what was then Orange County was not unusual. Nor was it out of the ordinary that he had virtually nothing in the way of material possessions awaiting him at his home. Even the relatively few Southerners who were rich before the Civil War faced destitution in the summer of 1865, and Washington Duke had never belonged to that class anyhow. Poverty would be no novelty to him. The prospect of regathering and then rearing his four, motherless children must have been both heart-warming and frightening as he tramped homeward.

The eighth of ten children, Washington Duke was born to Taylor Duke and Diccy Jones Duke on December 20, 1820. Taylor Duke's father had been born in Virginia, where the family had come from England in the seventeenth century, but Taylor Duke was born in Orange County, North Carolina, on the eve of the American Revolution, and Dicey Jones was of Welsh ancestry. Other than that they owned and tilled their modest farm along the Little River near his birthplace, only a few scattered facts are known about Taylor and Dicey Jones Duke. As a captain of the militia in his district and a constable, Taylor Duke was clearly a person of substance and one respected by his neighbors.[1]

Washington Duke later recalled that he grew up in a section where there were no extremes of wealth or poverty. He meant, of course, that everyone had enough to eat, since beyond that, life was hard. Hillsborough, the nearest town and the county seat, was some twelve miles away, and Raleigh, the state capital, about twice as far. In the early part of the nineteenth century, the lack of transportation facili-

1. B. N. Duke to James T. White and Company, January 6, 1897, in the Benjamin N. Duke MSS, William R. Perkins Library, Duke University. Memorandum by the late Dr. Virginia Gray on "The Dukes in America, 1670–1870," in the Washington Duke MSS. Certified copy from Orange County Court Minutes, 1815–1818, in Charles Caldwell Research Papers, James B. Duke MSS. All manuscripts cited, unless otherwise noted, are to be found in the Manuscript Department and the University Archives, Perkins Library, Duke University.

ties bought special problems and hardships for North Carolinians in the Piedmont and mountain regions, and Washington Duke had little choice but to spend most of his early life behind a plow. "I have made more furrows in God's earth than any man forty years old in North Carolina," he later declared.[2] Receiving only a few months of formal schooling, he spent his days laboring. For some years prior to his eighteenth birthday, he and one of his brothers lived with their oldest brother, William James Duke, who was born in 1803, but Washington Duke soon began to farm on his own.

Renting land at first, he worked hard and lived frugally. When he married Mary Caroline Clinton in 1842, her father gave the couple land, and by the time of the Civil War Washington Duke owned some 300 acres, on the cultivated parts of which he grew corn, wheat, oats and, on the eve of the war, a little tobacco. Two sons were born to the young couple, Sidney Taylor Duke in 1844 and Brodie Leonidas Duke in 1846. When the latter was only a little more than a year old, his mother died.

With his small sons in the care of relatives, Washington Duke toiled away on the land. In the early 1850's he built a modest frame house of hand-dressed lumber and brought to it in December, 1852, his second wife, Artelia Roney, from nearby Alamance County. A year later, a daughter, Mary Elizabeth, was born and then two sons, Benjamin Newton on April 27, 1855, and James Buchanan on December 23, 1856.

Tragedy soon again struck Washington Duke, however, for his oldest son Sidney died of typhoid fever in the late summer of 1858, and the same disease killed Artelia Roney Duke some ten days later. Two of her unmarried sisters, first Elizabeth and later Ann Roney, with Malinda Duke, a maiden sister of Washington Duke, took turns helping with the four children, and the three youngest may have spent some time with their Roney grandparents in Alamance County. Having grown up motherless, all four were to display in their later lives, as will be shown, a special sympathy and benevolence toward orphans.

Outside of his family, clearly the most important institution for Washington Duke and the one which exerted the greatest influence on him from his childhood was the Methodist church. The impassioned evangelical movement that swept through American Protestantism in the early decades of the nineteenth century retained its

2. Washington Duke to John W. Wright and the Union Bethel African Methodist Episcopal Church, November 1, 1890, in Durham *Daily Globe*, November 5, 1890.

full vigor in Piedmont North Carolina during Washington Duke's youth. Converted at an early age in Mount Bethel Church at a crossroads settlement known as Balltown (later Bahama), he, like so many of his kinspeople and neighbors, enjoyed both the spirited singing of such hymns as "Amazing Grace" and the fiery preaching that characterized early Methodism. William J. Duke so liked one particularly moving hymn, "The Old Ship of Zion," that he acquired the nickname of "Uncle Billy of the Old Ship."

In the latter part of the 1830's, William J. Duke constructed an arbor on his land where outdoor services and "protracted meetings," or extended revivals, could be held. Then about 1840 he donated an acre of land and helped to build a rough log structure which became the home of the small congregation of Mount Hebron Church, to which Washington Duke and his family belonged.[3] Served by circuit-riding preachers who made up in zeal what they lacked in formal training, Methodism of the variety that he embraced from his childhood gained a powerful and lifelong hold on Washington Duke.

The Church not only provided the spiritual focus for Washington Duke's early life but also served as the principal center for socializing. With its "dinners-on-the-grounds" and all day meetings, a church like Mount Hebron understandably loomed large in this simple, rural society.

Civic and reform activities were apt to be church-based, too. Reflecting a widespread, national movement against the alleged evils of intoxicating drink, William J. Duke early in 1842 presided over a meeting that organized the Mount Hebron Temperance Society. Among the members of the standing committee for the society was twenty-one-year-old Washington Duke.[4]

Alongside the crusade for temperance another important reform movement of the era was reflected in the strong hunger for schools that many North Carolinians were beginning to manifest. With its high rate of illiteracy and steady out-migration of population, North Carolina had become known to many outsiders as "the Rip Van Winkle state." One who determined to change that situation, and the most famous educational pioneer in North Carolina, was Calvin H. Wiley, a native of nearby Guilford County. While Wiley fought his

3. M. R. Dunnagan's historical sketch of Mount Hebron Church, which became Duke's Chapel after Wm. J. Duke's death in 1883, in Greensboro *Daily News*, October 24, 1926.

4. *Hillsborough Recorder*, January 20, 1842. Mrs. Jean Anderson kindly provided the lead for this information.

successful battles in the state legislature and became the first state superintendent of schools in 1853, Washington Duke and his neighbors struggled, with only limited success, to provide for their children the educational opportunities that they and the vast majority of Tarheels had never known.

In 1850 the *Hillsborough Recorder* reported that the board for the "common schools" of Orange County had met in Hillsborough and appointed committees in fifty-one districts to take a census of the white population between the ages of five and twenty-one years. In district number six, "W. Duke" was listed as one of the three committeemen, but whether that was Washington Duke or his older brother William is not known. In 1851 and 1852 "Wm. Duke" served on the school committee for the district.[5] At any rate, it is clear that, though genuine public schools for most rural North Carolinians were still at least a half century away, the idea was indeed alive. In the case of Washington Duke, he saw to it, through his own efforts combined with those of some of his neighbors, that his children at least received a bit more schooling than he had enjoyed.

With schools not yet in existence to rival the churches as key institutions, Methodism remained the true passion of Washington Duke's life, and unlike many of his contemporaries he apparently took little part in antebellum politics. Benjamin N. Duke later asserted that his father had been an "ardent Whig" before the Civil War.[6] Professor John Spencer Bassett, however, came to know Washington Duke rather well in the 1890's and wrote a biographical sketch of him which, according to Bassett, was based partly on their conversations. In that sketch, Bassett declared that up to the Civil War Washington Duke had "been a Democrat, and in his loyalty he had named his youngest son James Buchanan, after a Democratic President."[7]

Both Taylor Duke and William J. Duke in 1840, at a time when Washington Duke was still too young to be actively involved in politics, served on a "committee of vigilance" for the Democratic party and the presidential candidacy of Andrew Jackson's successor, Martin van Buren.[8] And as for the youngest son's name, William J. Duke later asserted that he had picked the name, with the "James" repre-

5. *Hillsborough Recorder*, February 13, 1850; January 8, 1851; and January 7, 1852.
6. B. N. Duke to James T. White and Co., January 6, 1897, B. N. Duke MSS.
7. J. S. Bassett, "Washington Duke," in Samuel A. Ashe, ed., *Biographical History of North Carolina* (Greensboro, N.C., 1905), III, 85–86; and Bassett to C. E. Mapes, August 29, 1927, J. B. Duke Estate Papers.
8. *Hillsborough Recorder*, June 4, 1840.

senting his own middle name and only the "Buchanan" representing the new president.[9]

The fact that Washington Duke became a staunch and well-known Republican soon after the Civil War is firmly established. Republicanism was, at least in its economic orientation toward a high protective tariff and "sound" currency, much closer to pre-Civil War Whiggery than to Jacksonian Democracy. Thus Benjamin N. Duke may simply have unconsciously "read backwards" when he identified his father with the Whigs. The scanty evidence suggests that before the war Washington Duke belonged, however tenuously, to the Democratic party that he came to oppose bitterly later in the century.

However little he may have involved himself in the stormy politics of the 1850's, Washington Duke, like the vast majority of his fellow North Carolinians, opposed secession. Nevertheless, the Confederate firing on Fort Sumter and President Abraham Lincoln's ensuing call upon the various states for troops to be used against "rebels" seemed to leave North Carolinians no alternative but to throw in their lot with their fellow Southerners.

Not until the Confederacy in late 1863 moved to draft men up to forty-five years of age did Washington Duke make his preparations to enter the Confederate service. With a teenage son, Brodie, and three small children to care for, he may well have resented the necessity that confronted him. But on October 7 and 14, 1863, the following advertisement—one of many of a similar kind as men readied to leave for the war—appeared in the *Hillsborough Recorder*:

PUBLIC SALE

I will sell at my residence, on the 20th of this month, about one hundred bushels of corn, my entire stock of Cows, Hogs, Farming Tools and Wagon, Oats, Fodder, Hay, Wheat, and many other articles too tedious to mention; and perhaps some eight or ten likely NEGROES will be sold the same day.

Terms made known on the day of the sale.

Washington Duke

The announcement about the "eight or ten likely NEGROES" poses another problem, for before the war Washington Duke briefly owned only one slave, not necessarily because he may not have wished to own more but because he did not have enough money.

9. Mrs. J. C. Angier to C. E. Mapes, November 29, 1927, J. B. Duke Estate Papers.

7

Benjamin N. Duke's later contention that his father was "opposed to slavery and [was] a Union man" is not as convincing evidence as the census returns for 1850 and 1860. These listed no slave property for Washington Duke, though the census of 1850 showed that a "mulatto laborer" by the name of Alexander Weaver lived on the premises, and "laborer" clearly meant hired hand rather than slave.[10]

Also arguing against his ownership of any eight or ten slaves is the fact that during the war Washington Duke hired the use of a slave named "Jim," a practice that was widespread throughout the South. When "Jim" ran away, apparently briefly or at least not permanently, Washington Duke notified the owner. And then as the Confederate draft threatened, Duke sent the following letter to the owner of "Jim":

> Having to brake [sic] up and go into the Service, I let Mr. Wm. E. Walker have your boy Jim until his time would be up— he, Jim, went to sulking last night and is absent this morning, his clothes is gone. I expect therefore he will go to see you—if he should you will please send him down to Mr. Walker who will take care of him until his time is up—unless he should run off.
>
> Yours respectfully
Washington Duke[11]

The census returns, the hiring of "Jim," and the tentativeness of the wording in the advertisement— ". . . and *perhaps* some eight or ten likely NEGROES will be sold the same day"—suggest that Washington Duke, possibly hoping to attract more people to his own sale, allowed one of his neighbors or an acquaintance to employ the occasion for the sale of the slaves.

At any rate, he had to "brake up." The three small children were sent to live with their Roney grandparents on their farm in Alamance County, and Brodie, weighing only ninety-six pounds and too thin

10. B. N. Duke to E. L. Vaughan, February 25, 1925; certified copies of the census returns of 1850 and 1860 for W. Duke, J. B. Duke Estate Papers. On October 15, 1855, at a sale of slaves in Hillsborough, Washington Duke purchased a slave woman named "Caroline" for $601.00. "Orange County Estate Records, Inventories, Sales and Accounts (1853–1856)," p. 390, North Carolina Department of Archives and History. Though Washington Duke had apparently sold or freed "Caroline" before the census of 1860 was taken, a black woman named Caroline Barnes was a longtime cook for the family.

11. W. Duke to James W. Cox, June 15 and October 27, 1863, James W. Cox Papers, Southern Historical Collection, University of North Carolina at Chapel Hill.

for the regular army, served with a Major Gee in the Confederate prison at Salisbury, North Carolina.

With the children arranged for, Washington Duke departed for the war. On April 4, 1864, he signed a receipt for a private's uniform at Camp Holmes in Raleigh.[12] Many North Carolina conscripts received some basic training at Camp Holmes before being sent to the front; in Washington Duke's case he either requested or was assigned duty in the Confederate navy. Some time shortly after the middle of June, 1864, he reported for duty aboard a Confederate receiving ship in the besieged port of Charleston, South Carolina.

Many years later a wartime comrade wrote that he had been aboard the *Indian Chief* at Charleston with Washington Duke and would be glad to see him and "talk about old times in the Confederate navy."[13] But reminiscing about the war was not, apparently, something that Washington Duke enjoyed. Perhaps because the Confederate veterans' organization acquired in later years a partisan Democratic tinge (as the Grand Army of the Republic in the North became a powerful ally of the Republican party), Washington Duke never became a professional "Wearer of the Gray." Few stories of his wartime experiences survive.

One story that does survive, and which has the ring of truth about it, concerns his dread of a certain part of the duty involved on the receiving ship. At night small boats were secured to long beams of the ship, and the beams extended high over the water. Washington Duke, who had probably never seen the ocean before the war, nervously observed the men who had to go out on the beams and disconnect the lines holding the boats. When the dread day came and an officer ordered him to proceed out on the beam, the Orange County farmer at first refused and declared that it was impossible for him "to walk that sleek log." When the officer began to curse and finally to threaten punishment, Washington Duke summoned his courage and, probably praying to the God of all good Methodists, executed the order.[14]

His duty at Charleston was cut short, however, by needs that grew out of the desperate situation of the Confederate forces near Rich-

12. The fullest and most accurate study of Washington Duke's Confederate service, and the source for the account which follows, is Dr. Virginia Gray, "Some Obscure Facts About the Military Career of the Man Whose Gift Brought the College to Durham," *Duke Alumni Register* (December, 1967), III, 23–25.

13. W. B. Fort to Washington Duke, October 14, 1898, W. Duke MSS.

14. *Durham Recorder*, April 16, 1900.

mond, Virginia. The James River squadron of the Confederate navy finally had to man artillery batteries on the banks of the river, and in September, 1864, Washington Duke, together with additional men from Charleston, was transferred to Virginia. There he became an able artillerist, was promoted to the rank of orderly sergeant, and survived the rain, mud, and flood waters that harassed the men at Battery Brooke on the James. Rear Admiral Raphael Semmes, the famed Confederate seaman who assumed command of the James River squadron late in the war, noted in his diary that supplies were exhausted and that the command was merely living "from hand to mouth."[15]

In the confusion surrounding the Confederate evacuation of Richmond on April 1 and 2, 1865, Washington Duke was captured by Union troops. He was imprisoned in Richmond only a week before General Robert E. Lee's surrender on April 9 at Appomattox Court House. Gaining his parole later in the spring or early summer, Washington Duke was sent by ship to New Bern. From there he walked home to his reunion with his children—Brodie, Mary, Ben, and "Buck."

A big man in his prime years, nearly six feet tall and with a large muscular frame, Washington Duke was a person of few words, dignified, and possessing a dry, laconic sense of humor. He would live to a venerable old age and be widely respected in his community and state, known to many as "Wash" Duke or "the Old Gentleman." But in 1865, as he approached forty-five years of age, he had a new life to start.

15. Gray, *op. cit.*, p. 25.

CHAPTER 2. BEGINNING ANEW IN 1865: THE EARLY PHASE OF W. DUKE, SONS AND COMPANY

Washington Duke, unlike more privileged Southerners of the antebellum upper class, had no reason at the end of the war for nostalgia about the "old days." It was true that the war had disrupted his family and left him penniless. But in starting over, he would labor under no psychological burden produced by a sense of a "golden age before the war" that had passed forever.

Most North Carolinians, especially in the hitherto undeveloped Piedmont region, would, in fact, find the new era which began after Appomattox less traumatic than it proved to be for many of their neighbors to the immediate north and south. Residing in an area sometimes known jokingly as the "valley of humility between two mountains of conceit," North Carolinians actually did not carry the burden of past glories—some quite real and some romantically fanciful—that oppressed many Virginians and South Carolinians.

Less than two decades after the war a campaign newspaper which Washington Duke helped to support, the *Durham County Republican*, boasted that the raw, new factory town of Durham had "no aristocracy but an aristocracy of labor." Durham, the *Republican* asserted, "is the pride of that middle class who when the shock of war had passed burned their bridges and set their stake forward. . . . Where now is the old slave-holding aristocracy? We answer, plodding along in the old ruts, clinging to past traditions, cursing the hand of destiny: their savings from the wreck held in [Confederate] government bonds —no ray of hope in sight; nothing to do but live in despair and vote the Democratic ticket for pastime."[1] If the partisan zeal be discounted, the campaign newspaper had a valid point, one that sheds light on both Washington Duke and Piedmont North Carolina.

The coming of the railroad, no less than the destruction of the old slave-holding society, made the new era possible for the Piedmont region of North Carolina. By 1854 the North Carolina Railroad, advancing westward from Goldsboro through Raleigh, had reached the land which Dr. Bartlett Durham had given for a station. Here a

1. *Durham County Republican*, July 29, 1884.

small village—known variously as Durhamville, Durham's Depot or Station, Durham's, and finally just Durham—grew up around the railway stop. When General William T. Sherman accepted the surrender of General Joseph E. Johnston and the last major Confederate force east of the Mississippi at a nearby farmhouse, Durham gained its first claim to the world's attention. Consisting of fewer than a hundred people at the end of the war, the hamlet lay some four miles to the south of Washington Duke's farm.[2]

In addition to the coming of the railroad, the development of a new variety of tobacco, bright leaf, had a great deal to do with the rise of Durham and the postwar career of Washington Duke. Pioneered by, among others, the four Slade brothers of Caswell county in central North Carolina along the Virginia border after the late 1830's, the new variety of tobacco flourished in relatively poor soil which contained silica. The best curing process, found only after much experimentation with charcoal and other fuels, proved to be a system of flues conveying heat from a wood fire throughout a simply built tobacco barn or shed in which the tobacco leaves were hung for curing. By the time of the Civil War, the lemon-yellow and mildly fragrant tobacco that resulted from the combination of the siliceous soil and careful curing was finding an ever-widening market, first as wrappers for plug or chewing tobacco and then especially for pipe-smoking. With bright-leaf tobacco and the railroad, Durham had both a product for the outside world and a method of getting it there.[3]

As a seller of tobacco, Washington Duke's first foray into the postwar commercial arena involved not the railroad but a wagon and two decrepit mules that he somehow acquired from the abandoned supplies of Sherman's army. While Brodie Duke, the oldest son, tried farming on shares with his uncle, William J. Duke, for a year or so, Washington Duke brought the three younger children back to the home he had been forced to break up in 1863–64.

Possessing in ready cash only a fifty-cent coin for which he had swapped a five-dollar Confederate bill with a Union soldier, Washington Duke found his farm stripped and bare—save for a quantity of dried leaf tobacco. One traditional story, which cannot be docu-

2. The standard source for the early history of Durham and the one on which the above is based, is William K. Boyd, *The Story of Durham* (Durham, 1925).

3. Nannie M. Tilley, *The Bright-Tobacco Industry, 1860–1929* (Chapel Hill, 1948), is definitive, and pages 3–36 provide detailed information on which the above is based. Joseph C. Robert, *The Story of Tobacco in America* (Chapel Hill, 1949, 1967), pp. 181–189, has a condensed version.

mented, has it that he had stored the tobacco after purchasing it with the proceeds from the sale of his livestock, grain, and farming tools in October, 1863. At any rate, Washington Duke, aided by ten-year-old Ben and nine-year-old "Buck," proceeded to launch his manufacturing career. In a crude log shed which stood close by the dwelling, they beat the tobacco with wooden flails, sifted it by hand, and packed it in cloth bags labelled "Pro Bono Publico." Loading the smoking tobacco and two barrels of flour in his wagon, which was also equipped with a "victuals box" for simple cooking along the roadside, Washington Duke in the autumn headed into the eastern part of the state and proceeded to peddle and barter.[4]

Selling his smoking tobacco at a good price, Washington Duke traded his flour for cotton and sold the cotton for $40.00 in gold. Some of the proceeds from the tobacco he invested in a side of bacon, which he sold in Raleigh. Then remembering that his children, like many other impoverished Southerners during the war, had gone without certain kinds of sweets for several years, he purchased a wooden bucket filled with brown sugar. He carried this prize home, placed it in the middle of the floor, and happily watched as his children attacked it with their spoons.[5]

Pleased with the results of his venture, Washington Duke continued to buy tobacco from his neighbors and to manufacture the "Pro Bono Publico" smoking tobacco. While father and sons, aided by occasional hired laborers, worked long hours in the "factory" and in the fields, young Mary Duke attended to many of the housekeeping chores. A glimpse of her at age eighteen has been provided by a traveler, who as a schoolboy in 1871, was making a trip by buggy in cold, rainy weather and stopped at Washington Duke's place to thaw out. "It was a simple house," the autobiographer remembered,

> two frame buildings of two stories each, joined by an open covered way (known as a "dog-trot" porch). We were hospitably taken into a room with a large open fireplace, where Sam [Samuel Tate Morgan, a friend of the Dukes] and I warmed ourselves against the further journey. . . . A young woman, I think Mr. Duke's daughter, sat at a table where, by the light of a lamp, she was filling little cotton bags from a pile of finely-shredded tobacco before her. These little bags, stuffed to bursting, were drawn up

4. The Durham *Recorder*, April 16, 1900, has a detailed account based on an interview with Washington Duke.

5. *Ibid.*

with a sturdy string run through the top and tied with a bow knot. From time to time she took a pen and wrote in ink "Pro Bono Publico" on an oblong yellow label which she pasted on the filled bag of tobacco. The lamplight on this table and her quiet deftness and complete absorption . . . held our fascinated attention. At last we were thawed and departed.[6]

That the family's tobacco business prospered, however modestly, is suggested by the fact that it required more and more space; finally a two-story frame building near the two older factories was constructed. Washington Duke later recalled that immediately after the war he and his sons could prepare from 400 to 500 pounds of smoking tobacco in a day; in 1866 they manufactured altogether some 15,000 pounds, which they sold for fifty to sixty cents a pound. But on every pound sold, they were required to pay a federal revenue or excise tax of twenty cents. By 1872 they were producing some 125,000 pounds a year.[7]

Although every member of the family worked hard, the children received some schooling too. Ben and Buck Duke attended sessions at the academy in nearby Durham, the only school then available in the village. And in 1871 Washington Duke enrolled Mary and Ben Duke in the New Garden School (later Guilford College), which was run by the Quakers and located near Greensboro. They enjoyed their year at New Garden, and shortly after returning home Ben exclaimed to a former classmate: "It has just been one month since I parted with all my dear friends at N.G. and it seems as though it has been 3 months . . . ."[8] Buck Duke, on the other hand, who was sent to New Garden in 1872, missed the farm and factory; and though he had earlier proved quick in his school work and especially in arithmetic, he had no interest in literary studies. Coming home from New Garden before the term was half completed, Buck Duke later attended the Eastman Business College in Poughkeepsie, New York. The bookkeeping and other skills which he acquired at the business school may have proved helpful to him, but Washington Duke's youngest son clearly learned most and fastest from his deep engrossment in the family's business—

6. Paul B. Barringer, *The Natural Bent: The Memoirs of Dr. Paul B. Barringer* (Chapel Hill, 1949), pp. 163–164.
7. Durham *Recorder*, April 16, 1900; Boyd, *Story of Durham*, p. 83.
8. B. N. Duke to Miss Katie Reynolds, June 24, 1872, B. N. Duke MSS.

in farming and in helping to produce and sell "Pro Bono Publico."

The first member of the family to move into Durham, however, was Brodie Duke. In 1869, at twenty-three years of age, he purchased a small frame building on Durham's Main Street, and while living in the upstairs room began to manufacture in the ground-floor room his own brands of smoking tobacco, first "Semper Idem" and then the more famous "Duke of Durham." He lived frugally on fried bacon and "ash pone" or hoe cake, with molasses on occasion. Brodie Duke, who at some point along the way acquired what would become for him a tragic taste for whiskey, was later described in this beginning phase of his life in Durham as a teetotaler, "his only beverage . . . the pure unadulterated ale of father Adam—branch water."[9]

Inspired by Brodie Duke's move and lured by the larger business opportunities offered by bustling little Durham, soon to be the self-styled "Chicago of the South," Washington Duke sold his farm and moved his family into town in 1874. Numerous others were moving into Durham in the 1870's, as is shown by the fact that the town's population of 256 in 1870 had jumped to 2,041 by 1880, and it would continue to climb in succeeding decades. With yet-to-be paved streets and all manner of livestock enclosures and vegetable gardens interspersed with the residences, Durham after the Civil War was repeating a process of urbanization that was almost as old as the nation, though a process that was accelerating in the late nineteenth century. Yet in Durham's growth, tobacco provided a distinctive element.

Washington Duke and his sons built their frame factory on the south side of Main Street, approximately where a large plant of the Liggett and Myers company would stand in the next century. At first a partition separated that portion of the building to which Brodie Duke removed his business from the half where Washington Duke and his two younger sons established themselves. This arrangement was later replaced by separate, adjacent buildings, but the business from the first was a family affair, with Washington Duke selling goods for his son Brodie and vice versa.[10]

As wagon-borne peddler in 1865 and then a "drummer" or traveling salesman in the 1870's, Washington Duke covered many thousands of miles selling the family's various brands of tobacco. One of the ledgers for the 1870's lists the names and addresses of dozens of tobacconists from Maine to California with whom the Dukes did busi-

9. Durham *Recorder*, April 16, 1900. 10. Boyd, *Story of Durham*, p. 85.

ness.[11] In St. Louis, Missouri, some years after the name of Duke had become famous in connection with tobacco, a retailer remembered that his first contact with the firm had been through Washington Duke. As the Missourian recalled it, one cold morning an elderly gentleman, wearing a broad brim hat and soberly dressed, opened the door to the tobacco shop in St. Louis, walked half way down to the office, turned deliberately, and walked back to shut the door. Then, speaking slowly in a droll, broad accent, he said, "Good morning. I did shut the door and I'm from North Carolina." After putting down his worn black carpetbag, Washington Duke continued, "I've got some mighty good smoking tobacco in here and believe you could sell a heap of it if you had some of it in your store."[12]

Washington Duke was not the only member of the family who "drummed the trade," for young J. B. Duke also took to the road in the late 1870's. On one of his trips in 1880, when he was nearly twenty-four, he wrote Ben Duke a long letter, which is the earliest of J. B. Duke's letters known to survive as well as the longest of his few extant personal letters. "I have been very much discouraged ever since I left home," he declared, "knowing that I was not paying expenses, but there is one consolation[:] I have done my duty whether it was successful or not, & shall put in some very hard work from now until I reach home & if I do not succede better this shall be my last Trip. I will stay at home & work."

Even as he travelled, however, young "Buck" Duke pondered how the family firm might move ahead in the industry. He wrote his brother that he had thought up a process that would make the "finest smoke out." He would put the tobacco in a dry room and thoroughly dry it so that there would be no water left in it. Then he would dip it in boiling, flavored rum that would "give it a pleasant flavor & make it smoke sweet & uniform."

Most of his long letter was not about tobacco, but rather about the fine time he had just had visiting the family of his uncle, John Taylor Duke, in Milan, Tennessee. Among other things, J. B. Duke said he had met the *"liveliest girl I think God ever put breath in."* There were also two young girl cousins about his own age, and the hilarity had ranged from water fights to much teasing, all of which he described in great detail. "We walked about 2 miles in the country one night to Church,

11. Ledger, 1873–1877, Washington Duke MSS.
12. Edward F. Small, "A Correct Version of the Beginnings of a Trust," unpublished memoir in the Edward Featherston Small MSS, Duke University Library.

16

a Camp Meeting & had a big time," he continued. "Cousin Lockie gave us plenty of wine & I got a gallon besides so we kept the crowd jolly all the time & it was a regular tare for 3 days & nights. . . ."[13]

James B. Duke, as a young man, clearly did not grind away at his tasks all the time, even though he was a prodigiously hard worker for most of his life. Through the labors and skill of Washington Duke and his three sons, in fact, they built a modestly successful business in the 1870's despite the fact that after 1873 there was an acute economic depression. But they were only one of about a dozen tobacco manufacturers in Durham—and the firm that stood far ahead of all others, the one which had first made the town widely known, was W. T. Blackwell and Company, with its globally-famed "Bull Durham" smoking tobacco.

The antecedents of the Blackwell company reached back to the eve of the Civil War and a brand of "Best Flavored Spanish Smoking Tobacco" produced in Durham. When marauding Union and Confederate soldiers confiscated the tobacco in the turbulent days at the end of the war, the product accidentally received a vast amount of advertising, and orders for more of the same tobacco came back from many scattered points. The proprietor of the business by this time, John Ruffin Green, set out at the war's end to produce a high-quality product and rejected the exotic reference to Spain in the old name. Inspired by a picture of a bull's head that appeared on a widely used variety of mustard made in Durham, England, Green chose as his trademark a Durham Bull, "a happy inspiration," as one historian has pointed out, "in a still predominantly rural society and for a product designed for male purchasers."[14]

Before his death in 1869, Green took as a partner William T. Blackwell, who had been a storekeeper in Roxboro, North Carolina, before the war. Then after Green's death Blackwell purchased the entire business from the Green estate and soon gained as one of his partners Julian Shakespeare Carr. The son of a merchant in nearby Chapel Hill, Carr was twenty-five years old when he moved to Durham. Though he served as a private in the Confederate army, he would become well known in his later life as "General Carr" through his activities as a Confederate veteran.[15]

13. J. B. Duke to B. N. Duke and Mrs. B. N. Duke, August 18, 1880, B. N. Duke MSS. Misspellings in the original.

14. Robert, *Story of Tobacco*, p. 123.

15. An early sketch of Carr may be found in Hiram V. Paul, *History of the Town of*

Successfully defending their trademark and brand name in a series of tedious but important legal battles in the 1870's, Blackwell and Carr also pioneered in the techniques of advertising their "Genuine Bull Durham" tobacco. Huge sums of money, for that day, went into advertisements in weekly newspapers, as well as in the larger daily ones, and prizes or premiums, ranging from a small item such as a razor to a more costly mantle-clock, were offered to purchasers. Most spectacular of all, huge painted signs of the Durham Bull appeared all over the United States, in Europe, and even at one point on the pyramids of Egypt.

The Bull Durham plant ultimately became, at least for a time, the largest smoking-tobacco factory in the world, and in 1874, the same year in which Washington Duke moved into Durham, the Blackwell company built a large new brick factory equipped not only with the increasingly expensive machinery that tobacco manufacture had begun to require but also with a large steam whistle designed to imitate the bellow of a bull.[16]

The Bull's whistle could be heard for miles around Durham, but one may be sure that the members of the Duke family took no pleasure in the sound. Competing against a neighboring firm with such a commanding head start, and in a business characterized by "dog-eat-dog" methods, was no simple task. The Dukes gained additional strength in 1878, however, when their firm was formally organized as W. Duke, Sons and Company, and a new partner, one who would remain closely associated with the Dukes for the remainder of his life, was taken into the business.

George Washington Watts moved to Durham from his home in Baltimore, Maryland, in 1878. Born in 1851 and thus a few years older than Benjamin N. and James B. Duke, Watts had attended the University of Virginia and then worked in his father's wholesale tobacco business. His father, seeking a likely place to help his son launch himself in business, provided the $14,000 with which young Watts purchased a one-fifth interest in W. Duke, Sons and Company. Quiet, sober, and hard-working, George Watts brought to the firm more than just capital, much as that was needed. He possessed considerable

Durham, N.C. (Raleigh, 1884), pp. 133–137; a fuller one is by Samuel A. Ashe in Ashe, *Biographical History of North Carolina*, II, 51–59.

16. Boyd, *Story of Durham*, pp. 58–68. In the twentieth century the old Bull Durham factory became a part of the American Tobacco Company's large plant in downtown Durham.

business ability, and for a number of years he and Benjamin N. Duke would handle most of the important correspondence and run the front office while James B. Duke interested himself in production and selling. Like his father, he put in many long days "drumming the trade" across the country.

Perhaps Washington Duke at age sixty had wearied of the "drummer's" life and felt that the time had come when he might stay at home in Durham to enjoy the Methodist church and his involvement in local Republican politics. At any rate, in 1880 he sold his interest in the business for $23,000. The purchaser was Richard Harvey Wright, a young man who had come from the family farm in nearby Franklin County to seek his fortune in Durham.[17] Born in 1851, Wright ran a general store and then opened a small tobacco factory in Durham in the late 1870's. Single-minded in his attention to business and eager to get ahead as so many of his fellow townsmen were, Wright became a principal salesman for the firm. For more than two years he headed a branch office in Chicago and covered much of the West for W. Duke, Sons and Company; then in June, 1882, he set out on a globe-circling tour through Europe, South Africa, India, the East Indies, Australia, and New Zealand to introduce the Duke tobacco products.[18]

Even before Wright could report from Europe on the growing popularity there of the new-fangled cigarettes, W. Duke, Sons and Company had begun producing them. "My company is up against a stone wall," young James B. Duke is reported to have said. "It can not compete with the Bull. Something has to be done and that quick. As for me, I am going into the cigarette business."[19]

Popular in the Spanish-speaking parts of the world much earlier, cigarettes did not appear widely in France and England until the decades immediately before the American Civil War. Immigrants and the limited number of the American elite able to afford travel in

17. Since the matter would become involved in Wright's subsequent break with the firm, it should be noted that he only paid $1,500 in cash to Washington Duke and gave five notes, due on the first of each year for the next five years, to cover the balance; the notes were secured by various pieces of real estate which Wright owned in Durham. Agreement and Indenture between Wright and W. Duke, January 1, 1880, Richard H. Wright MSS, legal papers of 1880's.

18. A biographical sketch of Wright may be found in *History of North Carolina*, IV: *North Carolina Biography* (Chicago, 1919), pp. 198–199.

19. Boyd, *Story of Durham*, p. 76. Boyd got the statement from a lawyer who heard it, and while the exact words may not have been used by J. B. Duke, especially the first person singular, the gist is correct.

Europe helped introduce the new fad into the United States, and by 1864 the manufacture of cigarettes had begun in New York City. It was there that the practice of smoking them caught on first, and there that the American cigarette industry was centered until 1875 when John F. Allen and Lewis Ginter began their manufacturing business in Richmond, Virginia.[20]

The new bright-leaf tobacco of North Carolina and Virginia proved ideal for use in the cigarette and would soon far outdistance Turkish and other types of tobacco, even in Europe. The golden leaf could be obtained more easily and cheaply, in fact, than cigarettes could be made by hand, for the first hand-rollers had to be brought over from Europe to train American workers. When the Duke company entered the business in 1881, more than a hundred skilled cigarette-makers from New York, many of them Jewish immigrants from eastern Europe, were brought to Durham. The hand labor involved in cigarette manufacture was obviously expensive, yet manufacturers in the state of New York in 1880 produced over 384,000,000 cigarettes, almost three-quarters of the total in the country, while W. Duke, Sons and Company only produced 9,800,000 cigarettes in their first year of making them.[21] The Duke company, however, was only beginning to be heard from in the tobacco world.

Aggressive salesmanship and advertising of a quality product laid the basis in the 1870's for the rise of the Duke firm. The decade of the 1880's, a time of vast expansion and prosperity for much of industrial America, brought the company a new preeminence. With their "Duke of Durham," "Pin Head," and "Cross-Cut" brands of cigarettes, among others, the Dukes and their partners, Watts and Wright, moved ahead vigorously.

A glimpse of the inside operation of the business at this crucial stage of its growth is afforded by letters from the company to one of its best salesmen, Edward Featherston Small. The intense secrecy which surrounded so much of the tobacco industry did not really originate from paranoia, as some observers have charged, but from the ruthless competitiveness that characterized the business. In the spring of 1884, as Small worked Atlanta, the home office informed him that he was being sent a sample of "Pin Head," which had been gotten up especially to run against a rival brand. The claim was that "Pin Head" was

20. Tilley, *Bright-Tobacco Industry*, pp. 504–510, gives the detailed story and background.
21. *Ibid.*, p. 510.

"finer & lower-price[d] than the rival, while 'Old Rip' [another rival] ain't worth within 50¢ to 75¢ per M [thousand] as much as 'Pin Head.' " On the back of this letter, James B. Duke, who was always eager to bypass the old-time commission merchants and wholesalers, scribbled an urgent query to Small about the reaction of retailers and consumers to the company's brands. "I want to know how the sales of retailers compare on our Duke [of Durham] with other brands both with the prominent retailers & the smaller ones," Duke demanded.[22]

"Our cig[arette] business was never so good," the home office soon boasted, "orders ranging from 200 M to 400 M daily while the Bull has purchased stamps this month for only 250 M altogether; if you mention this do so in confidence or you might get our Collector [of Revenue] in trouble." Small was advised that circulars for each retailer in Atlanta would be on the way to him shortly and that the company was "also preparing some other physic for the Bull which we will administer from time to time."[23]

As Small moved on to Savannah, the office notified him that a case containing 20,000 pieces of advertising matter and 99 packs of playing cards, among other things, was on the way. That, in addition to the cards and posters sent earlier, ought to give Small a "pretty good send off in Savannah." The home office urged: "We want the city and surrounding country worked for all it is worth. We sincerely hope you will create a big boom in Savannah & we don't want you to leave there until you make every possible effort to create such."[24]

Creating a "big boom" was something Small proved himself adept at doing, for he hit on a sensational move in Atlanta. A well known French actress of the day, one Madame Rhea, was playing in the Georgia capital, and the city was covered with advertisements about her, including life-size lithographs. Small inquired of Madame Rhea if she would consent to have the life-size lithograph of herself reproduced with a package of Duke cigarettes in her hand and the caption "Atlanta's Favorite" printed beneath. When the actress promptly agreed and the dazzling picture appeared in the most popular tobacco store in the city and then in a large advertisement in the Atlanta *Constitution*, Small had achieved a salesman's dream of gaining the

22. W. Duke, Sons and Company to Small, March 20, 1884, Edward Featherston Small MSS.
23. *Ibid.*, April 11, 1884.
24. *Ibid.*, May 8, 22, 1884.

public's attention. With sales soaring in Atlanta and its environs, the office in Durham responded: "We think you made a happy hit with Rhea. Give the Bull's tail another twist."[25]

The juxtaposition in advertising of beautiful women and cigarettes proved to be a long-lived development despite the shock it caused initially to millions of Americans. The sexual slant was clearly designed to appeal to the male market. Sophisticated society women in New York might privately use cigarettes, as the novels of Edith Wharton reveal, but the day of any widespread public acceptance of cigarette-smoking by women was several decades in the future. Meanwhile, Small had the further inspiration of hiring an attractive widow in St. Louis as a pioneer saleswoman for the Duke cigarettes. Not only did this attract much free publicity, as in the case of Madame Rhea, but the home office, after receiving a photograph of the widow, reported to Small that she had "made a mash" on Washington Duke and another man in the plant. Small "need not be surprised any day to have one or both of these gentlemen reach St. Louis to succeed" him.[26]

Clearly the astute salesman had a flair for capitalizing on the feminine angle, but he did not fall into a stale pattern. When roller-skating on indoor rinks became a wildly popular fad in the mid-1880's, Small secured the services of a "polo club" on skates, outfitted them handsomely as the "Cross Cut Polo Club of Durham, N.C.," and had them play widely noted matches in Ohio and Michigan. In Cincinnati where the "Cross Cuts" played in a leading rink, the match took on an aspect of the South once more "battling against the North for the honors of the hour." Headlines in newspapers and handbills played up the "desperate battle between the North and South" as they also advanced the interests of W. Duke, Sons and Company. One newspaper reported that the "Cross Cut club have won many hands [of applause] by their gentlemanly acting, and the only thing to be avoided tonight is the possibility of both clubs doing the slugging act. It was bordering on it last night." Presumably the "slugging act" was avoided, and as the spectators left the rink each gentleman was given a five-cent package of ten Duke "Cross-Cut" cigarettes and each lady a set of five small photographs.[27]

25. Small's unpublished memoir, pp. 2–3, Small MSS.
26. W. Duke, Sons and Co., to Small, April 4, 1885, *ibid.*
27. Small's unpublished memoir, pp. 12–13, and undated newspaper clipping, Small MSS.

Roller-skating "polo clubs," photographs of presidents and monarchs and of just about everything else imaginable, a chair to every dealer who gave an order for a certain number of cigarettes—all these and more were the schemes used by the Dukes as well as by their competitors.[28] Part of the struggle also involved price-cutting.

One of the bolder moves of the Duke company in the realm of pricing came in 1883 when the federal excise tax on cigarettes was cut to less than a third of what it had been, from $1.75 to 50 cents per thousand. Immediately upon passage of the new tax law and even before it was put into effect, the Dukes announced that they would reduce their prices by the full amount of the tax cut. Advertising stressed that "the Dukes are ambitious for a very large cigarette business, and to obtain such are *dividing their profits* with the dealers and consumers."[29]

Even though the price-cutting move of 1883 helped increase sales dramatically, W. Duke, Sons and Company continued to respond quickly whenever the market seemed to demand it. When W. S. Kimball and Company of Rochester, New York, came out with a "cheap cigarette" called "Old Gold," the Duke company, complaining that "some few jobbers and retailers want low priced cigarettes regardless of quality or the opinion of the smoker," concluded that the only thing to do was "to accommodate all such parties and meet competition, and . . . we will at once put the price of Pin Head down. . . ."[30]

Though James B. Duke believed in advertising as much as any one, when the office sent Small the 10,000 "cabinet photographs" that he had requested Duke cautioned that the photographic cards cost half as much as a package of ten cigarettes and "must be used very judiciously." As for himself, James B. Duke added that he was introducing the company's "Cameo" brand of cigarettes in New York City and that they were "catching on very nicely without any effort on our part so far," but "I am going to push them hard from now on."[31]

With a vigorous president such as J. B. Duke, who was not yet thirty years old, and salesmen like Small and Richard Wright, not to men-

28. An excellent study, including many illustrations, of the Duke's advertising is Patrick G. Porter, "Advertising in the Early Cigarette Industry: W. Duke, Sons & Company of Durham," *North Carolina Historical Review*, XLVIII (Winter, 1971), pp. 31–43.

29. *Nowitzky's Magazine*, as cited in Tilley, *Bright-Tobacco Industry*, pp. 557–558. Italics in original.

30. W. Duke, Sons and Co., to Small, February 6, 1885, Small MSS.

31. J. B. Duke to Small, January 27, 1886, Small MSS.

tion the quiet but efficient managerial and executive talents of Ben Duke and George Watts, the firm of W. Duke, Sons and Company began by 1884 to pull up alongside Blackwell's Bull Durham company, which also made cigarettes but continued to emphasize smoking tobacco. "The cig[arette] business with us continues splendid," the home office reported to Small. "We are getting repeated orders from every section of the country when [our cigarettes] are once tried, [and we] expect to ship more this month than ever before & keep on increasing until we make it 500 M per day." And shortly afterward, the management chortled, "Our orders on the glorious 4th [of July, 1884] were 1,905,000 cigtts."[32]

The very success of the Duke products brought new problems. The company congratulated Small on his sales and advertising feats but confessed that production was three weeks behind orders, so "at present it is useless for us to endeavor to enlarge the territory." There was, however, relief in sight: "We are now [October, 1884] opening a factory in New York from which to supply our Northern trade and as soon as we get that to running all right, we hope to be able to supply all our Southern trade promptly from here [Durham], as that factory [in New York] will relieve us of 3 to 400 M per day."[33]

With a new branch factory going up and its trade thriving in general, the business which Washington Duke had launched so modestly twenty years earlier had indeed gone far. But margins were still painfully close. "Only $200 in mail today & with nothing in Bank I don't know how I am to pay what has to be paid this week[,] say $12,000 . . . ," moaned Ben Duke. He requested Richard Wright in New York to try and arrange for the renewal there of the company's note for $5,000, and then he, Duke, would see what could be done about a short-term loan from the bank in Durham. "Money is awful tight here," Duke explained, " & it will require several days notice or they cannot aid us." Meant as a cheerful note, no doubt, was the information that there were orders on hand for 340,000 cigarettes.[34]

The new factory in New York, where James B. Duke would make his headquarters after 1884, was only part of the company's response to its success—and to the problems which accompanied that success. Much more important for the future was the decision that the partners were considering late in 1884 of moving increasingly toward the pro-

32. W. Duke, Sons and Co., to Small, May 23, July 7, 1884, Small MSS.
33. W. Duke, Sons and Co., to Small, October 4, 1884, Small MSS.
34. B. N. Duke to R. H. Wright, December 22, 1885, Wright MSS.

duction of machine-made cigarettes. At a time when the users of cigarettes gave every indication of liking the hand-rolled variety—and according to most of the manufacturers the customers strongly preferred hand-made cigarettes—the switch to a machine-made product would involve great risk for W. Duke, Sons and Company. Moreover, a completely satisfactory machine to make cigarettes had not yet appeared, although the race to make such a machine had been on for several years. The ambitious partners of the Duke company, and especially James B. Duke, were nevertheless ready by 1885 to take a large gamble and give the cigarette machine invented by James A. Bonsack of Virginia more than just a casual try. W. Duke, Sons and Company would be the first manufacturers of cigarettes to take such a step—and it would pay off handsomely, even if no one could know that for a certainty in 1885.

CHAPTER 3. JAMES B. DUKE, THE BONSACK CIGARETTE MACHINE, AND THE ORIGINS OF THE AMERICAN TOBACCO COMPANY

Letterbooks of James B. Duke that came to light in 1973 afford a close, inside view of the most dynamic sector of the American cigagrette industry during the late 1880's and underscore the key role of the Bonsack machine not only in the rise to preeminence of W. Duke, Sons and Company but also in the organization of the American Tobacco Company. Developments in the years between 1885, when W. Duke, Sons and Company decided to bet heavily on the Bonsack cigarette machine, and 1890, when the American Tobacco Company was officially launched, have remained obscure. The transactions of the latter firm after 1890 were extensively revealed in the first decade of the twentieth century by the federal government's Bureau of Corporations and by the Department of Justice in its successful antitrust action. But the phenomenal growth of the firm headed by young James B. Duke, who turned thirty late in 1886, and the actual negotiations that led to the formation of the great combination in 1890 may now be much more clearly understood from the letterbooks.[1]

The firm of W. Duke, Sons and Company arranged for the installation of a Bonsack cigarette machine in its Durham factory in the spring of 1884. First tested in the Richmond factory of Allen and Ginter, then the largest cigarette producers in the country, the ma-

1. Late in 1941, after the United States entered World War II, the officials of The Duke Endowment in New York shipped a number of their records to be placed in a special storeroom of the Endowment on the campus of Duke University. Among these records was a large wooden box marked "Box A—Property of James B. Duke," and together with the cash books, ledgers and other such material within the box were ten letterbooks, which the present writer first saw and helped to transfer to the Manuscript Department of the Perkins Library, Duke University, on August 9, 1973. The first three volumes, which are a chief source for this chapter, are not conventional letterbooks but consist rather of the original letters that came to W. Duke, Sons and Company and to James B. Duke from the officials of the Bonsack Machine Company from 1884 to 1890. The letters are pinned to the pages of the letterbook, and two sheafs of typed copies of the letters from the Dukes to the Bonsack Company are placed inside the first and third volumes. Mr. John Day, secretary of The Duke Endowment, and Mr. John Spuches of the law firm of Perkins, Daniels, and McCormack in New York kindly revealed the existence of this material upon their learning of it on the above date and allowed its transfer to the Perkins Library.

chine was theoretically capable of producing in a day about as many cigarettes as forty-eight skilled hand-rollers could make. The Bonsack Machine Company, the joint-stock company which had been organized to produce and handle the invention, leased the machines on a royalty basis of approximately two-thirds of the cost of producing cigarettes by hand. In other words, the Bonsack Company charged thirty cents per thousand cigarettes for "plain work" and thirty-three cents per thousand for "printed work," with the Bonsack Company installing the machine and furnishing an operator for it.[2]

Two major obstacles blocked acceptance of the Bonsack machine: it worked only sporadically and imperfectly and, second, most manufacturers clung to the strong belief that consumers preferred the hand-rolled cigarette which had become popular in the country since the Civil War. Overcoming the machine's imperfections was a triumph for the persistence and ingenuity of James B. Duke, but even more was it his great good luck when the Bonsack Company sent him William T. O'Brien, an Irish-American mechanic from Lynchburg, Virginia. Working tirelessly and patiently, O'Brien made no fundamental changes in Bonsack's complicated invention; more importantly, the young mechanic gradually made it work effectively. Ben Duke conceded guardedly to the president of the Bonsack Company, D. B. Strouse, of Salem, Virginia, that "O'Brien has done fairly well on his six machines this week . . . ," but James B. Duke insisted flatly to Strouse that O'Brien could run the complicated machine better than "any other man you now have or may have hereafter."[3]

The importance of O'Brien and his mechanical skill should not be underrated, since the South, still overwhelmingly agrarian in the 1880's and 1890's, sorely needed such talent for the industrialization that was already underway in the region. The feeling was growing among Southerners, according to one observant businessman, "that we must make what [we] use and use what we make in the South," but the shortage of mechanical skill posed a problem. "The shops north owe their success largely to the mechanics in their employ," he

2. Tilley, *Bright-Tobacco Industry*, pp. 568–576, has the fullest account.

3. B. N. Duke to Strouse, June 6, 1886, and J. B. Duke to Strouse, June 18, 1886, sheaf in J. B. Duke letterbook no. 3. Reflecting his faith in O'Brien as well as a life-long policy of giving his coworkers a stake in success, James B. Duke eventually employed O'Brien directly and gave him first three cents per thousand, then four cents per thousand for all cigarettes made on the machine. O'Brien later surrendered this commission as excessive and was made superintendent of the factory in 1897. Tilley, *Bright-Tobacco Industry*, p. 574.

continued, but "down here anybody who can pull a monkey wrench & pound his machine with a hammer & cuss the builder for making such a machine is called a mechanic."[4]

Perhaps O'Brien's unusual skill with the Bonsack machine helped convince James B. Duke that his firm could overcome the second great obstacle to widespread acceptance of Bonsack's invention, namely the alleged consumer resistance to machine-made cigarettes. At any rate, by late 1884 James B. Duke urged P. A. Krise, secretary-treasurer of the Bonsack Company and a banker in Lynchburg, to come to Durham "on important business . . . [that] would be to your interest as well as our own." Duke hoped that the Bonsack people would "reconsider the proposition" he had made some time earlier.[5]

Despite the Bonsack Company's keen interest in seeing the machine fully tested and more widely employed—and only the Duke firm had so far afforded hope for that—apparently neither Krise nor Strouse, the president, was ready for hard bargaining with James B. Duke. Moreover, the Duke firm and its thriving business encountered a new and serious problem in 1885 that seemed for a while to threaten their very existence. Organized as a five-man partnership in 1878, the company found in Richard H. Wright, who had purchased Washington Duke's share in 1880, an unhappy partner who threatened drastic action.

The immediate cause of Wright's discontent sprang from the call of the other partners, led by James B. Duke, for more capital to plow into the expanding enterprise. A deeper cause probably arose from Wright's dislike of playing second fiddle to James B. Duke, who was four and a half years younger. Every bit as hard-working and ambitious as Duke, Wright proved to be in the early years of his career a proud, strong-willed man who ended up in litigation involving a number of those with whom he associated in business. In 1885, James B. Duke, his brothers Ben and Brodie, and George Watts were given a painful lesson in the hazards of the partnership form of business organization and the advantages of the joint-stock company or corporation.

The partnership, as it had been renegotiated on January 1, 1884, for one year, was a strange one anyhow. At that time each of the five

4. John W. Petty in Durham to Richard H. Wright, November 18, 1889, R. H. Wright MSS.

5. J. B. Duke to P. A. Krise, December 24, 1884, from sheaf in J. B. Duke letter-book no. 3.

partners had pledged to contribute $20,000 to the capital of the firm and none was to engage in any other business, although Brodie L. Duke in "consideration of being allowed to engage in other business and to devote his time thereto agrees to contribute to the firm Two Thousand Dollars per annum in lieu of his services." Another unusual item, which was also apparently related to the habits of Brodie Duke, was the pledge of each partner to "conduct himself in such manner as to reflect credit upon the firm and not to drink liquors to intoxication." Furthermore, each partner agreed that if he should "violate any one of the obligations, covenants or stipulations for one time, except that relating to intoxication, and as to that a violation of five times during any one year, such violation shall dissolve this co-partnership so far as the party making such violation is concerned" and the remaining partners would pay to "such offending member" the sum of $8,000 in full settlement for his interest in the firm.[6]

The firm of W. Duke, Sons and Company, despite impressive strides in the tobacco industry, clearly had its problems at the executive level; but Brodie Duke's proclivity for drink was as nothing compared to the threat from Richard Wright. Upon returning from his global selling tour early in 1884, Wright made his headquarters in New York, where the firm opened a branch factory later in that year. If his partners suspected any difficulty, the records do not reveal it, for just before Christmas, 1884, Ben Duke sought Wright's help in a sensitive matter through two long, friendly letters. Ben Duke feared legal action from Allen and Ginter concerning patents on a small line of mouthpiece cigarettes produced by W. Duke, Sons and Company and requested Wright to seek advice and assistance from two other large cigarette manufacturers, Kinney Brothers in New York and Kimball and Company in Rochester. Ben Duke thought that since "nearly every cigarette manufacturer in the U.S. is down on" Allen and Ginter, the other firms "would rather see us in a position to whip them than to have us abandon the case and leave the field open to A. & G." Actually, the Duke firm sold the mouthpiece cigarettes only in New Orleans, Ben Duke continued, but to lose a lawsuit about them "might injure our trade on cigarettes all over the country, as Allen & Ginter would most assuredly make a big advertisement of it and use it against us everywhere." Ben Duke apologized for pressing the matter so close to the holidays and explained that "Buck would

6. Articles of copartnership, January 1, 1884, in R. H. Wright MSS, legal papers of 1880's.

have gone [to New York] if he could possibly have left, but he is now busily engaged in getting the new factory [in Durham] ready to be occupied Jan. 1st . . . and it was impossible for me to go because of the addition of another boy to my family."[7]

What action, if any, Wright took in the matter of the mouthpiece patents is unknown. Though he, as a rival cigarette manufacturer, would later seek to bring legal action concerning the mouthpiece cigarettes against W. Duke, Sons and Company, he appears to have had more urgent matters in mind as 1885 opened. His attorney in Raleigh, North Carolina, John W. Hinsdale, informed him early in the year that when a partnership continued after the expiration of the term prescribed for its duration—as was the case of W. Duke, Sons and Company after January 1, 1885—it did so at the will and pleasure of the partners and was dissolvable by any one of them. "If your partners will not give you a *full* price for your interest," Hinsdale added, "you can make it to their interest to come to terms. You have the game very much in your hands."[8]

Thus assured by his attorney, Wright proceeded coolly to play the "game." James B. Duke sought to increase the company's capital from $100,000 to $150,000, but Wright demurred. He had not yet paid Washington Duke for his share in the company, which Wright had purchased in 1880, and the head of the Duke family was ultimately forced in May, 1885, to foreclose the mortgage on real estate in Durham which Wright had given as security for his note to Washington Duke.[9]

Prior to the public sale of a portion of Wright's real-estate holdings, he and his partners had begun negotiating cautiously, and abortively. According to the Dukes and George Watts, they sought various ways to keep Wright in the firm while at the same time increasing the capital: they would persuade Washington Duke to release the mortgage he held on the real estate, which Wright could then mortgage to raise his share of the proposed increase, but Wright declined; he also rejected, they claimed, the proposition that those partners who could add additional capital should do so, each partner then to receive such proportion of the net profits as his contribution bore to the whole

7. B. N. Duke to R. H. Wright, December 20, 22, 1884, R. H. Wright MSS.

8. J. W. Hinsdale to Wright, January 13, 1885, *ibid.*

9. Agreement and indenture of January 1, 1880, between Richard H. Wright and Washington Duke, with endorsement of May 16, 1885, in R. H. Wright MSS, legal papers of the 1880's.

capital. The other partners offered to incorporate the business and to allow Wright to purchase an equal quantity of stock by using the stock that would be issued to him upon incorporation as collateral for a loan sufficient to pay for enough additional stock to make him equal with his partners; Wright again declined.[10]

According to Wright, he first made an offer to sell his interest in the firm to George Watts, who declined to pay the price asked but made a counteroffer to sell his interest, which Wright rejected. Some time thereafter, Wright, Watts, and Ben Duke negotiated in vain. Wright refused to allow his brother-in-law, William T. Blackwell, to act as a disinterested party to appraise the value of Wright's interest in the firm because, in Wright's words, "Blackwell had two years previously shown his ignorance of the value of a brand & good will as he owned the Bull Durham brand exclusively—his partner having no interest in it— & he sold it for $100,000.00 when he could easily have gotten three to five hundred thousand for it. . . ."[11]

With negotiations between Wright and his partners at an impasse, he began, as he put it, "to look outside for capital to buy my interest or to join me & buy them all out on a give or take proposition. . . ."[12] In other words, Wright made overtures to some of the major tobacco companies in the country, including a couple of the largest cigarette manufacturers, about their possible interest in buying into or buying out W. Duke, Sons and Company.[13]

Wright's behavior no doubt complicated matters for James B. Duke, but the youngest and shrewdest of the Dukes did not let such distractions prevent his pursuit of the main goal, which in the spring of 1885 was a special deal with the Bonsack Machine Company. Responding to another overture from Duke, D. B. Strouse, president of the Bonsack Company, avowed, "You are our largest patron and we

10. Brief for defendants in *Richard H. Wright against J. B. Duke, B. L. Duke, B. N. Duke, and George W. Watts,* Supreme Court, City and County of New York [1891], B. N. Duke MSS, 1966 addition, legal papers, 1834–1899. Hereinafter cited as Brief for defendants.

11. R. H. Wright to William J. Curtis, May 10, 1893, R. H. Wright letterbook.

12. *Ibid.*

13. M. E. McDowell and Co., Philadelphia, to Wright, June 29, 1885; Marburg Brothers, Baltimore, to Wright, July 6, 1885; W. S. Kimball and Co., Rochester, to Wright, July 11, 1885. Theo. E. Allen, a prominent tobacco man in New York and friend of Wright's, wrote that the possible buyer whom he had found wanted to buy only the goodwill and brands of the Dukes, they agreeing not to manufacture for themselves or for anyone else either cigarettes or smoking tobacco. Allen to Wright, July 6, 1885, Wright MSS.

feel disposed to forward your interests in every possible way." He expected to visit Durham soon to see what could be worked out to their mutual advantage and, in the meantime, congratulated Duke "upon the wonderful success of your firm."[14]

The negotiations between J. B. Duke and Strouse apparently began in April and culminated in New York in May, 1885. Eager for a wide market for the Bonsack machine as well as for its use in the manufacture of some of the better, more expensive brands of cigarettes, Strouse had good reason to woo James B. Duke and to fear certain companies that scorned the Bonsack machine and advertised the alleged superiority of the hand-made cigarette to the machine-made one. Duke well knew what his firm could do for the Bonsack Company and was determined that Strouse should pay accordingly.

The verbal agreement that the two men negotiated would be reduced to writing in two later stages and was one of the pivotal secrets of the tobacco industry in the late 1880's. It called for W. Duke, Sons and Company to utilize at once two of the Bonsack machines on their best brands and gradually to increase the number of machines as fast as practicable in light of the popular prejudice against machine-made cigarettes and the necessity of phasing out the hand-rollers and trying to avoid labor trouble. Strouse, for his part, agreed that the rate of royalty on the machines at the Duke factory should at once be reduced from thirty-three cents per thousand for printed cigarettes and thirty for unprinted ones to twenty-four cents per thousand on all cigarettes; furthermore, when and if all cigarettes produced by the Duke firm were made by machines the rate would be reduced to twenty cents per thousand; and, finally, if the Bonsack rate of royalty to any other manufacturer should ever be reduced below the standard rate of thirty-three and thirty cents respectively, W. Duke, Sons and Company should have its rate proportionately reduced so that it would always be charged 25 percent less than any other manufacturer.[15]

Adept from an early age at the businessman's art of masking his emotions, James B. Duke may or may not have expressed any satisfaction when he told Richard Wright about the contract with the Bonsack Company within twenty-four hours of the time that Duke and Strouse had finally struck their agreement. Wright, who later claimed to have been an early and ardent champion of the Bonsack

14. Strouse to Duke, March 24, 1885, J. B. Duke letterbook.
15. Brief for defendants, p. 7, B. N. Duke MSS. See also R. H. Wright to W. J. Curtis, May 10, 1893, R. H. Wright letterbook.

machine, minimized Duke's achievement by suggesting, "Hell, he [Strouse] ought to have given you the twenty-cent rate at once." Wright urged that the Duke firm should decline to accept the proposition, not install any more machines for a while, and thereby bring Strouse to offer even better terms.[16]

Wright and Duke later disagreed as to whether Duke actually had revealed the final part of the contract, that is, the pledge of a rate for W. Duke Sons, and Company that would always be 25 percent less than that of any other manufacturer. The two men agreed, however, that Duke had promptly told Wright about the negotiations with Strouse and that Wright had scoffed at the whole thing. Regardless of Wright's opinion, James B. Duke intended to gamble on the Bonsack machine; accordingly, after going to Lynchburg, Virginia, to pick up the contract from Strouse, Ben Duke reported, "We have all three machines busily at work from morning till night and expect to continue them the balance of the year." In fact, he expected that the firm would soon be ordering an additional machine.[17]

With machine-made cigarettes pouring out in an ever-swelling stream and with the favorable contract with the Bonsack Company, W. Duke, Sons and Company was ready to advance—except for the problem of the disgruntled partner, Richard H. Wright. True, Wright was having great personal problems around May and June, 1885, for the young wife whom he had married about a year before died after giving birth to a sickly daughter, who would herself die at the age of four. Wright was not one to neglect his business affairs, however, and his refusal to go to Durham for the conference which his partners urgently requested was clearly inspired in large part by the legal advice he had initially received about a "game" which his lawyer had assured him was "very much in your hands."

Facing up to the gravity of the situation, his partners also retained counsel, and, after a final abortive effort in late June to come to terms with Wright, they issued a public notice on July 2, 1885, that the old

16. The quotation is from the Brief for the defendants, p. 8, B. N. Duke MSS, and Wright's detailed corroboration may be found in Wright to W. J. Curtis, May 10, 1893, R. H. Wright letterbook.

17. Ben Duke to D. B. Strouse, June 15, 1885, sheaf in J. B. Duke letterbook no. 3. Ben Duke and George Watts were unaware of exactly what J. B. Duke and Strouse had agreed on in New York. Not until January, 1885, did James B. Duke ask to see the contract while on a visit to Durham and discover that it lacked the last part concerning the 25 percent lower rate for W. Duke, Sons, and Company. He accordingly demanded and got the supplemental clause from Strouse, who travelled to Durham on January 19, 1886. Brief for defendants, p. 9.

five-man partnership, "having expired by effluxion of the time limited for its duration," was from thenceforth dissolved. "The business of manufacturing Smoking Tobacco and Cigarettes will be continued without any break at the old stand by" Brodie L. Duke, Benjamin N. Duke, James B. Duke, and George W. Watts.[18] Securing the services of disinterested parties to inventory the firm's "physical, tangible, perishable assets," the Dukes and George Watts invited Wright or his representative to be "present to see that everything is properly and correctly listed."[19]

Although Wright ignored the invitation, he allegedly told James B. Duke on July 2, 1885, that he, Wright, would sell his share of the firm "to a rival who would buy, to wreck the business and get the Dukes out of the way."[20] Wright had been advised by his attorney, John W. Hinsdale, that "a suit in the U.S. Court, asking for a dissolution [of the firm] & settlement, and in the meantime a *receiver*," would quickly bring Wright's partners to terms. Hinsdale noted that some of the federal courts were "very liberal in the appointment of receivers" and that such a course would not only be "very distasteful to your partners" but "calculated to cause much alarm." Even if the court refused to appoint a receiver, the lawyer continued, it would unhesitatingly order a "speedy settlement," and that "would necessitate a sale of everything, and the third parties, to whom you referred, could become competitors for the brands, trade marks &c &c." Hinsdale suggested that "the *firm name* is one of the most valuable" assets of W. Duke, Sons and Company, and the "good will includes the *firm name*." The goodwill being of such obvious value in the case, it too would have to be sold, and, Hinsdale asserted, "a court will protect the purchaser by injunction if necessary."[21]

Sure enough, Wright filed his bill in equity in Federal District court in Greensboro, North Carolina, in mid-July, 1885, and only the elusiveness of James B. Duke, who managed somehow to avoid being served a subpoena, slowed Wright's legal maneuvers aimed at the appointment of a receiver and the forced sale of the firm. Hinsdale assured his client, who had misgivings about the public's reaction to the affair, that the suit was "not to be tried by public opinion, and

18. Printed announcement of July 2, 1885, R. H. Wright MSS.
19. Brief for defendants, pp. 3–4.
20. *Ibid.*, p. 5.
21. J. W. Hinsdale to R. H. Wright, June 15, 30, 1885, Wright MSS. See Hinsdale to Wright, July 23, 1885, about a possible suit for damages as well.

if it were, a true statement of the facts would satisfy any reasonable man that you are in the right."[22]

A settlement out of court, one closer to the price asked by Wright, was probably what he wanted all along. To one intermediary who reported that the former partners were ready to buy Wright's interest for $40,000, Wright intimated that earlier he had offered to sell for that sum but had been turned down; now he would sell for $42,500, and for $5,000 extra would agree not to engage in the manufacture of smoking tobacco or cigarettes for five years.[23] Hinsdale assured Wright that his former partners' charge of blackmail was "simply to create a diversion & to call attention away from their hoggish behavior towards you," and Wright's sister hoped, vainly as it turned out, that he might split the ranks of his opponents: "Secure Watts' *friendship*. Now is your time—Strike while the iron is hot, if the cost will not be too great. . . ."[24]

Despite such counsel, Wright edged toward a settlement. The Dukes and Watts offered to pay him $36,000 or—and this was a part of the ritual in such business tangles—they would sell each of their interests to him at that price. Wright replied on September 14, 1885, that he desired to avoid the "expense and vexation" of further litigation; that his interest in the firm at the first of the year "amounted to, say, $22,500" and that sum added to one-fifth of the $100,000 that one party had offered for the goodwill and trademarks came to $42,500; but to "arrive at an amicable settlement, I will sell to you my interest in the good will, trade-marks, effects, assets and property, real and personal, of the firm for $39,750."[25]

Wright's partners promptly accepted the offer and were, no doubt, relieved to have escaped from a painful, dangerous dilemma. They had by no means heard the last of Richard Wright, however, for he immediately invested heavily in the Lone Jack Cigarette Company of Lynchburg, Virginia, and became a principal stockholder of the company as well as its manager. He intended, as he put it, "to outstrip the Dukes" with the Lone Jack brand. It had become famous since the Civil War as a smoking tobacco and was now to be pushed vigorously in a line of cigarettes, for Wright knew the tobacco industry

22. Hinsdale to Wright, July 18, 21, 23, August 3, 5, 18, September 7, 1885, Wright MSS. Quotation from letter of August 3.

23. [Wright] to Theodore E. Allen, August 1, 1885, Wright MSS.

24. Hinsdale to Wright, August 18, 1885, and Mrs. J. R. Ball to Wright, August, 1885, Wright MSS.

25. In Brief for defendants, pp. 5–6.

just as well as did his former partners. Furthermore, since one or two of the principal officers of the Lone Jack Company were also officers of the Bonsack Machine Company and because the Bonsack Company used the Lone Jack factory for certain experiments and trial runs, Wright obtained a special and highly secret contract from D. B. Strouse. It provided that the Lone Jack Company would pay not the standard royalty rate for the Bonsack machine of thirty-three or thirty cents per thousand cigarettes, but a mere fifteen cents per thousand, which was significantly lower than even the secret rate James B. Duke had negotiated. Not for nearly five years would Duke learn of the Lone Jack's rate, but when he did legal fur began to fly in all directions.[26]

These secret contracts became known in the tobacco world around 1890. By then, W. Duke, Sons and Company, reorganized in 1885 as a joint-stock company, had forged to the top of the cigarette industry. James B. Duke served as president of the firm, Ben Duke as vice-president, and George Watts as secretary-treasurer; Washington Duke and Brodie Duke were also listed on the company's letterhead, since they were equal stockholders even if not officers. Characterized by an economic historian as "the leading innovator in the American cigarette business during the 1880's," James B. Duke vigorously led his firm in making "entrepreneurial contributions in marketing, in purchasing, and in production which were the driving force for change."[27] In an era when many entrepreneurs, large and small, looked admiringly at John D. Rockefeller and his vast Standard Oil Company, the nations' first great trust, twenty-nine-year-old James B. Duke early set his course toward a "combination."

The Bonsack cigarette machine, which the Duke firm demonstrated to be preeminently successful, played a key role in James B. Duke's strategy and tactics. Among the larger cigarette manufacturers, both the Allen and Ginter Company of Richmond and the F. S. Kinney Company of New York were late in switching from hand-rolled cigarettes, to which their advertisements attributed great superiority, but by 1887 they too were forced to turn to the Bonsack machine.

26. For Wright's move to Lynchburg, see P. A. Krise to Wright, September 12, 1885; Wright to Isaac N. Link (whom Wright tried in vain to lure from the Duke factory in Durham), November 17, 1885. Wright MSS and letterbook. For the Bonsack contract with the Lone Jack Company, see D. B. Strouse to J. B. Duke, June 28, 1890, sheaf in J. B. Duke letterbook no. 3.

27. Patrick G. Porter, "Origins of the American Tobacco Company," *Business History Review*, XLIII (Spring, 1969), p. 65.

Two other large manufacturers, Goodwin and Company of New York and W. S. Kimball and Company of Rochester, New York, used machines that were rivals to Bonsack's invention, Goodwin employing the Emery machine and Kimball the Allison.[28]

Learning that the Kimball Company was pushing its "Old Gold" brand at a fearfully low price, James B. Duke complained to Strouse, who had claimed that the Allison machine at Kimball's plant infringed on certain Bonsack patents, that if Kimball were not checked it would "necessarily shut out the manufacturers who use your [Bonsack] machines from making a cheap cigarette and give him a monopoly on that class of goods, which will cut you out of a big revenue." Duke argued that if the Bonsack patents were being infringed, Strouse should take prompt action. "If they are not infringing you," Duke threatened, "I must see if I can't put myself in shape to get my goods made so that I can compete."[29]

Wishing to keep down the number of producers in the fiercely competitive industry, James B. Duke began pushing Strouse as early as 1885 to restrict the use of the Bonsack machine to the major manufacturers. "Please let me know as soon as possible," Duke wrote, "what proposition you will be able to make, looking to a concentration of the business, and I will do what I can to bring about such a move." Duke thought it would be wise for the Bonsack Company to make "just as close a figure as possible [on rates], so as to induce those who are using other machines which you claim are infringements, to drop them rather than go into litigation over the matter."[30]

The "concentration of the business" which Duke referred to would be the American Tobacco Company and would take more years and effort than perhaps he initially realized, but in the meantime W. Duke, Sons and Company clamored for more Bonsack machines than Strouse could supply. Too, there was constant worry about fire. "We think it very important, for your sake, as well as ours," George Watts admonished Strouse, "that you should always keep duplicate machines to those that we use, for in case of a fire here [in the Durham factory] and the destruction of your machines we would be in a bad way, unless we could immediately secure the same number of other ma-

28. Tilley, *Bright-Tobacco Industry*, pp. 574–576.
29. J. B. Duke to D. B. Strouse, October 13, 1885, sheaf in J. B. Duke letterbook no. 1. As far back as March 24, 1885, Strouse had tried to assure Duke that the Allison machine posed no threat and would be limited to Rochester. "They admit that we have them in our power," Strouse declared. J. B. Duke letterbook.
30. Duke to Strouse, November 26, 1885, *ibid*.

chines from you. A few months' inability to supply our cigarettes might destroy our trade upon them, as the smokers would not wait upon us, but try other goods and probably become addicted to using the next best brand that they could find."[31]

If the threat of loss from fire increased with the switch to the Bonsack machine, so did the problem of maintaining a contented labor force. The Jewish emigrant hand-rollers, who had been brought down from New York to Durham in the early 1880's when the Dukes first began to produce cigarettes and some of whom ate their meals at the home of Washington Duke, greeted the first machine in 1884, and W. T. O'Brien, the expert mechanic, with threats and open hostility. Since the single machine worked so imperfectly, however, and the demand for cigarettes kept the hand-rollers fully occupied, the initial friction with the workers passed. By late 1885 and 1886, the machine in the Duke plant had clearly triumphed, and the leaders among the rollers, as Washington Duke later recalled, gave the company "no end of trouble." Well might the hand-rollers protest, for they were early victims of the technological revolution that would eventually eliminate the jobs of carriage-makers, blacksmiths, and countless other groups. "We have today notified our hands of a reduction in the price of making [cigarettes] and many of them may leave," the Duke firm informed Strouse in early 1886, "in which event we would need at least one more machine at once."[32]

Most of the Jewish workers did indeed return to New York. The Durham *Tobacco Plant* reported on September 15, 1886, that all save two had departed. "Their places," the *Plant* added laconically, "will be supplied by 'Natives' and machines." What the *Plant* did not explain, since it went largely without saying at that time and place, was that the "Natives," both black and white, male and female, young and old, were desperately eager for regular employment and would long constitute a remarkably vulnerable and unorganized labor force.

Confident of being able to handle whatever problems might arise from the workers, J. B. Duke in New York in 1886 pressed Strouse for additional Bonsack machines: "We are needing them badly now, as we are having to work at night to keep up with orders." Like his partners in Durham, Duke reminded Strouse of the importance of

31. Watts to Strouse, November 21, 1885, sheaf in J. B. Duke letterbook no. 3.
32. Tilley, *Bright-Tobacco Industry*, pp. 519–520; Washington Duke is quoted in the Raleigh *News and Observer*, April 5, 1896; W. Duke, Sons and Company to Strouse, February 8, 1886, sheaf in J. B. Duke letterbook no. 3.

quick replacements in case of fire and added the information that "our new brand [Cameo] is cleaning up things here, and I think will be a great success." Then remembering himself, Duke added: "I must ask that you keep strictly confidential what we write you, as we don't want any one to know how many machines we have or intend to put in; with the present state of things it is best for us both."[33]

From Durham, Ben Duke too pushed for additional machines. "Our trade is suffering on account of our inability to turn out goods fast enough to meet the increased demand for our cigarettes . . . ," he complained. He suggested, confidentially of course, that with prospects what they were, the firm would probably want to have at least twelve machines altogether in the Durham plant. (Actually, there were fifteen by the end of the year and 750 laborers.) When the Duke firm had unfilled orders for four additional machines at the very moment when one arrived at the old rival and neighboring Blackwell plant, George Watts thundered: "We do most emphatically object to your giving anyone preference over us, as you have admitted to us that we were the most profitable factory that was using your machines."[34]

As the Duke firm kept a sharp watch on the Bonsack Company's dealings with other manufacturers, so did Richard Wright and his Lone Jack Company. Despite his own company's highly favorable contract with the Bonsack Company, Wright complained bitterly and frequently about the alleged favoritism shown by Strouse to the Duke firm. "I think you do me a wrong in this matter," Strouse answered on one occasion; "I have not failed to do any possible thing for the Lone Jack Co. nor do I intend to." Wright resented Strouse's sending a mechanic from the Lone Jack plant to the Duke factory, but the Bonsack president argued that Lone Jack, with three machines, was running on half time "while the Dukes are behind orders and if they can't make their goods they will open another house [employing hand-rollers?] in New York." Strouse assured the irate Wright that Lone Jack's welfare would be protected, "but our [Bonsack] interests at Duke's are *so great*, that it would be more than suicidal to let our interest there fail."[35]

As Wright struggled against what he regarded as unfair treatment

33. Duke to Strouse, March 17, 1886, sheaf in J. B. Duke letterbook no. 1.
34. B. N. Duke to Strouse, March 30, 1886, and George Watts to Strouse, April 2, 1886, sheaf in J. B. Duke letterbook no. 3.
35. Strouse to Wright, May 31, 1886. R. H. Wright MSS, legal papers of 1880's.

from Strouse, the Lone Jack Company's energetic salesmen joined their boss in combatting the Dukes. "There appeared a new spot on the moon this morning," one salesman reported to Wright, when the Duke firm's salesman "started out with Cameo at $3.65 per M [thousand] and a chair with every M." The salesman concluded: "I suppose [the] Dukes think if we are trying to kill them they will die kicking (and kicking high)."[36]

Another Lone Jack salesman advised from eastern North Carolina that he was fighting Duke with "all I know how, and think it will tell." With all the posters he was having put up, he added, people often took him for a circus man. From Kansas City, a Lone Jack salesman insisted that "the Cleveland hangers" he was distributing had "flies" on them because Grover Cleveland had "become a chestnut." "We want something *new*," the salesman argued, something like the new Duke poster which he had mailed back to Wright and of which he bet there were "not less than 5 M now in this city hung up." In response to Wright's demand for greater push, this salesman retorted: "I have more business sense than to advertize Duke. 'Take notice.' I hate them just as much as you do and will work just as hard to down them." The salesman asserted that only by vast amounts of advertising "will we down Mr. Duke" and promised to spend the next night writing Lone Jack advertisements in yellow and blue chalk on the sidewalks of Kansas City. "It is not allowed," the salesman added, "but I think I can do it and not get 'run in' .... Wright[,] we are forced to catch the eyes of the smokers."[37]

Wright and his Lone Jack Company did everything conceivable to give the Duke firm a good race, but by late 1887 Wright apparently saw the hopelessness of the situation. Offering his resignation as manager of the Lone Jack Company, he claimed to have combatted many obstacles, "chief among which is the unfair and unjust treatment of the Bonsack Company at the commencement and during the busy season of each year. . . ." Though Wright delayed his actual withdrawal from the managerial post until the end of 1888, he was ready to move on to what he believed would be greener pastures.[38]

36. B. R. Allen to Wright, June 18, 1886, R. H. Wright MSS.
37. J. S. Walker to Wright, August 31, 1886, and —— Egbert to Wright, March 12, 1888, R. H. Wright MSS.
38. Wright to Edmund Schafer, August 16, 1887, and December 12, 1888, R. H. Wright letterbook. Wright's disagreement with the other officers of the Lone Jack Company about his desire to sue the Duke firm concerning an alleged patent in-

For all Wright's complaints about the Bonsack Company—and at one point he privately referred to James Bonsack the inventor and a principal stockholder in the company, as "a dirty little sneak" and to D. B. Strouse and his associates as a "dirty black-livered lot"—Richard Wright had decided to seek his fortune not with the manufacture of tobacco but with the machinery used in the tobacco industry.[39] Having travelled around the world as a salesman for W. Duke, Sons and Company in the early 1880's, Wright, far ahead of many American businessmen of the time, easily thought in transoceanic terms, and he obtained the exclusive agency from the Bonsack Company to sell the Bonsack cigarette machine in Africa, particularly South Africa and Egypt, and in Asia. He would operate at his own expense and pay the company one half of the gross receipts after deducting the cost of the machines laid down in the foreign country.[40]

James B. Duke, no less than Richard H. Wright, also thought in global terms, and when Strouse made the arrangement with Wright concerning Africa and Asia, Duke roared in anger. "The world is now our market for our product," J. B. Duke declared to Strouse, "and we do not propose sitting idly down and allowing you or any one else to cut off any of the channels of our trade by establishing factories where there have been none and tying up your machinery with them, and afterwards you could say to us, 'You must manufacture your goods in the United States; this country and that country is taken.'" If such really was to be the Bonsack Company's policy, Duke vowed that he and his associates would have to encourage an inventor "to get up a better machine" which would be "controlled solely by W. Duke, Sons & Co."[41]

Strouse, insisting that he thought Duke would be pleased to have Wright packed off to distant parts, defended himself as best he could. "Between you and Kinney," Strouse asserted, "I have the darnedest time that ever a poor mortal did have." The Kinney Company

fringement, which the other officers doubted, may be traced through the Wright MSS for 1886.

39. The quotations are from Wright to Fabius H. Busbee, July 15, 1892, and Wright to W. A. Hulse, August 24, 1892, R. H. Wright letterbook.

40. D. B. Strouse to Wright, December 3, 1888, and April 2, 1889, R. H. Wright MSS. Early in 1889 Wright made the first of many foreign voyages in connection with his Bonsack agency.

41. J. B. Duke to D. B. Strouse, March 20, 1889, from sheaf in J. B. Duke letterbook no. 1.

wanted "to send the Bonsack Machine Co. to the lower regions because of the 'enormous advantages' which W. Duke, Sons & Co.
have . . ." and still it appeared that that advantage did not satisfy
Duke. "You know that for two years," Strouse continued, "I have
been doing all I could to get the Lone Jack Co. out of your way. . . ."
How could the sale of a machine or two in South Africa affect Duke's
trade? The Bonsack machine had been in England since 1882 but
had not the importation there of American cigarettes continuously
increased? Had not a machine gone to Sydney, Australia, over two
years earlier without adversely affecting the trade of the American
manufactures?[42]

To this letter from Strouse, James B. Duke fired back that since
he was not Kinney's guardian he was "not responsible for any trouble
that he [Kinney] may cause you," and if Strouse's actions caused
Duke to give trouble, Strouse had "no one to blame" but himself. As
for the advantage enjoyed by the Duke firm, James B. Duke inquired
tartly if it amounted "to as much as the big royalties which you are
getting from the Bonsack machines"? If it did not, how could Strouse
"in good taste" harp on any advantage of the Duke firm. "We have
more than earned this by introducing and making a market for your
machines," Duke declared, "and I say openly, if it had not been for
us to-day, the Bonsack machine would be a smouldering wreck."

Concerning the Lone Jack Company, Duke insisted that his firm
had never feared competition with the Lynchburg-based business.
But if it or any other company had "been moved one inch out of the
way we have done it by preventing their getting a market for their
goods." Then, "after we have accomplished this and they or some of
them tire of the fight with us in the U.S., you gather them up and
send them to some other country to try their best against us there."
Instead of sending agents abroad to sell machines, Strouse, according
to Duke, might "better use your time and money to stop the infringe-
ment of your own rights in the U.S."

As for the sale of American cigarettes in England, Duke confessed a
rare failure by pointing out that his firm's sales there had been falling
for two or three years. Moreover, he noted that his company had
"received more objections to machine-made cigarettes from England
than any other country." Receiving instructions from wholesalers

42. D. B. Strouse to J. B. Duke, March 23, 1889, J. B. Duke letterbook. Despite
Wright's pleas, Strouse had refused to give him Australia because of pressure from
Duke as well as from Allen and Ginter.

not to ship any more machine-made cigarettes to England, the Duke company had gone ahead and done so. Yet, Duke concluded, "we did not succeed in making a market there for our goods, which was our first failure to get a sale on our goods in any market."

In Cuba, where an entirely different kind of tobacco from the famed Carolina-Virginia bright leaf was used, Duke had no objection to the introduction of the Bonsack machine. "But where mild cigarettes are sold or wanted," he insisted, "the U.S. leads the world in their manufacture," and Strouse could not "in good faith to us and your other patrons carry out your intentions to open up competition for us."[43]

Despite all of the protests of James B. Duke, Strouse stuck by his contract for Africa and Asia with Richard Wright; and for all of Duke's tirades against Strouse, the Bonsack Company's president continued to play a key role in the realization of Duke's long-standing hope for the "concentration" of the nation's cigarette manufacture. As the Duke firm moved toward the installation of the Bonsack machines in the New York branch of the company, Strouse in the summer of 1887 sent Duke a "Personal & Private" message from Rochester, New York: "Kimball is in favor of a combination which will restrict the machines to the large factories—so is Ginter. I can easily arrange matters all around here. Can you see as to Kinney and Emery[?]"[44]

Duke, expressing to Strouse his satisfaction that the other major producers of cigarettes thought "favorably of the arrangements which I have advocated to you for quite a while," felt more confident than ever that concentration would be best for the Bonsack Company as well as for the cigarette manufacturers. He had suggested the idea to F. S. Kinney early in the year, and since nothing more had been done by Kinney, Duke thought the matter should be left quietly to ripen. The young tobacco magnate indulged in a rare burst of near-philosophizing: "It requires time to get competitors to see things in the same light, but it requires hard work to smother out a good idea, and if you [Strouse] are prepared to be patient (since you already have a good thing with Kimball, Ginter and Duke to rest upon), you can rest assured that time will bring the others in. We were the first to give you substantial support, and I told you at the time, that our doing so would bring the others in, and you see that my predictions

43. Duke to Strouse, March 27, 1889, sheaf in J. B. Duke letterbook no. 1.
44. Strouse to Duke, July 8, 1887, J. B. Duke letterbook.

are coming true to the extent of two large manufacturers, and you now have more than three-fifths of the business on account of making it an inducement to us to handle your machines."

With five large cigarette manufacturers who had most of the business, Duke saw no chance for any new firm to compete "unless they are willing to sacrifice $1,000,000 on chances of being successful." Despite "the sharpest competition" in 1887 that he had ever seen in the business, Duke noted that his company had "made the largest increases" in its history. "Our aggregate orders now are 2,000,000 [cigarettes] per day," he declared, "and if we keep on at the present rate of increase, it will not be long before they greatly exceed this amount." Ordering five Bonsack machines for the New York branch, with five more to follow upon the installation of the first batch, Duke could not resist a boast: "I claim that our house is the leader in the business, and it certainly is in enterprise, and the others must follow us or find that they will gradually be left. These are facts, but I would not make use of them, unless I believed that you would keep them STRICTLY CONFIDENTIAL." Reiterating his constant theme to Strouse, Duke insisted that the "fewer number of hands you have the machines in, the more you will make."[45]

Despite pronouncements about patience and a visit to Lynchburg for a conference with Strouse, J. B. Duke was not satisfied with the pace of developments. "It certainly strikes me that it is time for you to come down off the fence and take either one side or the other and let us know what your platform will be," he wrote Strouse early in 1888. As for the Duke firm's buying out the Lone Jack Company, as Strouse had suggested, that would be a simple matter of proving that it would "be money in W. Duke, Sons & Co.'s pockets to run a factory in Lynchburg" and would not conflict with any of the firm's existing establishments. The Lone Jack goodwill and trademarks, Duke explained, would be worthless to W. Duke, Sons and Company, and, he added, "it is my opinion that it will be worth less than nothing to them to continue running."[46]

45. Duke to Strouse, July 19, 1887, sheaf in J. B. Duke letterbook no. 1. Duke's attention to important details, apart from the larger matter of the combination, is shown in his letter to Strouse of August 23, 1887, where he ordered five printing dies each of the Cameo and Cross-Cut brands so that all five of the first machines in the New York factory could produce either brand, depending on the calls of the trade that varied from day to day. He also had outlined the switching of full production, including operators, between the Durham and New York factories in case of fire at either plant.

46. Duke to Strouse, January 21, February 2, 1888, ibid.

After a conference of J. B. Duke, Lewis Ginter, and D. B. Strouse in Richmond in early February, 1888, Duke learned that a Bonsack machine was being shipped to the Hess Company of Rochester, New York. "You ought to countermand such orders as far as possible at once," he urged Strouse. "You have a good arrangement with Ginter and ourselves and you will be proud of it in a very short while but you must keep off the mosquito[e]s."[47]

Responding to Duke's demands, Strouse, after conferring with the other officers and directors of his company, finally wrote identical letters, which he termed the official "agreement between us," to the Duke firm and to Allen and Ginter. The Bonsack Company pledged to supply the two houses with as many machines as they desired, "you paying the same royalties you now pay." The Bonsack Company also agreed "not to place any of our machines in any house in the United States in which we have no machines now, and not to place any more machines in any house in which they are now in the United States, unless in our judgment we are legally or honorably bound to do so, and that as the opportunities may occur to remove the machines from the other factories in the United States, in which they now are, we will remove them, so that such removal shall not be in violation of good faith and fair dealing with such houses, not obligating ourselves however, to purchase the right to make such removals." The Bonsack Company's condition for the preceding arrangement was that "at least one half of the cigarettes made in the United States during 1888 and each year thereafter, be made on our machines, and whenever we shall find that such is not the case, we shall have the right at our option to cancel this agreement."[48]

Although J. B. Duke had finally gained a large part of what he wanted from Strouse and the Bonsack Company, there was a fly in the ointment having to do with Strouse's phrase about the Duke firm's, as well as Allen and Ginter's, "paying the same royalties you now pay." Duke's original contract of 1885 called not only for a reduction in the royalty rate from twenty-four to twenty cents per thousand cigarettes when machines were employed exclusively in the Duke factories, toward which condition Duke was moving after mid-1887, but there was also the final clause, added to the written contract early in 1886, concerning the 25 percent lower rate for the Duke firm than

47. Duke to Strouse, February 2, 1888, *ibid.*
48. Strouse to W. Duke, Sons and Company, February 8, 1888, J. B. Duke letterbook.

charged to any other manufacturer. Strouse clearly had hoped to escape from that original contract, but James B. Duke seems to have grown up reading fine print—as well as between the lines. He replied to Strouse: "We don't want this [new] contract to, in any manner[,] interfere with the one which we have with you regarding use of machines, royalties &c. We don't know that it does as we are not lawyers and have not consulted any." Duke also suggested that Strouse's phrase about the Duke firm's and Allen and Ginter's being allowed the "continuous use" of the Bonsack machine be changed to the "exclusive use" of it.[49]

"The restriction to the royalties as *now paid*," Strouse then admitted, "was an item that induced us to make the agreement." Strouse pointed out that Allen and Ginter had agreed to it (as well they might, since the Duke firm's special rates were highly secret). Assuring Duke that the Bonsack Company would remove the machines from the other, smaller houses as soon as possible consistent "with what we shall regard as fair dealing," Strouse pressed for early acceptance of the terms he had offered.[50]

Duke finally responded in a lengthy letter: "I have been taught by experience that in settling difficulties the surest mode of success was to use perfect candor and fair dealing. In that spirit I am determined to treat you on this occasion and shall be disappointed if it does not bring you to treat us justly, and give us what we feel we are so clearly entitled to by reason of the risk and hazard we took upon ourselves in testing and proving the merits of your machines, by which you were so much benefited." Duke then repeated the circumstances surrounding his firm's original gamble on the Bonsack machine and the gradual triumph of the machine-made cigarette which followed. The reduction of the force of hand-rollers had necessarily proceeded slowly, Duke pointed out, "to avoid all possible danger of doing injustice to our employees and all risk of collision with labor organizations," and Strouse had been "humane enough and considerate enough to recognize the truth that we were moving as fast as good judgement and sound policy dictated for us."

Now that the time approached when the firm could do all of its work on the machine "without doing injustice to any of our dependents," Duke insisted upon "a faithful performance of that contract

49. Duke to Strouse, February 16, 1888, sheaf in J. B. Duke letterbook no. 1.
50. Strouse to Duke, February 29, 1888, J. B. Duke letterbook. When no reply came, Strouse wrote again on March 7, 1888.

[of 1885] on your part, by promptly giving us such a drawback as will reduce our royalty to 20¢ per M cig[arettes]." Slipping away from the lofty tone, Duke termed the new contract about rates which Strouse had proposed as "absolutely childish" and a matter that had not been discussed at all in conferences at Richmond and elsewhere. "When you are prepared to offer a contract carrying out the understanding as it was made," he concluded, "then we are ready to entertain it; otherwise we have no further time to waste with something entirely foreign to our understanding."[51]

With Duke adamant in his refusal to relinquish any of the terms of his old contract, matters hung fire as Strouse engaged in legal battles to protect the Bonsack Company's patents, and Duke coped with labor troubles in his New York factory. Finally Strouse, sending Duke a revised contract to sign, declared: "With this contract I don't care who knows what you pay, for you will see that I have set out the true grounds ample to sustain it. You will stand just as you do now and I will be free from any embarrassment." A contract for the Kinney Company had been prepared, and Strouse had successfully resisted Kinney's effort to include a clause stipulating that he should have all the advantages that anyone using the Bonsack machines had.[52] Duke apparently signed the revised contract, for he subsequently reminded Strouse that the Bonsack Company had pledged to the Duke firm and to Allen and Ginter that the Bonsack-controlled machines, which eventually included not only the original Bonsack invention but also the Emery and Allison rival machines, would not be placed in the United States outside of the five major houses, that is Duke, Allen and Ginter, Kinney, Goodwin, and Kimball.[53]

Even larger developments loomed in the cigarette industry as the pace quickened in 1889 toward the combination which James B. Duke had urged for nearly five years. When Strouse informed him that some of the manufacturers had suggested a meeting to be held in New York "with a view to the organization of a consolidated cigarette company," Duke replied warily: "I am perfectly willing to meet the manufacturers at any time to discuss any matter for our common good, but if you mean by consolidated cigarette company that there is to be another factory started or a trust formed, and want us to take stock in them, I am opposed to anything of the kind, as we

51. Duke to Strouse, March 16, 1888, sheaf in J. B. Duke letterbook no. 1.
52. Strouse to Duke, May 4, 1888, J. B. Duke letterbook.
53. Duke to Strouse, December 12, 1889, J. B. Duke MSS.

want the full control of our own business, which we could not have with a trust. If there is any other proposition to discuss I will meet if called."[54]

In light of his later role and reputation, James B. Duke's disdain for "anything" like a trust was ironic. Strouse, after conferring with Kinney and explaining to him why Duke wanted no part of any absolute consolidation of the various firms, informed Duke that Kinney was most eager to get out of the advertising madhouse in which the cigarette industry had come to operate and to end what Kinney termed "this damned picture business." Strouse agreed that the business was undoubtedly "being greatly degraded" by all the advertising stunts and suggested that eventually an agreement might be worked out among the big five "on a basis of the number of cigarettes [produced] or gross sales."[55]

Duke soon replied that he had seen Lewis Ginter, who agreed to meet with the other four large manufacturers, and that a meeting had accordingly been called at the Fifth Avenue Hotel on April 23, 1889, at 3:30 P.M. "It will perhaps be well for you to be in the city at this time" Duke advised Strouse, "to see if you can settle your machine difficulties."[56] Many meetings and much hard negotiating would continue through 1889 as the American Tobacco Company was being born, but far from settling his "machine difficulties," D. B. Strouse and the Bonsack Company encountered a host of new problems as lawsuits swirled about them.

Like a hive of bees made angry by some intruder, various tobacco manufacturers stirred themselves into legal action around 1890. Many of the cases were compromised, but not before various secrets were spilled—and additional lawsuits thus inspired. James B. Duke heard rumors of the Lone Jack Company's preferential treatment by the Bonsack Company at least as early as 1888. After he complained, Strouse assured him that what Duke had heard was false. "The Lone Jack Co. pays us for *every cigarette they make*," Strouse pledged, "though they have not done work enough during the last two months to employ one machine constantly."[57] Duke no doubt fully understood the limitations of Strouse's guarded explanation, but when

54. Strouse to Duke, March 23, 1889, and Duke to Strouse, March 27, 1889, J. B. Duke letterbook.
55. Strouse to Duke, April 8, 1889, J. B. Duke letterbook.
56. Duke to Strouse, April 20, 1889, sheaf in J. B. Duke letterbook no. 1.
57. Strouse to Duke, June 2, 1888, J. B. Duke letterbook.

the Lone Jack Company initiated legal action against the Bonsack Company in May, 1890, Duke, as well as all the other cigarette manufacturers, began to learn the facts about the Lone Jack Company's fifteen-cent rate. Duke, thereupon, demanded under his original contract, with its provision for a 25 percent lower rate for the Duke firm, that the Bonsack Company owed his company a refund of around $237,000 in allegedly excessive royalties, since Duke claimed that the rate to his firm should have been not twenty-four cents (or perhaps finally twenty cents) per thousand cigarettes but eleven and one-fourth cents. The Bonsack Company insisted that the lower rate charged to the Lone Jack firm was justified by real and substantial services rendered to the Bonsack Company, just as was the special rate charged the Duke firm. James B. Duke refused not only to accept Strouse's defense of the Lone Jack rate but also to pay any further royalties at all to the Bonsack Company until the matter was settled. Allen and Ginter, likewise aroused by Strouse's favoritism both to the Lone Jack and the Duke houses, balked at further payments to the Bonsack Company.[58]

When the Bonsack Company sued first Allen and Ginter and then W. Duke, Sons and Company, to collect the unpaid royalties, and both firms filed counterclaims, the cases were eventually compromised out of court. In the Duke case, however, where the Bonsack Company reportedly paid around $130,000 to settle the claim against it, James B. Duke testified before the case was dropped that Richard Wright had not known in 1885 of the Duke-Bonsack contract; Duke later insisted under oath that he had meant that Wright had not seen the written contract but that he, Duke, had promptly told Wright all about the terms Strouse had agreed to in the late spring of 1885, when Wright had suggested holding out for a more favorable contract. More significantly, a letter written by George Watts to Strouse on September 7, 1885, a week before Wright finally came to terms with his former partners, was introduced as evidence in the Bonsack-Duke suit. Watts, fearing that Wright's efforts in federal court to force the dissolution and sale of the Duke firm might succeed, wanted to make sure that the Dukes and he would have the Bonsack machines in the

58. The R. H. Wright MSS shed much light on this legal tangle, but the clearest summaries may be found in *Wright* v. *Duke* 36 New York Supp. 853 (1895), *Bonsack Machine Co.* v. *S. F. Hess and Co.* 68 Federal Report 119 (1895), and in other legal documents cited below. The first three unconventional letterbooks in the J. B. Duke MSS, as well as the two sheafs of copies of letters therein, were obviously compiled in 1890 in preparation for litigation.

new cigarette business which they expected promptly to launch in such a contingency. "If we can get these machines, soon as we should want them" Watts stated, "and under the same arrangements as now (of which Mr. Wright knows nothing) we would endeavor not to employ any hands to roll cigarettes."[59]

Wright had actually been contemplating legal action against his former partners even before James B. Duke's testimony and George Watts' letter were put on record. After that happened, however, Wright sprang into action. Because the statute of limitations barred his suit in North Carolina, he moved from Durham, where he had returned in the fall of 1890, to New York in order to establish legal residence there in August, 1891, and to bring suit charging fraud and deceit against his former partners. Retaining Sullivan and Cromwell, one of the nation's leading law firms, Wright told his Raleigh lawyer, John W. Hinsdale, that no mistake could be risked in the case because "it would afford the Dukes too much pleasure to defeat me in the suit." Wright hoped to "make them stink in the nostrils of honest people."[60]

In testimony and in the brief filed for the plaintiff, Wright hammered away at the thesis that the spectacular prosperity of W. Duke, Sons and Company between 1885 and 1890 had only one explanation, the Bonsack contract, and that his former partners had practiced fraud upon him in concealing the existence of such a valuable asset. "The sum [for damages] must be large," the plaintiff's brief suggested, "and if there be difficulty in estimating it, that difficulty is no more than frequently exists and never would have arisen but for defendant's original fraud. . . . Judgment should be rendered for plaintiff with substantial damages equal to one-fifth of the full actual value of the contract."[61]

Wright's brief, however, failed to mention his efforts to seek a court-ordered sale of the Duke firm. Moreover, in attributing the entire success of that firm between 1885 and 1890 solely to the Bonsack contract, Wright and his lawyers conveniently neglected to mention that in those same years the Lone Jack Company had actually

59. Watts to Strouse, September 7, 1885, sheaf in J. B. Duke letterbook no. 3.
60. Wright to Hinsdale, July 31, 1H. 981, R. Wright letterbook.
61. Brief for plaintiff, *R. H. Wright v. J. B. Duke, B. L. Duke, B. N. Duke, and G. W. Watts*, Court of City and County of New York, in R. H. Wright MSS, legal papers of 1890's.

enjoyed an even more favorable Bonsack contract than had the Duke house, yet Lone Jack had certainly not prospered.

The testimony of James B. Duke as well as the printed statement for the defendants presented Wright's various actions throughout 1885 from a different perspective, of course. J. B. Duke insisted that he had fully informed Wright of all the terms agreed to by Strouse in the spring of 1885. As for the letter of September 7, 1885, Watts swore that he alone was responsible for it; that the firm had to consider the possibility of launching a new business if Wright forced a sale of the existing one; and that the phrase about Wright's not knowing of the then existing "arrangements" between the Duke house and the Bonsack company was more or less an afterthought added toward the close of the letter and intended to reassure the Bonsack Company that it need not worry about Wright's disclosing the terms of the contract to Allen and Ginter and other cigarette manufacturers.[62]

Privately, Wright had expressed great confidence in his case. "I have no fears about winning my case vs. the Dukes," he informed a friend in Durham. He may even have expected a compromise settlement before the start of the trial, for he added: "I expect them to die hard & try to save the odium a suit for fraud will cast on them." When the judge actually found against Wright and ordered him to pay costs, he ordered his brother in Durham "to keep quiet on it & not express any opinion one way or the other about it."[63]

The crux of the judge's decision against Wright was that the Duke-Bonsack contract of 1885, if viewed in its actual context rather than from the hindsight afforded by more than five years, involved a real gamble and could only have had a potential or prospective value. The matter of successfully marketing machine-made cigarettes, declared the judge, was "still in supposition and it would have been simply impossible to place any value on the prospect . . . subject to so many contingencies of experiment and risk." Furthermore, the judge held that even if one assumed that the Bonsack contract had some sort of value as of September, 1885, when Wright sold his interest, the plaintiff admitted knowing about J. B. Duke's negotiations with Strouse in New York (though there was disagreement about a

62. Statement [of defendants], in case as cited above, B. N. Duke MSS, 1966 addition, legal papers.
63. Wright to R. I. Rogers, March 18, 1893, and Wright to Thomas D. Wright, November 2, 1893, R. H. Wright letterbook.

key detail), and yet "during the whole time the settlement with his partners was under consideration, [Wright] never seems to have exhibited the slightest interest in or concern about the relations of his firm with the Bonsack Company."[64]

The leading trade journal in the industry, *Tobacco*, declared (November 17, 1893) that Wright had merely been envious of his former partners and that the abortive suit had grown out of "the success of the cigarette, and is but one of a series of legal battles brought on by the unsuccessful to make those who were successful divide the spoils." There the matter rested as far as the public then knew, though Wright presented his own version of the affair in a letter to the trade journals.

What few people knew at the time, or since, was that Richard Wright, who was not one to give up easily, appealed the decision. Hinsdale had advised from Raleigh that he saw little to be gained from an appeal. "I think your want of recollection and your own contradictions of yourself are mainly the reason of your failure," Hinsdale declared. He claimed to have warned Wright that if he resumed the stand and told the judge what he, Wright, had told Hinsdale, then the case would be lost. After Wright's testimony, Hinsdale said he heard one of Duke's lawyers tell another one, "Surely he [Wright] has delivered himself into our hands."[65]

Despite such pessimistic counsel, Wright persevered, and after considerable, and amusing, negotiations with the lofty firm of Sullivan and Cromwell about the fee they would charge him, the slow mills of justice were set to grinding again in 1894. All along, Wright seems to have hoped that a profitable compromise settlement would be worked out. While his appeal for a retrial was still pending, he had his old acquaintance, Theodore E. Allen, approach James B. Duke about a possible settlement out of court. Allen reported on his talk with Duke: "He said you was wasting money by appealing. He was sure to win, but that the whole matter was in the hands of his counsel [Williamson W. Fuller] and any settlement or arrangement must be done through his counsel."[66]

In early 1895 Wright again utilized Allen, who worked for a contingency fee, in an attempt to bring off a compromise settlement.

64. Copy of Judge Patterson's finding in case cited above, R. H. Wright MSS, legal papers of the 1890's.

65. Hinsdale to Wright, November 9, 1893, R. H. Wright MSS.

66. Allen to Wright, November 20, 1894, *ibid.* Aside from the normal delays in such legal affairs, Wright prolonged the case by his frequent trips abroad on his business affairs.

Wright authorized Allen to settle the matter if the Dukes and Watts would pay Wright "one fifth of what they actually recovered from the Bonsack Company in their suit with said co. for breach of the contract under which I claim a one fifth individual interest," each party to pay his own costs in the case. Once again Allen failed when W. W. Fuller, who had moved from Durham to become chief counsel for the American Tobacco Company, refused to compromise but offered merely to recommend that the judgment of over $2,000 against Wright be cancelled if he would withdraw all proceedings.[67] To the undoubted dismay of the Dukes and Watts and the obvious glee of Wright, late in 1895 he won the right to a retrial by order of the Supreme Court of New York.[68]

The mating dance of whooping cranes could not be more elaborate or humorous than the tortured negotiations that ensued as the various parties crept cautiously toward a compromise. None other than D. B. Strouse, he who had negotiated all the controversial contracts in the first place, played a pivotal role as intermediary. In his initial interview about the matter with W. W. Fuller, Strouse was surprised to learn that during the original trial one of Wright's lawyers, when asked by the judge what damages the plaintiff claimed, had replied "some where from $6,000 to $25,000." Strouse, therefore, advised Wright that the figure of $100,000 which he had mentioned was probably out of the question and that even $50,000 was dubious. Nevertheless, Strouse mentioned $75,000 to Fuller, who replied that he would not even suggest such a figure to his clients. "If Wright sees fit to make an offer to accept a very small sum, and will fully retract his charges," Fuller stated, "I will . . . receive such offer confidentially and consider it respectfully." Wright promptly retorted to Strouse: "You may say to Mr. Fuller that I have no proposition to make and *nothing to retract.* . . . If my retraction is a condition his clients haven't enough money combined to induce it. . . . I can stand it if they can."[69]

Despite Wright's defiant posture, he obviously felt nervous about

67. Wright to Allen, February 26, March 7, 1895, and Allen to Wright, March 3, 1895, R. H. Wright MSS and letterbooks. Wright gained additional evidence of the wisdom of compromise early in 1895 when he settled a dispute with the Bonsack Company for around $50,000 from them, and the following day the court ruled against Wright in the case.

68. *Wright* v. *Duke*, 36 New York Supplement 853 (1895).

69. Strouse to Wright, July 29, August 19, September 4 (enclosing Fuller to Strouse), 1896; and Wright to Strouse, September 5, 1896, R. H. Wright MSS and letterbook.

the gamble involved in another trial and the mounting legal expenses, and he wrote two simultaneous letters to Strouse—one that could be shown to Fuller and one for Strouse's own guidance. Strouse thought $25,000 was as high as the Dukes and Watts would go; Wright held out for $100,000, though he asserted that whether the sum was "large or small, it convicts them for all time of fraud in a transaction with a partner in business which would be or ought to be very humiliating to millionaires, especially to one of whom [George Watts] who now pretends to set himself up as a leader in the church, & it is his letter which he can't repudiate which will convict him & through him the others."[70]

Early in 1897, as Wright's lawyers moved tentatively toward scheduling the retrial, Wright asserted in his letter to be shown to Fuller that it was "useless to consider further the possibility of our coming together" and that "the court must fix the amount." Privately Wright advised Strouse, "If you can work him up to $75,000 I would consider it." A few months and several letters later, Wright had come down a bit: "I will order the suit dismissed if they will pay the court costs in the case & pay me $50,000.00 net cash besides. . . . In the event of a settlement on the above basis the public is to know nothing of the settlement." Once Strouse convinced Wright, and it took considerable effort, that the bill charging fraud would have to be withdrawn and another bill substituted—in other words, that Wright would have to formally withdraw his charge against his former partners, the wheels of compromise began to accelerate in the summer and fall of 1897. Finally in November, 1897, Wright sacrificed his psychological pleasure by formally withdrawing all charge of fraud, and enriched his bank account by the $50,000 which the Dukes and Watts, through Fuller, finally agreed to pay. D. B. Strouse, who early in 1897 severed his connection with the Bonsack Company and went into "evangelistic work," received $5,000 for his efforts.[71]

70. Strouse to Wright, September 7, October 9, 16, 24, 1896; Wright to Strouse, October 10, 17, 1896, *ibid.*

71. Wright to Strouse, January 17 (first quotation), April 1 (second quotation), June 29, July 20, September 7, October 13, 1897; Strouse to Wright, February 10, June 21, July 3, 23, August 18, October 2, 14, 25, November 1, 3, 9, 1897, *ibid.* Wright's subsequent negotiations with his lawyers were also rich in human interest. When Hinsdale billed him for $1,750, Wright, recalling Hinsdale's advice against the appeal and subsequent aloofness from the long-drawn affair, retorted: "I owe you absolutely nothing in equity, in morals, in law, or in fact & I am utterly surprised at your demand." Sullivan and Cromwell fared better than Wright, but their parting word was: "We hope that in the future you will select counsel in whose ability you

54

The rough-and-tumble tobacco world, from whence Strouse had fled, was one in which James B. Duke thrived. As president of the American Tobacco Company, he was, in fact, the "king of the mountain" in tobacco by the late 1890's. Popular feeling against the "tobacco trust" was rising, however, and more dangerous law suits than Richard Wright's had begun to assail Duke and his associates. Thus they had compromised with Wright and turned to more serious problems of the ever-growing tobacco empire that had been born in 1890.

---

will have more confidence and of whose services you will have more appreciation." Wright to Hinsdale, November 15, 1897, and Sullivan and Cromwell to Wright, December 30, 1897, *ibid.*

CHAPTER 4. BUILDING A COMMERCIAL EMPIRE: THE AMERICAN TOBACCO COMPANY, 1890-1904

Ironically enough, in 1890, the same year in which the American Tobacco Company was organized, the Sherman Anti-Trust Act, with its prohibition of combinations or conspiracies in restraint of interstate commerce, became the law of the land. Apathetic federal administrations and a conservative, probusiness Supreme Court, however, largely left the new law to gather dust throughout the 1890's except when it was used against labor unions. Then during the presidency of Theodore Roosevelt, things changed, and in 1907 the federal government proceeded to use its antitrust weapon against the American Tobacco Company.

James B. Duke, president of the company from its inception in 1890, testified early in 1908. When asked what motives lay behind the initial creation of the American Tobacco Company, Duke replied: "Well, the principal reason was to get an organization. We [that is, W. Duke, Sons and Company] had a large business and I had very little assistance to help conduct it. Another reason [was] I thought we could make more money and handle the business to better advantage by establishing a larger concern." J. B. Duke explained in more detail how his brother, B. N. Duke, and George Watts were in poor health in the late 1880's and how his father, Washington Duke, was quite old and his half-brother, B. L. Duke, had nothing to do with the business. Then James B. Duke reemphasized his belief that "in selling our business to the American Tobacco Co. in connection with the other manufacturers we would get a good organization of people who would be of assistance in conducting the business, and then besides that I expected to make a profit by it because you can handle to better advantage a large business than a small business."[1]

While James B. Duke was correct about the illnesses of Ben Duke

1. Testimony of James B. Duke, in *United States* v. *American Tobacco Company*, U.S. Circuit Court, Southern District of New York, Equity Case Files, 1907–1911, Record Group 21, Files E1–216, vol. V, pp. 3288–3289, Washington National Records Center. Hereinafter cited as Circuit Court MSS. A xeroxed copy of the 238 page typescript of Duke's testimony is also available in the J. B. Duke MSS.

and George Watts around 1890, the president of the American Tobacco Company hardly told the full story in his testimony. He was
candid enough about making "more money," the advantages of a
large business over a small one, and the pooling of the best managerial
talent in the cigarette industry. But by 1908 he had conveniently forgotten his long scramble in the late 1880's to gain exclusive control
throughout the United States of the Bonsack cigarette machine, as
well as of the two chief rival machines, for the nation's five major
cigarette manufacturers. Not only had the goal of that exclusive control been realized, but in a series of meetings in New York City,
beginning in April, 1889, and continuing intermittently throughout
the remainder of the year, James B. Duke and his former leading
rivals hammered out the organization of what one economic historian has termed "one of the first giant holding companies in American industry."[2]

The "tobacco trust," as the American Tobacco Company soon
came to be widely known and bitterly attacked, was not, technically
speaking, a trust in the sense that John D. Rockefeller's original model
of that form of business organization, the Standard Oil Company, had
been. That is, W. Duke, Sons and Company and the other four firms
did not turn over the stock in their concerns to trustees in exchange
for trust certificates. Rather, the five formerly competing businesses
were sold outright to the American Tobacco Company in exchange
for its stock. And as one would expect, the thorniest problem faced
by James B. Duke and his new associates concerned the apportionment
of that stock among the owners of the five old firms.

James B. Duke, though regarded as something of a Tarheel upstart
by Major Lewis Ginter of the proud Virginia firm of Allen and Ginter,
clearly was not a person, even at age thirty-three, to take a back seat
to any one. Basing his claim on the assets of his firm and on past as
well as prospective earning records, Duke held out for parity with
Allen and Ginter, and in the end, got it, along with the presidency of
the new company. Chartered under New Jersey's accommodating
incorporation law early in 1890, the American Tobacco Company was
capitalized at $25,000,000—$10,000,000 in preferred stock and
$15,000,000 in common. W. Duke, Sons and Company and Allen
and Ginter each received $7,500,000 in stock—$3,000,000 in preferred and $4,500,000 in common. The share of the Kinney Company
of New York City was $2,000,000 in preferred stock and $3,000,000

2. Porter, "Origins of the American Tobacco Company," p. 73.

in common; and Kimball Company of Rochester, New York, and the Goodwin Company of New York City each got $1,000,000 in preferred and $1,500,000 in common.[3]

Boasting privately late in 1889 that the five combining firms controlled "between 90 and 95% of the entire paper cigarette business of the U.S.," James B. Duke, however unintentionally, spotlighted the economically powerful base from which the American Tobacco Company launched its operations.[4] Keeping prices to consumers at their existing levels, and in some instances lowering them, Duke and his talented associates proceeded to rationalize an industry that had been chaotic in the 1880's. Many of the policies and practices that had earlier helped W. Duke, Sons and Company achieve its rapid rise were now extended to the national scope of the American Tobacco Company. For example, James B. Duke immediately inaugurated a vigorous system of cost accounting throughout the company. Eliminating many of the less profitable brands of cigarettes and smoking tobacco, as well as closing some of the less efficient factories, the firm soon reduced its costs per unit sold. Although the constituent firms continued for some time to keep their old identities as branch factories of the American Tobacco Company, the New York office increasingly made the important decisions and coordinated the advertising, sales, and other aspects of the business.[5]

The firm of W. Duke, Sons and Company had long preferred to buy its tobacco directly from the farmers in warehouse auction sales. The American Tobacco Company followed that same practice, which James B. Duke would have been mystified to hear described in the economist's term as "backward integration," that is, backward toward the industry's raw material. The result was that various leaf-dealers and speculators in tobacco were infuriated by being thus bypassed. They helped to stir up and keep alive much of the popular, and especially agrarian, resentment against the "tobacco trust."[6]

With controversy growing about the new company, especially at first in Virginia and North Carolina, James B. Duke not only re-

3. U.S. Bureau of Corporations, *Report of the Commissioner of Corporations on the Tobacco Industry* (Washington, 1909), pt. I, 65–66. Richard B. Tennant, *The American Cigarette Industry: A Study in Economic Analysis and Public Policy* (New Haven, 1950), also has an historical summary in the beginning portion of his book.

4. Duke to D. B. Strouse, November 19, 1889, sheaf in J. B. Duke letterbook no. 1.

5. Porter, "Origins of the American Tobacco Company," p. 74.

6. One of the important themes in Tilley, *Bright-Tobacco Industry, passim*, concerns the fight of the leaf dealers against the American Tobacco Company.

mained coolly on the job in New York, but was clearly doing what he most enjoyed—working strenuously himself and also keeping his associates and employees on their toes. From the meager room on Manhattan's Lower East Side which he had first rented in 1884 for $3 a week he had progressed by 1889 to a room on Gramercy Park for which he paid $10 a week. Arriving at his office in time to see the factory workers report for duty, he made frequent forays through the plant, carefully selected various kinds of advertising, and pored over a special record book he kept in his office which showed "Sales by Brands by Towns." Many years later, one of the men who had worked in his factory in the late 1880's wrote to the New York *Evening Post*: ". . . I, as well as the rest of his employees, found 'Buck' Duke (as we always termed him) [but certainly not to his face!] one of the most kindly, affable men we have ever met. Considerate in all ways, his employees' interests were his, and his kindly word and genial smile were the factors which kept the Rivington Street hands with him until years later when a fire wiped out the plant at 39th Street and First Avenue."[7]

The passing years had no doubt softened the worker's memory of the young J. B. Duke, but his dignified, direct, and quietly confident manner impressed many who knew him. Actually, neither he nor his brother, Ben Duke, used cigarettes, and perhaps as a concession to urban life J. B. Duke shifted from the chewing tobacco which he enjoyed during his early years in New York to cigars, which Washington Duke also smoked. Never a reader of much beyond business material, James B. Duke, after his twelve-hour or longer day in the office, tramped the streets of New York to visit tobacco stores for lengthy conversations and observation. As he walked with eyes cast downward, he counted the number of discarded cigarette packs of the various brands which he could spot—and, for good luck, picked up any straight pins he saw and stuck them behind his lapel.[8]

After becoming the president of the American Tobacco Company, Duke changed certain aspects of his private life, but even then he was remarkably restrained for the 1890's, the flamboyant era of Lillian Russell and 'Diamond Jim' Brady. Like so many persons in the pre-automotive age, the young executive took pride in his horses. On a

7. As quoted in John Wilber Jenkins, *James B. Duke: Master Builder* (New York, 1927), pp. 83–84.

8. *Ibid.*, p. 80. Jenkins obtained much of his personal information about Duke from interviews with a number of persons who had known him well.

visit to New York, George Watts reported to Ben Duke: "Buck is enjoying his horses, his mate to Maud is a fine one so he has a dashing team now. He spends the evenings talking & planning his new stable. . . ."[9]

James B. Duke subsequently moved to a hotel, the Hoffman House, where B. N. Duke also stayed on his frequent business trips to New York. In 1893 the young bachelor president of the American Tobacco Company also met a handsome, sociable divorcee, Mrs. Lillian Fletcher McCredy. With a fine figure in the hour-glass style of the period, Mrs. McCredy dressed well, possessed a trained voice and quick wit, and apparently enjoyed flirtation and the company of men. The fact that her husband had filed a countersuit for divorce in 1892, and won it in a trial featuring a series of alleged infidelities on the part of Mrs. McCredy, must not have bothered J. B. Duke—at least not initially, for his niece, Ben Duke's daughter Mary, at one period added "Lillian" as her middle name in honor of "Uncle Buck's sweetheart." And Mrs. McCredy herself moved into a five-story graystone house on West 68th Street owned and frequently visited by James B. Duke.[10]

Washington Duke, whom his sons deeply venerated, for a long time knew nothing about his youngest son's private life. When the "old gentleman," as many in Durham referred to the patriarch of the Duke family, did apparently hear something about his son's relationship with Mrs. McCredy, the president of the American Tobacco Company received a peremptory parental summons to Durham, and a dire chain of events was set off. But that would come early in the twentieth century. In the 1890's Washington Duke had only to worry about some of the advertising material used by the American Tobacco Company—to be specific, about the small pictures of actresses clad in acrobatic tights and other such costumes that were distributed with cigarettes and avidly collected by millions of Americans. "My dear Son," Washington Duke began his letter, "I have received the enclosed letter from the Rev. John C. Hocutt and am very much impressed with the wisdom of his argument against circulating lascivious photographs with cigarettes. . . ." The senior Duke noted that he had "always looked upon the distribution of this character of advertise-

9. Watts to B. N. Duke, March 30, 1892, B. N. Duke MSS.

10. New York *American*, December 19, 22, 1905; John K. Winkler, *Tobacco Tycoon: The Story of James Buchanan Duke* (New York, 1942), pp. 89 ff. Winkler has a number of facts, plus a good bit more, concerning Mrs. McCredy.

ment as wrong in its pernicious effects upon young man[-] and woman-hood, and therefore [it] has not jingled with my religious impulses." Insisting that "we owe Christianity all the assistance we can lend it in any form, which is paramount to any other consideration," Washington Duke went on to note that "this mode of advertising" would be used against cigarettes and strengthen the arguments against them "in the legislative halls of the states." Concluding with the statement that he would be much pleased to learn of a change in advertising policy, Washington Duke remained "Affectionately, your father."[11]

Although James B. Duke could hardly end the time-hallowed use of pictures of curvaceous women in cigarette advertising, he no doubt made some sort of conciliatory gesture to his father, possibly in the form of a message by one of the sizable group of tobacco executives who increasingly travelled back and forth between Durham and New York. After 1890 James B. Duke wrote fewer and fewer business letters and only quite rarely took the time for a personal letter. When Ben Duke, for example, wondered if he should run up to New York for what promised to be an important meeting of the directors of the American Tobacco Company, he wrote W. W. Fuller: "I wish you would do me the kindness to ask Buck if he does not think I should come. I would write him myself but know he does not answer letters and I do not care to trouble him with one."[12]

Happily preoccupied with his work, James B. Duke eschewed recreation as well as letter-writing. The nearest thing to a hobby for him was the farm near Somerville, New Jersey, which he purchased in the summer of 1893. Starting with 327 acres, he eventually owned a tract of some 2200 acres, which he gradually converted into a magnificent estate as well as the site of his favorite residence. Like his father and brothers, he deeply loved trees and flowers; and water, especially cascades and fountains, held a lifelong fascination for him. As some of America's rich men in the late nineteenth and early twentieth centuries cultivated their aesthetic natures through the acquisition of paintings by the "old masters" of Europe, James B. Duke lavished his attention—and money—on horticulture and landscaping.

11. Washington Duke to J. B. Duke, October 17, 1894, B. N. Duke letterbook.

12. B. N. Duke to W. W. Fuller, June 16, 1896. Fuller replied the next day that J. B. Duke thought that both B. N. Duke and George Watts should be present for the meeting. J. B. Duke's casual treatment of his mail is also shown by B. N. Duke's suggestion on a communication of January 1, 1896: "Do not leave this letter on your desk where it can be read by visitors."

Although the scale of operations increased dramatically around the turn of the century, he began modestly enough in the mid-1890's by bringing up from Durham an old friend of the family's who was a former Methodist minister and horticulturalist, Reuben Hibberd. After Hibberd's work on what came to be known as "Duke's Farm" was well underway, he reported to Ben Duke that J. B. Duke seemed "very pleased with my work so far." With a "big force of hands and teams," Hibberd expected "to make a very pretty job." But he had certain reservations about the undertaking: "I shall be very glad to get back into Christian civilization again. All the hands I work 'Cuss.' The Newspaper man 'Cussed.' The fountain man in New York cussed and I think the whole crew cuss from the boys on the street to the city Mayor. The Methodist Preacher did not cuss perhaps he *couldn't*[;] neither could he preach, perhaps for the same reason. New York for money, Durham for Christianity & Brotherly Love."[13]

The Durham native was perhaps too sweeping in his indictment of metropolitan morals, but he was indeed correct in asserting, "New York for money." Certainly James B. Duke and his associates in the American Tobacco Company found it so. From all over the nation and growing portions of the rest of the world, the profits of the American Tobacco Company poured into the home office in New York. After paying 8 percent on the preferred stock and 12 on the common in 1891, the company had a surplus of nearly $1,300,000; the next few years proved even more lucrative despite the panic of 1893 and the grim depression which continued until late in the decade.

Not content with the success already achieved, the American Tobacco Company early embarked on a course of expansion that eventually led to control of about four-fifths of the entire tobacco industry, except for cigars. But this very expansion also led to the federal government's successful antitrust action and the eventual dissolution of the company. Initially the company derived most of its income from cigarettes, less from smoking tobacco, and least of all from plug or chewing tobacco. As late as 1904, however, only five cents out of every sales dollar received by the United States' tobacco industry was derived from cigarettes; snuff, which brought in only two cents of the sales dollar, was even less important than cigarettes, but chewing and smoking tobacco accounted for thirty-three cents, while

13. R. Hibberd to B. N. Duke, April 24, 1895, B. N. Duke MSS. The name of the estate was originally Duke's Farm, but it was subsequently changed to Duke Farms.

sixty cents was derived from cigar sales.[14] To gain a larger slice of the U.S. tobacco sales dollar, the American Tobacco Company moved early in the 1890's to expand its share of the business in chewing and smoking tobacco by purchasing various firms in Baltimore, Louisville, and elsewhere.

Asked in the antitrust proceedings of 1908 why the company had embarked so promptly on its program of expansion, James B. Duke replied: "We wanted to have a full variety . . . of the different styles of tobacco. . . ." Pointing to the fickle nature of the public's taste, Duke argued that if "one style [of tobacco product] went out of fashion we would have another style ready for the public to take up. . . ." Too, sentiment against cigarettes reached large proportions in the mid-1890's, and, Duke noted, for a few years at least sales of the bright-leaf cigarette declined. "Well, I was the one that promoted the idea that we should go into the plug business," Duke declared, "and some of [the other officers and directors] didn't seem to favor it very much. . . ."[15]

The so-called "plug war" between the American Tobacco Company and the older, established manufacturers of chewing tobacco did not reach its climax until late in the decade. As early as Christmas, 1892, however, James B. Duke was already so caught up in the early stages of the competitive battle that he was unable to return to Durham for the holidays. In a handwritten note to his brother, he explained why he had to remain in New York: "1st Because ½ dozen plug salesmen from the west will be here next week & I must see them. We are making Rome howl on Plug & are making preparations to do great work the 1st of the year[.] We will make the Plug Mfgrs hustle like we once did Cigarette Mfgrs. . . . I will invest the 30 M [thousand] you send me for Pa next week. Wishing you all a merry Christmas & happy new year. I am your devoted Bro."[16]

"Making Rome howl on Plug" was achieved by Duke and his allies in a variety of ways, many of which were later to figure prominently in the antitrust action. To encourage jobbers, that is wholesale merchants, to handle only the products of American Tobacco, the company resorted to rebates. When this aroused widespread protests as well as various legal actions against the company, the rebates were

14. Robert, *Story of Tobacco*, p. 173.
15. Circuit Court MSS, vol. V, pp. 3295–3299.
16. J. B. Duke to B. N. Duke, December 24, 1892, B. N. Duke MSS.

temporarily dropped despite the opposition of James B. Duke. Then the system was revived in another form until mounting difficulties led the company to abandon it in 1897.[17]

By the middle of the decade the "plug war" raged in earnest, with the Liggett and Myers Company and the Drummond Company, both of St. Louis, teaming up with the Pierre Lorillard Company of Jersey City to fight back against the moves of the American Tobacco Company. With "Battle Ax" as the fighting brand of chewing tobacco, Duke was able to sell it well below manufacturing cost, spend vast sums on advertising, and absorb the losses from the large profits made on cigarettes. John B. Cobb, once closely associated with Ben Duke in the company's leaf-purchasing operations in North Carolina and Virginia and then like so many other Tarheel tobacco men transferred to New York to become a top executive in the American Tobacco Company, reported correctly in 1895 that "indications now are that there will be a considerable quantity of cheap cigarettes put out in the next year or so." To explain why this was so, Cobb continued: "The big Western [i.e., St. Louis] Plug Factories are certainly going into the business and its going to be a lively fight." Cobb believed that American Tobacco had "a good advantage and if the 'Conservatives' don't bother Mr. J. B. D. we will whip the life out of them." Business was "good in nearly every line," Cobb assured Ben Duke. Moreover, the president of the company, who Cobb said was working harder than ever, reminded him of "the war-horse that scents the battle . . . I really believe he enjoys the prospect of the fight."[18]

Not long afterwards, Cobb conveyed the news that James B. Duke had just returned from the company's large plug-producing branch in Louisville and that the branch would in a short time be able "to turn out full 100,000 lbs of Plug per day." Orders were running about 125,000 pounds a day, Cobb noted, and the company was about a million pounds behind in orders. "You never saw people appear so glad that they have a business as the A[merican] T[obacco] people are of the Plug business today," he declared. "You know the Plug Factory has been regarded by some of our Co. as a sort of cancer and now we would be almost 'one-legged' without it. Well its just still another proof of Mr. J. B. D.'s farseeing wisdom. I never saw a more confident

17. Glenn Porter and Harold C. Livesay have a concise account in their chapter on the tobacco industry in *Merchants and Manufacturers: Studies in the Changing of Nineteenth-Century Marketing* (Baltimore, 1971), pp. 209–210.
18. J. B. Cobb to B. N. Duke, August 12, 1895, B. N. Duke MSS.

man than Mr. J. B. and he has got everybody around here in the same mood. . . . There can't be but one result, we will down them sure."[19]

True to Cobb's predictions, the St. Louis manufacturers did begin to produce cigarettes, the Drummond Company distributing coupons redeemable for cigarettes with packages of its chewing tobacco. Liggett and Myers, the largest of all the plug producers, also pushed its new brands of cigarettes. It was able to do so because not only had rivals to the Bonsack cigarette machine been developed, but as a result of adverse judicial decisions the Bonsack Company in 1895 lost certain important patent rights. The American Tobacco Company, therefore, ceased to have exclusive use of the Bonsack machine. As a result of the changes in the machine aspect of the cigarette industry and of the fierce competition between the American Tobacco Company and its rivals in St. Louis, that city led the country in cigarette production in the latter half of 1897, making 15 percent of the total output.[20]

Consumers of tobacco products no doubt enjoyed their cheaper and cheaper puffs—and chews—as the "plug war" raged. No consumer relished the struggle more, however, than did one manufacturer, James B. Duke. He explained to one of his allies in St. Louis that Ohio was being worked "on the Knife Scheme by giving a card to consumer to attach 12 tags to," along with a sample of "Battle Ax" and a spiel on its merits. Then sixty tag cards were distributed "to hold the fellows that have gotten a knife with 12 tags." Duke declared that "all reports are of the most encouraging nature, and I believe that we have hit upon the best scheme ever tried to make chewers." He conceded that the plan was "slow and expensive at the start" but insisted that it would be cheap in the long run. Once Ohio was "captured," the campaign would be shifted to other states. As for the lowering of the price of "Battle Ax," which had once sold for fifty cents a pound, to fifteen cents a pound in combination with jobbers' purchases of other products of the company, Duke argued that it was "a great benefit to other brands, and we are killing two birds with one stone."[21]

19. Cobb to B. N. Duke, August 26, 1895, *ibid.* W. W. Fuller, who had recently moved from Durham to New York to become chief counsel for American Tobacco, also reported to Ben Duke that his younger brother was "a great general." Fuller to B. N. Duke, October 28, 1895, *ibid.*

20. Bureau of Corporations, *Report on Tobacco*, pt. I, 67, 97.

21. J. B. Duke to James G. Butler, January 1, 1897, J. B. Duke letterbook.

When the "knife scheme" was used in Indiana to help introduce "Dragoon," another of the American Tobacco Company's brands of plug, a less enthusiastic but still revealing report came from Brodie Duke's older son, B. Lawrence Duke, who was at that time working for the company as a salesman: "My opinion is that 60% of those chewing Dragoon . . . are doing it simply for a knife, 20% because they like it, [and] the other 20% for no reason at all. These last ones are those who when asked what kind they chew, tell you any kind."[22]

Regardless of whether J. B. Duke or his nephew was correct about the "knife scheme," the larger and undisputed fact was that J. B. Duke and his associates by 1898 were close to a victory in the "plug war." In 1894 the American Tobacco Company had sold only nine million pounds of chewing tobacco; by 1897 sales had reached thirty-eight million pounds and were still climbing. In other words, from 5.6 percent of the total plug-tobacco production in 1894, the American Tobacco Company had jumped to nearly 21 percent. The company's losses on plug tobacco in 1896 alone totalled more than a million dollars, but profits from cigarettes and other products made that tolerable. Consequently, "it was but natural," the United States Bureau of Corporations later noted laconically, "that competitors should become disposed to make peace by combining with the American Tobacco Company interests."[23]

The trend toward the formation of "combinations," small ones as well as vast ones, reached epidemic proportions in the United States around the turn of the century. Before the new combination in the plug-tobacco industry could be achieved, however, James B. Duke met and largely overcame a new kind of challenge to his leadership of the American Tobacco Company. In order to effect many of the combinations of previously competing companies, enormous amounts of capital were required, and this need for capital opened the way to control of a number of key industries by investment bankers. In steel, farm machinery, and shipbuilding, for example, control shifted from manufacturers to financiers. But in the case of the American Tobacco Company, as one historian has stated, "the financiers apparently shared the goals of James Duke, for he remained president of the firm."[24]

22. B. L. Duke to H. A. Hersey, January 17, 1898, enclosed with G. W. Russell to Washington Duke, January 25, 1898, W. Duke MSS.
23. Bureau of Corporations, *Report on Tobacco*, pt. I, 97–98.
24. Porter, "Origins of the American Tobacco Company," p. 75.

One of the keys to Duke's ultimate success lay in the understanding which he reached with Oliver H. Payne, a multimillionaire who had grown rich in Standard Oil. Working through James R. Keene, then one of the shrewdest operators on Wall Street, Payne and his associates quietly purchased large blocks of stock in the American Tobacco Company and prepared for a showdown at the annual meeting of the board of directors. James B. Duke sought an interview with Payne, made clear his determination to manage the business in his own manner—or to get out and launch a new, rival business—and ended up by gaining additional and important support from Payne and his friends. A prominent New York banker soon apprised Ben Duke of the situation: "I spent last night with Colonel Payne on his yacht, and it gave me great pleasure to hear him express his opinion of the President of the Tobacco Co. He thoroughly recognizes his great ability and regards him in all respects with the highest esteem. He has made up his mind that he is the kind of man that he is willing to be harnessed up with."[25]

Payne did indeed become "harnessed up with" James B. Duke, and before 1898 ended the new plug-tobacco combination, known as the Continental Tobacco Company, was formed. The American Tobacco Company, which purchased two of the independent plug businesses in St. Louis in the early fall of 1898, next sold its four plug-tobacco branches to the Continental Company in exchange for stock in the latter company. Six other independent producers, including the Lorillard Company which was allowed to continue its separate organization, also sold out to the Continental Tobacco Company. Although the American Tobacco Company did not own a majority of the stock in Continental, James B. Duke was elected its president also. He later insisted that he had neither planned nor desired to head the new plug combination, which also produced considerable smoking tobacco as well as some snuff, but that "quite a contest" developed between Pierre Lorillard, Harry Drummond, and one or two others who were candidates for the presidency. Payne and one of his associates came and urged Duke to accept the post. "At first I declined," Duke later explained, "and they then said that we had a large interest in the concern and that they did not believe that these fellows would ever be able to organize and run that thing and that . . . we would lose

25. Dominick and Dickerman [W. B. Dickerman?] to B. N. Duke, August 19, 1898, B. N. Duke MSS. For J. B. Duke's earlier efforts to reach agreement with Payne, see J. B. Duke to H. L. Terrell, May 27, June 10, 1898, J. B. Duke letterbook.

a lot [of money] unless I did." Duke added that many of his friends "spoke to me and told me I ought not to, but I did it."[26]

Liggett and Myers alone of the important manufacturers of plug tobacco remained out of the new combination, but not for long. In 1898 a group of powerful financiers, including Thomas Fortune Ryan, Peter A. B. Widener, William C. Whitney, Anthony N. Brady, and others, organized the Union Tobacco Company. Buying up Blackwell's Durham Tobacco Company and the National Cigarette Company of New York, which was one of the last independent manufacturers of any importance in that line, the Union Tobacco Company also secured an option on the controlling portion of the Liggett and Myers stock. Aside from the firms which the Union Tobacco Company had rounded up, the financial resources represented by the men involved—all immensely wealthy and richly experienced tycoons of New York and Philadelphia—made the new organization one to be watched closely.[27]

The former partner and then unyielding adversary of the Dukes, Richard H. Wright, watched with pleasure as the men behind the Union Tobacco Company readied their plans. "They are quietly getting ready to make it hot for Duke," Wright advised James A. Bonsack. Having become interested in various patented machines and inventions used in the tobacco industry, Wright declared that he "should like nothing better than to work these fellows against each other & force $200,000 a year at least out of one or the other for a monopoly" of one of the inventions in which he was interested.[28]

To Richard H. Wright's disappointment, he could neither play off one company against the other nor have the satisfaction of seeing J. B. Duke downed. Despite a flurry of excitement in the tobacco world and in the trading done in tobacco stocks on Wall Street, James B. Duke soon came to terms with the powerful challengers. In New York for these exciting developments, Ben Duke sent word back to Durham: "Tell Pa the business of both the Continental & A[merican] T[obacco] Co is fine. The stocks have been sold down by Union Tob[acc]o people & those who are alarmed at the competition they fear." A

26. Circuit Court MSS, vol. V, p. 3325.

27. Bureau of Corporations, *Report on Tobacco*, pt. I, 4–5, 73–74.

28. Wright to J. A. Bonsack, November 18, 1898, R. H. Wright letterbook. To G. P. Butler, one of those involved in the Union Tobacco Company, Wright expressed regret that he had not been more fully informed about the new company, which he might have been able to aid. "*You know my love for Duke and his Durham Associates,*" Wright added. Wright to Butler, January 5, 1899, *ibid.*

few days later, Ben Duke reported: "Confidentially Union Co will be ours. Tob[acc]o was never in so strong a position. I expect to see it sell at $200 soon, [and] it was up to 178 today."[29]

Ben Duke's satisfaction resulted from the purchase of the Union Tobacco Company by the giant firm headed by his brother. The American Tobacco Company paid heavily—$12,500,000 in its common stock—but J. B. Duke argued that it "was largely a trade to get people, financiers and moneyed people[,] into our concern, and they had of course also bought the Blackwell's Durham concern which was a very old established [firm] and one of the best brands in the country. . . ." Duke always regarded the purchase of the Union Tobacco Company as a special case, as he later admitted somewhat defensively: "I never bought any business with the idea of eliminating competition; it was always [with] the idea of an investment except probably in that one case of the Union Tobacco Co[mpany] and in that case we had an idea . . . of getting in with ourselves a lot of rich financial people to help finance our properties."[30]

The "rich financial people" to whom James B. Duke referred— Ryan, Widener, Brady, and others—became directors of the American Tobacco Company as well as of the Continental Tobacco Company in the spring of 1899. The cigarette manufacturers, such as Lewis Ginter, Francis Kinney, and the others who had helped launch the American Tobacco Company in 1890, had already ceased to be directors, and some had disposed of their stock in the company. Only J. B. Duke, together with his brother Ben and their longtime partner George Watts, remained of the original group of tobacco men, but they, and especially the president of the two great combinations, were pivotal figures in the ever-expanding tobacco empire.

That empire reached even grander dimensions with the American Tobacco Company's acquisition of Liggett and Myers. To purchase Liggett and Myers, J. B. Duke, O. H. Payne, and H. D. Terrell joined Thomas F. Ryan's group of financiers in forming a syndicate. For the assets of Liggett and Myers and $5,000,000 in cash, the Continental Tobacco Company exchanged $17,500,000 of its common stock and the same amount of its preferred. The total capitalization of the plug combination, the Continental Tobacco Company, thus became and remained $97,690,700. The American Tobacco Company, which

29. B. N. Duke to J. E. Stagg, confidential secretary and agent in Durham, February 10, 21, 1899, B. N. Duke MSS.

30. Circuit Court MSS, vol. V, pp. 3341, 3357.

had initially been capitalized at $25,000,000 in 1890, paid to the holders of its common stock in 1899 a stock dividend of 100 percent, or $21,000,000, from the company's accumulated surplus and the profits of the sale of its plug business to Continental. The stock dividend, together with the $12,500,000 in common stock paid for the Union Tobacco Company, added $33,500,000 to the American's capital stock. From 1899 down to 1904, therefore, the American Tobacco Company was capitalized at $54,500,000 in common stock and $14,000,000 in preferred.[31]

For the Continental Tobacco Company's control of "western" chewing tobacco, which was made of the burley tobacco produced in Kentucky and nearby states, the purchase of Liggett and Myers was important. But for the "eastern" or "southern" variety of flat plug, less sweet than the western variety and made from bright-leaf tobacco, the acquisition of the R. J. Reynolds Tobacco Company of Winston-Salem, North Carolina, was equally important. Although the Continental Tobacco Company acquired about two-thirds of the outstanding capital stock of the Reynolds Company in 1899, the Winston-Salem subsidiary enjoyed a high degree of autonomy; through the acquisition of a number of the smaller plug factories, the Reynolds Company, in the words of the Bureau of Corporations, "accomplished a consolidation of the manufacture of plug tobacco in the South somewhat similar to that brought about by the Continental Tobacco Company in the West."[32]

According to James B. Duke, Richard J. Reynolds came up with the proposal to sell his business to Continental. "I personally told Reynolds," Duke continued, "that the Continental Tobacco Company had no organization to manufacture, or that knew how to manufacture[,] his style of goods and that I would not favor buying it unless

31. Bureau of Corporations, *Report on Tobacco*, pt. I, 3–5. The question of over-capitalization or "watered stock" is an old and thorny one. A recurring theme in the dry recital of economic data gathered by the Bureau of Corporations in its *Report on the Tobacco Industry* has to do with the alleged over-capitalization that resulted from the large sums charged up to goodwill, that is brand names and trademarks. A more modern economic historian, noting that in 1908 goodwill accounted for 55.5 percent of all assets in the American Tobacco Company's domestic tobacco manufacture, nevertheless concludes: ". . . From the point of view of investors, none of the goodwill, except in the case of the cigar group, represented 'water,' for adequate profits were earned on it." There follows an interesting discussion of the nature and origin of goodwill, with distinctions that were not made by the Bureau of Corporations. Tennant, *The American Cigarette Industry*, pp. 36–37.

32. Bureau of Corporations, *Report on Tobacco*, pt. I, 103–104, 236.

he should stay and run it. . . ." Duke added that in discussing the business he had always told Reynolds, "you run it any way you like."[33] Reynolds accepted Duke's terms and proceeded to build an increasingly important business.

Thus in chewing and smoking tobacco, as earlier in cigarettes, James B. Duke and his associates had achieved dominance by 1899. Next to be conquered was snuff, and after a price war between the Atlantic Snuff Company, a combination of four companies formed in 1898, and the Duke-led producers, the American Snuff Company was organized in March, 1900, with a capital of $23,000,000. Less than half of that went to the American and Continental Companies for their snuff interests, and James B. Duke, for a change, served as a mere director of the new company rather than as its president. Controlling about 80 percent of the nation's snuff production when formed, the American Snuff Company raised that figure to over 96 percent in a decade.[34]

Compared with the cigar business, however, snuff was small potatoes indeed. As mentioned earlier, sixty cents of each sales dollar received by the nation's tobacco industry in 1904 was derived from cigars, and in an effort to gain a larger share of that lucrative business, Duke and his allies organized the American Cigar Company in 1901. Despite intensive efforts, it never gained dominance in the cigar industry, because of its many small and scattered producers who continued to depend largely on hand-rollers. The American Cigar Company's share of the national output never rose above about 16 percent, and, as one economic historian has put the matter, the "persistence of industrial decentralization in cigars indicates the importance of the Bonsack machine in making possible the heavy concentration of the cigarette industry."[35]

Even without control over the cigar industry, Duke and his associates enjoyed ever-increasing profits. The combination bought up subsidiary companies that produced licorice paste, tin foil, cotton bags, wooden boxes, tobacco machinery, and acquired control of the 392 retail outlets of the United Cigar Stores Company organized in 1901.[36] As if all the expansion—forward, backward, and even side-

33. Circuit Court MSS., vol. V, pp. 3375–3379.
34. Bureau of Corporations, *Report on Tobacco*, pt. I, 141–145; Tennant, *The American Cigarette Industry*, p. 31.
35. Tennant, *The American Cigarette Industry*, pp. 32–33.
36. *Ibid.* The United Cigar Stores were careful to carry the goods of independent

ways—were not enough, James B. Duke and the inner group that controlled the combination pulled a complicated maneuver in 1901 that was to be short-lived and yet to play a part in bringing down the antitrust club of the federal government on the combination. That maneuver was the formation of the Consolidated Tobacco Company.

Much of the vast expansion of both the American Tobacco Company and the Continental Tobacco Company had been accomplished through the exchange of blocks of stock in the two companies for the various properties being acquired. Ownership was, therefore, scattered. Furthermore, with dominance achieved after about 1900 in much of the tobacco industry, save for cigars, every prospect was for increased earnings for the combination. There was also an immediate need for additional capital for expansion, both in the cigar industry and in foreign countries. Accordingly, James B. Duke and the financiers who had joined him in the late 1890's organized the Consolidated Tobacco Company in June, 1901, with a capital stock of $30,000,000 which was paid for in cash. The sixteen directors of the new company, who included Ben Duke and George Watts as well as its president, J. B. Duke, and a New York financial house which had worked closely with the combination for a number of years, Moore and Schley, held 94 percent of the Consolidated stock.[37]

Consolidated offered to exchange its 4 percent bonds for equal par value of the Continental Company's common stock and at the rate of $200 for $100 of the American Tobacco Company's common stock. Since Continental had not paid a dividend and had been selling on the stock market for $20 to $30 a share, the holders of Continental common were naturally glad to make the exchange and have the guaranteed 4 percent from the Consolidated bond. The American Tobacco Company had paid 6 percent annual dividends on its common stock after the 100 percent stock dividend of 1899, and the Consolidated bond promised 8 percent. Consolidated's offer was quickly accepted by almost all of the stockholders in the other two companies.

The men who owned Consolidated thereby acquired effective control of both the American and Continental companies. They also became entitled to all the profits of both companies in excess of the

manufacturers as well as those of the combination. See Bureau of Corporations, *Report on Tobacco*, pt. I, 315.

37. The above, as well as the account which follows, is based on Bureau of Corporations, *Report on Tobacco*, pt. I, 7–9, 114–127; and Tennant, *The American Cigarette Industry*, pp. 34–36. The capital was subsequently raised to $40,000,000.

fixed amounts that would be required for the dividends on the preferred stock and for the interest on Consolidated's bonds. That profits would increase substantially was a strong bet. The costly expenditures of the battles in plug and snuff were now a thing of the past, and the taxes on tobacco products that had been raised in 1898 at the time of the Spanish-American War were scheduled for reduction. In fact, Congress passed the act reducing the taxes before Consolidated was organized. The prices of the combination's products were not correspondingly reduced, and much of the sharp increase in earnings of the tobacco companies went to the men who owned the Consolidated Tobacco Company. It lasted only a little over three years, but during that time the earnings of the American and Continental companies were sufficient to pay dividends on preferred stock, interest on the Consolidated bonds, and to leave a profit of around $30,000,000 to the Consolidated Tobacco Company on its investment, which was initially $30,000,000 but subsequently raised to $40,000,000. Put another way, Consolidated paid $6,000,000 in dividends, accumulated a surplus of $17,000,000, and, in the words of the Bureau of Corporations, "substantially became entitled" to the increase in the surpluses of the American and Continental companies, which amounted to over $7,000,000.[38]

While the formation of the Consolidated Tobacco Company enriched those who owned it, the new capital furnished by Consolidated played a vital role in the foreign expansion of the American Tobacco Company. Even before the formation of that company in 1890, American manufacturers of smoking tobacco and cigarettes had aggressively developed foreign markets. James B. Duke had asserted early in 1889 that "the world is now our market for our product. . . ." That policy had been vigorously continued after 1890: subsidiary companies were organized in Australia in 1894, and the American Tobacco Company of Canada was established in the following year. Foreign expansion received particular attention around the turn of the century, however.

Asian countries were tempting markets for American cigarette manufacturers not only because their vast populations had long used

---

38. Bureau of Corporations, *Report on Tobacco*, pt. I, 9. James B. Duke, Brady, Payne, Ryan, Widener, and Whitney each held 8.3 percent of the total issue of Consolidated stock, or approximately half. Ben Duke, owning 5 percent, came next, and George Watts owned 2.5 percent. Moore and Schley held 23.5 percent of the stock for customers. *Ibid.*, p. 119.

tobacco in one form or another, but also because the famed bright-leaf tobacco of America was quite different from the huge crops of tobacco grown in India, China, and elsewhere in Asia. James B. Duke, along with Richard Wright and other pioneers in the American cigarette industry, played a key role in creating a world market for one of the most important agricultural exports of the United States.

Japan, for example, attracted American tobacco salesmen in the late nineteenth century. When the Japanese government, which had a monopoly on the importation of leaf tobacco, imposed a prohibitive duty on imports of manufactured tobacco products in 1899, the American Tobacco Company purchased a controlling interest in one of the established Japanese tobacco firms, Murai Brothers Company, and proceeded to manufacture and sell its products in rough-and-tumble American style. A veteran tobacco man from Durham, Edward J. Parrish, went to Japan in 1899 as the representative of the American Tobacco Company and vice-president of the Murai Company, of which Kichibei Murai was president.

Dignified and courteous in manner, Parrish seems to have worked harmoniously and effectively with his Japanese colleagues. He assured the New York office that the "Messrs. Murai and Mr. Matsubara are even more anxiously concerned about the business . . . than ever before." Remembering James B. Duke's hard-working habits, Parrish added: "We all get to [the] office at 8:30 every morning: office hours begin at 8:30 with understanding of an hour for lunch, and after 5:30 any one could feel at liberty to go home." He was satisfied that he and his coworkers in Tokyo were agreed on one thing: "We must have the *cigarette* business of Japan, and even if we cannot make much profit. . . ."[39]

A great believer in the merits of bright-leaf tobacco, Parrish advised the Leaf Department in the New York office that the Murai company would always want about half of its purchases of leaf to be "of the Henderson, Oxford [North Carolina] types—old tobacco belt tobaccos." The Japanese, according to Parrish, liked "a mild, mellow smoke," and he subsequently amplified this by explaining that "our Japanese people do not eat much meat, or strong food like we Ameri-

39. Parrish to J. B. Cobb, first vice-president of the American Tobacco Company, April 23, 1900, E. J. Parrish letterbook. S. H. Matsubara was the secretary of the Murai company.

74

cans, their principal diet being rice, fish, vegetable[s] &c, and therefore a strong cigarette attacks their *stomachs*."[40]

Building a new factory modelled closely after the plant of W. Duke, Sons and Company in Durham, the Murai company advertised and promoted its goods with all the verve and vigor that the Dukes had earlier shown in the American industry. "We are preparing to advertise our leading brands by street parades in principal cities with banners and music and *Sandwiched men*, distributing circulars," Parrish informed the New York office. An exposition at Osaka, Japan, afforded the company an opportunity to make a splash, and Kichibei Murai reported on it: "I am glad to say that everything we have exhibited is beautifully made, and that the fact that we used special care over our exhibits is clearly seen if we compare our things with the small exhibits of [the rival] Iwaya and Chiba companies, which are right next to ours." Murai noted that the company's ten or more "free smoking stands" scattered around the exhibition grounds were quite popular and always crowded. His greatest praise, however, was reserved for the "Advertising Tower" which he thought was "beautifully finished" and made a "quite gigantic" show. "I felt delightfully when I myself was on the top of the tower and looked down upon the whole of Osaka city," Murai declared. "The electric illumination of the tower at night is so beautiful that not only myself but all who have a chance to witness the scene will be surprised by the great advertisement of our company."[41]

Not all was sweetness and light in the fiercely competitive Japanese cigarette business. One of the Murai company's brands of cigarettes, for example, was named "Hero." A sharp rival company, capitalizing on the Japanese difficulty with the English letter "l" which usually resulted in an "r" sound, came out with a brand called "Hallo." Though the rival allegedly admitted that "*morally* he [was] guilty, but not legally," the rival brand was not withdrawn. Attacks by competitors on the Murai company as "unpatriotic" and "foreign" and on American tobacco leaf as "poisonous" did not prevent Parrish and his Japanese colleagues from building a profitable business.[42]

40. Parrish to W. L. Walker, October 19, 1900, and Parrish to J. A. Thomas, June 20, 1901, E. J. Parrish letterbook.

41. Parrish to W. R. Harris, second vice-president of American Tobacco Company, February 20, 1902, E. J. Parrish letterbook; and K. Murai to Parrish, March 19, 1903, E. J. Parrish MSS, 1973 addition.

42. Parrish to W. R. Harris, May 30, 1900, March 15, 1902, E. J. Parrish letter-

James B. Duke, though he never visited Japan himself, took a keen interest in the affairs of the Murai company. Not only were various other officers in the American Tobacco Company periodically dispatched to Japan, and Murai officials brought to New York, but Duke conveyed advice and recommendations about many aspects, large and small, of the Murai company's affairs. When he summoned Parrish to come home on a visit in 1903—a visit for which Parrish prepared elaborately by collecting detailed data on every conceivable aspect of the business in Japan—Duke invited Parrish, Mrs. Parrish, and their daughter to the Farm for a weekend. "When Mr. Duke was through asking the many questions that an ordinary man would not have even thought of, and of making suggestions that only Mr. Duke is capable of making," Parrish reported to the senior Murai, "he said that he would answer your letter himself, and that he would have a still more extended talk with me relative to these matters, before I returned to Japan." Parrish then went on for eight typewritten pages to convey J. B. Duke's ideas about various aspects of the business in Japan.[43]

When the Japanese government established a monopoly on tobacco manufacture in 1904 and purchased the Murai company, Duke and his associates shifted more of their attention to China. James A. Thomas, a native of North Carolina and another veteran of the tobacco trade, became the key representative in China after a stint in India and Singapore. Thomas, who became well acquainted with J. B. Duke as well as an intimate friend of Ben Duke and his family, later wrote two memoirs about his career in the Far East. He recalled his first interview with James B. Duke, who had unintentionally acquired a considerable mystique by the turn of the century: "I went into Mr. Duke's office with as much awe as if I were meeting the President of the United States, wondering all the while what he would say. . . . After being in his presence for five minutes, I felt as though I had known him all my life. I realized that I could tell him in detail what I was undertaking in the Far East, because I was certain that he would be interested and would give me the benefit of his great mercantile knowledge."[44]

book. When one of the Japanese rival firms that had attacked American leaf as "poisonous" later switched to the production of cigarettes using American leaf, Parrish and his associates gleefully took out after their competitor.

43. Parrish to K. Murai, April 25, 1903, E. J. Parrish MSS, 1973 addition.

44. James A. Thomas, *A Pioneer Tobacco Merchant in the Orient* (Durham, 1928), pp.

Thomas recounted in his first memoir many incidents that illustrated J. B. Duke's keen interest in China and his business acumen even in such an exotic context. Thomas correctly noted, too, that the global organization which Duke headed "developed a remarkable *esprit de corps*, which he nursed continually." On one occasion, Duke asked Thomas how many men he had working under him in the Far East who could take his place if that necessity should arise. When Thomas in a few minutes handed Duke a list of twelve names, the latter considered a moment and declared that if Thomas had trained twelve men to take his place, he deserved a raise in salary, which he promptly got.[45]

One of the most interesting points made by Thomas in his account of James B. Duke is that Duke "put the same amount of energy and business ability into the Far Eastern trade that he did into the domestic business." In fact, Thomas recalled that Duke had once told him that he "expected soon to have the domestic business so thoroughly organized that if it were not for the Far Eastern trade he would have nothing to do."[46] The Far Eastern phase of James B. Duke's career in the tobacco industry became most notable with the formation of the British-American Tobacco Company in 1902, and that company was the direct outgrowth of Duke's efforts about a year earlier to expand his company's share of the market in Great Britain.

The vast new capital that became available upon the organization of the Consolidated Tobacco Company in 1901 not only facilitated expansion in the Far East and in Cuba, but it also was essential when Duke and his allies determined upon an intensive campaign to gain a more significant portion of the lucrative British market. In the face of trade restrictions which favored British manufacturers of tobacco products, the American Tobacco Company suffered declining sales for several years and then actually lost money in its important London depot by 1900. To combat the situation, James B. Duke made what was apparently his first trip abroad in the fall of 1901 when he and two of his associates went to London and, for something more than $5,347,000, purchased Ogden's, Limited, one of the major tobacco firms in Britain.[47]

38–39. Thomas' subsequent book was *Trailing Trade A Million Miles* (Durham, 1931). The James A. Thomas MSS contain relatively little on the early phases of Thomas' career.

45. *Ibid.*, pp. 51, 54–55.

46. *Ibid.*, p. 41.

47. Bureau of Corporations, *Report on Tobacco*, pt. I, 166–167.

The shock of being abroad must have influenced James B. Duke, for he wrote by hand a letter, a relatively long one for him, to his aged father. Though J. B. Duke would subsequently change his mind about England, he sounded like the typical American chauvinist at the outset when he declared that he was "not very much impressed with this country" and thought the people were "back numbers" who were "narrow minded & slow." After pointing to America's favorable balance of trade and England's excess of imports over exports, Duke got to the purpose of his trip: "We have bought one of the best concerns in England & it has raised a great howl[;] they call us the American invaders & are ap[p]ealing to the people to repel us. I don't know how much public prejudice will affect our business but fear it is going to make it hard for us." Duke noted that he had "worked very hard" since his arrival but hoped to get off shortly to Paris and "from there to Italy for a couple of weeks to see if I can get some ideas to further develop the Farm."

After mentioning that his eczema had "been worse than usual" for ten days or so but that otherwise his health was splendid, Washington Duke's youngest son closed on an affectionate note: "I regret exceedingly that business is such that I can't be more with you & when I get back I want you to try & come up & pay me a long visit at the farm. I know that it must be very lonely for you since Ben is away from home so much. I hope to be able to see more of you when I return, & that your health may continue good. With much love to your dear self & all the family, I am your devoted Son."[48]

J. B. Duke's fear that attacks on the "American invaders" would complicate his British plans proved entirely correct. Alarmed by the intrusion of the Americans, thirteen of the largest manufacturers in Britain and Ireland, led by the important old firm of W. D. and H. O. Wills of Bristol, scurried together to form a great combination, the Imperial Tobacco Company. Urging smokers to "Buy British," the Imperial company demonstrated a mastery of many of the techniques which American manufacturers, and especially James B. Duke, had long used. In March, 1902, as the battle between the Imperial company and the American-owned Ogden's, Limited, raged, Imperial offered large bonuses to jobbers and other tobacco merchants who pledged not to sell American goods for a term of years.

Duke and his allies countered by issuing a circular in which they,

48. J. B. Duke to Washington Duke, October 27, 1901, W. Duke MSS.

or actually the Ogden's company, offered to their customers among the jobbers their entire net profit on British business for the next four years, and £200,000 a year in addition. And the final sentence of the circular attracted a great deal of sympathetic attention: "To participate in this offer we do not ask you to boycott the goods of any other manufacturer."[49]

The struggle between Imperial and Ogden's reached into distant parts of the world. E. J. Parrish in Japan noted that the American Tobacco Company's agent in Calcutta was being bothered by "cheap cigarettes [made] by Wills and others." Parrish advised the home office: "We have no doubt the English Combination is disposed to force things in India, the Straits and China. We have no doubt the A[merican] T[obacco] Co., with our help, will be able to make it very interesting for England's manufacturers in that territory."[50]

Both in Britain and the Far East, the Americans succeeded, as Parrish expressed it, in making things "interesting" for the Imperial company. As a countermove against the Americans, the British combination threatened to invade the American market and reportedly began considering sites for factories in the United States in the summer of 1902.

Just as similar struggles in the United States had ended by the coming together of the antagonists, so too what might be termed the "tobacco war in the English-speaking world" was terminated by a far-reaching, global agreement in September, 1902. James B. Duke returned to London to help negotiate a deal whereby the American Tobacco Company and its affiliates relinquished all of their business in Britain and Ireland. The Imperial Tobacco Company, in turn, agreed not to manufacture or sell tobacco in the United States, any of its dependencies, or Cuba. Then, to carry on the tobacco business in the world outside of Britain and the United States, the British-American Tobacco Company was incorporated under the laws of Great Britain, with the Duke-led companies receiving approximately two thirds of its stock and the Imperial company the remaining third.[51]

Warming up to England as it entered its Edwardian heyday, James B. Duke gave an elaborate dinner in honor of his new British associates. To his father he sent a cable: "Have just completed great deal with British manufacturers covering world [and] securing great

49. Bureau of Corporations, *Report on Tobacco*, pt. I, 169.
50. Parrish to W. R. Harris, March 28, 1902, E. J. Parrish letterbook.
51. Bureau of Corporations, *Report on Tobacco*, pt. I, 10, 165–176.

benefit to our companies." And to Sir William Henry Wills, Duke declared: "I strongly believe that the business combination made by your Company and mine, will prove to be very advantageous to both companies, and its consummation, I feel sure, was largely due to your practical wisdom and foresight."[52]

As Duke had suggested, the British-American Tobacco Company did indeed prove to be advantageous to those behind it on both sides of the Atlantic. In succeeding years, Duke's interest in the company and its global organization grew larger, and he served as chairman of British-American for more than a decade later in his life. His satisfaction in the global as well as domestic expansion made possible by the creation of the Consolidated Tobacco Company was tempered, however, by developments in the United States having to do with President Theodore Roosevelt and his trust-busting inclinations.

In 1904, in an epochal and trail-blazing case, the Supreme Court of the United States upheld the federal government's contention that the Northern Securities Company, a vast holding company involving J. Pierpont Morgan and other of the most powerful magnates in the country, was an illegal device for restraining trade and therefore in violation of the Sherman Anti-Trust Act. The Consolidated Tobacco Company, also a great holding company, was not unlike the Northern Securities Company—and James B. Duke and his associates moved quickly in an attempt to avoid trouble from Roosevelt and the Department of Justice.

Theodore Roosevelt was not beloved by the J. P. Morgans and J. B. Dukes of America. Duke's all-time favorite president, in fact, was none other than the late William McKinley, a ten-foot-high bronze statue of whom Duke commissioned in Italy and installed on his estate near Somerville. Moreover, when Senator Mark Hanna, McKinley's close friend and ally, died early in 1904, Duke conveyed his deepest sympathy to the family "because I feel the loss of a personal friend to whom I had become attached, and feel also that the country has lost its most useful citizen."[53]

The "good old days" of McKinley and Hanna had faded, however, and the Consolidated Tobacco Company was an embarrassment in

52. J. B. Duke to W. Duke, September 27, 1902, W. Duke MSS; J. B. Duke to Wills, January 7, 1903, J. B. Duke letterbook.
53. For the statue see R. B. Arrington, executive secretary, to Prof. Chevalier Trentanove, June 15, 1906; J. B. Duke to H. M. Hanna, February 16, 1904, J. B. Duke letterbooks.

view of the Northern Securities case. Moreover, investors on Wall Street and elsewhere in the nation had been confused all along by the tangled relationships between the American, Continental, and Consolidated companies. In October, 1904, therefore, the three companies were all merged into one company called the American Tobacco Company. All intercompany holdings of securities were canceled, and the securities of the reorganized American Tobacco Company were exchanged for the remaining securities of the old companies. The preferred stock of the old companies was exchanged for 6 percent bonds of the new company, and the Consolidated bonds were exchanged, half for 6 percent preferred stock and half for 4 percent bonds of the new company. Common stock in the new American Tobacco Company was swapped for Consolidated common stock, and, in the words of one historian, "the previous concentration of control was perpetuated and strengthened in the new arrangement."[54]

The abandonment of the holding-company arrangement of the old Consolidated Tobacco Company did not suffice, of course, to remove the vast tobacco empire headed by James B. Duke from the scrutiny of the aroused Justice Department. One may be sure that as Theodore Roosevelt began his own, full term in March, 1905, Duke and his associates eyed the president warily. Well they might, for the American Tobacco Company was headed for trouble with the federal government.

That trouble, which began in 1907, would not be resolved until 1911. From that point on, much of the remainder of James B. Duke's life would acquire a Southern, and particularly a Carolina emphasis. The developments leading to that later shift were rooted in the activities of Washington Duke and especially of Benjamin Newton Duke in the 1890's. While James B. Duke led in the formation of the tobacco empire, his father and older brother devoted large amounts of their time and energy—and progressively larger portions of their incomes—to philanthropic causes in North Carolina.

54. Tennant, *The American Cigarette Industry*, pp. 35–36; Bureau of Corporations, *Report on Tobacco*, pt. I, 11–12.

CHAPTER 5. "DURHAM IS ON THE WAY TO HEAVEN REJOICING": EARLY PHILANTHROPY OF THE DUKES

Washington Duke came to philanthropy via the Methodist church. His children, and especially Benjamin N. Duke, followed the same route, and their multimillion-dollar giving in the 1920's followed lines that were clearly discernible as early as the 1890's, when both their wealth and their gifts were yet modest. As James B. Duke in New York took the principal leadership role in the family's tobacco interests, Benjamin N. Duke remained in Durham, and, while also working in the American Tobacco Company and other business ventures, he attended to a growing number of charitable concerns for the family.

Americans of a later day have come to accept income taxes, along with death, as great inescapable facts of life. Moreover, the relationship between deductible gifts for charitable purposes and the income tax has become so pervasive that some persons cannot conceive of philanthropy divorced from the reward of a tax deduction. The fact remains, however, that there were no income taxes in the United States in the 1890's, and thus other inspirations and motives for philanthropy must be sought in the case of the Dukes.

When Washington and Benjamin N. Duke began to work at philanthropy, their motives were no doubt mixed, as is the case in most human affairs. Although they generally acted quietly when that was possible and never hungered for publicity, they sought, certainly in some measure, the approval of their fellow Tarheels and were comforted thereby when their philanthropic gifts began to attract notice.

After the storm of angry opposition to the tobacco trust arose in the 1890's, some critics, and particularly John R. Webster in his weekly newspaper published in Reidsville, North Carolina, charged that the philanthropy of the Dukes represented nothing more than an attempt to "buy off" or silence an aroused public. The simplest rebuttal to that suggestion, however, lay in the large amount of time, thought, and worry, even more than money alone, that Benjamin N. Duke gave to charitable causes, and he began doing so before the American Tobacco Company was even formed.

Pride in Durham and a desire to help enhance its respectability and progressive "modernity" played a part in some of the family's early giving. The Dukes were not alone, of course, in their strong sense of family and community; but in their case money began to give increasingly tangible expression to the sentiment.

When all cautionary qualifications are made, however, the simplest answer seems to be the principal one: the Dukes gave because the Methodist church emphasized the desirability, even the necessity, of giving on the part of those who were able. In a time when the Southern churches still kept the new social gospel at arm's length and concentrated on the actions and responsibilities of individuals, the old doctrine of the stewardship of wealth remained alive. Those who possessed wealth had the dual responsibility, according to the teachings of the church, of both using and giving it wisely.

Just as Washington Duke had imbibed and accepted those teachings from an early age, so did his children. The records kept under the heading of the "tithe account" began early. All joined the Methodist church when quite young, and even before the family moved to Durham in 1874 they had attended services there in what became Trinity Methodist Church, where Washington Duke after the war served as a steward, or church officer.

As Durham grew around its various factories, new churches were needed in both the eastern and western parts of the town, and in the spring of 1886, as the first step toward a new Methodist church in what was then western Durham, a Sunday school of some thirty-three members was organized in the Duke factory. Then that same autumn the new Main Street Methodist Episcopal Church, South, opened its doors in a building given largely by the Dukes, on a lot provided by Brodie L. Duke in the block just to the west of the factory. Since Washington Duke and his sons moved their membership from Trinity to the Main Street church and were among the seven trustees of the church, and Washington Duke was the supervisor of the Sunday school, which Benjamin N. Duke served as secretary-treasurer, it is clear that the family took more than a casual interest in the church which they had built for many of their workers as well as for themselves.[1]

The Dukes were in no way unusual in their religious zeal. Julian S. Carr gave liberally to the new Carr Methodist Church in eastern

1. "Manual of Main St. M.E. Church (South), Durham, N.C., 1889," B. N. Duke MSS; Boyd, *Story of Durham*, pp. 188–191, 197–198.

Durham, which was dedicated at the same time as the Main Street church. George Watts became a lifelong and dedicated member of the First Presbyterian Church, where he served as a deacon and then an elder and as superintendent of the Sunday school from 1885 until his death in 1921. And though Durham, like so much of the South, was still overwhelmingly Protestant, William T. O'Brien took the leadership in the organization of the first Roman Catholic congregation in Durham in 1887 and ultimately gave the site and a generous contribution toward the first church building.[2]

Religion was not, of course, just the province of a few well-to-do individuals. Simultaneously with a spiraling economic boom in 1888, Durham, or much of it at least, tingled with the excitement created by the revival services being conducted by one of the well-known evangelical preachers of the day, Samuel Porter Jones, better known as plain Sam Jones. In the midst of a business letter, one of Richard Wright's associates in Durham declared: "We have had the best [revival] meeting here for ten days I have ever seen or heard tell of, two or three hundred people have professed. . . . *Durham is on the way to heaven rejoicing. . . .*" Business was at a standstill, this letter continued, for "no one seemed to think of anything but for the good of the meeting & to save the dying sinners in and around Durham." The decidedly over-sanguine conclusion was that "if whiskey is sold here now, the Barkeepers will have to be imported from some where else."[3] The cashier of a Durham bank further informed Wright that William T. Blackwell, who had earlier sold his share of the Bull Durham company to a Philadelphia concern and gone into banking and various kinds of speculation, had been publicly converted by Sam Jones and, in the evangelist's words, Blackwell had " 'a good case from his hat to his heels.' "[4]

Unfortunately for Blackwell, his newly found salvation did not help him when a severe economic storm burst on Durham later in the fall of 1888. Heading the list of a group of prominent businessmen who had to assign, that is put their property in trust for the benefit of their creditors, was William T. Blackwell. In the gloom of the economic morning-after, one Durhamite commented bitterly: "The whole amount of it all—Durham is on a 'Bust'—got more than she knows

2. Boyd, *Story of Durham*, pp. 194, 198–202.
3. Robert I. Rogers to Wright, October 30, 1888, Wright MSS. Italics in original.
4. W. S. Halliburton to Wright, October 30, 1888, Wright MSS.

what to do with, and needs a guardian until she becomes of age, or takes the 'pledge'. She has been drunk with excitement for six months." A Tobacco Exposition, Sam Jones, the fall elections, and Durham's increase of business, this observer noted, "were more than her youthful nerves could stand, and now she has the delirium tremens of Bankruptcy . . . a youthfull indiscretion she will out grow, before she arrives at the years of virility."[5]

Durham may or may not have arrived at "the years of virility," but the town did recover from the economic setback of late 1888. And with its baseball games, picnic parties transported in wagons and buggies on Easter Monday, "brilliant hops" at the local hotel attended by the "beauty and chivalry" of the town, and occasional parades by the Negro Fire Company "in full uniform with brass band attachment," the upstart factory town had its attractions.[6] Certainly all of the Dukes save perhaps the youngest son, James B. Duke, felt strong ties with Durham, for there they married, lived, and reared their children.

Brodie L. Duke, with more extensive real estate holdings in Durham than any of the family—Benjamin N. Duke called him jokingly the "great real estate king of the town"—also remained through his life closely tied to his home town.[7] He married Martha McMannen, daughter of a Durham minister, and they had three children—two daughters, Mabel and Pearl, and a son, Lawrence. After the death of his first wife in April, 1888, Brodie Duke in 1890 married Minnie Woodward of Gadsden, Alabama, and a son, Woodward, was born of this marriage, which ended in divorce in 1904.[8]

For all of his dashing appearance, frequent charm, and prominent role in helping to build Durham, Brodie Duke encountered serious difficulties in his life. The local newspaper announced early in 1892 merely that he was about to return from Dwight, Illinois, but a friend of his reported privately that Brodie Duke had returned "sober as

5. O. R. Smith to R. H. Wright, November 19, 1888, Wright MSS. The misspellings are in the original.

6. Durham *Tobacco Plant*, April 13, 1887.

7. B. N. Duke to B. L. Duke, February 4, 1893. B. N. Duke letterbook.

8. The most convenient source for this information is in Walter G. Duke, compiler, *Henry Duke, Councilor: His Descendants and Connections* (Richmond, Va., 1949), pp. 283–284. The copy in the Manuscript Department, Duke University Library, has important corrections and additions by the late Dr. Virginia Gray, who extensively studied the genealogy of Washington Duke.

a judge" and that it was a "grand institution that can stop a fellow getting drunk & even [make him] dislike whiskey."[9] The "grand institution" referred to was the Keeley Institute, and Dwight, Illinois, was the home of Dr. Leslie E. Keeley, who originated a once-famous treatment for alcoholism and other types of drug addiction. One enthusiastic observer no doubt went too far in hailing the Keeley Institute as "the vestibule of the Church of God."[10] Yet in a day when society at large scorned alcoholics and made no provision at all for their treatment, the "Keeley cure" at least held out hope, albeit only for those who could afford to pay for the treatment.

Impressed by the experience of Brodie Duke and of one or two other citizens of Durham that had made the trip to Dwight, Illinois, Benjamin N. Duke, James B. Duke, and George Watts put up most of the $15,000 required in 1892 to establish a Keeley Institute in Greensboro, North Carolina.[11] Some two years later, and after the principal owners had themselves helped to send numerous patients to Greensboro, the director there noted: "The Keeley Institute of N.C. has contributed about $20,000.00 towards the cure of drunkards since it started and . . . there is never a day but there are charity patients in the house."[12] After nearly seven years of operation, the Institute had treated some 2500 persons, and of that number the director claimed knowledge of about 1800 who had not relapsed.[13] Unfortunately, Brodie Duke did not belong in that reformed category.

He nevertheless involved himself in Durham's textile manufacturing, railways, mercantile establishments, and real estate. "I tell you fellers that we can't stick like the bark on a tree—so d——d tight it won't come off," he declared to a gathering of businessmen in Durham in 1890. "We've got to be like the branches of the tree—we must expand—we must make Durham bigger and we must expect to put up the coin if we expect to get men to come here."[14] Brodie Duke put up his share of "the coin" in developing his hometown, but he also indulged a dangerous taste for speculation in the commodity market and especially in cotton futures. In the massive depression that began

9. Durham *Daily Globe*, January 19, 1892; R. I. Rogers to R. H. Wright, February 7, 1892, Wright MSS.

10. Durham *Recorder*, April 16, 1900.

11. G. Watts to B. N. Duke, March 8, 1892, and B. N. Duke to N. M. Jurney, May 2, 1892, B. N. Duke MSS.

12. W. H. Osborn to Washington Duke, December 17, 1894, B. N. Duke MSS.

13. Charlotte *Observer*, as quoted in the Durham *Recorder*, January 19, 1899.

14. Durham *Morning Herald*, February 5, 1919.

in 1893, he finally became so entangled and financially embarrassed by immediate debts that he had to assign his assets to trustees and be bailed out gradually by help from his father and brothers as well as by his own endeavors.[15]

The financial troubles of the oldest son were bad enough, but earlier in 1893 Washington Duke had suffered a greater tragedy in the death of his only daughter. Mary Duke had married Robert E. Lyon, a dealer in leaf tobacco in Durham, and they had five children, Mary, Benjamin, George, Bertha, and Edwin ("Buck") Lyon. A devout worker in Trinity Methodist Church, Mary Duke Lyon also possessed business abilities, for she managed a phase of the work of W. Duke, Sons and Company concerned with making the cloth bags in which smoking tobacco was packed.[16] Brodie Duke in 1891 had been the first member of the family to visit Europe, but the hope that Mary Duke Lyon's health would benefit from travel was one of the inspirations for the "Grand Tour" taken in the summer of 1892 by Washington Duke, the Lyon family, Dr. A. G. Carr, the family physician, and Benjamin N. Duke and his family. Neither travel nor, a bit later, specialists in New York could check Mary Duke Lyon's physical decline, however, and her death in the spring of 1893 at the age of thirty-nine occasioned widespread mourning in Durham.

The constitution of Benjamin N. Duke was never robust either, and as a child he suffered from serious illnesses. Nevertheless, from his early manhood until the last fourteen years of his life he generally managed to overcome the worst of his health problems. Not long before his twenty-second birthday in 1877, he married Sarah Pearson Angier of Durham. Their first child, George Washington Duke, died at the age of two, but two other children were born to the young couple, Angier Buchanan Duke on December 8, 1884, and Mary Lillian Duke on November 16, 1887.

Since the bulk of Ben Duke's, and indeed the entire family's papers, do not begin until 1890, it is impossible to know the full range of the family's charitable activities prior to that time. Moreover, while they were certainly well off in the 1880's as compared with the vast majority of poverty-stricken Southerners, the Dukes had by no means moved at that time into the ranks of the conspicuously rich, such as George W. Vanderbilt who built his famed baronial estate, Biltmore, in

15. Durham *Daily Globe*, December 13, 1893; B. N. Duke to W. R. Hall, January 16, 1894, and other letters in B. N. Duke MSS.

16. See R. E. Lyon to B. N. Duke, January 1, 1894, in the B. N. Duke MSS.

western North Carolina in the 1890's at a cost of several million dollars. When Ben Duke in the late 1880's built a new frame house in Durham in the fashionable "Victorian" style, the local newspaper effused about the interior woodwork, the plastering, and the fact that the house would be equipped with such modern improvements as a furnace, hot and cold water, and electric lights. The reporter judged that the "cost all told will probably exceed $25,000," but actually Duke had agreed in 1887 to pay the builder $8,000 to erect the house.[17]

Washington Duke as well as Ben Duke and his family paid summer visits not to the famous resorts of the Gilded Age but to Buffalo Lithia Springs and Chase City Springs, two old-fashioned resorts in Virginia where they "took the waters." The Dukes and a number of their business associates and friends also owned a modest fishing camp near Newport in eastern North Carolina which was organized as a stock company and known as Carteret Lodge. Like his younger brother in New York, Ben Duke acquired a farm in the early 1890's. It was located a few miles out from Durham, and when he decided to build a summer cottage there, he also wished to have a house built for the pastor of the Main Street Methodist Church. "I do not want the parsonage to cost over $2000 & my country cottage over $2000 to $2500," Duke instructed. "Building can now be done here 20% less than a year ago."[18]

Ben Duke's concern about the parsonage illustrates the fact that the Main Street Methodist church of Durham was always a prime concern of the Dukes, but they early began extending aid to other congregations in North Carolina, not always but primarily to those that were Methodist and in the rural areas and villages. "We are so very anxious to have some little repairs done on [our Methodist church]," one woman wrote; "it has never been painted neither in nor outside, and our little 25 cent Lamps makes but a poor light . . . and there is such a small band of us—and all of very limitted [sic] means. . . ." A minister wrote that one of his churches consisted of forty-five members who had to worship in an "uncomfortable, unfinished school house belonging to the community." The members were all poor, he explained, "no one being assessed over $2.00 [per year] for the support of the ministry, and are unable to build without

17. Durham *Tobacco Plant*, January 25, 1889; contract of May 13, 1887, in B. N. Duke MSS.

18. B. N. Duke to George F. Barber and Company, February 21, 1894, B. N. Duke MSS.

88

a good deal of outside help." Then he added: "We have about 9000 feet of lumber, a few nails and a small amount of money promised, and $55.50 cash, $50 of which was given by the Board of Church Extension, but here we are at a standstill for lack of more funds. Our need is sore. . . ."[19]

To such appeals as these the family, acting through B. N. Duke, usually responded with a contribution, often in the early years a small one ranging from five to fifty dollars. "I am continually applied to by people from all over the country for money to aid in the erection of churches, etc.," Washington Duke explained on one occasion, "and I would not be justified in contributing any large amount to one enterprise. Before making a contribution I would want to know what the people interested are doing to help themselves, and if I have satisfactory assurance that money enough will be raised to complete whatever is undertaken, then I am willing to make a contribution; otherwise I cannot."[20]

While the physical arrangements for many Methodist congregations were poor enough, the plight of most ministers in the depression-wracked 1890's was even worse. "I have not received but $25.00 off of my work this year, as a support," one preacher declared. "I have not been living, but staying here. . . ." Another wrote that he had been paid $79.80 for the year but with a new assignment coming up he would be compelled to have a horse and to buy one he needed to borrow $100. From a textile-manufacturing area one Methodist minister, who served churches in three separate towns, reported that his total salary was supposed to be $475 per year. "To help me support my family," he confessed, "I had to take my only son from school and put him in the cotton mill. There are seven of us to support."[21]

Despite the gloomy tone of the appeals that came to the Dukes, there was also evidence that many churches did the best they could for their ministers. For example, one ministerial friend reported that upon arriving at his new charge, he and his family were met at the

19. Mrs. M. E. M. to B. N. Duke, April 2, 1894, and the Rev. G. T. Simmons to B. N. Duke, January 26, 1897, B. N. Duke MSS. Many dozens of such letters may be found in this collection.

20. Washington Duke to O. L. W. Smith, April 8, 1892, B. N. Duke letterbook. The letter was actually written by B. N. Duke in all probability. For two examples of numerous donations on two separate, mail-answering days, see April 8, 1892, and February 28, 1894, B. N. Duke MSS.

21. The Rev. J. A. Peeler to "Brother Duke," August 9, 1894; Rev. Edward Kelley to B. N. Duke, December 18, 1894; Rev. John C. Hocutt to W. Duke, March 30, 1898, B. N. Duke MSS.

railway station and carried to a comfortable, well-furnished parsonage where several ladies served as a welcoming committee. "A blazing wood fire and a well prepared, bountiful dinner greeted us," he continued. "I tell you these good people gave us a royal reception & made us feel that we had come among friends. The pantry was supplied for days to come. There stood a barrel of flour, then lard, meat, sausage, coffee, sugar &C [and] in the wood house we found coal & wood, in the yard ten or eleven chickens." The enthusiastic minister added, however, that he had four churches in his care and would require a horse and buggy. "I preach three Sundays [morning and night] in the month in Hertford," he explained, "but two of these I preach at 3 P.M. in the country, so that these two Sundays I preach 3 times. I have two churches 12 & 15 miles from town where I preach morning & afternoon. I hold prayer meetings every Wednesday night in town, so you see I have plenty of work on hand."[22]

Because Washington Duke had from an early age come to love the Methodist church and its circuit-riding, itinerant ministers and had raised his family to share his feeling, the Dukes responded to the plight of the hard-working, pitifully underpaid clergy. In the late nineteenth century, when American individualism and unregulated capitalism reached their apogee, the old notion that "those who can, do, and those who can not, teach—or preach," had by no means died out. One young businessman, for example, warned his sister about her daughter's marital prospects: "For God's sake don't let her marry a preacher. Of all lives I think that of a preacher's wife is the least to be desired. . . . Most preachers follow the business as an easy way of living without work & as a respectable way of begging of other people."[23]

The Dukes, for all of their own competitive and money-making instincts, did not regard preachers as "respectable" beggars. Washington Duke sympathized with the plight of those who preached and that was undoubtedly the initial reason why he and his family became entangled with Trinity College, North Carolina Methodism's struggling institution for the higher education of men. Ben Duke led the family into contact with Trinity when he gave the nearly bankrupt institution $1,000 in 1887.[24] He certainly did not know it at the time,

22. Rev. F. A. Bishop to B. N. Duke, December 24, 1894, B. N. Duke MSS.
23. Richard H. Wright to Mrs. J. R. Ball, June 30, 1893, R. H. Wright MSS.
24. Durham *Tobacco Plant*, August 10, 1887.

but with that $1,000 he had, in fact, cast into the church-and-college pond a pebble that would end up causing some sizable waves.

Located in Randolph County some seventy miles to the west of Durham, Trinity College in the late 1880's, like most other educational institutions in the South at that time, lived precariously on the bare bones of poverty. The college traced its beginnings to the late 1830's when some Quakers and Methodists in the area cooperated to launch an academy known as Union Institute. Passing through several phases, including a state-supported emphasis in the 1850's on the training of school teachers, the institution was adopted by the Methodists of North Carolina in 1856 and took the name of Trinity College in 1859.[25]

Proud of its service to "poor boys" who could pay little and most of whom tended to become preachers and teachers, Trinity College managed to hang on through the years of the Civil War and even during the Reconstruction period, when the University of North Carolina had to suspend operation for some five years. The extraordinary leadership of Braxton Craven, president of the college and a Methodist minister himself, and a slowly growing body of loyal alumni were the principal assets of early Trinity College. After Craven's death in 1882, however, only the heroic intervention of three Methodist businessmen, including Durham's Julian S. Carr, saved the college from collapsing before a new president could be found in 1887.

The naming of twenty-nine-year-old John F. Crowell as the new president of Trinity College was of the greatest significance for the institution, both because of what Crowell would accomplish and of what the appointment symbolized. At a time when defensive sectionalism still characterized much of the South, Trinity College chose a native Pennsylvanian who had done both his undergraduate and graduate work at Yale University and who was completely caught up in the ferment of reform that was reshaping American higher education in the last quarter of the nineteenth century. More than any other one institution, perhaps, the new Johns Hopkins University in Baltimore, Maryland, had blazed a trail that Harvard, Yale, and other old colonial colleges were eagerly following. Now, here came Crowell to Trinity College—which was located in an agrarian community some five miles from the nearest railroad, telegraph, or tele-

25. The early history of the college is covered in Nora C. Chaffin, *Trinity College, 1839–1892: The Beginnings of Duke University* (Durham, 1950).

phone—with the audacious idea of having the struggling college catch up with the educational vanguard.

Changes and reforms came fast in the raising of academic standards and modernizing of the curriculum, but none was so far-reaching as Crowell's notion, reached in his second year at Trinity, that the college should be moved from the bucolic fields and woods to a city. There, in the cities, according to Crowell, operated "the main creative forces in modern society," and there perhaps Trinity College might truly move along the progressive and, for the South at that period, unconventional lines that Crowell and his allies envisioned. After successful struggles in the board of trustees and the North Carolina Conference of the Methodist church, Crowell prepared to lead the college in a move to Raleigh, where Methodist and civic piety had combined to offer a site for the college and $35,000 for the buildings.[26] Pushy little Durham also coveted a college, and when the state's Baptists invited offers for the location of a Female Seminary (which ultimately became Meredith College), Durham outbid Raleigh. Thus Durham's embarrassment was all the greater when the Baptist institution chose as its home the older state capital rather than the upstart factory town.

Stung by this affront to Durham, Washington Duke conferred with his family, particularly with his son Ben Duke, and informed a Methodist minister, who had all along been ardently urging Trinity's cause on the Dukes, that he, Washington Duke, would personally guarantee that Durham not only would match Raleigh's offer of $35,000 for Trinity but would also provide an additional $50,000 for endowment. Alerted by the minister, Crowell wasted no time in visiting Washington Duke, whom he then met for the first time. He also saw Julian Carr, who offered some fifty acres of land on the western edge of Durham known as Blackwell Park as a site for the college. Informing Washington Duke of the land offer, Julian Carr added graciously, "I shall ever feel proud to point to you as a fellow townsman. . . ."[27]

With Raleigh's consent and the trustees' approval, Crowell began to prepare for the move to Durham, "the supreme opportunity," he assured Washington Duke, "of placing the college upon the highway to success in the service of humanity."[28] Crowell was understandably

26. Chaffin, *Beginnings*, pp. 478 ff.; John F. Crowell, "Personal Recollections of Trinity College, North Carolina, 1887–1893," ch. 4, unpublished memoir in the John F. Crowell MSS, Duke University Archives.

27. J. S. Carr to W. Duke, March 6, 1890, W. Duke MSS.

28. Crowell to W. Duke, February 24, 1890, copy in Crowell MSS.

elated, but his vision or dreams of Trinity's future far outstripped the cold realities. The Dukes, along with Julian Carr and other citizens of Durham, had indeed been generous to Trinity: Washington Duke's gift was widely hailed as the largest single philanthropic gift of money up to that time in the state's history. The Dukes, quite understandably, expected their fellow Methodists throughout the state to rally around the college, which was their college, once it was moved and launched on the road of revitalization. Crowell certainly shared this hope and, in addition, he had grandiose ideas both as to what the Dukes themselves could or would do for the college and as to what Trinity College could afford to undertake.

The move to Durham, for Crowell and others, signalled the opportunity to build "The Greater Trinity," by which was meant nothing less than a true university, one with a college of liberal arts flanked by a new-style graduate school as well as professional schools for theology, law, engineering, and medicine.[29] The dream was a grand one whose influence would linger on, but it was also, alas, not rooted in reality and far in advance of its time. Serious trouble, rather than quick expansion, lay directly ahead for Trinity.

In the meantime, Washington Duke headed the building committee, which, because he was seventy, meant that Benjamin N. Duke had acquired a heavy, new set of responsibilities. The building committee of ten members, opening their meetings in Washington Duke's office with prayer, set to work in the spring and summer of 1890, and the Main Building, which was later to be known as the Washington Duke Building, began to take shape in 1891.[30]

While Ben Duke bore the brunt of the fast-multiplying problems of Trinity's imminent move, another member of the family, Brodie Duke, gained an interesting new perspective on collegiate architecture, a perspective that his youngest half-brother, James B. Duke, would later come to share. Touring Europe for the first time, Brodie Duke had typical American complaints about the lack of the "latest modern improvements" in Parisian hotels and the absence of "the push and enterprise" that he regarded as characteristics of the United States. But Westminster Abbey, Notre Dame, and other European cathedrals led Brodie Duke to confess: ". . . I tell you we are far behind in

29. Crowell, "Personal Recollections," ch. 23; Earl W. Porter, *Trinity and Duke, 1892–1924: Foundations of Duke University* (Durham, 1964), pp. 25–26.
30. Copy of the Building Committee's Minute Book in Crowell MSS; Porter, *Trinity and Duke*, pp. 29–30.

church structure in America. They are grand beyond description covering whole Squares & every kind of carvings outside & inside. . . . I only wish Pa had come with us. I know he would have loved it, & here I want to say I know we are going to miss it on Trinity. Oh! if Crowell could see the college Buildings & Chapels at Oxford England he would have changed Trinity. He is hurrying things too much. It ought to have taken 3 years to build the main building. . . . But our people need Traveling."[31]

Although Crowell alone should not be blamed for "hurrying things too much," the collapse of the Main Building's brick tower in August, 1891, delayed the moving of the college for another year. The fallen tower was the most dramatic sign of trouble, but it was by no means the most fundamental. Money, or rather the lack of it, had that distinction. By the time Trinity College began operations on its new Durham campus in the fall of 1892, with a total enrollment of 180 young men, some faculty salaries for the previous year were yet unpaid, and there was no money in sight to pay either salaries for the new school year or various overdue bills for coal, furniture, insurance premiums, and other pressing items. While expenses for the year were estimated at $17,900, the income from tuition would be only $4,500, including $2,300 still due for the term that had opened.[32]

"No man knows how heavy the load has been since you left," Crowell declared to Ben Duke upon the latter's return from Europe in the fall of 1892. "Single-handed and with triflingly small resources have I stood at my post. Hence it will be a glad day when you return." Crowell was not alone in looking to Ben Duke for help. One of the leading trustees and a Methodist presiding elder who had helped persuade the Dukes to help move Trinity to Durham, E. A. Yates, admitted to Ben Duke that too much money had been "swamped in Buildings," and while the Methodists of the state had contributed their mites for the college, the simple fact was that most of them were desperately poor. "The truth plainly spoken is," Yates concluded, "we are in a bad condition. We are really in *danger of a collapse*. It will be a disgrace to us for this to take place."[33]

Perhaps because Ben Duke was yet in New York and appalled by the troubled prospect of college affairs that awaited him in Durham,

31. Brodie Duke to B. N. Duke, May 21, 1891, B. N. Duke MSS.

32. Porter, *Trinity and Duke*, pp. 35–36.

33. Crowell to B. N. Duke, September 23, 1892, and E. A. Yates to B. N. Duke, October 7, 1892, B. N. Duke MSS. Italics in original.

he took a cold, hard line. "I do not think the Methodist denomination of North Carolina deserve[s] to own a College," he asserted to Yates. The people of Durham, and especially his father and Julian Carr, had acted nobly for Trinity College, yet other Methodists in North Carolina, including some at least who were well-to-do, were "sitting idle and letting their institution starve for the want of the necessary financial food." Ben Duke feared that the failure of the college was "inevitable sooner or later," and, he added grimly, "I think the sooner the better." Expressing his personal sympathy for Crowell and Yates, he concluded: ". . . I can say frankly, that no enterprise with which I have ever been connected has caused me half the trouble and worry and loss of sleep, as my short connection with the work [of the college] since it began operations at Durham."[34]

Once back in Durham and confronted with the painfully human aspects of the problem, Ben Duke relented. Perhaps the interest in the college of his ill sister, Mary Duke Lyon, and the approach of Christmas helped soften him too. At any rate, after toying with an abortive idea of gaining an endowment for the college through an insurance plan, he offered on behalf of himself, James B. Duke, and Mary Duke Lyon to give the college $7,500 per year for three years if the college would raise an additional $15,000 in each of the years. Part of the Dukes' gift would be spent for sixty scholarships. With the prompt acceptance of the offer by the North Carolina Conference of the Methodist church and by the recently split-off Western North Carolina Conference, Trinity College had gained breathing space, at least. But its difficulties were far from over.

President Crowell had recruited for the faculty several able young scholars equipped with the relatively new Ph.D degree from Johns Hopkins, Yale, and a few other Eastern universities. Unfortunately, he not only failed, admittedly through circumstances beyond his control, to see that their modest salaries of $1,200 per year were paid, but he also antagonized some, as one of them later explained, ". . . by his attempt to absorb all the power into his own hands and by not paying any attention to the experience and requests of his colleagues."[35] Crowell had also introduced intercollegiate football to Trinity and the state, and while many of the college's supporters were thrilled by some of the early victories over the nearby University of North Carolina,

34. B. N. Duke to E. A. Yates, October 14, 1892, B. N. Duke letterbook.
35. Charles L. Raper, *The Church and Private Shcools of North Carolina* (Greensboro, 1898), p. 192.

the Western North Carolina Conference voiced anxieties about various aspects of the increasingly popular game. When Crowell dealt with the matter in a somewhat lofty and undiplomatic fashion in his report to the Conference late in 1893—and to the dismay of many of the Methodist brethren devoted more pages to the matter of athletics than to the religious life of the students—the Conference voted in a manner that Crowell interpreted as a condemnation of him and his administration. Inwardly stunned, he kept quiet but prepared to resign. When the board of trustees unanimously refused to accept his resignation in May, 1894, he stood firm, and the board finally yielded.[36]

Ben Duke had kept scrupulously aloof from various moves against Crowell a year earlier and admired him as a dedicated, progressive educator. An enthusiastic advocate of faculty and student awareness of and involvement in contemporary issues and affairs, Crowell drew occasional attacks from Democratic newspapers, which certainly did not lessen his stock in the Republican eyes of the Dukes. When Crowell published his views about a railroad commission for North Carolina, young Josephus Daniels, then editing the Raleigh *State Chronicle*, suggested that Crowell run his college and let "the people," unassisted by any Yankee, run the state. A bit later when the Wilmington *Daily Messenger* attacked a professor at Trinity College for his activities in the new Populist party and urged that the college should oust him, Crowell fired back: ". . . I cannot regard your words involving the sacrifice of freedom of thought in this College as anything less than a species of intolerable arrogance to which an excess of partisan zeal has led you. You must learn, herewith, that the purpose of Trinity College is to influence public thought, and that it is beyond reason to suppose that, when a man becomes a member of its Faculty, he thereby surrenders a whit of his freedom to act or think in matters political."[37]

While Ben Duke could not know at that time just how much Crowell's legacy to Trinity and his ambitious plans would influence the future course of the institution, the businessman had gained an invaluable, and also painful, introduction to higher education and philanthropy. Another thing that Ben Duke probably did not realize as he approached his fortieth birthday in 1895 was that in his close association with Trinity College—and its never-ending problems, needs, and human kaleidoscope—he had stumbled on to one of the great passions of the remaining years of his life.

36. Porter, *Trinity and Duke*, pp. 38, 49–53.
37. Crowell, "Personal Recollections," ch. 15; Porter, *Trinity and Duke*, pp. 14, 35.

CHAPTER 6. "TRINITY COLLEGE IS THE BEST INSTITUTION OF LEARNING IN THE SOUTH": THE PHILANTHROPIC PATTERN TAKES SHAPE

Ben Duke's service as the family's agent for philanthropy, as well as the range of the family's charitable concerns, is neatly shown in a letter he wrote to James B. Duke in New York shortly after Christmas, 1893. The amounts of money mentioned were yet small, but there would be a striking continuity of purpose between the small-scale gifts of the 1890's, the larger donations of the 1900's, and the immense bequests of the 1920's. "Dear Buck," Ben Duke wrote:

> I am much disappointed at not seeing you here [in Durham] this Xmas, but I suppose your business would not allow you to leave N.Y. I want to talk to you about money matters. During the past year I have paid out money as follows
>
> | | |
> |---|---|
> | Trinity College (on account of our offer to the conference last year) | $7500 |
> | All other church & charity | $4016 |
> | | $11,516.00 |
>
> I believe it was understood that Mary, you and myself were to share in this Trinity College expenditure. The other item of $4016.00 was expended about as follows: contributions to the poor fund of the town during the severe weather last winter, amounts given to the pastor of our church for the poor during the year which he used in doctoring the sick, burying the dead &c, &c (all of which he rendered itemized statement of) Oxford Orphans Asylum, current expenses of our church of every kind. Colored School at Kittrell N.C. $500. Worn out Preachers of the N.C. Conference $500. To poor churches over the state &c &c. What I mention is in addition to what Pa gave or rather it is two-thirds (2/3rds) of the total of such payments, the total being $6024.00. I expect you have given away money individually during the year—if so & you are disposed to assist me as usual with these expenses you should have credit for such amounts as

you have expended. The total amount I've paid ($11,516.00) looks large but $7500 of it went in one place & I do not see how I could have made the other items less, as the pressure from the poor &c has been urgent, & as for myself I feel better for having given it than if I had not done so. Of course this does not include money I've given to favor kin people. . . .[1]

James B. Duke paid his share. While he did, as his brother had suggested, occasionally make charitable contributions on his own, he generally had no time to spare for the correspondence involved in philanthropic work, much less the tiresome hours of conferring with educators, Methodist preachers, and assorted other petitioners. Ben Duke, on the other hand, took the trouble to answer, even if negatively, the hundreds of requests that poured in to him and his father, requests that became especially voluminous after the announcement of any of their larger gifts to Trinity College. He also became personally involved in a number of institutions other than Trinity.

One of the early and special concerns of Ben Duke and the family was the Orphan Asylum at Oxford, North Carolina, which is mentioned in Ben Duke's letter to his brother. Owned and operated by the Grand Lodge of North Carolina Masons, to which Washington Duke but not Ben Duke belonged, the asylum limped along on donations from churches and other organizations as well as from the Masons. Ben Duke's involvement with the orphanage began with special Thanksgiving offerings for the institution, state-wide offerings in which Durham's Main Street Methodist Church far outpaced all others in the 1890's. "My father and self have in mind the advisability of giving a Christmas tree to the Orphans under your care," he wrote the superintendent in 1893, "and now write to get your views in the matter." Word of his appointment as a director of the asylum reached Ben Duke before his $200 check for the Christmas tree could be mailed.[2]

Ben Duke shortly afterward sent $100 "with which to buy the books for the Asylum Library" and offered to be personally responsible if necessary for paying for dormitory partitions and windows that were needed for ventilation. "You do not know how much I thank you and

1. B. N. Duke to J. B. Duke, December 29, 1893, in B. N. Duke letterbook. This letter was written by hand and the letterpress copy pasted in the back of the letterbook.
2. B. N. Duke to Dr. W. Black, November 28, 1893, B. N. Duke letterbook, and S. F. Telfair to B. N. Duke, December 2, 1893, B. N. Duke MSS.

your father for coming here, spending the day with me and looking over things so carefully . . . ," the superintendent wrote. With no heat in either the boys' or the girls' dormitories and "no place for the boys to be on a rainy day except where they sleep," the superintendent felt overwhelmed by the needs of the orphanage. Moreover, he added, "I have written and talked with a good many people since you were here trying to see if I could not raise $2500, but I have not had a single favorable response." The "financial condition of the country" was simply too depressed.[3]

The panic of 1893, as Ben Duke well knew, had thrown the country into a prolonged and massive depression. When he requested a fellow North Carolinian who had become a banker in New York to supply a list of transplanted Tarheels who might contribute to a Christmas fund for the orphans, the banker replied: "North Carolinians in New York have not fared very well during the last two years, and while they have the greatest affection for their old state and anything connected with it, I am afraid they would not be disposed to contribute much for the purchase of Christmas things, outside of what they will be forced to do at home."[4]

Ben Duke took care of the Christmas tree again, but more importantly he decided to tackle the problem of the asylum's woefully inadequate physical facilities. If the Masons and other North Carolinians would raise $5,000 for the institution in 1895, he would give a similar amount. The offer being promptly accepted, new dormitories for the boys and other improvements soon materialized. The problems were far from solved, however, for the superintendent informed Ben Duke early in 1897 that applications were increasing, "the destitution is simply distressing," and no more children could be admitted unless others were first discharged. As for a poverty-stricken family in Durham which Duke had investigated, the superintendent concluded that since the eleven- and twelve-year-old girl and boy, both illiterate, had jobs in a textile factory it was "a great deal better" to let them help support themselves than to send them to the overcrowded orphanage. The superintendent added that during a recent two-week spell of cold weather the water tank at the orphanage had frozen and every bit of water used at the boys' building and at the girls' building,

3. B. N. Duke to Dr. Black, February 21, 1894, and B. N. Duke to N. M. Lawrence, September 10, 1894, B. N. Duke letterbook; Lawrence to Duke, October 11, 1894, B. N. Duke MSS.
4. James H. Parker to B. N. Duke, November 26, 1894, B. N. Duke MSS.

where there was no well, had to be hauled in barrels or brought from the well "near the farmer's house in buckets."[5]

Ben Duke continued to interest himself in various aspects of the orphanage, from little things such as shades for the windows in the dining room and terra-cotta pipes to prevent dampness in the basement to planning and paying for much-needed new buildings. As would happen in many other instances of the family's philanthropy, he also arranged to involve a close friend and soon-to-be business associate, Clinton W. Toms, in the affairs of the asylum. Still unhappy about the poor facilities at the orphanage, Ben Duke announced early in 1898 that he would contribute $7,500, once again on a matching basis, "to be used in building and furnishing cottages for the girls, similar to those now occupied by the boys, and for such other buildings and improvements as may be deemed necessary."[6]

Thanks in part to Ben Duke's concern, the institution was significantly improved. When the Oxford Orphanage became involved in the fiercely bitter politics of the late 1890's, however, Ben Duke and his allies on the board of directors and in the management of the institution fell under attack from certain Democratic quarters. In 1901, on the eve of his establishing part-time residence in New York, Ben Duke resigned as a director of the asylum, but neither he nor the other members of his family lost interest in the larger, permanent social problem with which he had grappled closely for some ten years.[7]

While the Oxford Orphan Asylum was maintained at the time for white children only and the walls of the "Jim Crow system" for the segregation of black people were rising rapidly to new heights throughout the South around the turn of the century, the Dukes also contributed to orphanages and other institutions maintained by and for Negroes, Kittrell College being an early and long-continuing example. In fact, the relationship of the Dukes to the black minority was both complicated and interesting.

Having acquired money and with it power and social status by the last decade of the nineteenth century, the Dukes also displayed those paternalistic and benevolent attitudes toward black people on which

5. B. N. Duke to N. M. Lawrence, December 29, 1894, B. N. Duke letterbook, and Lawrence to Duke, February 8, 1897, B. N. Duke MSS.

6. C. W. Toms to B. N. Duke, August 16, 1897; B. N. Duke to John C. Drewry, January 8, 1898. B. N. Duke MSS and letterbook.

7. For the political attacks, see Governor Daniel L. Russell to B. N. Duke, January 10, 1899, and other letters in that year, and for Duke's resignation see Governor Charles B. Aycock to Duke, May 29, 1901, B. N. Duke MSS.

upper-class Southern whites traditionally and many times unwarrantedly prided themselves. But in the case of the Dukes there was an unusual aspect of the relationship that transcended paternalism, and it was rooted in politics. The overwhelming majority of Negroes in the years after the Civil War were Republicans and so also, beginning with Washington Duke in the era of Reconstruction, were the Dukes. If blacks knew all too well what it meant to be a minority, so too, in an admittedly different way, did the Southern whites who became Republicans after the Civil War. To Washington Duke, one of the despised "scalawags" in the eyes of the Democratic majority, blacks were political allies as well as, in many cases, friends. The relationship influenced not only his sons and the family's philanthropy but even had an impact on Trinity College after 1890.

Reconstruction set the pattern of Southern politics that persisted for many decades. Democrats, having learned the power of racist appeals in that bitter postwar era, long continued to use the shibboleths and tactics that had proved so successful in restoring "the white man's party" to power in the 1870's. In 1888, for example, the Durham *Recorder* prepared its readers for the elections of that year in this fashion: "White men of Durham, those who have any respect for the Anglo-Saxon race, will you fail to do your duty on the 6th of November? Will you allow negro rule or a white man's government?" Since the Republicans of Durham County had made nominations for five offices and only the nominee for county coroner was a Negro, one can see what Southern Democrats means by "negro rule."[8]

The Durham *Tobacco Plant*, a Democratic paper owned by Julian Carr, was twitted by another newspaper for having declared that the "one issue" in the election was the protective tariff when Josephus Daniels in the Raleigh *State Chronicle* had insisted that the "one issue" was "negro supremacy." The *Tobacco Plant* recovered neatly by asserting that the "one issue in national politics is the tariff, and the one in State politics is the negro question."[9]

Such time-hallowed and stale "issues" served the Democrats well for two decades. Then in the 1890's, when the long-simmering economic discontent of Southern and Western farmers exploded into the Populist revolt, the Democrats faced their most serious challenge in a generation. The new Populist or People's party was especially vigorous

8. Durham *Recorder*, October 3, 1888. Durham County was created by the legislature in 1881.

9. Durham *Tobacco Plant*, July 11, 1888.

in North Carolina, and in 1894 it cooperated with the Republicans with the result that the two groups gained control of the legislature. In 1896 not only did the "Fusionists," as their opponents first labeled them, keep control of the legislature, but they also elected a Republican as governor, Daniel L. Russell, who became a friend and debtor of Ben Duke.

While the Dukes were especially jubilant about the election of William McKinley as president in 1896, they also took pleasure in the triumph of Tarheel Republicanism. Russell urged Washington Duke to come stroll with him around the Governor's Mansion so they could give the "Bourbon Democrats" a symbolic demonstration of the new day that had arrived. "We admit their partnership," Russell declared, "but decline to acknowledge their superiority or mastery."[10] The satisfaction of the Dukes, Russell, and other Republicans about state affairs was short-lived, however. In 1898 the Democrats, led by Furnifold M. Simmons of New Bern and Josephus Daniels of the Raleigh *News and Observer*, among others, mounted their great "white supremacy" campaign and in a frenzy of unrestrained racism and intimidation of black voters regained control of the state legislature. With his own life threatened by a Democratic mob at one point and with his hometown of Wilmington the scene of a bloody political and racial *coup* by local Democrats against blacks, Governor Russell confessed wearily to Ben Duke that "the irritations incident to being a Republican and living in the South, are getting to be too rank to be borne."[11] Disfranchisement of the great bulk of the black voters in the state came with the Democratic victory of 1900, and North Carolina, along with the rest of the South and indeed much of the nation, wallowed in harshly discriminatory treatment of the black minority.

White Republicans did not, certainly, suffer as did the blacks, yet the treatment white Republicans received was often degrading and cruel. Ben Duke's brother-in-law and fellow Republican, John C. Angier, reported after the heated election of 1896 that certain people in Cary, a small town near Raleigh, had "tried every way possible to insult me and my family" and even had his children crying at school on one occasion. "Last Sunday I was in my place in Sunday School as usual," he added, and "I shall be in my place at prayer

10. Russell to B. N. Duke, November 30, 1896, B. N. Duke MSS.
11. D. L. Russell to B. N. Duke, December 2, 1898, B. N. Duke MSS.

meeting to-night and will be at Sunday School again next Sunday and propose to do my duty and fight it out along this line."[12]

More serious than the problem of social ostracism of white Republicans were the cases of men who lost their jobs because they voted "wrong". After the "white supremacy" campaign of 1898, a friend sought Ben Duke's assistance in finding another job for a veteran employee in a bank in eastern North Carolina. The employee had resigned and was contemplating moving to another section of the country because he was "a Republican by conviction" and something of a local political leader. "You know how much feeling has been stirred up in the east on the race question and so many of the bank's customers criticized" the employee, the friend explained to Ben Duke. Shortly afterward another white Republican in eastern North Carolina informed Ben Duke that local Democratic businessmen had petitioned to have his brother's job as correspondent for a newspaper in Norfolk, Virginia, taken away from him. "This they succeeded in doing," the letter continued, "and not only that but have completely ostricised [sic] us all from society, and will use measures to take the business I am engaged in away from me."[13]

The foregoing suggests the atmosphere of repression and intolerance in which the relationship of the Dukes and their Negro friends must be viewed. When Washington Duke supplied the money for his black allies to print a campaign newspaper in Durham in 1896, that was politics.[14] But when he and his sons contributed regularly to various Negro churches, colleges, and other institutions, that was white philanthropy—with a difference.

Echoing the shrewd accommodationist approach that a foremost black leader, Booker T. Washington, made famous in the years around the turn of the century, a Negro preacher wrote Washington Duke on the eve of the 1892 election:

> I was with a committee of colored men at your gate one night last week. We desired to formally thank you for your great kindness to our poor race, and to request your council [sic] in some matters of public importance. But the thought came to us that

12. John C. Angier in Cary, N.C., to B. N. Duke, November 11, 1896, B. N. Duke MSS.
13. Thomas H. Battle to B. N. Duke, November 22, 1898, and Paul P. Cobb to B. N. Duke, December 2, 1898, B. N. Duke MSS.
14. James E. Shepard to W. Duke, April 20, May 20, 1896, W. Duke MSS.

your daughter was not strong, and you, too, might be weary with care and business; so we moved around your block, looking at the friendly lights streaming from the windows and returned to our homes. I hope it may be your pleasure to receive us soon. . . . I hope you walked around the church in Hayti [a black community in Durham] which your generosity has enabled us to push as far as it is. . . .[15]

The black preacher was being diplomatic in giving Washington Duke so much credit for the new church, for the truth was that black leaders in Durham took the initiative and bore the primary responsibility for building their own institutions. These included, as one example, an insurance company, the North Carolina Mutual, which grew in the twentieth century to be one of the largest Negro-owned businesses in the world. Here the role of the Dukes was that they befriended in various ways the men who launched the company in the late 1890's.[16]

One of the black leaders involved in the insurance company was a physician, Dr. Aaron M. Moore, who wanted a hospital for his people. In 1895 George Watts had given a general hospital, one of the early ones in the state, to the white people of Durham. For blacks, however, medical facilities were sorely lacking until Dr. Moore set to work. He persuaded Ben Duke and J. B. Duke to give Lincoln Hospital to the black community of Durham in 1901, at an initial cost of more than $8,000. As with many other instances of Duke philanthropies, much larger sums for Lincoln Hospital would be forthcoming from the family in the years ahead.[17]

Although Ben Duke served on the board of Watts Hospital and the family contributed to its support, Lincoln Hospital was the first and

15. Andrew J. Chambers to W. Duke, October 31, 1892, W. Duke MSS. B. N. Duke to G. W. Watts, May 23, 1892, explains that B. N. and W. Duke had agreed to pay one-fifth of the cost of the African Methodist church building "to cost not exceeding $7,000" providing the Negroes raised the balance themselves, B. N. Duke MSS.

16. W. G. Pearson to B. N. Duke, June 19, 1897; see also J. E. Stagg to B. N. Duke, November 7, 1897, for B. N. Duke's payment of $500 for J. B. Duke to John Merrick on account of St. Joseph's African Methodist Church. For B. N. Duke's role as a member of the Durham school board who helped to launch the "Colored Graded School," see B. N. Duke to Gurney Heater Comp., June 16, 1896, and W. G. Pearson to B. N. Duke, September 26, 1896, B. N. Duke MSS and letterbook.

17. Trustees of Lincoln Hospital to Messrs. W. Duke and Sons, February 9, 1901, and J. C. Kilgo to B. N. Duke, July 6, 1901, B. N. Duke MSS; J. E. Stagg to John W. Merrick, November 25, 1901, B. N. Duke letterbook.

for a time the only major venture of the Dukes in the field of medical care. Methodist churches and colleges continued to be their primary philanthropic concerns. In addition to Trinity College, the family contributed to a number of other educational institutions. To save Louisburg Female College, a Methodist-sponsored school in Louisburg, North Carolina, in 1891 Washington Duke acquired title to the property, and after his death Ben Duke in 1907 conveyed it to the North Carolina Conference of the Methodist Church "without conditions, other than that it must be used for school purposes."[18] When Greensboro Female College, another Methodist school located in Greensboro, North Carolina, faced a crisis in 1901 Ben Duke furnished $5,000, and a few years later he gave $10,000 for the endowment fund of the college.[19]

Guilford College, the Quaker institution which had grown out of the New Garden School attended by the younger Dukes back in the 1870's, had a special claim on the family's philanthropy. President L. L. Hobbs of Guilford began to request an urgently needed "Duke Hall of Science" in 1896, but Ben Duke dodged with the explanation that "we are right heavily burdened with Trinity College at present." He explained that the family had paid for most of the buildings and other improvements at Trinity and added that "since the day the College opened here, I have, personally, paid one third of the entire running expense of the institution." All this was more, Duke noted in a nice understatement, "than we contemplated in the beginning, and thus we are hampered in carrying out some of our other ideas along this line. . . ." When, after all of his talk about the burden of Trinity, Ben Duke tentatively inquired what the probable cost of a science building at Guilford would be, President Hobbs no doubt realized that he had practically landed a prize catch. Sure enough, in the spring of 1897, Ben Duke informed President Hobbs that he had conferred with James B. Duke and that they together would give $10,000 for the building. As for the suggestion that it be named "Mary Duke Hall" in honor of the late Mrs. Lyon, Ben Duke countered with the proposal that it be named simply "Memorial Hall," with a plaque or tablet inside commemorating Mary Duke Lyon. And as for pictures

18. J. A. Thomas to W. Duke, March 31, 1891, W. Duke MSS; W. Duke to Louisbrug Female College, August 18, 1894, B. N. Duke letterbook; B. N. Duke to J. B. Hurley, November 23, 1907, B. N. Duke letterbook, and other correspondence.

19. Dred Peacock to B. N. Duke, July 3, 8, 9, 1901, and A. P. Tyre to B. N. Duke, December 11, 1908, B. N. Duke MSS.

of the donors for the newspapers, Ben Duke had earlier explained: "My brother has never allowed a likeness of himself published, and under the circumstances, I prefer that mine be left out."[20]

As the case of Memorial Hall at Guilford illustrates, the Dukes generally resisted oft-made suggestions that all sorts of buildings and institutions be named for them. This was probably not so much because they were any less vain than other mortals but because they were hard-headed businessmen as well as philanthropists, and they learned early that one good deed called for another, and another, and so on, ad infinitum. Their name on an institution or even a building advertised a responsibility which they might or might not choose to bear at a later time or in different circumstances.

In the case of Guilford College, President Hobbs succeeded a few years later in tapping Ben Duke for a portion of the salary of a chemistry professor who used Memorial Hall. In 1905 Guilford needed help with matching offers, including one for $45,000 from Andrew Carnegie, and Ben Duke and J. B. Duke came up with $15,000. There were other gifts to Guilford College to come later.[21]

Guilford College had managed to obtain help from the Dukes, but a number of other institutions were not so fortunate. Vanderbilt, the first significantly endowed private university south of Baltimore, then served the Methodist Episcopal Church, South, throughout the region and urgently plead in vain for aid from the Dukes in the field of theological training. Even the Methodist world's heaviest artillery, in the form of the bishops of the church, failed to procure from the Dukes anything more than sympathetic letters. Pleas from Methodist bishops for the newly established American University in Washington, D.C., likewise were in vain, and while Bishop Warren A. Candler of Atlanta did obtain occasional help for mission work from Washington Duke and Ben Duke, he failed to get from them the $30,000 he wanted for a Protestant church in Havana, Cuba.[22]

20. L. L. Hobbs to B. N. Duke, April 7, 1896; Duke to Hobbs, May 11, 1896, and March 25, 1897; Duke to T. G. Pearson, April 8, 1897; J. Elwood Cox to Duke, August 17, 1897; Duke to Cox, August 31, 1897, B. N. Duke MSS and letterbook.

21. L. L. Hobbs to B. N. Duke, May 22, 1902; J. A. Arrington, executive secretary of B. N. and J. B. Duke, to J. E. Cox, November 22, 1905, B. N. Duke MSS and letterbook. B. N. Duke also made gifts to the Baptist Female College (Meredith College) in Raleigh, as shown in W. N. Jones to B. N. Duke, August 11, 1905, B. N. Duke MSS.

22. Wilbur F. Tillett, dean at Vanderbilt, wrote J. B. Duke, April 27, 1897, but was answered by B. N. Duke, October 25, 1897; see also Tillett to Washington Duke, May 18, 1899, Chancellor J. H. Kirkland to W. Duke, May 22, 1899, and Bishop

In refusing pleas even from Methodist bishops, Washington and Ben Duke had not abandoned philanthropy, but they had undergone after late 1894 a reawakened enthusiasm about Trinity College. The explanation centered around the man who became Trinity's new president, John Carlisle Kilgo. An impassioned Methodist preacher and controversial fighter for the causes in which he believed, Kilgo became a key link in the chain that tied the Dukes to Trinity College.

Just as Ben Duke had remained aloof from various quiet maneuvers among some of the trustees against President John F. Crowell, he likewise left the selection of Crowell's successor in other hands. ". . . I do not care to enter the contest of the approaching election [of a new president]," Duke informed a friend in the summer of 1894, and, "I do not propose to let such matters bother and harass me longer."[23] Although Ben Duke had been ill and was recuperating in New York when he declared his aloofness from Trinity's problem, the deeper truth was that both he and, probably to an even larger extent, his father had grown weary of the college's unending financial crises, the problems between Crowell and some faculty members and trustees, and the continued failure of other Tarheel Methodists to come to the aid of the institution. While Ben Duke and his family enjoyed the most cordial personal relations with Crowell and his wife, and would continue to do so for many years, Washington Duke as he approached seventy-five had apparently grown tired and disillusioned about the complex, seemingly insoluble problems of Methodist higher education. One story, often told and probably correct, has it that he drove the new president, Kilgo, in his buggy out to see the college and upon arriving there declared, "Well, there it is. I never expect to give another dollar to it, and I wish I had never put a dollar in it."[24]

Fortunately for Trinity College, Kilgo was not one to be easily discouraged, even when confronted with such grim news from Washington Duke. A thirty-three-year-old native of South Carolina, Kilgo had attended Wofford College in Spartanburg, South Carolina, and, after several years as a Methodist minister, became the financial agent

O. P. Fitzgerald to W. Duke, May 31, June 2, 1899; W. Duke to Tillett and Fitzgerald, June 2, 3, 1899. Bishop Candler to W. Duke, August 1, 1898, and W. Duke to Candler, August 5, 1898, and correspondence in 1899. W. Duke MSS and B. N. Duke MSS and letterbook.

23. B. N. Duke to N. M. Jurney, June 20, 1894, B. N. Duke letterbook.

24. Edwin Mims, "Trinity College: A General Sketch," *The Trinity Archive*, XV (November, 1901), 105.

or fund raiser for Wofford as well as a professor of philosophy and political science there. Possessed of a rich, musical voice, he was a wiry man of medium height whom the student magazine described as having a "frank and open" countenance and being "plain and unostentatious in his manners."[25] A sharp administrator who realized that Trinity had to live within its pitifully limited means, at least until those means might somehow be expanded, Kilgo cut expenses wherever possible but insisted that the salaries of the able, young professors whom he had inherited from Crowell must at all costs be paid. They would receive $1200 per year, plus a house or lodging. Kilgo lost no friends among the faculty members when he suggested $1500 per year as a goal.

The ambitious academic standards and goals of the Crowell era were retained by Kilgo, but he added a new emphasis on the relationship of the church and the college. Making himself a veritable apostle of "Christian education," whose great duty it was to produce "the highest and noblest type of man," Kilgo readied for battle. He not only fought for Trinity but against increased state appropriations for public colleges and universities at a time when a public elementary and secondary school system barely existed in North Carolina. With the agrarian revolt of the 1890's approaching its climax in the pivotal election of 1896, Kilgo quickly became a prime target for the various groups in North Carolina who bitterly attacked the "tobacco trust," the "wicked cigarette," Republicans—especially rich ones like the Dukes—and Trinity College.

The Dukes quickly learned to love Kilgo, combative controversialist that he was. He preached in Durham's two Methodist churches on his first Sunday in town, and while Washington Duke was not given to advertising his views, he seems to have shared the reaction of another man who wrote to Kilgo: "My appreciation of your ability is unlimited. When I listen at your speeches and sermons I am so afraid you will quit it makes me nervous."[26] Within a few weeks of Kilgo's arrival in Durham Ben Duke reported, "He is a very strong man in every way and is admirably fitted for the position he holds." As the first academic year under Kilgo approached its end, Ben Duke waxed even more enthusiastic in a long letter to a Trinity professor who was

25. The Trinity Archive, VIII (October, 1894), 1; Paul Neff Garber, John Carlisle Kilgo (Durham, 1937); and Porter's chapter on "Kilgo: The Holy Wars, 1894–1903," in Trinity and Duke are the best studies of Kilgo.
26. J. C. Rowe to Kilgo, March 10, 1898, Kilgo MSS.

studying in Germany: "I have never felt so confident about the success of Trinity College as I do at present. There was entire harmony during the last year among faculty and students, and the only problem now to solve is that of finance, and I am satisfied Prof. Kilgo will be able to solve that." Ben Duke believed that "the hand of God must have been in Kilgo's selection as President of the Institution," for he was "one of the greatest and best men in every way I have ever known . . . ." Kilgo, in less than a year according to Ben Duke, had preached sixty times in different parts of the state and delivered eighteen lectures "besides putting everything in order out at the College, and has completely captivated, not only Methodists, but people of all denominations and of no denomination." Ben Duke vowed that he looked "for great things for the College in the future." For the present he and his father had authorized Kilgo, in pursuance of one of the family's pet interests in the college, "to put our campus and grounds in splendid shape." "We wish," Duke explained, "to make it an attractive place not only for the students, but a pleasant park for the citizens of our community."[27]

Serving on the executive committee of the trustees and closely involved with many phases of the college's life, Ben Duke at age forty was generous with the time, worry, and service he gave. Though he continued to come up with cash at all sorts of crucial junctures and to meet specific needs, he encouraged his father to give the larger donations of money for Trinity at this stage. Accordingly Washington Duke in 1895 informed the trustees that he would give $50,000 toward the endowment for professorships, about which Kilgo spoke so often and urgently, if others would come up with an additional $75,000.

Gratified by this first monetary encouragement from the head of the Duke family since the initial gifts of 1890, Kilgo and the trustees energetically set to work to raise the necessary matching funds. With approval from the two Methodist conferences in North Carolina, a ministerial trustee and fund raiser, Andrew P. Tyer, tackled the job but soon grew discouraged, as Earl Porter has put it, "about the Methodists' matchless inclinations." In a letter to Ben Duke, who had personally covered the college's deficit in the summer of 1896, Tyer noted that the "spirit of benevolence has never been largely manifested in the south" and that Tarheels in particular "have never given much to endow colleges." He believed that the Methodists of North Caro-

27. B. N. Duke to Solomon Pool, October 10, 1894, and to Professor A. H. Meritt, May 2, 1895, B. N. Duke MSS.

lina would never put much money in an endowment for Trinity until the institution were made secure and then they would give. "There has always been a feeling of insecurity about Trinity College," Tyer candidly suggested, and so it was "with all colleges without endowment . . . which is the basis of permanence." Tyer, resigning from his thankless post, made one last appeal: "The only hope that Trinity College has of ever being endowed is to be found in the Dukes. I therefore ask that you give the college five hundred thousand dollars as endowment and allow the Trustees to name it 'Duke College.' "[28]

If Ben Duke responded to Tyer's proposal, he must have done so orally and emphatically in the negative. He and his father had clearly decided, however, that the family's support for the college would have to be continued and made permanent, regardless of what others might or might not do. Accordingly, Washington Duke informed Kilgo late in 1896 that while he was disappointed in the failure of the campaign to raise the $75,000 needed to match the $50,000 he had offered in 1895, he had nevertheless concluded to give $100,000 to Trinity on the condition that it would "open its doors to women, placing them in the future on an equal footing with men." Washington Duke added that the confidence he had "in the present administration of the affairs of the college, and the hope that it will be continued along the same lines, has been the main influence in encouraging me to make this offer."[29]

Although Trinity College had awarded degrees to a few women beginning as early as 1878, the idea of coeducation had certainly found no widespread acceptance in the South or even in the East by the 1890's. Most so-called colleges for women in the South at the time were in reality secondary or finishing schools, though there were beginning to be a few exceptions, such as the Methodist-related Randolph-Macon Woman's College in Lynchburg, Virginia. Washington Duke gave no explanation for the condition on which he had made his gift, which the trustees of Trinity quickly accepted, but he and

28. A. P. Tyer to B. N. Duke, November 16, 1896, B. N. Duke MSS.
29. W. Duke to J. C. Kilgo, December 5, 1896, B. N. Duke letterbook. Although Washington Duke's idea concerning the admission of women was promptly met, as mentioned below, he formally withdrew the condition in 1903, not because he had ceased to favor the policy but because the gift had been the only one "which in any way affects your policies in the management of the College" and he wished to leave the trustees free to "adopt such a policy as may, in your judgment, seem wisest." Porter, *Trinity and Duke*, p. 103.

Ben Duke probably were influenced by the memory of the late Mary Duke Lyon. They also could hardly have missed the increasing demand for equal educational opportunity on the part of intelligent women, and their champions such as Kilgo. President Crowell, during his last year at Trinity, had urged the establishment of a full-fledged coordinate college for women in connection with Trinity, and while that was a generation away from realization the idea was one that remained very much alive.[30]

Washington Duke declined the vice-presidency of the National Suffrage Association that was proffered him in the wake of his conditional gift, but he stood by Trinity College. In 1898 he informed Kilgo that, "moved by a desire to build up our people and advance the Kingdom of Christ," he wished to give another $100,000 for the endowment fund.[31] At the same time, Ben Duke's assistance to the college continued to be quiet, regular, and crucial. In 1896, for example, when Trinity's professor of English, Edwin Mims, went to Cornell University to complete the work for his doctorate, his temporary replacement was a young Shakespearean scholar fresh from Harvard with his Ph.D. degree, William Preston Few. A gentle, unassuming native of South Carolina and graduate of Wofford College, Few had qualities of intelligence, loyalty, and conscientiousness which impressed Kilgo and others. But with Mims returning to Trinity at the end of his year away, how could young Few also be retained? Ben Duke agreed to pay his salary, as he would in the case of many other important additions to the faculty, and Edwin Mims was more prophetic than he could realize when he declared that Few's retention was "one of the most important steps that Trinity has made."[32]

For almost a decade, Ben Duke had given Trinity College much more than money, although that had helped and would continue to help at critical times. As his wealth increased by the late 1890's, he accordingly gave $50,000 to Trinity College in 1899, which went for a

30. Durham *Daily Globe*, April 7, 1894.
31. W. Duke to Kilgo, June 6, 1898, B. N. Duke letterbook. Washington Duke also gave another $100,000 in 1900. The significance of the money that the Dukes gave to Trinity in the early years is pointed up by the fact that the state's appropriation to the University of North Carolina for 1899–1900 was $25,000, and the university's total income from all sources for that year was $48,000. Louis R. Wilson, *The University of North Carolina, 1900–1930: The Making of a Modern University* (Chapel Hill, 1957), pp. 31, 36.
32. Edwin Mims to B. N. Duke, May 5, 1897, B. N. Duke MSS.

science building, new dormitories, improvement of the grounds, and a house for the president.[33] For the new library, which the faculty and Kilgo especially coveted, Ben Duke, possibly aided by his father, scored a special triumph in 1902 by persuading James B. Duke to foot the bill not only for the handsome library building but also for $10,000 worth of books to go in it.

For his first major gift to Trinity, James B. Duke had indeed met a vital need. Echoing the sentiments of John Spencer Bassett, Trinity's brilliant young professor of history and avid friend of the library, Kilgo had declared many times that the library was "the one department that measures the future development of the College."[34] When the time came for the dedication of the new library, however, James B. Duke maintained his usual policy of refusing to make a speech, or even a ceremonial appearance. Instead he dispatched to represent him Walter Hines Page, a native Tarheel who had become a prominent publisher in New York and editor of *World's Work*. Page reported to the audience at Trinity College on February 23, 1903, that he had called on James B. Duke before leaving New York and asked, "What shall I say?" Duke replied vigorously, according to Page, "Tell them every man to think for himself." Page accordingly dedicated the new library "to free thought, reverent always, always earnest, but always free."[35]

Such a message fell on receptive ears at Trinity College, where a critical attitude toward the triumphant Democratic party and its rabid racism was at least possible. In North Carolina at the turn of the century, and even more so in states further to the south, free inquiry or discussion about certain racial matters was as rigidly tabooed as in the days of slavery. Trinity, with its private sources of support, could be different, though the winds of an angry, aroused "public opinion" could blow fearfully at times.

Furthermore, it was more than just the money from the Republican Dukes that lay behind Trinity College's challenge to prevailing racial and political orthodoxies. Faculty members such as Bassett, Mims, and Few—and there were others like them—were native Southerners, but they were also superbly trained as professional, truth-seeking scholars from the best graduate schools that the United States had at the time. From the perspective of the late twentieth

33. J. E. Stagg to Kilgo, May 8, 1900, B. N. Duke letterbook.
34. Porter, *Trinity and Duke*, p. 91.
35. Original manuscript of Page's address, Kilgo MSS.

century many of their limitations would become apparent, but in the context of their own time the matter was quite different. Because of the quality of its faculty, Trinity College aspired to higher academic standards for itself and the region. It gradually helped to achieve them after 1895 as one of the six charter members of the Association of Colleges and Preparatory Schools of the Southern States. By the turn of the century, in a number of fields of study such as English and history for example, a few students were being accepted for graduate work at Trinity and were awarded the Master of Arts degree. Kilgo and his associates planned for a law school as the first professional school to be developed, moved cautiously toward the idea of a coordinate college for women, and backed away from the notion of a medical school, as much as the state needed one, unless even greater resources were available. A decade after its inauspicious transition to Durham, the "Greater Trinity" was gradually becoming a reality.[36]

Ben Duke, of all the family, best understood and gloried in Trinity's evolution. "Trinity College has reached that point of capacity and efficiency to warrant the claim," he declared to an old friend in 1902, "that it is the best institution of learning in the South." The college, he continued, "has a strong faculty, a sufficient number of students, every necessary equipment and is turning out brains versus numbers as compared to a good number of other institutions around us." Touching on another important Trinity characteristic that he cherished, and one which he had helped to nourish, Ben Duke pointed out a little later that the college stood "for the new forces working now very rapidly for the upbuilding of the whole South and tending to break up the sectional isolation and make the South a part of our common country."[37]

With his son Angier Buchanan Duke a graduate of Trinity in 1905 and his daughter Mary Duke in the class of 1907, after both had attended the public schools in Durham, Ben Duke had many contacts with the college other than those that came through his active membership on the executive committee of the trustees. Various faculty members were often in his home, as they were also in that of Washington Duke for Sunday afternoon calls. Ben Duke's wife, Sarah P. Duke, joined with Edwin Mims, Robert L. Flowers (a popular young mathematics teacher who had joined the Trinity faculty in 1891),

36. Porter, *Trinity and Duke*, pp. 72–77, 88–91.
37. B. N. Duke to E. J. Parrish, February 4, 1902, and B. N. Duke to Senator J. C. Pritchard, May 6, 1902, B. N. Duke letterbook.

William P. Few, and others from the town and campus to organize the bimonthly Canterbury Club for "study and appreciation of the best literature" and later the Shakespeare Club, which featured the reading of scenes from the Bard's plays as well as papers on various aspects of his work.[38]

All the ties of personal friendship together with Ben Duke's intimate knowledge of the operation and needs of Trinity College led to his pride in the institution and to his and the family's ever-increasing generosity to it. Aside from the various buildings that he and other members of the family gave and his constant attention to the beautification of the grounds, Ben Duke by 1907 was contributing $13,500 per year to the operating budget of the college.[39]

Perhaps the most crucial demonstration of Ben Duke's relationship to the college came in 1903 in a famous episode that has come to be known as the "Bassett Affair." All the complex political, racial, and economic currents that had flowed around both Trinity College and the Dukes since the early 1890's came to a sharp, dramatic focus in this event. Ben Duke, conservative businessman though he was, played a key role in helping the college to transform the Bassett Affair into a nationally important milestone in the history of academic freedom in the United States.

One of the important antecedents of the 1903 affair reached back into the late 1890's when President Kilgo fell into a sharp disagreement with one of Trinity's trustees, Walter Clark, a justice of the North Carolina Supreme Court and champion of antitrust legislation, free silver, and other economic and political causes. Kilgo's battles for "Christian higher education" led him into early conflict with Clark, Josephus Daniels, and other friends of the state-supported colleges. But after a committee of the trustees headed by Clark disapproved Kilgo's recommendation of four-year tenure for the faculty, the two men, both able and fierce fighters, began in 1897 and 1898 to exchange letters that grew steadily angrier. After Clark charged, among other things, that Trinity College was likely to corrupt its students with "political heresy [Republicanism] foreign to the faith of their fathers" because of the Dukes' gifts, Kilgo presented the correspondence to the trustees who, after a committee had reviewed the matter, endorsed Kilgo and suggested that Clark should resign. Clark

38. Undated clippings in the B. N. Duke MSS, 1966 addition.
39. R. B. Arrington to J. E. Stagg, December 27, 1907, B. N. Duke MSS.

not only refused to do so but protested that the "trial" had been conducted in his absence.[40]

When the matter reached the newspapers in 1898, charges back and forth between Kilgo and Clark began to escalate, with Clark charging that Kilgo's reputation in the Carolinas was that of "a wire-puller of the ward politician type" and that he was not fit to be a college president. Kilgo, insisting that his character had been defamed, demanded an investigation by the trustees, and in the late summer of 1898 the trustees of the college suffered through another investigation that resulted in Kilgo's being upheld on all counts.

Learning that Clark had acquired certain derogatory allegations about Kilgo from an elderly Methodist minister and church book-agent, Thomas J. Gattis, the sharp-tongued president of Trinity thereupon let loose with a characterization of Gattis that became famous in North Carolina: "Behind a pious smile, a religious walk, and a solemn switch of the coat tail, many men carry a spirit unworthy of them."[41] Kilgo's words, plus some others, inspired Gattis early in 1899 to launch a suit for slander against Kilgo, Ben Duke, and two other well-to-do trustees. Though many suspected that Judge Walter Clark was the true plaintiff, the "Kilgo-Gattis controversy" raged on and off in North Carolina for seven years. The phrase became so familiar in the newspapers that there were even reports of a child or two named "Kilgo-Gattis Controversy." The upshot of the whole affair, which cost Ben Duke as well as his antagonists substantial sums in legal fees, was that the North Carolina Supreme Court, on the third occasion that the matter came before it, upheld the dismissal of the case once and for all in November, 1905.

As protracted as it was, the Kilgo-Gattis imbroglio was not the most epochal event in the state around the turn of the century. The Democratic party's crusade to end "Negro domination" and to restore "white supremacy" held the honor of primacy, and that was the more immediate setting for the Bassett Affair. The faculty members at Trinity, sensitive to the repeated charges that they were dominated by wealthy Republicans, kept their political affiliations largely to themselves. Three members of the trustees' executive committee,

40. Partisan accounts may be found in Garber, *Kilgo*, and Aubrey Lee Brooks, *Walter Clark: Fighting Judge* (Chapel Hill, 1944), but Porter, *Trinity and Duke*, pp. 79–84, has the best balance in treating what he sees as the "mixed elements of comic opera and war to the knife."
41. Porter, *Trinity and Duke*, p. 82.

however, were active Democrats and the chairman, James H. South-gate, was a prominent leader of the Prohibitionist party.

On the matter of the Negro, however, the Trinity College community was outspoken for the time and place. Kilgo invited Booker T. Washington to speak on the campus in 1896, and the students responded enthusiastically. John Spencer Bassett, thirty-six-year-old professor of history at Trinity, published in the late 1890's pioneering studies of the institution of slavery and of antislavery leaders in North Carolina. Though he was a native of eastern North Carolina, where racial passions raged almost as in the deep South, Bassett had confessed to one of his former teachers in 1898, after the Democratic victory of that year and the bloody *coup* in Wilmington, that he did "not have the honor to agree with my fellow Anglo-Saxons on the negro question."[42]

Kilgo was almost as outspoken in his racial views as Bassett, and when it came to the right of academic persons to enjoy free inquiry and free speech, rights that were widely denied and violated throughout the nation around the turn of the century, the president of Trinity held unshakeable convictions. Declaring that the college had "set its life" against provincialism, Kilgo told the alumni in 1902 that "no dread of unpopularity, no fear of small attendance, no criticisms" or even hatred could divert Trinity from its mission.[43]

Emory College, a Methodist institution in Oxford, Georgia, meekly accepted the resignation in 1902 of a professor who had offended opinion in Georgia by an article in the *Atlantic Monthly*. The professor had brought down the wrath of newspapers and some of Emory's patrons by attacking the mounting brutality of whites toward blacks and the political exploitation of racism. Firing off a long, impassioned protest to Bishop Warren A. Candler, Kilgo declared that the "supreme question in the South is, shall we be a free people or shall we be the slaves of a vile partizanship?" The state-supported schools, Kilgo argued, had "been bound hand and foot and are the vassals of this bondage," and he cited actual examples in Kansas, Texas, and North Carolina. With church colleges "marked for the slaughter" and other private institutions yielding as Emory had done, Kilgo concluded: "Well, Trinity shall be free tho' all the Bishops, preachers, politicians, and wild women on earth decree otherwise, and I will get out only

42. Bassett to Herbert B. Adams, November 15, 1898, as quoted in *ibid*.
43. Raleigh *Morning Post*, June 8, 1902.

when whipped out, and then I will leave the church on record for a crime, the stench of which will never cease to rise to heaven."[44]

Kilgo could not know it, but the crucial testing time for Trinity lay close at hand. It came with the vigor of a hurricane in the fall of 1903 when Professor John Spencer Bassett published an article, "Stirring Up the Fires of Racial Antipathy," in the *South Atlantic Quarterly*, a magazine launched at Trinity the previous year and edited by Bassett.[45] In his article, which was closely reasoned and which contained the crystallization of ideas Bassett had been formulating for several years, there were numerous important points, but the key theme, as intimated by the title, was that politicians and political newspapers of the Democratic party were exploiting the race issue for partisan ends. All the political agitation, which had not ceased with the disfranchisement of the blacks in 1900 but had continued unabated, was "awakening a demon" of racial hatred in the South. Some day, Bassett predicted, Negroes would win equality, and dire conflict between the races lay somewhere in the future unless whites substituted a "spirit of conciliation" for their insistence on the inferiority of the blacks.[46]

A passing phrase in Bassett's article, but one which his critics soon made famous, concerned the foremost Negro leader of the day, Booker T. Washington. Wishing to make the point that Washington was not a typical but an exceptional Negro, Bassett resorted to a sweeping statement: "Now Washington is a great and good man, a Christian statesman, and take him all in all the greatest man, save General Lee, born in the South in a hundred years. . . ."

The reaction to Bassett's article came quickly once Josephus Daniels, editor of the Raleigh *News and Observer* and powerful Democratic partisan, got his hands on it. Having expressed about all the "outrage" that could be squeezed out of President Theodore Roosevelt's famed dinner at the White House with Booker T. Washington in 1901 and a more recent dining incident in Hamlet, North Carolina, in which the black leader was involved, Daniels was eager for fresh grist for his

44. Kilgo to Candler, August 14, 1902, Kilgo MSS.
45. The best treatment, and the one on which the following is partially based, is in Porter, *Trinity and Duke*, pp. 96–139.
46. *South Atlantic Quarterly*, II (October, 1903), 297–305; Bassett's article, together with other key documents, is reprinted in William B. Hamilton, ed., *Fifty Years of the South Atlantic Quarterly* (Durham, 1953).

mill. Bassett's article was reprinted in full, with certain portions in uppercase print: bold headlines proclaimed the Trinity professor's prediction of equality for the Negro. A two-columned editorial blasted Bassett for the contempt he had displayed toward "the attitude of nine-tenths of the Southern people" and insisted that the Democratic white-supremacy campaigns of 1898 and 1900, like those of the Reconstruction era, had been necessary to restore peace, order, and "good government" after an alleged orgy of Republican and Negro misrule. The professor had best repudiate his freakish ideas, the powerful editor suggested, or the reaction of the Southern people would be impossible to anticipate.[47]

Then, in a manner that had grown familiar in numerous instances after 1895, Daniels waited for other Democratic daily and weekly newspapers in the state, and elsewhere in the South, to pick up the scent, so that the *News and Observer* might reprint choice quotations and report mounting popular indignation. He did not have long to wait. For six weeks most of the Democratic press in North Carolina engaged in a storm of abuse and vituperation directed against "bAssett" as a "slobbering" lover of blacks and, in many cases, against the institution that harbored such a traitor to the South.

From Reidsville, North Carolina, *Webster's Weekly*, long one of the *News and Observer*'s pet sources for quotable matter, thundered that "Duke's money has made it possible for Trinity's teacher of history to fling defiance in the face of Southern ideals and call on the young men of the South to forsake the faith of their fathers and worship at the shrine of a negro." Daniels wrapped up the argument by concluding that if Bassett's ideas became widespread "then the civilization of the South is destroyed." The Trinity professor had indeed "committed the only unpardonable sin."[48]

From the vantage point of nearly three-quarters of a century later, one has difficulty comprehending both the near-hysteria of the many critics of Professor Bassett and the genuine dilemma of an institution that had to consider its "clientele," for it was a time when colleges had to worry about recruiting students rather than students worrying about being admitted to a college. In the face of the clamor, Bassett offered to submit his resignation, and the critical question became whether the trustees of Trinity, meeting in a specially called session

47. Raleigh *News and Observer*, November 1, 1903.
48. *Webster's Weekly*, November 12, 1903, and Raleigh *News and Observer*, December 3, 1903, as quoted in Garber, *Kilgo*, p. 248.

on December 1, 1903, would acquiesce to the storm and sacrifice the professor.

Though the students, faculty, and president at Trinity College rallied wholeheartedly in defense of Bassett's right to free speech, the final power of decision lay with the trustees, and no trustee was more crucial in the matter than Ben Duke. Not only was he a veteran member of the executive committee, but he was also a close personal friend and business associate of the chairman of the board, James H. Southgate of Durham, and of other trustees. Never given to speech-making or dramatic gestures, Ben Duke moved quietly but, under the circumstances, with incomparable influence. His longtime friend, Walter Hines Page, argued strongly in several letters for a courageous stand by Trinity. Page thought it "of the highest importance that a professor from Trinity College should be allowed to hold and to express any rational opinion he may have about any subject whatever. . . ." Page admitted that professors "in Southern institutions have many times lost their places and been driven from home for offenses less than this," but Trinity's refusal to oust Bassett would be "a splendid tribute to the college, and to its atmosphere," which, Page added flatteringly, was "one of the excellent results of your identification with it." Ten days later, Page urged Ben Duke again not to let Bassett "be driven out on the cry of 'nigger' " and insisted that "Trinity must stand, as you stand, for free thought & free speech."[49]

How much influence the letters from Page as well as from others, such as ex-president Crowell, may have had on Ben Duke is not known. He, in consultation with James B. Duke, who had come to Durham to visit their fast-failing father, may have made his decision on his own and possibly not so much personally on the abstract ground of academic freedom as on the more familiar refusal to be bulldozed by Josephus Daniels and his fellow Democrats. At any rate, after a dramatic meeting where Kilgo gave an impassioned plea for Bassett and free speech and Furnifold M. Simmons, United States senator and Trinity alumnus and trustee, waged what he regarded as a "last fight for white supremacy," the trustees balloted in the early morning hours of December 2, 1903. The result was eighteen to seven for Bassett and academic freedom at Trinity. Although four of the nine Methodist ministers who were trustees and in attendance at the meet-

49. W. H. Page to B. N. Duke, November 12 and 23, 1903, B. N. Duke MSS. Page, who had also been in touch with Edwin Mims about the affair, wrote Ben Duke again on November 26, 1903.

ing voted with the majority, the greater part of Bassett's defenders came from the businessmen on the board, that is from Ben Duke and his associates.[50]

Pleased by what came to be known as "Trinity College's finest hour," Ben Duke telegraphed the news to his brother in New York. When the Baltimore *News* and Springfield, Massachusetts, *Republican*, along with many other newspapers and magazines throughout the country praised the action of the trustees and the ringing statement they had issued, Ben Duke sent copies of the editorials to a number of his friends.[51] And when President Theodore Roosevelt stood on a platform facing the Trinity campus in October, 1905, and hailed the institution for its stand in behalf of academic freedom, one may be sure that Kilgo and his faculty were no prouder than was their staunch friend and ally, Ben Duke.

When Kilgo in 1910 finally won the election to the Methodist bishopric which he coveted and for which Ben Duke as well as other of Kilgo's friends had long been working, the soft-spoken Shakespearean scholar and dean, William P. Few, was elected to the presidency of Trinity College. For his inauguration, Trinity College capitalized on the dramatic possibilities inherent in such academic occasions, and Ben Duke, who with his wife hosted a large reception in their new house in Durham, enjoyed to the hilt the college's great occasion. "I felt prouder of Trinity than ever before," he declared. "There were representatives here from the leading colleges and universities in the United States, and they were as much astonished at what they saw and heard as they were pleased at the reception given them. It was a great day for not only Trinity and Durham, but for the entire State."[52]

Trinity and its new president, William P. Few, had undergone many changes in the years since 1897, when Ben Duke had agreed to pay the salary for the additional professor of English at the college. While absolutely loyal to Kilgo, Few had his own unique style as president, and those who predicted that the end of the Kilgo era would also mark the end of the Duke family's support of the college proved to be totally incorrect. A conciliator and peacemaker where Kilgo had been a flamboyant fighter, Few quickly impressed Ben Duke and many others as exactly right for his job. Only a year after

50. Porter, *Trinity and Duke*, pp. 124–139.
51. See B. N. Duke MSS for December, 1903.
52. B. N. Duke to R. B. Arrington, November 11, 1910, B. N. Duke letterbook.

the new leader took over, Ben Duke, who was by then giving $20,000 a year to Trinity's operating budget alone, confided to a friend that Few was "making a rousing good college president." Trinity had opened in the fall of 1911, Duke boasted, "with the largest number of students it has ever had; in fact, the number is so large that it is almost impossible to take care of them."[53] Trinity's needs, as Ben Duke implied and as he had learned all too well since 1890, kept growing. But the Duke family's wealth, derived first from tobacco, then from textile manufacturing, and finally from the electric power industry, also grew apace. Ben Duke saw to it that a growing portion of that wealth went to a variety of charitable causes, but Trinity College always headed the list.

53. B. N. Duke to Mrs. W. G. McCabe, September 29, 1911, B. N. Duke letterbook.

CHAPTER 7. NEW MYTHS FOR OLD: THE DUKES AND THE TEXTILE INDUSTRY OF NORTH CAROLINA

Abandoning a number of ideas that had long gripped the minds of Southerners, the people of Durham, as in many other southern communities in the late nineteenth century, embraced what was for them a new set of beliefs and aspirations. Not the agrarian life of old but industrialization became the lodestar. Instead of the antebellum notion that "cotton is king," the belief became widespread that the cotton-textile factory would be the economic salvation of the community. In short, a significant number of Southerners, in Piedmont North Carolina as elsewhere, rejected certain of the myths of the Old South and became enthusiastic converts to the national or American myths of Progress and Prosperity via industrialization.

Historians are not in agreement on the significance and impact of the industrialization that occurred in the South prior to World War I. One influential view is that, despite all the oratorical tub-thumping for factories, Southern industrialization in the late nineteenth and early twentieth centuries did not actually amount to much. Urbanization, for example, has been the almost universal accompaniment of industrial development; yet, according to Professor C. Vann Woodward, "the sum total of urbanization in the South was comparatively unimportant," and the South on the eve of the First World War remained what it had been, "by far the most rural section of the Union." To be sure, manufacturing did increase in the South in this period, but it increased as well in the rest of the nation. The end result was that the South in the early twentieth century had about the same proportion of the factories and capital of the country as it had in 1860.[1]

Far from minimizing the impact of admittedly limited industrialization, another historian has asserted that by 1914 "the American South had been 'northernized' to a degree only hoped for by the most ambitious of the Reconstructionists [after the Civil War]." A permanent change because it was one that was voluntarily accepted, South-

1. C. Vann Woodward, *The Origins of the New South* (Baton Rouge, 1951), pp. 139–140.

ern industrialization was, according to this latter view, "the Reconstruction that took," and it "signified the beginning of the integration of the South into the nation." Not only had a decisive break with the agrarian tradition been made, but "the re-creation of the South in the image of the North was begun."[2]

Regardless of which of these views is correct, such abstract considerations were not paramount in the minds of Tarheels in the lean and hungry years after the Civil War. There is abundant evidence, moreover, that many of them were indeed frantically eager to bow before the American national gods of Progress and Prosperity. "The life of Durham and Henderson is Progress," an orator proclaimed when a new railway linked the two towns in 1889. ". . . 'Tis this that distinguishes them from most of their sister towns, Progress, Progress, Progress." What had made it possible? They were the homes of "the Bright Golden Tobacco of the World." Carried away by his own eloquence in old-time Southern style, the speaker spiralled into the empyrean: "Tobacco! Oh thou mighty dispeller of care, and gracious dispenser of pleasant reveries and brightest hopes. Thou Son of the American wilderness, thou hast demeaned thyself so well since Walter Raleigh first made known thy virtues, that thou has now become the Adopted Son of all the nations of the earth."[3]

Tobacco had indeed been the making of Durham, as of a number of other towns in North Carolina and Virginia; but even if it had become the "Adopted Son of all the nations of the earth," Durhamites were too canny to pin all of their hopes on one product. The clamor for a textile mill, the New South's foremost symbol of industrialization, began early in Durham. Pointing to the vast amounts of cotton then grown in eastern North Carolina and some even in Durham County, the Durham *Tobacco Plant* asked: "Why should not this staple be manufactured here, where there will be no freights [freight charges] to get cotton and no freights required to send the manufactured article to market, for in a town where a million dollars a year is paid upon granulated tobacco for internal revenue it must of necessity sustain a manufacturing establishment of no mean proportions." Besides, the newspaper noted, Southern cotton factories were reportedly paying profits in the range of 15 to 25 percent annually.[4]

2. Carl N. Degler, *Out of Our Past: The Forces that Shaped Modern America* (New York, 1959, 1962 edition), pp. 254–257.
3. Durham *Recorder*, May 1, 1889. The orator was W. R. Henry.
4. Durham *Tobacco Plant*, January 25, 1882.

Others in Durham shared the editor's reasoning, and in 1884 Durham got its first textile mill, the Durham Cotton Manufacturing Company. Capitalized at $130,000, it was in part the creation of Julian S. Carr, whose money came from his interest in the Blackwell tobacco company, and of the Odell family of Greensboro and Concord, North Carolina. W. H. Branson, also from Greensboro, moved to Durham to become the secretary-treasurer and actual manager of the pioneer venture.

Despite the "intense heat" of July, 1884, the newspaper reported that a large crowd gathered for the laying of the cornerstone of the factory, around which the new village of East Durham was growing. The choir of the Methodist church "rendered in fine style an appropriate hymn, followed by an impressive prayer by Rev. T. A. Boone." A minister from Concord then delivered an address filled with "valuable information." The news story concluded, "It was a joyous day for all true Durhamites."[5]

Unaware of the host of new problems that would come with the "mill village" and its woefully underprivileged white population, Durham rejoiced in its cotton factory and strove to prove to the rest of the world, and particularly to any Northerners who came through, that a Southern community could indeed keep up with the awe-inspiring progress of the modern world of steam and the factory whistle. When a group of Northern newspapermen visited Durham in 1886 they were greeted at the railway station by the "clanging of bells and the screaming of whistles." From the piazza of the local hotel they were welcomed by James H. Southgate, pioneer insurance man and spokesman for the Tobacco Board of Trade and the Commonwealth Club, an organization of those who promoted Durham's economic development. The visitors were taken to the Duke factory among other places, and the newspaper proudly reported: "Everything was in ship shape. Not a jar occurred anywhere, and our northern friends were enabled to see for themselves what order, push, [and] cleanliness could prevail in a southern factory. . . ." After an "elegant lunch in the spacious dining hall of the Hotel Claiborn," which included "oysters, turkey, ham, tongue, salad, celery, native wines, with the ordinary side dishes . . . ," a spokesman for the visitors addressed the gathering. He declared that he rejoiced to discover that Northerners

5. Durham *Tobacco Plant*, as reprinted in *The Truth*, July 1884.

had misunderstood the Southern people and that he hoped the visit would "help fill and cover up the broad deep grave into which all, both north and south, were hurling whatever bitterness, prejudice, sectional feeling and misunderstanding that heretofore have existed."[6]

Though the oratory of such occasions always included exaggeration and excessive optimism, Durham, like other towns of the "New South," did have less time and emotional energy to spend on the past and its bittersweet memories than other more traditional Southern communities. Durham craved factories. When a newspaper in Richmond, Virginia, poked fun at Lynchburg, a hustling town in the Piedmont like Durham, for allegedly desiring a chewing-gum factory, the Lynchburg *Virginian* retorted: "Money's money whether it is made in iron or soap, pig's feet or pickles, chewing tobacco or chewing gum; and just so a man or community makes enough of it the world will not be fastidious about the manner of making it." The Durham *Recorder* expressed admiration for Lynchburg's pluck and added: "The community that is ever looking out for new industries and developing new resources is the one that will make the most rapid strides in material wealth."[7]

A recurring theme in the campaign of the Durham newspapers for more cotton factories was that many people above and beyond the stockholders would benefit. "There is money in these enterprises for the owners, work for our laboring people, and general advantage to the community at large," the *Tobacco Plant* argued.[8]

The economic distress of farmers, who were the overwhelming majority in the South, added urgency to the campaign for industrialization. Long before the panic of 1893 threw so much of the nation into a massive depression, farmers suffered from declining prices of cotton, tobacco, and other important crops. As the militant new Farmers' Alliance swept across North Carolina in the late 1880's, the Durham *Recorder* commented: "The farming interest is now at its lowest ebb. We should rejoice to see it revive; but we can give no advice that will help, except to work the harder." Later, after noting the mounting number of sheriff's sales because of unpaid taxes and the

6. Durham *Tobacco Plant*, November 3, 1886.
7. Durham *Recorder*, February 6, 1888.
8. September 14, 1888. The same theme is developed in the paper on September 21, 1888.

"depressed condition of farming," the *Recorder* pleaded: "Durham needs more enterprises right now. Let's be like Noah of old: in his great wisdom he entered the ark and was on the safe side."[9]

To learn about the distress of farmers the Dukes did not have to rely solely on newspapers, for their incoming mail contained pathetic and firsthand evidence, and some of it came from their own kinfolk. A cousin, seeking help with the education of the oldest of her seven daughters, wrote: "We are making a good crop this year in the way of something to eat, but nothing to bring any money."[10] When Washington Duke sent Christmas checks to his numerous nephews, nieces, and other kin in 1894, a nephew in Tennessee who had received a check for $1,000 wrote that he had rested "mighty good on Xmas eve night . . . ," but with corn at thirty cents a bushel and cotton at five cents a pound he would make "nothing after expenses paid."[11]

The situation for farmers hardly improved as the decade wore on. One of the Tennessee relatives reported that their land had been sold but no factory jobs were available. Nor did the prospect of renting a farm have any appeal: "It is all that farmers in this country can do to make a living on their own land, while the renters don't live, but just partially breathe."[12] One of the hundreds of letters from job seekers that Ben Duke regularly received and answered epitomized nicely the farmers' plight: "Tis said 'Cotton is King.' If so 'the Lord help us.' I am in the center of a cotton belt and the price has made everything here depressing. Can't you make me an offer of a position of some kind, some place, some where."[13]

Even Ben Duke himself failed at farming, though the losses hardly hurt him as they did the millions of people in the South, black as well as white, who remained dependent on the land. When his secretary

9. Durham *Recorder*, February 20, April 24, 1889.

10. Fannie Duke Lyon to James B. Duke, November 4, 1893; B. N. Duke replied, November 23, 1893, that the daughter "should go to a first-class school" at his and his brother's expense. J. B. Duke MSS and B. N. Duke letterbook.

11. James M. Duke to Washington Duke, December 25, 1894, Washington Duke MSS. The letters to the various kin are in the B. N. Duke letterbook, December 21, 1894. One great-nephew, Willie J. Duke, wrote (December 31, 1894): "My habits are not so verry good nor so verry bad I dont drink any whiskey but I am not any member of the chirch but I pray that I will be outside of that my habits are verry good. . . ."

12. Pattie Duke to Washington Duke, November 11, 1897. W. Duke MSS. Washington and B. N. Duke subsequently bought farms for several of their relatives.

13. E. N. Morris of Franklinton, N. C., to B. N. Duke, March 1, 1899. B. N. Duke MSS.

and agent in Durham balanced the accounts for Ben Duke's farm near Durham for the year 1909, during a period when farm prices were higher than they had been in the 1890's, the loss was something over $2,700. The executive secretary in New York responded: "Mr. Duke has seen the statement and thinks there is not much money in farming in North Carolina. The loss for the past year was considerably larger than it has been for any year previous to this for five or six years."[14]

Though one of a number of industrial islands in an agrarian sea in the late nineteenth century, Durham could not have escaped awareness of the farmers' plight even if its leaders had so wished. The opportunity for farmers and their families to work in a factory was obviously an escape from, rather than a solution to, the agrarian problem. Grim though the route of escape was, hundreds of thousands of economically marginal farmers in the South were ready to take it. In advocating more factories, the Durham newspapers were certainly not thinking primarily of the farmers and their plight, but the connection was inescapable. With one textile mill prospering after 1884, the Durham *Recorder* hailed the hum of the whirling spindles, "the ceaseless anthem which goes up to Providence of a restored and reawakened people." The *Tobacco Plant*, however, issued a challenge to the home-grown capitalists of Durham: "It is time for some of those people whom Durham has made what they are to help make her better than she is. Our town must continue to grow, and she looks for aid from those of her citizens who have grown fat by her rapid strides and the increase in value of her real estate."[15]

Quite apart from the rhetoric of the newspapers, the cool calculations of the entrepreneur emphasized advantages that Durham possessed for the potential investor. Richard H. Wright, himself interested for a few years in a mill venture in Durham, sought in 1891 to persuade a British acquaintance to invest money in a new textile enterprise there. Wright explained that the existing cotton factory in Durham had run successfully for more than six years, the owners "clearing a net profit annually of from 25% to 30% on their capital."

14. R. B. Arrington to Miss E. A. Childs, January 18, 1910, B. N. Duke letterbook. Ben Duke ultimately sold his farm and did so before the recession after World War I sent land values in the South plummeting downward. "The farm brought more than I expected," he noted. "I am glad it is off our hands." B. N. Duke to Miss E. A. Childs, June 28, 1919. B. N. Duke MSS.
15. Durham *Recorder*, December 25, 1889; Durham *Tobacco Plant*, January 26, 1889.

Good cotton grew nearby, Wright continued, rail transportation was excellent, and the climate was "all that can be desired." He noted that coal was obtainable at from $3.15 to $3.25 per ton and added the inevitable, clinching argument concerning labor for the textile factories: "Girls can be had at from $2.50 to $4.00 per week."[16]

Wright failed, at least at that time, to gain the substantial profits that he believed could be made from the textile industry, but the Dukes and George Watts, once they decided to move into textile manufacturing, made large profits for many years. These potential profits, and not the exhortations of the Durham newspapers or the plight of poor farmers seeking factory jobs, led them to launch the venture in 1892. Yet the fact that they launched it in Durham should be duly emphasized. Opportunities for capitalists to invest their money abounded in America in the late nineteenth century, with Wall Street in its unregulated, wild-and-woolly glory as the Mecca for a large number of rich men. The Dukes and Watts were offered many, diverse opportunities to invest their money. But when an acquaintance tried to tempt Ben Duke into a gold mining proposition in Alaska, he noted that he had washed his hands of "that kind of business," for "Alaska is too far from home." Earlier and much closer to home, a South Carolinian inquired if Ben Duke and his associates could be induced to build a cotton mill there provided a twenty-five acre site were donated, immunity from town taxes given for ten years, and 60 percent of state and county taxes rebated for the same period. Duke replied, "Sorry I cannot."[17]

Clearly, Ben Duke took the lead in the family's move into textile manufacturing, and like his younger brother in the tobacco industry, Ben Duke showed great talent in picking the right man to do the job. William A. Erwin was thirty-six years old when Ben Duke secured him in 1892 to manage the new textile enterprise in Durham. A native of Burke County in western North Carolina, Erwin was a grand-nephew of Edwin M. Holt, founder of an important antebellum textile enterprise, and for a decade or so prior to moving to Durham Erwin had

16. R. H. Wright to A. C. Watts in London, August 11, 1891. Wright letterbook. The Commonwealth Cotton Factory, in which Julian S. Carr and Wright were involved, got off to a slow, faltering start; when Brodie Duke offered to buy their shares for seventy-five cents on the dollar, Carr thought it "a very lucky escape." See Carr to Wright, December 10, 16, 1892, and Wright to Carr, December 17, 1892. R. H. Wright MSS and letterbook.

17. B. N. Duke to W. B. Hall, May 18, 1910, and J. T. Pinnix of Mullins, S. C., to B. N. Duke, March 17, 1900. B. N. Duke MSS and letterbook.

served as the treasurer and general manager of the famous E. M. Holt Plaid Mills in Burlington, North Carolina.[18]

Early in the negotiations Erwin assured Ben Duke about the profitability of the proposed venture. "Of course I can not tell what the future will be in the manuf[acturin]g business," Erwin wrote, "but if I had the plant in operation *now*, that I should like to build, I *know* that I could make it turn out at least at the rate of 40% *net profits*. This I know sounds large, but with the facts before me, and having a true knowledge of the business, I think I am safe in saying this is a conservative estimate, as I can show you."[19]

After further conversations with other cotton manufacturers and additional correspondence with Erwin, Ben Duke signified in April, 1892, that he was quite satisfied and ready to commence work at the earliest possible moment. The company would be capitalized at $125,000 initially, with Erwin putting in $40,000 or "his all," as Ben Duke put it, and with the balance coming from the Dukes and George Watts.

Concerning the naming of the new enterprise, the historian of Durham, William K. Boyd, has a nice story that has the ring of truth. When Ben Duke and Erwin visited a Durham lawyer (probably W. W. Fuller, who had not yet moved to New York) to talk about articles of incorporation, the question of a name for the mill arose and, Boyd relates, "on that point Mr. Duke was at sea." At that juncture, the attorney reportedly remarked, "Let us name it for this young man [Erwin]; then if it fails the onus will be upon him; and if it succeeds, it will be to his glory."[20]

The Erwin Cotton Mill did indeed succeed and, as the lawyer predicted, it was to the "glory" of its secretary-treasurer and general manager, W. A. Erwin. Ben Duke served as president of the company until his death and enjoyed close, frequent association with Erwin in the venture. When Erwin informed his former employers of his decision to move to Durham, they paid him high tribute: "My experience is that in a life time we seldom find an 'all round' man," L. Banks Holt declared to Ben Duke, "one of extensive business capacity[,] entirely reliable, 'as true as steel,' and with all a Christian gentleman." After a business association with Erwin of some seventeen

18. W. S. Person, "William Allen Erwin," in Samuel A. Ashe, ed., *Biographical History of North Carolina* (Greensboro, 1905), III, 114–128.
19. Erwin to B. N. Duke, March 29, 1892, B. N. Duke MSS.
20. Boyd, *The Story of Durham*, p. 122.

years, Holt continued, "I can not part with him without saying to you that I can not find words that will express too strongly my good opinion of him. . . ."[21]

Erwin began to live up to his advance billing by travelling north to visit the textile selling agents in New York and to make the important selection of machinery in New England. From New York he advised Ben Duke that he would learn all he could from the largest commission agents and then proceed to Lowell and other points "as mapped out by us." Already tired out on leaving New York, Erwin talked "plans and machinery" all day with the people in one machine works in Massachusetts and, when he next reported to Duke, was headed for Lowell to "obtain all from them I possibly can & then make for home & hope to see you Monday, as I must have your approval & advice on plans, your help in laying off our grounds for Factory site, Tenement houses, etc. before you leave for N.Y. . . . ." The biggest question, as expected, Erwin continued, concerned what type of cloth was best to produce in the new mill. "And when we come here, in New England & find the big mills changing their products *all the time*," Erwin noted, "it is not strange that it is a hard question with us." But, he concluded, "I have all the points noted that I was able to obtain, & will lay the whole question before you on my return with suggestions & advice."[22]

Reflecting the carefulness and conscientiousness that Erwin showed in his letters, the mill and the village of West Durham, just to the west of the new campus of Trinity College, began to materialize in late 1892. When the wheels were ready to turn in the spring of 1893, a satirical editor, Al Fairbrother, who both amused and outraged Durham for several years, reported that "Uncle Wash Duke touched off the business," that is, started the machinery running, and "the anti-trust shriekers went into their closets and wept bitterly over the hopeless degeneracy of the times, painfully and pathetically recalling with regret the good old days when every man made his own homespun, dined on ash cake and drank sassafras tea for breakfast."[23]

"Anti-trust shriekers" there were indeed in North Carolina, as elsewhere, but the day of homespun had long passed. B. N. Duke, acting for the family, became increasingly important in the campaign to place North Carolina among the leading textile-manufacturing

21. April 20, 1892, B. N. Duke MSS.
22. Erwin to Duke, May 9, 12, 1892, B. N. Duke MSS.
23. Durham *Daily Globe*, March 30, 31, 1893.

states in the nation. Convinced that the cotton mill had, as he expressed it, "a big future in the Southern States," he sought to interest New England manufacturers in North Carolina. "We have recently invested in several mills and are well pleased with the result," Duke explained, "but the mills are all comparatively small and cannot meet with that degree of success that would be possible in plants of larger capacity with ample capital. . . ." He believed that "most of the mills throughout this section have struggled along with capital entirely inadequate to successfully operate even the small plants that have been erected." Turning to the advantages offered by his native state, Ben Duke asserted that the "Piedmont belt in North Carolina is the most healthful locality in the South and there are many inducements for the location of such a mill as I would like to see erected." The state has "splendid water power," and an "abundance of cheap white labor. . . ." All that was required "to utilize these advantages successfully and profitably is money and men with experience in the business."[24]

Failing to attract help from New England, where the long-established textile manufacturers nervously and jealously watched the growth of the Southern mills, Ben Duke and his associates relied on their own resources and moved only gradually toward obtaining the "very large mill" that they envisioned. The various textile mills which the Dukes, George Watts, and Erwin controlled in the Erwin Cotton Mill Company would ultimately be capitalized at approximately $10,000,000, but in 1893, as the original Erwin Mill began operation, Ben Duke notified his brother in New York and George Watts, who was visiting the World's Fair in Chicago, that $50,000 in additional capital was required immediately. "We will pay in the additional fifty thousand from time to time as it is needed and dividing it up among the present stockholders in proportion to their present holdings," Ben Duke explained, "it will work no harsdhip on anyone." Watts promptly replied that instead of adding merely $50,000 to the original investment of $125,000, why did they not add $75,000 to ensure an adequate working capital. "Besides," Watts added, "a large capital would give us prestige with everyone."[25]

The "prestige" may or may not have interested Ben Duke, but

24. B. N. Duke to Charles F. Lovering of Lowell, Mass., February 4, 1893, B. N. Duke letterbook.

25. B. N. Duke to G. Watts and J. B. Duke, June 16, 1893, and Watts to B. N. Duke, June 20, 1893, B. N. Duke letterbook and MSS.

the success of the Erwin Mill most certainly did. He confessed to another manufacturer in the neighboring town of Henderson that "next to our tobacco business [the Erwin Mill] will be one of our pet enterprises, and we propose to make it a success if it is possible to do so." Though the mill was just starting, he added, "we already have contracts for enough goods to keep us running several months, and which will pay quite a nice profit."[26]

The business acumen of W. A. Erwin contributed mightily to the success of the enterprise. Though the mill initially produced the type of muslin cloth used in bags for smoking tobacco, it soon expanded into the manufacture of denim, which up to that time had not been manufactured widely or successfully in the South. The Erwin Mill soon became one of the largest producers of denim in the nation.[27]

Erwin worked hard at merchandising as well as at manufacturing, and that fact played a significant part in the mill's success. Writing Ben Duke from Indianapolis, Erwin noted that he had been travelling at night and "drumming the trade" in the daytime. He had spent one day in Buffalo, the next in Detroit, and from Indianapolis would proceed to Chicago and then New York. "We have worked thoroughly the Jobbers and Cutters in each place," Erwin wrote, "and while 'Eastern mills' have been selling their goods at unheard of [low] prices, & have constantly drummed the trade in every place, am glad to report that by hard work, we have overridden prejudice in a great degree; and made most satisfactory sales in every city; though mostly for future delivery." Erwin added that he had advised the mill superintendent in Durham "to keep mum" about sales. There were already enough denim mills to compete with, and the "mill men in N.C. are so terribly jealous, constantly watching what their neighbors are doing." Erwin declared that he had "tried to keep both eyes open, as well as my ears, & have seen & heard much that will prove to our interest in the future, as well as [at the] present time."

A devout Episcopalian who taught a Sunday-school class in a mission in West Durham for many years, Erwin may have felt uneasy as he plunged into the cosmopolitan mercantile world of the north. At any rate, he concluded his letter to Ben Duke by expressing the hope that he, Erwin, would be spared to return safely to Durham, but "should Providence forbid this, I want you to know how much I appreciate your universal kindness and friendship shown, and proven to

26. B. N. Duke to John D. Cooper, June 16, 1893, B. N. Duke letterbook.
27. Boyd, *Story of Durham*, pp. 122–123.

me, and my family, for whom I bespeak your continued interest and friendship."[28]

Pleased with all the hard work and good results, Ben Duke and his associates raised Erwin's salary to $6,000 a year in 1896. More importantly, the Erwin Mill, which employed 375 workers on 11,000 spindles and 360 looms in 1895, more than doubled its capacity in 1896. With 1,000 workers, 25,000 spindles, and 1,000 looms it became by far the largest of Durham's four textile mills and one of the larger ones in North Carolina.[29]

In addition to the Erwin Mill, the Pearl Cotton Mill which Brodie L. Duke had launched in 1892 came under the management of W. A. Erwin and his brother, J. Harper Erwin, after the death of W. H. Branson in 1899. When Brodie Duke, overextended in various enterprises in and out of Durham and caught short in his speculation in cotton futures, had to assign his assets to trustees during the panic of 1893, the family moved in to help him out. To a businessman in Memphis, Tennessee, where Brodie Duke was involved in a railway project, Ben Duke explained that the family, unable to complete and underwrite all of Brodie Duke's enterprises, had decided that investments "to help along his affairs" would be best made in Durham. Accordingly, the capital of the Pearl Mill was increased from $100,000 to $175,000, with Washington, B. N., and J. B. Duke, together with George Watts paying the new subscription. In 1895 with 200 workers, 10,000 spindles, and 160 looms for making extra-wide sheeting, the Pearl Mill also became a highly successful venture.[30]

The success of Durham's textile factories was related not only to the availability of local capital and the managerial talent of the Erwin brothers but also to the low price of both raw cotton and labor. Wages in Durham, as elsewhere in the South, were lower than in the rest of the country. In 1890 North Carolina reported that skilled men re-

28. W. A. Erwin to B. N. Duke, October 2, 1894, B. N. Duke MSS.

29. B. N. Duke to W. A. Erwin, January 30, 1896, B. N. Duke letterbook; Durham *Daily Globe*, July 18, August 15, 1895.

30. B. N. Duke to W. R. Hall in Memphis, January 16, 1894; B. N. Duke to W. C. Houston, Jr., January 22, 1894, B. N. Duke letterbook. The Commonwealth Cotton Mill, another venture in which Brodie Duke invested heavily, began production early in 1893. In 1895 it employed 140 workers who made yarn and hosiery on 6400 spindles and 58 knitting machines. Late in 1897, Ben Duke wrote that the mill was in better shape than ever and making money. "I have been giving its affairs my personal attention this year," he noted, "and have recently made additions and improvements which cost about $30,000., and which will add one-third to its capacity." B. N. Duke to R. I. Cheatham, December 21, 1897. *Ibid.*

ceived average daily wages of from $1.00 to $2.50, skilled women from 40 cents to $1.00, and children from 20 to 50 cents. Not only were hours long, ranging from sixty-three to seventy-five hours per week in North Carolina before 1903, but a high percentage of the workers were women and children.[31]

The mill villages, such as grew up in East and West Durham, have been tellingly compared with antebellum plantations by historians. Though physical force and paternalism had been intertwined to keep the black slaves at work before the Civil War, paternalism combined with a wide range of economic sanctions characterized the mill villages of the white textile workers of the South. "Long hours, low wages, and poor living conditions awaited all who entered the mills," one historian has written. "Yet, they came, often in such large numbers that some were turned away. They came because the mills offered them the hope of a better life instead of the despair of farm life. . . ."[32]

W. A. Erwin, Ben Duke, and their associates were men of their times, and the Erwin Mill and the village that grew around it reflected many of the harsh realities of the period and of the industry. Yet in some ways Erwin, encouraged by Ben Duke, managed to do better than many of his fellow textile manufacturers. At a time when Durham itself had no city park, Erwin gave one to the West Durham community. In a grove of shade trees with a spring of cool water nearby, it was equipped with swings and "rustic seats." The movement to organize a brass band among the operatives in Erwin Mills obviously reflected another aspect of the role of the park in the community's life.[33]

More important than the park, which after all reflected the benevolent paternalism of many (but by no means all) mill owners, Erwin from the mid-1890's on managed to do better than the majority of his fellow textile manufacturers in the matter of the length of the working day—which was eleven hours at Erwin Mills in 1895—and in his refusal to employ underage children.[34] In the early twentieth

31. *N. C. Labor Report*, 1890, as cited in Melton A. McLaurin, *Paternalism and Protest: Southern Cotton Mill Workers and Organized Labor, 1876–1905* (Westport, Conn., 1971), pp. 22–26.

32. *Ibid.*, p. 39.

33. Durham *Daily Globe*, August 22, 1895.

34. J. E. Stagg to B. N. Duke, February 1, 1895, B. N. Duke MSS; Elizabeth H. Davidson, *Child Labor Legislation in the Southern Textile States* (Chapel Hill, 1939), p. 115. Another aspect of the child-labor problem is reflected in a number of letters in the B. N. Duke MSS. A woman with three children "deprived of a Father's care"

century, as public sentiment grew in North Carolina as elsewhere in the nation for more effective legislation against child labor and for compulsory school-attendance laws, Erwin lent his support to statutory changes. Reporting to Ben Duke on a meeting of large textile manufacturers and the state's Child Labor Committee, Erwin explained that "we agreed by unanimous vote to recommend that the present laws of the State be amended somewhat, increasing the age limit of children working at night to sixteen years instead of fourteen, approving of an inspector under the Educational Department of the State and a compulsory educational law between the ages of seven and fourteen."

Erwin confessed his concern about the provision for an inspector but declared that "some of the manufacturers in North Carolina have been working children much under the lawful age limit . . . and for this reason not only the Child Labor Committee, but many of the most conservative mill men in North Carolina have urged an inspector that the law might be complied with." Erwin concluded by noting that "the high ground we have tried to take since the opening" of the mill in Durham had been in thorough accord with Ben Duke's views, and the latter would certainly "cordially approve" of the changes Erwin had supported.[35]

Child-labor legislation gave concern to most textile manufacturers, even relatively enlightened ones such as W. A. Erwin and Ben Duke, but the idea of labor organizations for textile workers was far more frightening to the mill owners. The early moves to bring Southern workers into the Knights of Labor in the 1880's came before the Erwin Mills were begun, but when renewed efforts to organize Southern mill workers were launched by the National Union of Textile Workers in the late 1890's, Erwin joined his fellow manufacturers in successfully resisting the unionists.

"Organized labor did not fail to develop in Southern textile mills because the operatives were satisfied, or uneducated, or subservient to mill management," one historian has recently concluded. "Or-

---

wrote that the superintendent at the tobacco factory had insisted "that my little boys are too young, neither of them being thirteen." The woman added: "I have succeeded in getting the oldest one in a mill in Edgemont [East Durham] but now I have a little boy eleven and a little girl just eight. I can not do heavy work in a Factory and have decided to take a few Boarders, and after the boys are old enough put them in your Factory." Mrs. A. M. to B. N. Duke, May 12, 1903, *ibid.*

35. W. A. Erwin to R. B. Arrington, January 7, 1913, B. N. Duke MSS.

ganized labor failed because management took the offensive against it and destroyed it."[36] When, for example, the union gained some adherents in West Durham in 1900, Erwin posted a two-week notice for any workers affiliated with the labor organization and also closed the company store to them. Some of the workers thereupon went on strike, some stayed in the union and were fired after two weeks, and some remained on the job. When the unionists appealed to Erwin for credit at the company store, he declared that his quarrel was with "unwarranted interference" in the business rather than with individual workers and authorized the store to issue food to all of the mill hands, including those on strike. "This enlightened action seriously hurt the union's cause . . . ," an historian has concluded, and the Durham local disbanded.[37]

Uninhibited by labor organizations, therefore, and encouraged by the profits made in the 1890's, the Erwin Mills launched a vast enlargement early in the twentieth century. Ben Duke and his associates carefully studied the situation prior to launching the program of expansion. Duke conferred with various leaders in the industry, including a prominent selling agent in Philadelphia, Frederick L. Baily. "A mill in the South, built with the machinery that is obtainable today," Baily declared, would have "an enormous advantage over the New England machinery that was bought five, ten or twenty years ago. . . ." There would be further advantages in the site with water power, which Duke had described, in "the help that would be anxious for work, and every advantage that the South has in this class of business, from the very bricks that go into the mill construction, right straight up to the salary paid the President, the Treasurer, the Secretary, etc., ALL would be an ADVANTAGE that would give a very handsome return, even if New England were selling the goods at cost."

According to Baily, New Englanders were talking increasingly of moving their plants to the South. "But with such capital as you have at your command," he suggested to Ben Duke, "why should you allow any one to come into this section and reap the benefits of what you can have to their fullest extent if you will simply reach out your hand and take them?" Baily argued that people would always wear clothing

36. McLaurin, *Paternalism and Protest*, p. 211.

37. *Ibid.*, p. 156. Earlier, after an illness of two weeks, Erwin had written how glad he was to be out again and how "gratified I am that all our operatives seem glad to see me." Erwin to Ben Duke, May 10, 1899, B. N. Duke MSS.

"and even if the clothing is curtailed the last thing to go would be the cotton goods in the under garments. . . ." Getting down to specifics, he advised a mill at the outset with about 80,000 spindles and 2,000 looms built with a view to making "plain gray goods of what is called the print cloth construction." Baily concluded: "Now, Mr. Duke, if you can get a gentleman like Mr. Erwin . . . you would have the other essential to a successful mill enterprise, that is, a practical mill man of great force and energy, who will make a success of anything he undertakes in his line, and beside that a most agreeable gentleman to be associated with in business, and one to whom you could trust your affairs with perfect confidence, as you know; so that, with the Capital, with the Location and with the Brains, you ought to be in a position to make a handsome thing of it, if any one in the country can."[38]

If Baily's encouraging letter did not inspire Ben Duke to move ahead with the plans for expansion, it certainly did nothing to inhibit them. The emphasis on the advantages of a site with water power, which the original Erwin Mill had not possessed, should also be noted. The Dukes were in the vanguard of those who were realizing in the 1890's that hydroelectric power might just represent an important wave of the economic future.

The particular site with potential water power, about which Ben Duke had told Frederick L. Baily, was on the Cape Fear river in Harnett County, which is south of Durham in what was then a relatively undeveloped section of the state. Accompanied by Ben Duke's executive secretary in Durham, his brother-in-law John C. Angier, and an engineer, Erwin scouted the site in the spring of 1898 and reported that "the lay of the land was better than I expected to see, being high and healthful on the east side of the river. . . ." He had "learned after making a great many inquiries that they were not troubled at all with chills and malarial fever, and the people in that section seem very thrifty, though small farmers and poor, and conditions favor the securing of good operatives." The engineer was studying government statistics on the Cape Fear's water flow, and if his estimates proved to be accurate, Erwin believed that "we are in the way to secure a very valuable property at a very low cost. . . ."[39]

38. Frederick L. Baily to B. N. Duke, February 23, 1898, B. N. Duke MSS. Baily wrote a second letter urging expansion on November 24, 1899.

39. Erwin to B. N. Duke, May 20, 1898, B. N. Duke MSS. The executive secretary, J. E. Stagg, was equally enthusiastic in a letter of May 21, 1898, to Ben Duke.

The acquisition of options and then the securing of titles to various properties desired for the large venture in Harnett County took considerable time. There were also rival sites to consider, but the public announcement was finally made on August 1, 1902, that W. A. Erwin, acting for the Dukes and George Watts, would manage a large new mill to be built in Harnett County. When the matter of a name for the new mill village, which would soon have a population of 2,000 persons, arose, Ben Duke sought his brother's advice. W. W. Fuller replied that he and J. B. Duke had conferred on the matter and that the latter thought either the name "Erwin" or "Duke" would be proper for the new town. Since Erwin had charge there, J. B. Duke advised that the choice of the name be left to him and that "if Erwin should have any desire to have it named for himself" it would be "proper to conform to his preference."[40] Ben Duke preferred to name the village "Erwin," but when that gentleman thought otherwise the Dukes acquiesced, and the new town of Duke, North Carolina, was born in 1903. Ironically, when Trinity College became the core of Duke University some twenty-two years later and confusion began to arise between the new university and the mill town in Harnett County, President William P. Few requested that the name of the still-unincorporated mill village be changed. Accordingly Duke, North Carolina, became and remained Erwin, North Carolina.[41]

At the same time that Erwin Mill Number Two was under construction on the Cape Fear river, an even larger textile mill, which was to become Erwin Mill Number Three in 1906, was developed by the Dukes and their associates at Cooleemee, which lay to the west of Durham near Salisbury, North Carolina. Purchasing the interests of B. F. Mebane and Dr. G. A. Mebane in the Cooleemee venture, Ben Duke and his associates put the new mill under the supervision of Erwin early in 1901. Though it took some time, additional capital, and great effort on the part of the management, Erwin Mill Number Three gradually rounded the financial corner to profitability. By July, 1903, Erwin reported that he had 25,000 spindles and 800 looms operating at Cooleemee; in early 1905, the figures had risen to 40,000 spindles and 1,296 looms, and Erwin considered matters there in "excellent shape."[42]

40. W. W. Fuller to B. N. Duke, February 11, 1903, B. N. Duke MSS.
41. W. P. Few to B. N. Duke, July 11, November 24, 1925, W. P. Few MSS, Duke University Archives.
42. Erwin to B. N. Duke, January 3, 1901; George Watts to B. N. Duke, January 9,

Erwin apparently never indulged in false optimism in his frequent reports to Ben Duke, who saw to it that J. B. Duke was also kept informed on the family's growing involvement in the textile industry. Figures for the profits of Erwin Mills in the early years are not available, but they were no doubt sizeable. At the beginning of 1901, Erwin sent this undoubtedly cheering news to Ben Duke: "We have finished casting our accounts at this mill [in Durham], and find our profits for the past year to be about $195,000 or, 55% of the capital stock, which I tell you, since you have quit telling anybody about such matters, and which may make you feel more comfortable over your sale of Riverside [stock]. Mr. Watts told me of the extra 10% dividend from [Riverside common]."[43]

Early in 1903, Erwin reported a net profit of $187,000, which was about 53 percent on the capital or 20 percent on the capital and surplus. He had begun the new year, Erwin added, "with 4,100 bales of cotton in warehouse paid for, very good contracts for goods, and without owing one dollar, which places us in position for a good run this year."[44] In 1904 a stock dividend of 200 percent was declared by the directors, and Erwin advised that a net profit of $215,000 had been made.[45]

Matters did not always run as happily for the owners of Erwin Mills as they did in the 1890's and the opening years of the twentieth century. The price of cotton rose for one thing, and buying it became a tricky matter about which Erwin both worried a great deal and frequently sought advice on from B. N. Duke. In 1912 Erwin noted that it took 5,000 bales of cotton per month to supply the four Erwin Mills (the fourth having been built in Durham in 1910). The other mills which the Dukes and Watts controlled and Erwin helped to manage and for which he bought cotton—the Pearl Mill and Durham Cotton Manufacturing Mill in Durham, the Alpine Mill in Morganton,

---

1902; B. N. Duke to B. F. Mebane, April 28, 1902; Erwin to B. N. Duke, July 16, 1903, May 20, 1905. Numerous other letters concerning Cooleemee as well as the mill in Harnett county are in the B. N. Duke MSS.

43. Erwin to B. N. Duke, January 3, 1901, *ibid.* The Dukes and Watts had invested early in the famous Riverside (Dan River) Mills in Danville, Virginia, and around 1894 owned about $250,000 worth of the stock. As indicated in Erwin's letter, Ben Duke had sold his Riverside stock before 1901. For a detailed history of the important enterprise, see Robert S. Smith, *Mill on the Dan* (Durham, 1960).

44. Erwin to B. N. Duke and J. E. Stagg to B. N. Duke, January 9, 1903, B. N. Duke MSS.

45. Erwin to B. N. Duke, January 1, 14, 1904, *ibid.*

North Carolina, and the Oxford Cotton Mill in Oxford, North Carolina—used about 1,500 bales per month. Some of the mills, such as the Pearl Mill, required cotton grown in the deep South, Erwin observed, but at the Erwin Mills in Durham and in Harnett County some 27,000 bales of "local cotton" would be used if the price compared favorably with prices in the deep South. He expected to buy in the neighborhood of Cooleemee around 5,000 bales of the 17,000 bales that would be used there. "We are going over the whole situation very carefully," Erwin explained, "so as to determine from what points we can get the best staple at the lowest price, best suited for the fabrics that we manufacture."[46]

Some years before the purchasing of raw cotton became so crucial, however, textile manufacturing in North Carolina had run upon troubled times. For one thing, labor was not so plentiful as in the depression-wracked 1890's, and Erwin mentioned in 1906 his "desperate efforts to get more [workers] from the country at all the mills and train [them] in, which seems to me the only early solution of the problem." Subsequently, after reporting that health conditions at all the mills were good, Erwin noted that "it seemed expedient, in the light of our duty to our operatives, and with the hope of maintaining a kind relation with them, to cut down the hours of work to 62 hours and 40 minutes per week at West Durham and 63 hours and 55 minutes at No. 2 mills [at Duke] which we did, and the first of this year placed our No. 3 plant [at Cooleemee] on the same basis as our No. 2." All the mills shut down at noon on Saturday, Erwin added, and it was "specially gratifying" to him "to report the moral condition of all our plants good and the people seem generally contented and happy."[47]

That "the people" were so contented and happy may well be doubted, for improvements in their wages and working conditions were slow in coming. Yet Erwin's major headaches came not from the workers but from the depressed market for manufactured cloth. Early in 1908, while reporting a good previous year, he confessed that he had "sold almost no denims since October and have made no new prices on same, endeavoring to deliver goods already sold at last year's prices." If business did not improve, he insisted it would be "absolutely necessary for us to curtail production on account of the extreme high price of cotton." A few months later he was even gloom-

46. Erwin to B. N. Duke, August 13, 1912, *ibid.*
47. Erwin to B. N. Duke, November 22, 1906, January 22, 1907, *ibid.*

140

ier in a letter to Ben Duke: "You will pardon me for telling you . . . that we are passing through the worst time in manufacturing that we have ever experienced." Both in Durham and at the town of Duke the mills were only "running on four days time." Baily, the selling agent in Philadelphia, argued that the sole remedy was to curtail production, which Erwin insisted that he was doing, "struggling at each and every mill to cut down expenses at every possible point. . . ." Concerning the workers, he added: "Our people are not yet suffering. We are giving a good number of them work overhauling machinery, relining and levelling shafting, working on the building, chopping wood, etc." He was impressed that the operatives "were making the best of conditions."[48]

The slump in textiles continued, and in October, 1909, Erwin informed Ben Duke that the North Carolina Cotton Mills' Association and the American Manufacturers' Association were scheduling a conference "looking to a general curtailment [of production], not only for the United States, but abroad." Erwin believed that "conditions are so acute, and the prospects so grave as applied to cotton mills, that there is a good chance of succeeding in reducing in the next few months the consumption of cotton at least a million bales." At any rate, Erwin avowed, "the demand is so urgent that it is worth the honest effort that I propose to make to that end."[49]

Early in 1911 Erwin expressed his thankfulness for having come out "something better than 'Whole bones' last year," but he added: "Goods in our line are very much depressed and cotton manufacturing does not look bright. There is no question but there is over-production in almost all lines, notwithstanding we are starting our No. 4 Mill, hoping for better things later on." Ben Duke also reflected the prevailing gloom about the industry; when the manager of a textile mill in Greensboro, North Carolina, in which he and his associates had made large investments, reported the need for more capital, Duke replied: "I do not care to take another dollar in cotton mills anywhere, because the industry looks to me to be in very bad condition, and I am not encouraged to think there will be any improvements very soon."[50]

Erwin resorted to various strategies in his attempt to cope with the

48. Erwin to B. N. Duke, April 28, 1908, *ibid.*
49. W. A. Erwin to B. N. Duke, October 1, 1909, *ibid.*
50. Erwin to B. N. Duke, January 23, 1911, and B. N. Duke to G. O. Coble, January 25, 1911, B. N. Duke MSS and letterbook.

critical situation in cotton textiles that continued through 1911. For example, Ben Duke sent his friend James A. Thomas, the chief representative in China for the British-American Tobacco Company, to confer with Erwin about ways to increase textile sales in the Far East. Erwin prepared some miniature cotton sheets that could be widely distributed to advertise one of his important products in China and declared his readiness "to resort to all sorts of proper schemes" to sell his goods. Through the agency of one of the trading companies in China which dealt extensively with the British-American Tobacco Company, he had already sent from the Cooleemee mills 1,600 cases of canton flannels and some mottled flannels, and he was now taking an order from them for denims, which he thought might be among the first denims from the United States ever sold to China. But he was not optimistic, despite the increased sales in China, and he declared to Duke: "Am sorry to tell you that this month [July, 1911] has brought more 'knotty problems' than I have ever known in my 30 years cotton mill experience and . . . with prospects pointing with reasonable weather conditions to the best crop [of cotton] this country has ever grown, and consequently lower prices, buyers of cotton goods will not make contracts and will persist in waiting to see results."

Erwin explained that he was having "strenuous times" endeavoring "to hold up the price of cotton goods, and to avoid a stampede in prices, as well as to conjecture what the growing crop will turn out and what the price shall be." He believed that the majority of farmers would not sell their cotton at a price below ten cents a pound and thought too "that it would be unfortunate to the general trade if conditions favor a lower price."

To cope with the crisis, Erwin explained that at West Durham and Duke he was producing only enough denim to keep his "organization of hands" and would not start any more machinery in the new No. 4 mill in West Durham until conditions grew settled, though the new mill was turning out an "excellent fabric" of wide sheetings which were bleached and put into sheets and pillow cases "in the best manner. . . ." Cooleemee was running full time, producing mostly cantons for the China trade. After briefly reporting on the various other mills in which he and the Dukes were involved, Erwin noted that the mills had come out "a little better than whole, all of which goes to show [that] with any kind of times, at fair prices our mills are prepared to and would do well. . . ." He concluded: "We are trusting in the Lord and trying to keep our powder dry for such better days."[51]

Gradually, the "better days" for which Erwin longed, and for which he carefully planned, did return. Late in 1911, after acknowledging Ben Duke's telegram saying that he and J. B. Duke approved the selling arrangement with Baily for the next year, Erwin went on to explain that he had made an "absolutely confidential" arrangement with Baily to sell all the goods of the various mills on a 4 percent commission, with guaranteed sales. With that end of the business advantageously arranged, Erwin worked closely with the Dukes in the crucial matter of buying the vast quantities of cotton required by the mills.[52]

In addition to advising Erwin about cotton purchases, Ben Duke and J. B. Duke had long before learned in the tobacco industry the wisdom of watching Congress and lobbying discreetly when necessary. After the election of Woodrow Wilson to the presidency in November, 1912, and with the prospect of a special session of Congress in the spring of 1913 to deal with tariff reforms that the victorious Democrats had promised, Ben Duke sent advice to Erwin: "My brother and myself were talking over the cotton mill situation . . . and he suggested that I write you that we think it is important that the Southern Cotton Manufacturers get busy at once, looking to the protection of the cotton industry in any tariff legislation. . . ." Ben Duke, noting that Erwin was president of the Southern Cotton Manufacturers Association, figured that with the new Democratic administration the "Southern manufacturers will have quite a little influence in the matter of tariff legislation affecting the cotton industry." He hoped Erwin would "take the proper steps and put the necessary machinery in motion."[53]

Erwin replied the following day that he was already at work "trying to get forces in line to use every possible influence that our membership can muster, individually, through committees, and collectively as an Association." He explained that he had to move discreetly, but, nevertheless, intended "to do everything it is possible to do in this matter and hope to accomplish good results." Early in the new year of 1913, Erwin combined the news that he considered "our business in the best shape it has ever been" with the information that he was

51. Erwin to B. N. Duke, July 28, 1911, *ibid.*
52. Erwin to B. N. Duke, December 29, 1911, July 1, August 8, 13, 1912, *ibid.*
53. Ben Duke to W. A. Erwin, November 18, 1912, B. N. Duke letterbook.

headed for Washington to do all in his power "to avoid drastic legislation."[54]

Southern protectionists such as the Dukes and Erwin did not carry the day with the Democratic administration of Woodrow Wilson. The Underwood tariff of 1913 finally emerged as the first genuine, major reduction in this country's duties on imported goods since the Republican party assumed power at the time of the Civil War and launched the nation on a long era of highly protective tariffs. And though Erwin complained only mildly about Congressional "tinkering with the tariff and banking laws" in his annual report to the stockholders at the close of 1913, he noted that while it was too early to tell what the full effect of the new tariff would be, "thrown as we are in closer competition with the world, we realize the necessity of the most economical and intelligent management."[55]

Superbly capable of just such management as he had described, Erwin by 1912 had, in fact, come through the difficult period for cotton textiles that had begun around 1908. Reporting on the year 1912, he noted that the book value of the Erwin Mills common stock stood at $177 per share. Upon his recommendation the directors had declared the regular quarterly dividends of 1½ percent payable on April 1 and July 1, 1913, and also an extra dividend of 1 percent on the common stock on each of those dates. "With reasonable times we think we can hold to these dividends and carry a good amount each year to surplus," Erwin advised, "and we are going to try mighty hard to make the undivided profits after paying dividends stand over $2,000,000 at the close of the year."[56]

Ben Duke sent his hearty congratulations on Erwin's report. "My brother is also highly pleased," Duke added, "and joins me in the highest praise of your management of these properties." A year later Ben Duke was still delighted by the "wonderful showing" that Erwin had again made. In fact, Ben Duke, who was unable himself to attend the annual meeting of the company's directors, requested George Watts to "have the Erwin Mills Company to increase [Erwin's] salary from $20,000.00 to $25,000.00" and to let stand the $3,500 that Erwin received from the other mills which he managed. Frederick L. Baily of Philadelphia joined in the chorus of approval, declaring that

54. Erwin to B. N. Duke, November 19, 1912, January 18, 1913, B. N. Duke MSS.
55. Erwin to B. N. Duke, June 11, 1913, and Erwin's annual report at the end of 1913 folders, B. N. Duke MSS.
56. Erwin to B. N. Duke, January 27, 1913, *ibid.*

144

"of all the mills in the South The Erwin Cotton Mills Company has a place entirely by itself."[57]

Whether or not the Erwin Mills Company actually had "a place entirely by itself" is a question that economic historians will some day have to decide. Since so much of the economic history of the South since the Civil War has yet to be investigated, that decision may be long in coming. What is clear, at any rate, is that Ben Duke had indeed acted wisely back in 1892 when he selected young William A. Erwin as the man with whom the Dukes and George Watts would venture into cotton-textile manufacturing. Ben Duke continued to serve as president of the Erwin Mills Company until his death in 1929, but his close association with both Erwin and the company's affairs ended after 1914, when illness began to plague him. Erwin himself lived until 1932.

Though the Duke's largest and most significant involvement in North Carolina's textile industry was in connection with Erwin, they also played key roles as large investors in cotton mills in various other cities in Piedmont North Carolina, including Roxboro, Concord, Greensboro, and Spray. Moreover, Washington Duke in 1897 befriended a movement launched by Tarheel black capitalists to establish a cotton mill in Concord, North Carolina, that would be managed by blacks and employ blacks as operatives, since the existing textile mills in North Carolina, as elsewhere in the South, used blacks only in menial jobs. "It is my pleasure to subscribe one thousand dollars to the capital stock of the Coleman Manufacturing Company," Washington Duke declared in a statement intended for publication. "I commend the enterprise of the colored people in establishing a cotton mill for the employment of their people. I wish for the institution that success its worthiness merits."[58]

Making the bricks for the building, W. C. Coleman, the secretary-treasurer of the new company, and his associates persevered in their efforts to embrace the New South's favorite, all-American way to prosperity. Obstacles were many, however, the chief one being the shortage of capital. After a committee had conferred with Washington Duke and B. N. Duke in March, 1899, Coleman assured the latter

57. B. N. Duke to Erwin, February 3, 1913; copy of B. N. Duke to George Watts, January 23, 1914; F. L. Baily to Erwin, January 28, 1914, B. N. Duke letterbook and MSS.

58. W. Duke to R. B. Fitzgerald of Durham, president of the Coleman Manufacturing Company, March 10, 1897, B. N. Duke letterbook.

of "our highest appreciation" and added that it "was voted at the meeting yesterday to ask of you a loan of $10,000 or $15,000 and give the property as security." B. N. Duke's check for $10,000 was soon dispatched, but Coleman's delay in insuring the property, and thereby protecting the loan, finally led Duke to arrange for the insurance himself and to send the bill for it to Coleman.[59]

Ben Duke's involvement with the Coleman mill led to growing complications. "We are in need of some more money to get cotton," Coleman advised early in 1900. The plant had cost around $51,000, he stated, and the machinery was installed and ready to roll. But, he added, "we need the cotton and a few other things, and wanted to see if you would increase yours—that is your loan,—make us another."[60]

Though the interest at 6 percent on the first loan of $10,000 was unpaid, Ben Duke finally agreed, after much negotiation, to a second loan of $10,000 in 1901. In July, 1901, Coleman informed Washington Duke that the mill was operating successfully, but there were current expenses which had to be met. Coleman presented this argument: "There being a large number of delinquent subscribers we feel it our duty to ask the paid up stockholders to supplement their efforts in order to derive the direct benefit from what has been already paid in." Washington Duke declined to make an additional investment in the mill.[61]

The lack of adequate capital gradually proved the undoing of W. C. Coleman's experiment. Although Ben Duke granted a six-month extension for payment of the notes of the Coleman Manufacturing Company which he held, he grew increasingly concerned about the matter of inadequate insurance on the property. Morrison H. Caldwell, a white attorney in Concord who was also involved in the enterprise, reported that Coleman was trying to get additional insurance but could not because the mill was shut down on account of high-priced cotton. "This is characteristic of Coleman's management," Caldwell added, "and only shows the necessity of a change [in the management]."[62]

59. W. C. Coleman to B. N. Duke, March 8, April 20, May 3, 1899; J. E. Stagg to Coleman, April 22, May 5, 6, 1899, B. N. Duke MSS and letterbook.
60. Coleman to B. N. Duke, February 21, 1900, B. N. Duke MSS.
61. Coleman to J. E. Stagg, May 18, June 26, 1901; Coleman to W. Duke, July 25, 1901; W. Duke to Coleman, July 31, 1901, B. N. Duke MSS and letterbook.
62. M. H. Caldwell to B. N. Duke, June 23, September 14, 16, 23, 1903, B. N. Duke MSS. Quotation in letter of September 16.

Coleman gave another version of the insurance matter. "The fact being that the Insurance Companys refusing to *Insure* our mill on account of me being Colored, I have thought best to resign my office as Sec & Treas in order to protect you[r] and others interests," he informed Washington Duke. Coleman enclosed a copy of a letter from one insurance company to its agent in Concord which said that if the Coleman mill would in the future be "under the exclusive management of white people" and be put in good financial condition, then the company would gladly authorize the insurance; otherwise "we would not care to be interested again."[63]

Although Coleman was replaced late in 1903 by a white manager, B. N. Duke received no payments on the interest, much less the principal, of his loans totalling $20,000. Accordingly he took legal action to foreclose his mortgage on the property, which was advertised for sale late in June, 1904. To Edward A. Johnson, a black leader in Raleigh who was prominent in the venture and who had begged for more time, Ben Duke explained: "I have never had any disposition to have mortgages I hold foreclosed, as you must be aware from what has been stated to you, but it has become necessary for me to have this step taken out of sheer necessity to protect my interest. The question of insurance has become a governing one." Duke ultimately bought in the property at the sheriff's sale for $10,000 in 1904, and his secretary figured that he had lost up to that time more than $13,000 in the venture. When Duke sold the property for only $13,000 in 1906, his total loss climbed to something around $20,000.[64]

The failure of the black-sponsored Coleman mill, when compared with the success of Erwin's venture, points up the crucial inadequacy of capital available to the black leaders, but even more importantly, the episode underscores the plight of the blacks and the precariousness of their economic stake in the industrializing New South. The involvement of Washington Duke and B. N. Duke in the affair was both incidental and, in the last analysis, kept on a cool, businesslike basis. Yet even that kind of relationship was in stark contrast to the harshly discriminatory policies of disfranchisement and segregation of blacks that the Southern Democrats championed so successfully in

63. W. C. Coleman to Washington Duke, November 21, 1903, with enclosure, W. Duke MSS.

64. E. A. Johnson to B. N. Duke, May 30, 1904, and Duke to Johnson, May 31, 1904; J. E. Stagg to Rev. S. B. Hunter, July 1, 1904; B. N. Duke to C. M. Bernard and E. A. Johnson, February 20, 1906, B. N. Duke MSS and letterbook.

those same early years of the twentieth century. Just as Progressivism in the South in those years was for whites only, so, as the affair of the Coleman mill suggests, was most of the industrialization that occurred in the region.

In contrast to the Coleman mill, most of the Dukes' investments in the textile industry of the Carolinas paid off handsomely. In addition to the cotton mills themselves, Duke money went into banking and railway ventures that were related to the mills. In Durham the Dukes' money went into the Fidelity Bank in 1889. Ben Duke, who long served as president of the institution, indicated in a letter to Brodie Duke early in 1893 that banking, like textile manufacturing, could be profitable even when farming most decidedly was not: "The bank earned last year about 16½ percent net . . . ," Ben Duke wrote, "and there is no reason why it should not be made to earn this every year if the management of the bank is in the right hands and its business expanded."[65] Keeping its capital at $100,000, the Fidelity Bank by 1917 had a surplus of $500,000, made profits in 1916 of $51,886, and possessed the largest resources of any of the banks in Durham.[66]

The inauguration of another banking institution in Durham illustrates the relationship between the Dukes and their lifelong associate, George Watts. His only child, Annie Watts, married a young Tarheel lawyer, John Sprunt Hill, in 1899, and George Watts helped to get his son-in-law launched in business. "I want to organize the Home Savings Bank about June 2nd [1904]," he wrote to B. N. and J. B. Duke, "and write to know if each of you won't become stockholders in the enterprize." Of the $50,000 capital, Watts explained that he and Hill would put up half. The Duke brothers each subscribed $5,000 in the new savings bank. Later in the summer when Watts was ready to launch another new venture to be capitalized at $100,000, the Durham Loan and Trust Company, he again wrote to Ben Duke: "I should much appreciate it if you & Buck would take each $5,000—or $10,000. We might get such a combination of bank-

65. B. N. Duke to Brodie Duke, February 4, 1893, B. N. Duke MSS. The new cashier at Fidelity about whom B. N. Duke also wrote was John F. Wily, with whom Ben Duke had a long association in the bank's affairs and who ultimately succeeded him as president.

66. John F. Wily, vice-president of Fidelity Bank, to B. N. Duke, January 11, 1917, B. N. Duke MSS; Boyd, *Story of Durham*, pp. 118–119. In 1905 when the oldest bank in Durham, the Morehead Banking Company, was reorganized as the Citizens National Bank, Duke money was involved, and B. N. Duke was elected its president also. James S. Manning to B. N. Duke, April 20, 1905, B. N. Duke MSS.

ing business there that it would be a fine thing for Angier [Ben Duke's son] to go into in a few years. John Hill is learning fast & adapting himself to our ways of doing business & I believe he will prove a success." Once again, the Duke brothers complied with Watts' request, as he generally did with their suggestions.[67]

The Dukes and George Watts were close friends as well as business associates. Less than a year before the launching of the banking ventures in Durham, George Watts and Ben Duke had, in Watts' words, "made fools" of themselves in a venture on Wall Street. When James B. Duke learned of their plight and moved quickly to lend them money, Watts expressed his thanks in these terms: "You have no idea how humiliated & ashamed I feel of my experiences in Wall St., not so much that I have lost a fortune & cut my income in half, as because some of my bonds were sold contrary to our agreement, while you were worried & harassed to protect the bonds & other tobacco securities on the market. . . . I have admired you as a great genius, but I have esteemed you more as an intimate friend & I am glad my foolishness & blunders have not estranged you. I would sooner lose my arm than to lose your personal regard & friendship."[68]

The two Duke brothers and George Watts never had a serious falling out, as far as the available records indicate, and Durham was not the only Tarheel city where their money went into banking. Winston-Salem and especially Charlotte, in a later period, had banks in which the Dukes invested heavily, and even the new mill village of Duke saw the Bank of Harnett launched in 1904 with B. N. Duke as its president. A decade later, the cashier there rendered this glowing report: "In the ten years of operation sixty-nine percent of the original investment [of $10,000] has been returned in cash dividends, a surplus fund of two hundred percent has been set aside and still the undivided profits amount to more than seventy-five percent of the capital. From this you will see [that] in ten years the bank has earned three hundred and forty-four percent and now your stock is worth $375.23 per share."[69]

Banks were not the only institutions to grow out of the tobacco and

67. George Watts to B. N. and J. B. Duke, April 14, 1904; Watts to B. N. Duke, June 30, August 20, 1904; and I. F. Hill to B. N. Duke, August 29, 1904, B. N. Duke MSS. Angier B. Duke did not try his hand at banking in Durham, but John Sprunt Hill ultimately became an important capitalist in Durham and North Carolina in general.

68. George Watts to James B. Duke, August 30, 1903, in the J. B. Duke MSS.

69. E. P. Davis to B. N. Duke, September 23, 1914, *ibid.*

textile enterprises of the Dukes and George Watts. When John C. Angier, Ben Duke's brother-in-law and president of the Cary Lumber Company, wished to get timber out of Harnett County, Duke built the short Cape Fear and Northern Railway in 1898. It initially extended only a few miles eastward from Apex, North Carolina. When in 1903 the road was completed to the town of Dunn, which adjoined the mill village of Duke, Ben Duke's executive secretary and the vice-president of the railway, J. E. Stagg, described the celebration: "The Dunn depot looked imposing and pretty in its new coat of 'yaller' & red. The Governor (our Governor) [Washington Duke] enjoyed the trip and feels pretty well to-day."[70]

By the time the railroad was extended all the way from Dunn and Duke (later Erwin) to Durham in 1906, it had been reorganized as the Durham and Southern Railway Company with a capitalization of $1,000,000. Hauling freight from the cotton and tobacco factories of Durham to the Seaboard Air Line at Apex and the Atlantic Coast Line at Dunn, the Durham and Southern proved to be not only a profitable investment but an important transportation facility for the growth of an hitherto undeveloped section of North Carolina. As with numerous other family enterprises, Ben Duke helped to watch over the Durham and Southern. When operating income fell as expenses rose in 1910–11, he summoned the vice-president of the railway to New York: "Come prepared to explain the nature and necessity of these increases [in expenses]."[71] Ben Duke's caution did not go unrewarded, for by 1918 he noted that the railroad had "been a profitable enterprise, never having paid dividends of less than 7% upon its capital stock since the year 1909." He added that it was "absolutely free from debt," covered a route of "approximately sixty miles," and served "communities that are not served by any other line of railroad."[72]

Railroads, banks, and textile mills in North Carolina were thus spawned by money that originally came from the tobacco industry. They were important economic developments in themselves, especially the textile mills. Despite the social problems that came with them and the notoriously low wages which they paid, the mills played

70. Stagg to B. N. Duke, September 25, 1903, *ibid.*

71. F. S. Fuller to stockholders of Durham and Southern Railway Co., December 8, 1905; [B. N. Duke] to J. E. Stagg, August 30, 1911, B. N. Duke MSS and letterbook. See also Boyd, *Story of Durham*, pp. 148–149.

72. B. N. Duke to William G. McAdoo, July 6, 1918, B. N. Duke letterbook.

their part in the South's gradual movement in the twentieth century toward economic parity with the rest of the United States. "Augmentation of the incomes of the mass of the population was not the goal directly sought [by individual investors]," a distinguished economist has written about the South's industrial experience, "though this was achieved almost in proportion as enterprise succeeded."[73]

In the last analysis, perhaps the most important consequence of the Dukes' involvement in cotton mills was that it led them straight into the electric power industry. Seeking cheaper sources of power for their mills, they began to learn about electricity produced at water power sites. Hardheaded businessmen who had grown up knowing all phases of the tobacco industry, the Dukes soon learned fast and well about textiles. Finally, they began to learn about the multiple problems associated with hydroelectric power. W. A. Erwin, appropriately enough, played an important role in the movement of the Dukes toward their final important economic venture. Helping them to locate and then purchase various water power sites in the two Carolinas, Erwin wrote more prophetically than he could have known in 1905. "The main trouble with all these powers is the erratic rising and falling of the rivers, except the Great Falls of the Catawba [in South Carolina], where the river never rises above about eleven feet, and would give practically an invariable steady power. This is the greatest property in my opinion in the United States on this account, as well as on [account of] the very low cost of development it will require, and if it were mine, I would not turn it loose except at a good price for cash."[74]

The Dukes most certainly did not "turn loose" the site which Erwin described, for it became a pivotal feature of the family's venture into the power industry, a venture that played a major role in the twentieth-century transformation of the Piedmont section of the Carolinas. Before that final great economic move occurred, however, there were troubles, troubles in abundance, that the Dukes had to endure, for their rapidly accumulating wealth brought them no immunity from many of the woes that less affluent men and women suffer.

---

73. Joseph J. Spengler, "The New South: Exemplar of Hope Fulfilled," in A. R. Desai, ed., *Essays on Modernization of Underdeveloped Societies* (Bombay, India, 1971), II, p. 385.
74. Erwin to B. N. Duke, April 1, 1905, B. N. Duke MSS.

CHAPTER 8. A TIME OF TROUBLES—AND SPLENDOR ON FIFTH AVENUE

Washington Duke's withdrawal from the family business in 1880, a virtual retirement for the man who had so successfully launched his family as manufacturers, is puzzling. In that year, as he approached his sixtieth birthday, he sold his interest in W. Duke, Sons and Company to Richard H. Wright, and while Washington Duke repurchased the one-fifth interest in the family firm five years later, he never actually resumed an active role in business. Perhaps he was simply tired after all his bone-wearying labors, first as a small farmer and then as modest tobacco manufacturer. Yet he lived almost twenty-five years after 1880, mostly in good physical condition until the last year of his life. He remained, nevertheless, on the sidelines of the family's burgeoning empires in tobacco and textiles and contented himself with the affairs of his family, the Main Street Methodist Church, and the local Republican party. While his two younger sons, Ben Duke and James B. Duke, grew to be quite at home in New York City and travelled frequently to Europe in the halcyon days before the First World War, Washington Duke made his only visit to Europe in 1892. He simply lived out his days in Durham.

In the mid-1880's, after retiring, he built a large frame house in the then-popular "Victorian" style. Known as "Fairview," the house was located to the side and rear of the large factory of W. Duke, Sons and Company on Durham's Main Street, and was surrounded by handsome grounds and outbuildings. His deceased wife's maiden sister, Miss Ann Roney, served as housekeeper, and after the death of his daughter, Mary Duke Lyon, in 1893, the Lyon children also resided at "Fairview."

Having outlived his nine brothers and sisters, Washington Duke not only headed his immediate family but accepted certain responsibilities, especially monetary, toward a large number of nieces, nephews, and other kinfolk. While his lot was infinitely easier and more comfortable than that of most Southerners, white or black, in the late nineteenth century, Washington Duke had good reason to know the burdens and aggravations that inevitably accompanied the growing affluence of his sons and himself. Ben Duke, at least after 1890 and quite probably from an earlier date, answered most of the many importuning letters that came to Washington Duke. They arrived in largest numbers after each of his gifts to Trinity College, and all received a prompt, courteous reply, even if a refusal. "I am sorry that it will not be convenient for me to respond favorably," Washington Duke replied to one appeal. The recipient shot the letter right back with this pencilled notation: "Brother you have got it and to spare, and I need it so please send me ten dollars by Monday's mail. . . ."[1]

Despite such irritations, Washington Duke's days were also filled with bright spots. His great love and admiration for the impassioned preaching of John C. Kilgo renewed his interest in Trinity College after the mid-1890's. The young professors, such as William P. Few, Robert L. Flowers, and John S. Bassett, regularly made Sunday afternoon calls on Washington Duke. The college students also esteemed him, and one of them, who entered Trinity College when it opened in Durham in the fall of 1892, recalled seeing the main benefactor of the college drive his buggy "almost every afternoon through the campus." When a group of students went to the tobacco factory they found Washington Duke standing at the entrance. "We boldly asked him if he would not show us through the mill," the former student recounted, "which he did with the most fatherly kindness and interest one could imagine. . . . He impressed us then as being a most timid man, and I have carried that impression with me for these thirty-five years." On another occasion when some of the students spoke to the old gentleman in his front yard about the beautiful lawn and flowers he seemed to enjoy so much, Washington Duke replied: "It is all yours. It is as much yours as mine. Whenever you feel like it, come in and lie down on the grass and gaze into the sky to your heart's content."[2]

While Washington Duke thus enjoyed the students and drew closer to the college in the last years of his life, his first love among institutions remained the Main Street Methodist Church. Its doors seldom opened that he was not in his regular place down front, and all of the activities of the church, from the Sunday school to the choir, were of deep interest to him. On one occasion J. E. Stagg, Washington Duke's nephew who married Mary W. Lyon, sent this message to Ben Duke

1. W. Duke to G. W. S., April 22, 1903, B. N. Duke letterbook. Many similar examples could be cited.

2. Bruce R. Payne, president of George Peabody College for Teachers, in *Peabody Alumni News*, April 1, 1927; copy in William P. Few MSS, Duke University Archives.

in New York: "Uncle Wash says please get a B. Flat (with C attachment) cornet for Main Street Church and send it on. Says 'tell Ben to get it and make Buck and Jack Cobb pay for it.' "[3]

Next to being a Methodist, Washington Duke prided himself on being a Republican, even though that was neither an easy nor a popular thing to be in his time and place. As early as 1868, when the party that advertised itself as having "saved the Union and freed the slaves" first formally appeared in North Carolina, Washington Duke cast his lot with the Republicans. In the fall of that year when Ulysses S. Grant won the presidency and the Republicans led by W. W. Holden captured full control of North Carolina, Washington Duke served as the registrar of voters in Durham precinct.[4] He and his sons later grew to champion warmly the Hamiltonian economic policies of the Republicans. The initial inspiration for Washington Duke to join the party, however, probably lay in the belief, which was long held by more than a few Southerners, that the Southern Democrats had been primarily responsible for the tragedy of secession and Civil War. A young lawyer in Durham in the 1890's later recalled his almost weekly visits from Washington Duke: "The stout old gentleman, with shaven upper lip and short-cropped beard on his ample chin and face, wearing a stiff hat, about such as Oliver Cromwell would have worn, and dressed in a plain, untailored dark suit, would slowly enter my office and quietly sit and tell of his scant young days and of the folly of the old secession leaders, who had brought on the Civil War."[5]

Speaking with the young lawyer of events leading to the Civil War, Washington Duke recalled a speech by Samuel F. Phillips, a Tarheel who later served as Solicitor General under President Grant. The speech, delivered a few weeks before the first shots at Fort Sumter and while North Carolina yet refused to secede, impressed Duke as about the greatest one he had ever heard. " 'Abide in the ship! Abide in the ship!' was the substance of Phillips' speech," Washington Duke remembered, and he added: "What a pity we did not take his advice."[6]

3. J. E. Stagg to B. N. Duke, February 17, 1902, B. N. Duke letterbook.

4. "Registry of Voters in the Durham Election Precinct, County of Orange, N.C., Nov. 3, 1868," in N.C. Durham County Papers, MSS Dept., Duke University Library.

5. Robert W. Winston, *It's A Far Cry* (New York, 1937), pp. 224–225.

6. *Ibid.*, p. 255. As late as 1956 a filling-station attendant in Durham mentioned that he would not vote for the presidential candidate of the "Democratic war-party."

The majority of white North Carolinians did not, of course, agree with Washington Duke about the political parties and their respective roles in the Civil War and Reconstruction. Yet he never faltered in his loyalty to the Republican party at all levels, from the county and precinct to the nation. Ben Duke's father-in-law, "Squire" Malbourne A. Angier, was a prominent Democrat who served for a number of years as mayor of Durham, and informal but hot political debates between him and Washington Duke were regular entertainments for those Durhamites who were fortunate enough to catch them.[7] After one of Grover Cleveland's presidential victories, a Democratic farmer and friend of Washington Duke's was driving through the streets of Durham a wagon loaded with firewood for sale at $2.75 a cord. Spying Washington Duke, the staunch Democrat yelled gleefully, "Oh, yes, Uncle Wash, oh, yes, we've beat you, Uncle Wash, we've elected our man Cleveland." Washington Duke replied, in his slow, dry manner, "So you have, Sam. And four years from now you'll still be hauling wood to town at $2.75 a cord."[8]

Durham's Republicans occasionally gained control of both county and city governments before the Democrats disfranchised Negro voters in 1900, but Republican presidential victories were a more frequent source of satisfaction to Washington Duke and his political allies. When William McKinley won reelection to the presidency in 1900, an old Durham friend of Washington Duke's who had been moved to the New York office of the American Tobacco Company wrote jubilantly: "It is needless for me to tell you that the people around this office, including the head of this Company, are simply delighted, and as I stated to a friend today, who asked me how Mr. [J. B.] Duke liked the election, I said to him that if he could have seen him on Wednesday morning no questions along this line would have been necessary, as his countenance was as bright as an electric light of a thousand horse power." The friend confidently believed that "a company like ours, managed by the wise heads that are looking after its interests and financeering [sic], under a Government handled

---

When pressed, he explained that he had grown up in Western North Carolina and that he was referring not to World Wars I and II or the Korean War but, as his father and grandfather had taught him, to the Civil War.

7. Josephus Daniels, *Tar Heel Editor* (Chapel Hill, 1939), p. 479.
8. Winston, *It's A Far Cry*, p. 224.

by the present Administration, will soon have the 'world by the tail with a down hill pull on it.' " [9]

Although Washington Duke shared in the satisfaction of his sons and his friend about McKinley's reelection, he seldom displayed in public strong emotions of either pleasure or pain. He was, in fact, sometimes lonely and even on occasion depressed as he entered the last decade of his life. He enjoyed the company of younger people, especially young women whom he would take for sedate buggy rides around Durham, and he paid frequent visits to one or two old friends in the tobacco factory and to W. A. Erwin at the textile mill. "The Old Gentleman drove by this morning with a pretty girl," Erwin informed Ben Duke. "I told him I had just had a letter from you, and he wanted to know when you were coming back [from New York], and what you were doing up there. . . . Guess you had better write, or have Angier write him a letter, giving account of yourself." [10]

Angier Duke did occasionally write his grandfather, as Ben Duke certainly did (though few of the letters survive) and as J. B. Duke did only rarely. Replying to one of young Angier's letters, Washington Duke mentioned that he had recently attended and enjoyed a barbecue that his old friend and physician, Dr. Albert G. Carr, had given for some young people. "I have gone out driving several afternoons recently with young ladies," the seventy-five-year-old grandfather added, "and had a fine time." [11]

Washington Duke did not always maintain this brave front. To one of his kinsmen in Tennessee who faced the loss of his farm, Washington Duke in 1897 sounded a note that recurred in a number of his letters: "I am feeble and worried over everything, and not in a condition to say much or do much for you." Sending a check to another relative, this one in Missouri, who had appealed for aid, he declared: "I am getting old—too feeble to pay any attention to business—and there are a great many demands made on me by my relatives and others for money. I have already given very largely, and my days of usefulness are about over." [12]

Despite these sad moments of self-pity, Washington Duke still

9. W. L. Walker to W. Duke, November 10, 1900, W. Duke MSS.

10. Erwin to B. N. Duke, May 21, 1898, B. N. Duke MSS. For the almost daily visits to the tobacco factory, see C. A. Jordan to W. Duke, February 17, 1902, W. Duke MSS.

11. W. Duke to "My dear little Angier," June 29, 1896, B. N. Duke letterbook.

12. W. Duke to J. M. Duke, September 16, 1897; W. Duke to Mrs. Luena Price, September 23, 1897, B. N. Duke letterbook.

found pleasure in life even as he approached eighty. Reporting on a cakewalking contest in Durham around the turn of the century, a local newspaper noted that there "was some graceful walking and there was much that wouldn't be called graceful." As the lively music played on, two couples were soon clearly in the lead for first prize, and when Washington Duke and his lady edged out Julian S. Carr and his by a vote of sixty-six to sixty-five, the old Republican gentleman no doubt quietly relished his besting of the prominent Democrat.[13]

More serious satisfaction came to Washington Duke from the frequent and warm tributes paid to him by his friends among the black community. Many of these accolades took the shape of formal resolutions of thanks from various Negro churches and schools, but Washington Duke may have gained even greater pleasure from knowing that his own policy of friendly assistance to blacks occasionally had a pebble-in-the-pond effect. One of his longtime friends who had moved from the Durham branch of the American Tobacco Company to work for the American Cigar Company in Petersburg, Virginia, wrote to Washington Duke about an experiment in the new factory there: "Heretofore, Negroes have been allowed to work only in the dirty parts of tobacco factories, such as stemming &c, but our new factory expects to work them altogether. Petersburg is a great place for Negroes, and there are quite a lot of intelligent respectable ones who will not work in tobacco factories, and it is that class we expect to use in the cigar factory. I have interested a number of well to do Negroes like your [John] Merrick & [R. B.] Fitzgerald in the scheme, and they have promised to furnish us all the labor we need. I guess we'll get a lot of cussing from the 'Nigger haters' all around here, but we are not bothering ourselves about that."[14]

Knowing that he had done, or tried to do, some good in the world undoubtedly consoled Washington Duke as bouts of depression occasionally seized upon him in his last years. Clearly one source of mingled joy and hurt was his close relationship to his three sons. Ben Duke, in many ways, shouldered what portion he could of his father's responsibilities and worries. Yet Ben Duke was frequently in New York on business in the 1890's, and in 1901, while still maintaining and often occupying his home in Durham, he purchased a house in New York and moved his family there. His wife was less enthusiastic than his children about the move, but Ben Duke wished to be closer

13. Clipping dated June 19 [1900?], in Scrapbook, B. N. Duke MSS, 1966 addition.
14. C. A. Jordan to W. Duke, October 2, 1902, W. Duke MSS.

to his brother as well as to the financial and business hub of the nation. He also resented deeply the terroristic and racist tactics which the Tarheel Democrats had employed so successfully against the Republicans and Populists in 1898 and 1900. Accordingly, he delayed for about a decade building the new home in Durham about which he began talking in the late 1890's and moved to New York instead. "Uncle Wash rec[eiv]d photo of you in your N.Y. office," Stagg wrote Ben Duke, "and it pleased him very much. Has been laughing and showing it all around."[15]

Laugh though he did, Washington Duke clearly felt the partial loss of his second son to the great metropolis. James B. Duke had moved there in the mid-1880's, and while he made regular visits to see his father, Washington Duke frequently longed to see more of his youngest son. As Christmas of 1896 approached he wrote a special appeal to J. B. Duke: "My birthday is on the 20th of this month [December], your's is on the 23rd. I think it will be a very fitting thing for you to come home in time to celebrate both birthdays with me, and Christmas also. I think I would like to tell you something about your birth, and talk over the old ups and downs which have come along since that time. I am here trying to wear away the time. Sometimes, I go around among the young women, but it does not amount to much. Sometimes the time hangs mighty heavy. We are all well, and if you can find it convenient to come, I hope you will. Your affectionate father. . . ."[16]

James B. Duke most probably acceded to the request and went to Durham. He usually did when thus summoned; all who knew him well have left evidence about his great love and respect for his father. Washington Duke's feelings toward his youngest son were a bit more complicated. Though he had long recognized and admired James B. Duke's remarkable talent for business, there is evidence, in addition to a well-known tradition, that Washington Duke never fully understood—nor perhaps totally approved—all the complexities of J. B. Duke's maneuvers in building the tobacco empire. According to an oft-told story that may be true, Washington Duke once remarked: "There are three things I never could understand: electricity, the Holy Ghost, and my son Buck."[17]

15. J. E. Stagg to Ben Duke, November 25, 1901, B. N. Duke letterbook.
16. W. Duke to J. B. Duke, December 9, 1896, copy in the Mary L. D. Biddle portion of the Semans Family Papers.
17. Josephus Daniels, *Tar Heel Editor*, p. 471, relates this story as do many other accounts.

158

Washington Duke's failure to comprehend all the complexities involved in building the vast tobacco combination is understandable. Remaining in North Carolina and in close touch with popular sentiment there, he was also puzzled and worried about the storm of criticism against the "tobacco trust." J. B. Duke repeatedly and vehemently insisted that the American Tobacco Company was not responsible for the low prices which farmers received for leaf tobacco, a charge which inspired a major part of the agrarian attack on the company. Historians have subsequently agreed in large part with J. B. Duke on the matter of leaf tobacco prices, but Washington Duke could not know that history would at least partially vindicate his son. When newspapers, especially those that were pro-silver and Democratic, angrily and continually accused the American Tobacco Company of robbing and oppressing the poor tobacco farmers, Washington Duke winced and worried, even though the prices of cotton and most other farm commodities were even lower than the price of tobacco.[18]

Josephus Daniels, editor first of the Raleigh *State Chronicle* and then of the Raleigh *News and Observer*, specialized from an early date in flamboyant attacks on the American Tobacco Company and its alleged robbery of the farmers. When Washington Duke, who was in Raleigh on a Sunday-school picnic, stopped by to cancel his subscription to Daniel's paper because he felt that it was "always abusing" him, the editor invited the old gentleman into the inner office for a private conversation. After Daniels had made a lengthy presentation of his case against the American Tobacco Company, Washington Duke, according to Daniels' memory at a much later date, made a confession: "I am just talking to you now; I don't want you to say anything about this. I wish Buck had never put us into the [American Tobacco] company and that we could carry on our business like we used to do it. We were making lots of money and did not have any criticism."[19]

Although Washington Duke probably did feel anxiety about the charges against the American Tobacco Company, he was, at the same time, quite proud and fond of his youngest son, who worried not at all about what a later generation would refer to as his "public image."

18. The most important study concerning the relationship between leaf-tobacco prices and the American Tobacco Company is Tilley, *Bright-Tobacco Industry*, esp. pp. 251–308, 386–387. See also Tennant, *American Cigarette Industry*, pp. 53–54.

19. Daniels, *Tar Heel Editor*, p. 47.

The relationship of Washington and J. B. Duke was, in short, richly mixed and all too humanly complicated. This same relationship prevailed even in greater degree between Washington Duke and his oldest son, Brodie Duke.

Remaining in Durham all of his life save for frequent visits to New York and other cities, Brodie Duke was more gregarious than either of his half-brothers. This sociability was also his undoing, for "drinking with the boys" marred his life. Nevertheless, Brodie Duke visited his father regularly and after one visit Brodie Duke reported to Ben Duke: "I was in to see Pa yesterday evening. He said he had not been feeling so well yesterday, but I told him I thought it was the same old grunt and insisted upon his taking more outdoor exercise."[20]

If the oldest son cheered and entertained his aging father on occasion, Brodie Duke also caused certain embarrassment and worry. A Methodist evangelist holding a revival meeting in Durham in the late 1890's sought Washington Duke's support as well as his permission to hold prayer meetings in the tobacco factory during the noon hour. "Let us pray very earnestly for Brodie," the insensitive clergyman added. "I used to know him before I became a Christian. . . ."[21]

The clergyman was perhaps pharisaical, but Brodie Duke did have a peculiar talent for trouble. His son Lawrence Duke, when grown, frequently turned to Washington Duke or Ben Duke for advice and assistance, and on one occasion wrote, "I went up to see papa on business but I found out it was useless[;] he was too much taken up in 3 ave [bonds?] & selling August cotton."[22] When Brodie Duke's second wife, whom he had married in 1890 after the death of his first wife and by whom he had had a son, divorced him in 1904, Washington Duke was undoubtedly distressed, for divorce was rare and not regarded lightly in his nineteenth-century, Methodist world. Thus it was that as Washington Duke began to distribute a significant portion of his wealth to his children and other relatives around 1900, he carefully put Brodie Duke's share in trust in a New York bank. J. E. Stagg explained to Lawrence Duke that those securities in trust were expected to yield an income of about $28,000 per year, half of which would go to Brodie Duke during his lifetime and the other half to his four children; then after his death all the income would go to the children in

20. B. L. Duke to B. N. Duke, May 5, 1904, B. N. Duke MSS.
21. W. P. Fife to W. Duke, May 5, 1897, W. Duke MSS.
22. Lawrence Duke to Washington Duke, March 1, 1900, W. Duke MSS.

equal proportions until they reached specified ages when they were to receive the principal.[23]

Having disposed of much of his personal fortune and drawn his will, Washington Duke probably felt that he was approaching the end of what had been a long, long furrow. "The Governor is about as you left him," J. E. Stagg informed Ben Duke in September, 1904. "Asks frequently if anything has been heard from Ben & Buck." Then a few days later Stagg notified Ben Duke that his father wanted "you and Buck to come and spend a few days with him."[24]

The sons promptly went to Durham, and the probable consequences of the visit were indeed unfortunate. No doubt Washington Duke as well as his sons believed that his death was approaching. Only circumstantial evidence exists to prove the point, but it appears that the aged father had somehow heard rumors about his youngest son's long-standing relationship with Mrs. Lillian McCredy and that Washington Duke in September, 1904, exacted a promise that his son would marry her. It also appears quite likely that James B. Duke, for instinctive reasons perhaps, had not actually wished to marry Mrs. McCredy, whom he had known well for a number of years. Yet he did marry her, in a quiet ceremony in the home of Mrs. McCredy's aunt in Camden, New Jersey, on November 29, 1904.[25]

Washington Duke was spared the knowledge of how grim a mistake his forty-eight-year-old son had made, for the headline-making divorce case broke after the patriarch of the family had died. Before that death, however, Brodie Duke also stumbled into what was the most distressing episode of his life, and it may have been partly triggerred, at least psychologically, by J. B. Duke's marriage. Despite the popular attacks on the "tobacco trust," J. B. Duke by the turn of the century had become one of the swashbuckling giants of the American business world. These powerful millionaires, especially of the so-called "self-made" variety from humble origins, were as much folk heroes for some Americans as they were economic villains for others. Whereas Brodie Duke's independent business career had included some spectacular failures, especially in 1893, J. B. Duke from teenage on had displayed an uncanny ability to succeed on a large scale. Just what rueful,

23. J. E. Stagg to B. N. Duke, December 11, 1900; J. E. Stagg to Lawrence Duke, February 12, 1901, B. N. Duke letterbook.

24. Stagg to B. N. Duke, September 10, 15, 1904, B. N. Duke letterbook.

25. *New York Times*, November 30, 1904.

possibly amused thoughts the oldest son entertained about the marriage of the fair-haired youngest son to Mrs. McCredy may only be imagined. What is hard fact, however, is that a few days after J. B. Duke's wedding, Brodie Duke launched a marathon spree in a disreputable hotel in New York. After the gaiety had continued for two weeks or so, Brodie Duke and one Alice Webb, a woman of dubious reputation who had shared in Brodie Duke's extended party, appeared at the Madison Square Presbyterian Church on December 19, 1904, and were married by an assistant pastor.

Upon learning of the marriage and the spectacular prenuptial events, which included Brodie Duke's having signed several promissory notes to Alice Webb, Ben Duke summoned Brodie Duke's son, Lawrence, put private detectives and lawyers on the case, and the family obtained a warrant for Brodie Duke's commitment to a sanitarium on the ground that he was mentally irresponsible at the time because of intoxication. Brodie Duke eventually obtained his release on a writ of habeas corpus, again put his property under the control of trustees, and successfully sued for divorce. He argued that he had no recollection at all of the marriage and, moreover, that his wife had been unfaithful to him after that event.[26]

As Brodie Duke writhed through this most lurid escapade of his life and as James B. Duke and his bride took a honeymoon trip to Europe, Washington Duke suffered an accident that eventually led to his death. Late in January, 1905, he fell in his home and broke his hip. After cabling J. B. Duke in England, who promptly sailed for America, Ben Duke rushed to Durham, where J. B. Duke and his wife followed upon landing in New York. A physically strong man for most of his long life, Washington Duke rallied in the early spring and then died on May 8, 1905, at the age of eighty-four. A few months before his fall, he and John C. Kilgo had had a long, quiet talk about death, and Washington Duke had declared in conclusion, "The only thing that makes me hate to die is I do not want to leave the boys."[27]

Prior to the funeral, a reporter walking through the crowded, flower-filled rooms of "Fairview," Washington Duke's home, noted Brodie Duke "sitting on the staircase, out of the crush and watching

26. The story may be followed in the *New York Times*, January–June, 1905; Winkler, *Tobacco Tycoon*, pp. 187–189, also has details.

27. Kilgo's memorial address at Trinity College, June 4, 1905, as quoted in Mason Crum, "The Life and Times of Washington Duke," unpublished manuscript in the Mason Crum Papers, Duke University Archives.

the people file into the room where the casket lay." The newsman added: "He looked small and frail and pitiful, this son that the old man loved. . . ."[28]

Although Washington Duke had disposed of the bulk of his estate prior to his death, in his will he left money not only to his children, grandchildren, nieces, and nephews but to several institutions and causes in which he had long been interested. The two conferences of the Methodist Church in North Carolina received $10,000 each, half for the home-mission work and half for the "worn-out preachers" and their families for whom he had so long been solicitous. The two conferences in North Carolina of the African Methodist church also received $2,500 each. A benefaction of $3,000 went to the Watts Hospital in Durham, a similar amount to the Oxford orphanage and the Methodist orphanage in Raleigh, and $5,000 was left to the Kittrell Institute (later Kittrell College).[29] The benefactions made in Washington Duke's will, in addition to his gift of nearly a half million dollars to Trinity College at various intervals during his lifetime, not only recapitulated the dominant pattern of the family's philanthropy from the late 1880's on but also foreshadowed the pattern of the much larger giving that would be done by B. N. Duke and J. B. Duke in the twentieth century.

As one would expect, suggestions for memorializing Washington Duke by naming this or that institution or proposed building after him poured in to the family after his death. None of the proposals was accepted. But when the Main Street Methodist Church, which had outgrown its original building, set out to build a much larger new edifice in 1907, B. N. Duke and J. B. Duke gave a large proportion of the cost for what was initially called Memorial Church, in honor of Washington Duke, and which became Duke Memorial Church in 1925.[30]

28. Raleigh *News and Observer*, May 11, 1905.

29. Copy of will in B. N. Duke MSS, 1966 addition, legal papers; clippings of "Newspaper Tributes," scrapbook in the Washington Duke MSS.

30. For the initial naming of the Memorial Church, which was B. N. Duke's choice, see J. E. Stagg to B. N. Duke, October 12, 1907, and R. B. Arrington to Stagg, October 16, 1907, B. N. Duke MSS and letterbook. For the change to Duke Memorial Church, see W. P. Few to B. N. Duke, July 11, November 24, 1925, Few MSS. The church, which still stands on the northwest corner of Chapel Hill and Duke streets and is one of Durham's increasingly scarce "old" buildings, was and is remarkable for its architectural ungainliness. When it was finally completed in 1914, the candid minister wrote B. N. Duke: "The interior of the Church is very wonderful to me. I do not particularly admire the exterior but the auditorium atones for all. I know of

To honor Washington Duke on the campus of Trinity College, which also had attracted vital support from him because of its Methodist connection, friends of his contributed the money for a statue. T. J. Walker and A. T. Ragland, two tobacco men who had been transferred from Durham to Richmond, successfully sought modest contributions from a large number of donors rather than big gifts from only a few, as they explained to George Watts. With President Kilgo's approval, Walker and Ragland commissioned a famous sculptor in Richmond, Edward V. Valentine, to execute an unusual representation of Washington Duke seated in an armchair. When the bronze statue was completed, mounted on its pedestal, and dedicated in 1908, W. W. Fuller declared that its likeness to Washington Duke was "striking and strong."[31]

Reposeful the statue of Washington Duke may have been, but the old gentleman himself would have been agitated and heartbroken if he had lived to witness his youngest son go through the ordeal of the sensational divorce case that began in September, 1905. J. B. Duke, as suggested earlier, may never have wanted to marry Mrs. McCredy. After his father's death the newlyweds began to quarrel bitterly because of Mrs. Duke's aversion to residence at Duke's Farm. Then in the summer of 1905 J. B. Duke learned that his wife was secretly in communication with another man. After consulting his lawyers and arranging for surveillance of Mrs. Duke by private detectives as well as by one or two executives in the American Tobacco Company, Duke arranged to be summoned to London on business. During his absence, abundant and incontrovertible evidence of Mrs. Duke's close association with an aging man-about-town, one Frank T. Huntoon, was gathered by the detectives and Caleb C. Dula, a vice-president of the tobacco company. As a result, in September, 1905, Duke sued for divorce on the ground of his wife's alleged adultery.

The bitter contest that followed provided abundant grist for the mills of the sensation-mongering newspapers of the period. In addition to much testimony from servants and the private detectives, the evidence against Mrs. Duke included telegrams as well as "personals"

---

nothing in New York City to equal it for the sweep of its arches and for simplicity combined with beauty." L. P. Howard to B. N. Duke, February 16, 1914, B. N. Duke MSS.

31. Correspondence from and to T. J. Walker and A. T. Ragland, November–December, 1905, January and March 1906, in the John C. Kilgo MSS, Duke University Archives; W. W. Fuller to T. J. Walker, February 26, 1908, *ibid.*

that Huntoon placed in the advertising columns of the New York and Paris editions of the New York *Herald* as messages to Mrs. Duke during her honeymoon trip to Europe. "Oh, memories that bless and burn!" one of these strange advertisements proclaimed. "This separation is killing. Please don't wear low-necked dresses. Shall enjoy your house until Octopus [J. B. Duke] returns, when that pleasure shall cease."[32]

The New Jersey court found the evidence against Mrs. Duke overwhelming and granted James B. Duke a divorce in May, 1906. Since the trial brought out the fact that he had given his wife, over the period of their acquaintance, some $250,000 in securities and other property, there was no financial settlement. Though the first Mrs. James B. Duke tried unsuccessfully to press her claims at various later times, the subject was, understandably, one that J. B. Duke did his best to forget. Those around him did likewise. When his close associates of the last period of his life, George G. Allen and William R. Perkins, arranged for a Tarheel-born newspaperman, John Wilber Jenkins, to write the first biography of J. B. Duke, which was published after the subject's death, it contained only one terse paragraph concerning the disastrous first marriage.[33]

Trouble came to the Dukes not only in the form of the marital misadventures of Brodie and James B. Duke but also from the federal government. In 1907 the federal courts found a subsidiary of the American Tobacco Company, one that had a near-monopoly on licorice paste, guilty of violating the Sherman Anti-Trust Act. Then in 1908 there began the legal action which the leaders of the American Tobacco Company had feared at least since the Northern Securities case of 1904. The Department of Justice, increasingly zealous about the antitrust law of 1890, moved directly against the gigantic American Tobacco Company in the Circuit Court for the Southern District of New York. In a suit in equity against twenty-nine individuals and sixty-five corporations, the government sought either to force the dissolution of the tobacco combination or to enjoin it from operating in interstate commerce.[34]

Like J. P. Morgan in 1904, J. B Duke was no doubt outraged and appalled by the government's move against the American Tobacco

32. *New York Times*, September, 1905–May, 1906; New York *American*, December 19, 22, 1905; April 24, 27, May 4, 1906. The quotation is from Winkler, *Tobacco Tycoon*, p. 177.

33. Jenkins, *J. B. Duke, Master Builder*, p. 199.

34. Tennant, *American Cigarette Industry*, p. 59.

Company. Yet there is evidence, too, that some of the deep satisfaction he had earlier found in putting together the vast combination and rationalizing various facets of the industry had waned after most of the competitive contests had been won by him and his associates. Testifying in the antitrust suit early in 1908, Duke insisted, not too convincingly, that the continuous program of expansion on which the American Tobacco Company had embarked after its beginning in 1890 had been motivated by both prudence and a desire for additional profitable investments rather than by any idea on his part of eliminating or lessening competition. When asked why the company had wanted to make every variety of tobacco product, Duke replied "because after one style went out of fashion we would have another style ready for the public to take up. . . ."[35]

As for his company's alleged desire to swallow or destroy all potential rivals, Duke maintained, "I never bought any business with the idea of eliminating competition; it was always [with] the idea of an investment. . . ." He admitted, however, that the case of the Union Tobacco Company in 1899 had been special because, as he put it, "we had an idea for instance of getting in with ourselves a lot of rich financial people to help finance our properties."[36] Pressed about his company's secret purchase around 1903 of several formerly independent tobacco companies, Duke gave this answer: "Our crowd had about all they could handle and we concluded that the best way would be . . . to let them [the secretly purchased companies] continue an interest in it and they would manage it." Duke argued that he and his associates had "wanted them to push and drive hard against us." In fact, he admitted in a significant statement that "one of the mistakes the American Tobacco Company made in the beginning [was] that we didn't keep a separate organization for all of the principal businesses we bought." The company would have gotten "better service and better management," Duke believed, and "we would have had competition and would have built and extended the business."[37]

When queried about the alleged advantages of competition, Duke insisted that businesses not only grew more in such competitive circumstances but also made more money. "I know it in the case of the cigarette business," Duke continued, "because when we had so nearly all of it, [business] was cut in half in four or five years and as soon as

35. Circuit Court MSS, vol. V, p. 3296.
36. *Ibid.*, p. 3357.
37. *Ibid.*, pp. 3392–3393.

we had competitors we built it up again." There were plenty of Americans who consumed no tobacco products, Duke pointed out. "If there is enough [advertising] work put back of them we will make them all consumers."[38]

Duke's own testimony about the economic advantages of competition contrasted glaringly with one gigantic and incontrovertible fact: by 1906, on the eve of the federal government's legal action against the Duke-led companies, the tobacco combination controlled approximately four-fifths of the production in all lines of tobacco except cigars.[39] After voluminous testimony and the presentation of a veritable mountain of documentary evidence, the federal court, in a three-to-one decision, found the American Tobacco Company guilty of violating the antitrust law but exempted the United Cigar Stores, the Imperial Tobacco Company, and the British-American Tobacco Company. Except for those three companies, the other parts of Duke's vast combination were prohibited from engaging in interstate trade "until conditions existing before the illegal contracts or combination were entered into are restored."[40]

Both the federal government and the tobacco company appealed the ruling, and in May, 1911, the Supreme Court of the United States rendered a landmark decision of great importance. It ruled not only that the three companies excluded by the Circuit Court fell within the ban of the Sherman law but also that the tobacco combination had to be dissolved. Holding that the enforcement of an injunction against operation in interstate trade or the appointment of a receiver would be too prejudicial to the interests of both the stockholders and the American public in general, the Supreme Court declared:

> 1st. That the combination in and of itself, as well as each and all of the elements composing it, whether corporate or individual, whether considered collectively or separately, be decreed to be in restraint of trade and an attempt to monopolize and a monopolization within the first and second sections of the Anti-trust Act.
>
> 2nd. That the [Circuit] court below, in order to give effective force to our decree in this regard, be directed to hear the parties, by evidence or otherwise, as it may be deemed proper, for the

38. *Ibid.*, pp. 3397–3399, 3410.
39. A more detailed breakdown may be found in Bureau of Corporations, *Report on the Tobacco Industry*, pt. I, 28.
40. *United States* v. *American Tobacco Co.*, 164 F. 700, 704 (1908), as quoted in Tennant, *American Cigarette Industry*, p. 59.

purpose of ascertaining and determining upon some plan or method of dissolving the combination and of recreating, out of the elements now composing it, a new condition which shall be honestly in harmony with and not repugnant to the law.[41]

The man who more than any other single person had put together the combination turned out to be the principal unscrambler of the eggs. During months of incessant labor, James B. Duke and his lawyers hammered out a plan of dissolution which, with modifications urged by Attorney General George W. Wickersham, was approved by the court and issued as a decree on November 16, 1911. Beyond the severance of the more autonomous parts of the tobacco empire from the control of the American Tobacco Company, the business of that company itself and its closely related subsidiaries was divided into three major parts—the American Tobacco Company, a reorganized Liggett and Myers Tobacco Company, and a reorganized P. Lorillard Company.[42] Those three firms plus the R. J. Reynolds Tobacco Company were destined to dominate the domestic tobacco industry in the years ahead, and, in the terms of the economists, a monopolistic situation had been replaced by an oligopolistic one. Although, except for the British-American Tobacco Company, James B. Duke ended his personal involvement with the tobacco industry after 1911, his remarks in 1908 about the growth that could result from competition proved completely correct, for the American tobacco industry, especially that part of it involving cigarettes, grew enormously in the years after the dissolution of the combination. While the British-American Tobacco Company, with its headquarters in London, continued to involve and hold the interest of James B. Duke, after 1911 he more than ever turned to the electric power industry in the Carolinas and, for a while, in Canada.

By the time the Supreme Court ruled against the tobacco combination, both B. N. Duke and J. B. Duke had acquired splendid mansions on that part of New York's Fifth Avenue which around the turn of the century gained worldwide fame as "Millionaires' Row." J. B. Duke became a New Yorker long before his older brother became even a part-time one, but it was B. N. Duke and his family who led the way on to the Fifth Avenue scene.

In the spring of 1901 a realtor tried to sell Ben Duke a home over-

41. *United States* v. *American Tobacco Company*, 221 U. S. 186 (1911), as quoted in *ibid.*
42. Tennant, *American Cigarette Industry*, pp. 60–61.

looking the Hudson river on Riverside Drive. Arguing that Riverside Drive was the only street in New York that was "restricted to private carriages," the realtor insisted that it was one of the "most desirable locations" in New York for a person who disliked "5th Ave. with its noise, crowds—dirt & dust—and trucks."[43] Fifth Avenue may have been noisy and dusty, as the realtor suggested, but it was crowded with rich people, some of them wealthy for a few generations—like the Astors—and therefore self-styled "aristocrats," and some of them more recently grown rich—like the Vanderbilts—and pushing and spending their way into Society. At any rate, the extremely wealthy together with many more modestly well-to-do descendants of colonial New York families were building cheek-by-jowl on Fifth Avenue, which, north of 28th Street, then consisted mainly of residences and hotels. A few of the ornate mansions were faithful replicas of famous chateaux or palaces in France or Italy, but most were hybrid affairs that borrowed and mixed features from Versailles, Venetian or Florentine *palazzi*, and English castles and manor houses. One critic described the Renaissance, medieval, Byzantine and other types of mansions as "palatial plagiarisms."[44]

Neither Ben Duke nor J. B. Duke, fortunately for their reputations, took this ostentatious Society too seriously. Moreover, their Fifth Avenue homes were, in comparison with many of the mansions of the period, models of restraint and taste. Ben Duke purchased a residence at 1009 Fifth Avenue which faced on East 82nd Street and was directly across the avenue from the Metropolitan Museum of Art. Though he subsequently made extensive alterations and renovations in the handsome dwelling, which still stands in 1974, the house was not originally in the class of the great mansions, such as those built by Henry Clay Frick or Andrew Carnegie. Immediately after purchasing the house and before making any changes or installing furniture, Ben Duke considered insuring it for $150,000 and then lowered the figure to $75,000.[45]

Though Ben Duke apparently intended all along to build new residences both in Durham and on Fifth Avenue, he took his time about it. In the interval, he and his family enjoyed various aspects of life in New York, especially its theater and opera. Though he con-

43. V. S. Woolley to B. N. Duke, March 8, 1901, B. N. Duke MSS.

44. Allen Churchill, *The Upper Crust: An Informal History of New York's Highest Society* (Englewood Cliffs, N.J., 1970), pp. 141–143.

45. B. N. Duke to Mr. Harris, June 15, 18, 1901, B. N. Duke letterbook.

sidered disposing of his house at 1009 Fifth Avenue for $450,000 after various alterations had been made, he did not sell, and when J. B. Duke's first marriage fell apart, he made his home with his older brother's family.

The B. N. Dukes, in fact, rescued James B. Duke from the gloom and spell of sickness into which his divorce threw him. B. N. Duke himself was anguished by the affair, and his daughter's voice teacher, a Frenchman who became a close friend of the family's, offered this consolation: "I quite understand you there [about your brother's troubles] & sympathise with your Christian feelings about the matter & socially too. But [the] American public is always prepared to [accept] such scandals. Sloans and Vanderbilts had their own. Don't fret, your brother's reputation is unscathed in this whole matter & all good men must sympathise with him."[46]

Ben Duke and his wife, the sensible and sociable "Miss Sally" as she was known to her intimates in North Carolina, did another important favor for J. B. Duke when they introduced him to the woman who became his second wife and the mother of his only child. Though the Ben Dukes began around 1902 to pay brief visits in the summer to Newport, Rhode Island, they preferred such Southern resorts as Lake Toxaway in the mountains of North Carolina. There they met in 1906 a strikingly handsome and dignified widow, Mrs. Walker P. Inman, who had lived in Atlanta with her late husband and son but who was born Nanaline Holt in Macon, Georgia, in 1871. Although Mrs. Inman, like so many Southerners after the Civil War, had known genteel poverty in her youth, her first husband had left her with a modest competence, and she frequently travelled to New York and to such resorts as Lake Toxaway.[47]

Struck by the beauty and poise of Mrs. Inman, Ben Duke saw to it that his brother soon met her, and Mrs. Inman and her mother took up residence in a New York hotel. Ben Duke also may have had something to do with the fact that the publisher of *Town Topics*, the gossip sheet of New York's wealthy Society, instructed his staff to be "careful of anything said about Mrs. Inman of Atlanta." There was to be "nothing unpleasant."[48]

James B. Duke married Mrs. Inman in a quiet, private ceremony

46. M. Gaspard in Paris to B. N. Duke, October 26, 1905, *ibid*.
47. Winkler, *Tobacco Tycoon*, pp. 208–209.
48. As quoted in Dixon Wecter, *The Saga of American Society* (New York, 1937), p. 375.

on July 23, 1907. At the same time, Ben Duke, preparing to build his new homes in New York and Durham, turned over the house at 1009 Fifth Avenue to the J. B. Dukes, and a new era began for the man who built the tobacco empire. Though J. B. Duke never really cared for the social pattern that was an inevitable part of life on Fifth Avenue, Mrs. Duke enjoyed many aspects of New York; she apparently preferred it, in fact, to Duke's Farm or to any place in the South. For her, therefore, J. B. Duke acquired a lot on the northeast corner of Fifth Avenue and 78th Street and commissioned Horace Trumbauer, a famous architect of Philadelphia, to draw plans. Trumbauer's firm had designed outstanding residences for the Wideners, Elkinses, and Stotesburys in Philadelphia as well as numerous important public buildings there and elsewhere in the country. For James B. Duke, Trumbauer's staff came up with an elegantly restrained mansion in white marble which was built in 1909–10.[49]

Perhaps because Ben Duke was building two new homes, one on Fifth Avenue and one in Durham, he operated on a less grand scale than his brother. His new dwelling on Fifth Avenue and East 89th Street, which was built about the same time as J. B. Duke's home, cost around $341,000 to construct. In Durham, "Four Acres," which was diagonally across the street from Memorial Methodist Church and on the site where Ben Duke's previous residence stood, cost $136,000 to build. With handsomely landscaped grounds, "Four Acres" stood for about a half century as one of Durham's finest homes.[50]

In addition to mansions on Fifth Avenue there came other new developments for the Dukes. The Ben Dukes, and especially their daughter Mary, had begun to enjoy theater and opera in New York in the 1890's. Young Mary Duke, in fact, kept a "Theatre Record and Scrap Book" in the late 1890's, and she, accompanied by her brother

49. Richard B. Arrington to Horace Trumbauer, June 4, 16, October 9, 1909, J. B. Duke letterbook. Soon after J. B. Duke's death in 1925, the house was assessed at $1,600,000 and the furnishings at $600,000. In 1957 Mrs. Duke and Miss Doris Duke gave the house to the Institute of Fine Arts of New York University. *New York Times,* April 4, 1962.

50. Memorandum of August 29, 1911, about the New York house; R. B. Arrington to B. N. Duke, March 3, 1911, about "Four Acres," B. N. Duke MSS. After Mrs. B. N. Duke's death in 1936, her daughter gave "Four Acres" to Duke University, which used it as a guest house and reception center. In 1960 the university sold the property, and "Four Acres" was demolished; the North Carolina Mutual Life Insurance Company, one of the largest black-owned businesses in the nation, erected its headquarters building on the site. B. N. Duke's mansion on Fifth Avenue at 89th Street was sold and razed after his death and an apartment house built on the site.

or other members of the family, enjoyed "Faust" and "Il Trovatore" along with Maude Adams in "Romeo and Juliet" and Ada Rehan in "Merchant of Venice." About one "Parisian vaudeville-operatta," however, Mary Duke noted that "Miss [Marie] Dressler was very common but Mr. [Edwin] Foy was real funny."[51]

The "Diamond Horseshoe" of boxes in the Metropolitan Opera House, especially in the day of such singers as Enrico Caruso and Geraldine Farrar, was a far cry from Marie Dressler's operetta. Yet the B. N. Dukes in 1908 rented George Henry Warren's box on twenty Thursday evenings of one season for $2,000, and the J. B. Dukes paid $1,250 for "Mr. Belmont's box" on alternate Thursdays.[52] Renting a box and attending the opera were, of course, two different matters and whether J. B. Duke actually joined his beautiful wife for such occasions is not known. At any rate, he moved easily and confidently in those circles that did matter to him; on one occasion he sent 2,000 of the "best Havana cigars" to J. P. Morgan and on another John D. Rockefeller, Jr., invited him to visit the family's gardens on the estate at Pocantico Hills.[53]

For all their mansions, boxes at the Metropolitan Opera, and paintings by such British artists as Hoppner and Gainsborough, the Duke brothers may have had one true distinction among the residents of "Millionaires' Row": they regularly imported foodstuffs, especially freshly ground cornmeal, from Durham. Chicken and hams came up from the South, and on one occasion there was even a barrel of turnips.[54]

When they were in Durham, shipments to them from New York were of a quite different nature. The evidence suggests that neither B. N. Duke nor J. B. Duke drank much in the way of intoxicants, but they did like champagne, and Ben Duke enjoyed imported beer. Since North Carolinians were participating in a great prohibitionist crusade around 1908, B. N. Duke in Durham ordered from New York a case of "Pommery Sec [champagne]—vintage 1900," six bottles of

51. Scrapbook in B. N. Duke MSS, 1966 addition.
52. B. N. Duke to F. V. Dodd, July 22, 1908; R. B. Arrington to Dodd, July 29, 1908, B. N. Duke letterbook; Arrington to Dodd, October 28, 1909, J. B. Duke letterbook.
53. J. B. Duke to J. P. Morgan, June 22, 1908; J. B. Duke to J. D. Rockefeller, Jr., May 14, 1909, J. B. Duke letterbook.
54. R. B. Arrington to J. E. Stagg, May 18, 1909, J. B. Duke letterbook; B. N. Duke to I. A. Hogan, March 4, 1913, and E. A. Childs to Mrs. B. N. Duke, December 29, 1913, B. N. Duke letterbook.

gin, and two of dry vermouth—all to be sent in "plain packages (that is packages that will not show contents)."[55] When the brothers began around 1906 to rent private railway cars for their trips into North and South Carolina, usually in connection with the affairs of the electric power company, their secretary emphasized to the Pullman Company that "a liberal supply of champagne and cigars" would be required. To be sure that the eight persons in the party on one occasion had the beverages and smokes that they would want for the six-day trip, the secretary requested "two cases of Pommery Sec Pints, instead of one case, and *two* hundred and fifty Principe de Gales 'Sobranos' [cigars]. . . ."[56]

Seldom seen without his cigar, J. B. Duke at age fifty-seven took great pride and pleasure in becoming a father. On November 12, 1912, his wife gave birth to a daughter who was named Doris. Ben Duke gleefully telegraphed his wife in Durham: "I have a new niece this morning. Mother and child doing fine and father very happy."[57] Perhaps because he was of an age when many men become grandfathers, James B. Duke found a special, new satisfaction in his beautiful, fair-haired daughter. Preoccupied though he had been for so long with his business affairs, he actually possessed the same strong family feeling that Washington Duke and Ben Duke had always taken the time to cultivate and demonstrate. After the birth of his daughter, J. B. Duke too began to think of things other than his business affairs.

As J. B. Duke learned to play a father's role, B. N. Duke became a father-in-law. His son, Angier Buchanan Duke, more than any other member of the family perhaps, enjoyed the style of life that great wealth made possible in the years before the First World War. After graduating from Trinity College in 1905, Angier Duke briefly attended the same business school in Poughkeepsie, New York, where his uncle, J. B. Duke, had gone. Although helping to manage his father's affairs, Angier Duke felt no economic need to work. Dark, handsome, and amiable, he enjoyed life. The loss of his right hand in an accident with a gun late in 1905 did not prevent his becoming an early automobile enthusiast. Motor cars entered the family's life around 1905, and that summer Angier Duke, accompanied by his parents and sister,

55. R. B. Arrington to W. A. Taylor Company, March 28, 1908, B. N. Duke letterbook.
56. R. B. Arrington to J. C. Yager, September 26, 29, 1906, B. N. Duke letterbook.
57. November 22, 1912, B. N. Duke letterbook.

reported happily on one day's excursion of seventy-five miles in New England. Getting the car to Durham posed problems, however, because of road conditions; Angier Duke accordingly arranged to drive from New York to Charlottesville, Virginia, and to have the automobile shipped from there to Durham by train.[58]

One of the early cars owned by the Ben Dukes was a Pope, but late in 1905 he ordered from the Italian Fiat company a "24–32 H.P. car, fitted with a Demarest Limousine body, similar to the one built by Rothschild on Mr. J. B. Duke's 28 H.P. 'Mercedes'. . . ." Dark maroon and black in color, with red running gear and monogrammed panels, and other luxuries, the car cost $9,500.[59] A few years later the family had largely shifted to the British-made Rolls-Royce, and Angier Duke enjoyed a specially built five-seated "Torpedo-Phaeton" six-cylinder Rolls-Royce with "speed & brake levers . . . fitted in centre of front seat."[60]

Angier Duke joined a number of clubs, both in the city and in the suburban communities that had developed in Westchester County, New York, and in northern New Jersey. Although invited along with Harry L. Harkness, W. Vincent Astor, August Belmont, Jr., and others, to become a charter member of an "Auto-Polo Association," he declined.[61] Visiting the famous hot springs of western Virginia in the fall of 1913, Angier Duke made these arrangements with the family's executive secretary for his return trip northward: "I expect to leave here Thursday night for Philadelphia, and go from there to the Princeton-Harvard Foot Ball Game at Princeton. . . . I should like you to instruct Fox [the chauffeur] to bring the Rolls-Royce Limousine Car to Princeton, and be at the Princeton Inn not later than one o'clock on Saturday, as I am going to motor to the Rumson Country Club after the game that afternoon, and will want that car." Less than a year later he urged a friend to join him for a week at York Harbor, Maine, where he knew many people and where "some friends

58. A. B. Duke to R. B. Arrington, July 5, 1905; R. B. Arrington to J. E. Stagg, July 22, 1905, B. N. Duke MSS and letterbook.

59. C. H. Tangeman to B. N. Duke, December 18, 1905, *ibid.*

60. R. B. Arrington to Rolls-Royce Ltd., August 27, 1912, *ibid.* The cost was £1,191 or about $6,000. In 1915 Alex. H. Sands, who became the executive secretary after Arrington's death in 1913, reported to the Automobile Club, October 29, 1915, that J. B. Duke owned altogether four Rolls-Royce cars and a 1908 Hotchkiss, and that B. N. Duke owned four Rolls-Royces.

61. R. R. Sinclair to A. B. Duke, March 21, 1913, A. B. Duke to Sinclair, April 8, 1913, *ibid.*

of mine, the Biddles, are going to give a dance next Friday night. . . ."[62]

The Anthony J. Drexel Biddles of Philadelphia, whom A. B. Duke had met and liked, belonged to a well-known family in the Quaker City. This particular branch of the Biddles had more verve and social connections than money. The head of the family was a gregarious individualist who had founded an interdenominational "Biddle Bible Class" movement and who, along with a mania for physical fitness and jujitsu, did such impulsive things as keep a live alligator in a tank in the dining room of his home. The member of the Biddle family who most interested Angier Duke, however, was Cordelia Biddle. The marriage of the pretty and vivacious Cordelia, aged seventeen, to Angier Duke, who was thirty-one, took place in Holy Trinity Church on Rittenhouse Square, Philadelphia, in April, 1915, with Angier's sister, Mary Duke, as maid of honor.[63]

The interest of the public and newspapers in the elaborate wedding became even greater when the B. N. Dukes announced, shortly before the ceremony, that their daughter Mary was engaged to marry Anthony J. Drexel Biddle, Jr. An attractive, rather shy and serious young woman of twenty-eight, Mary Duke was almost ten years older than "Tony" Biddle. Graduating from St. Paul's school just prior to his marriage, he was a dashingly handsome youth with great charm and flair. Special trains brought the guests from New York and Philadelphia to Somerville for the wedding of Mary Duke and Anthony Biddle, which took place at Duke's Farm in June, 1915. Doris Duke, then two and a half years old, served as flower girl and Mrs. Angier B. Duke as matron of honor. Ben Duke, who had quickly taken a great liking to the Biddles, proudly sent the newspaper stories and pictures of his daughter's wedding to friends in Durham, and to one of them he wrote: "My brother's country place was ideal for such an occasion. All of our friends think it was one of the most beautiful country weddings that has ever taken place in this country and I myself think it was pretty nice."[64]

62. A. B. Duke to Alex. Sands, November 3, 1913; A. B. Duke to R. R. Hill, August 6, 1915. B. N. Duke MSS and letterbook.

63. Cordelia Biddle, in collaboration with Kyle Crichton, has written of her family in *My Philadelphia Father* (Garden City, N.Y., 1955), which was subsequently the inspiration for a play and then a movie entitled "The Happiest Millionaire." There are distortions and inaccuracies concerning the Dukes in the play and especially in the movie version.

64. B. N. Duke to Colonel Cameron, July 17, 1915, B. N. Duke MSS.

Thus the Dukes of Durham and New York had intertwined their lives with the Biddles of Philadelphia. Both B. N. Duke and his brother, J. B. Duke, had hopes that Angier Duke or Tony Biddle, or both, would become interested in electric power in the Carolinas, for that industry loomed larger and larger in the economic spheres of the Duke brothers' lives. The years ahead, however, would reveal that fate had decreed otherwise concerning Angier Duke and his brother in-law, Anthony Biddle.

ILLUSTRATIONS

111 Fulton St.

Washington Duke, about 1880, when he turned sixty.

Brodie Leonidas Duke

Mary Duke (Mrs. Robert E. Lyon)

Benjamin Newton Duke as a young man.

Sarah Pearson Angier (Mrs. Benjamin N. Duke)

James Buchanan Duke, about 1881, when he was twenty-five.

The house Washington Duke built for his second wife in 1852, and where Mary, Benjamin N., and James B. Duke were born. Though Washington Duke is shown seated on the porch, the photograph was apparently taken about 1900, a quarter of a century after he and his family left the homestead for Durham.

"Fairview," Washington Duke's house in Durham, on the left, with a portion of the factory of W. Duke, Sons and Company on the right and West Main Street running through the center of the picture.

(*above*) "Four Acres," Mr. and Mrs. Ben Duke's house in Durham. It stood on the southeast corner of the intersection of Chapel Hill and Duke Streets. (*left*) James B. Duke's mansion on the corner of Fifth Avenue and East 78th Street, New York.

Mary L. Duke and her brother, Angier B. Duke, in an early (1905?) automobile.

Brodie L. Duke and his fourth wife (the former Miss Wylanta Rochelle) in about 1912, in one of Durham's early Cadillacs. Brodie Duke's house, in the background, stood near the later site of Durham High School, on Duke Street. (Photograph courtesy of Mrs. Wylanta . . . Holt)

Mrs. James B. Duke (*nee* Nanaline Holt)

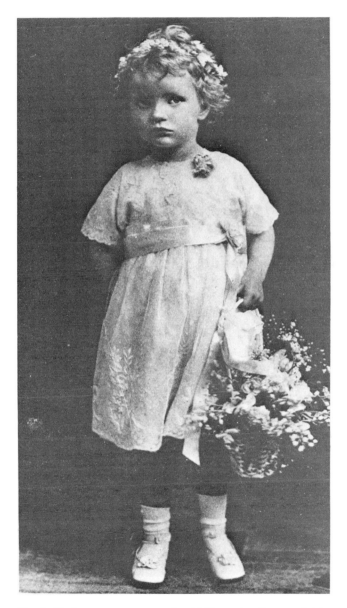

Doris Duke at age two and a half, as the flower girl in the wedding of her first cousin Mary L. Duke to Anthony Biddle, Jr., June, 1915.

(*above*) Angier B. Duke, his wife Cordelia, and Mary L. Duke (left to right). (*right*) James B. Duke and his daughter Doris at Newport, R.I., in August, 1919. On the back of this picture-postcard addressed to Benjamin N. Duke in Atlantic City, N.J., this message is printed in a child's hand: "I love you, Doris."

Angier and Tony Duke, sons of Angier Duke and Cordelia Biddle Duke, in a photographer's studio in St. Petersburg, Fla., where they visited their paternal grandparents, the Ben Dukes.

Ben Duke, his daughter Mrs. Anthony J. D. Biddle, Jr., and his grand-daughter, Mary Duke Biddle, II (Mrs. James H. Semans), spring, 1921.

James B. Duke and Benjamin N. Duke in the early 1920's.

Tony Biddle and his son Nicky, clowning at Palm Beach, Fla., in the 1920's.

CHAPTER 9. ELECTRIC POWER FOR THE PIEDMONT REGION OF THE CAROLINAS

One of the most enduring and creative phases of the Dukes' economic activities came in the last two decades of their lives. They then played pivotal and indispensable roles in launching a pioneering electric power industry that has been a major factor in the twentieth-century development of the two Carolinas. While Ben Duke had never completely left his North Carolina home, the venture in electric power ultimately led James B. Duke to return to his native state, and the move had far-reaching implications for the Carolinas. As in so many of the two brothers' activities, they moved jointly and worked together in launching their venture into electric power. The bolder and more far-seeing vision, however, belonged to James B. Duke, as his devoted older brother would have happily admitted; and, after the onset of Ben Duke's prolonged illness around 1915, J. B. Duke bore the entreprenurial burden of the power company without the assistance and counsel that his brother had always given.

Contrary to an oft-told tale, the Dukes did not go into electric power because of treatment given J. B. Duke's sore foot by Dr. Walker Gill Wylie in 1904. A prominent physician in New York, Wylie was also involved in an hydroelectric development in his home state of South Carolina. He and the Dukes did join forces, but not as a simple result of a chance conversation and an uninformed impulse on the part of J. B. Duke. The Duke brothers never proceeded impetuously in investing their wealth.

The Dukes became interested in the potentialities of hydroelectric power in the Carolinas as an outgrowth of their large investments in the textile industry. They were ever alert to the critical importance of economical sources of power for their factories. Moreover, they were among the vanguard of American businessmen who began to see as early as the 1890's that various technological developments were occurring and combining to foreshadow the day when the electric motor might largely replace the steam engine and when the vast, untapped energy of America's cascading rivers—nature's "white coal"— might richly supplement the fossil fuels buried in the earth.

One of the nation's earliest and, at the time, most widely noted ventures in the industrial use of electric power occurred in Columbia, South Carolina. There in the spring of 1894 a cotton mill began to utilize seventeen electric motors of sixty-five horsepower each, and the alternating current which ran them was furnished by a hydrostation located on a river about a thousand feet from the mill. At $15 per horsepower, the Columbia mill's power was said to be the cheapest in the country.[1]

A little more than a year after this trailblazing venture in South Carolina, a pioneer innovation in the centralized generation and transmission of electric power on a large scale was launched at Niagara Falls, New York. The first two generators there went into service in August, 1895, and the first purchaser of the power was the Pittsburgh Reduction Company, which later became the Aluminum Company of America. In order to be near a low-cost source of power, the Pittsburgh-based company led a veritable parade of industries that built plants at Niagara Falls to utilize the hydroelectric power.[2]

Just as J. P. Morgan and his associates played a key role in both the financing and basic planning of the important project at Niagara Falls, the Duke brothers, only a decade later, became the prime movers behind the building of one of the nation's early electric power systems. Aiming at an eventual comprehensive development of the water power of a region rather than at the prevailing pattern of random development of isolated sites, the Dukes and their associates pioneered in power technology, conservation of natural resources, and, finally, in connecting their own vast power grid with a number of smaller networks prior to the First World War. Thus they played an important role in the creation of the largest "system of systems" attempted in the world up to that time.[3]

As early as 1897, Ben Duke became aware of the growing interest of a few far-sighted North Carolinians in the possibilities of hydroelectric power. "I have it in mind to develop some of the enormous water powers in the Piedmont section of N.C. perhaps on the Yadkin or Catawba [rivers]," one entrepreneur wrote to Ben Duke, "bring the power out to a good point on the R[ail] R[oad] & build up a

1. Richard B. DuBoff, "The Introduction of Electric Power in American Manufacturing," *Economic History Review*, XX (December, 1967), p. 512.

2. Harold C. Passer, *The Electrical Manufacturers, 1875–1900* (Cambridge, 1953), pp. 293–294.

3. James E. Brittain, "Electricity and the Development of the South, 1880–1920," a paper read to the Southern Historical Association in November, 1973, a copy of which was kindly supplied by the author.

business, as durable as the Hills themselves." Compared to steam, "electro-water power" would mean, according to this man's calculations, a savings of $15,000 per year in every one thousand horsepower developed.[4]

Ben Duke apparently made no response to this initial overture, but within a year he and his brother began investigating and then buying various water power sites in both Carolinas. Though the large textile mill that they planned to build as Erwin Mill No. 2 was eventually located on the Cape Fear river in Harnett County, North Carolina, before the site was decided upon they had learned a great deal about water powers in the entire Piedmont region of the Carolinas and had actually purchased several of the sites. In view of later events, perhaps the most important was at the Great Falls of the Catawba river in South Carolina, some forty-five miles south of Charlotte, North Carolina.

Hiring their own engineer to advise in the new field of hydroelectric power, the Dukes also had the faithful, able assistance of W. A. Erwin. When the engineer occasionally revealed certain information to outside parties, Erwin, who shared the true businessman's penchant for quiet operation, complained: "I am of the opinion that 'much learning' makes hydraulic engineers and preachers mad: most of them need guardians. . . ." Erwin believed, however, that the engineer, whom he liked and regarded as quite competent, would learn to be "more politic." In addition to his calculations about a power site on the Haw river in North Carolina, from whence Erwin hoped to transmit "about 4000 H.P." to the factories and townspeople of Durham, he advised Ben Duke that he was "making an especial effort quietly to learn the status of the Catawba River Falls, which is unquestionably the biggest thing in the South. . . ." A little over a year later, in 1901, he had managed to acquire the coveted site for $41,973.17.[5]

After several years in which he had investigated numerous power sites and learned much from engineers and others, Erwin concluded that the "main trouble with all these powers" that he had seen in the Carolinas was the erratic flooding and drying up of the rivers in a region where periods of heavy rainfall often alternated with prolonged

4. John Q. Gant to B. N. Duke, December 15, 1897, B. N. Duke MSS.
5. Erwin to Ben Duke, November 13, 1899, and Erwin to J. E. Stagg, August 1, 1901, enclosing memorandum of cost of March 12, 1901, B. N. Duke MSS. Erwin obtained additional properties at Great Falls which brought the total cost to $90,000.

droughts. The one exception, in Erwin's view, was "the Great Falls of the Catawba, where the river never rises above eleven feet, and [which] would give practically an invariable steady power." It was, Erwin asserted, "the greatest property . . . in the United States on this account," as well as because of the low cost of development it would require, and "if it were mine, I would not turn it loose except at a good price for cash."[6]

In this same year, 1905, the Dukes were finally ready to launch at Great Falls their own venture in hydroelectric power. Prior to that time, however, they had already become associated with Dr. Wylie in his development on the Catawba river. They had also met and acquired the services of a brilliant engineer, William States Lee, who was to play a central role in the Dukes' involvement in the power industry. The work of Lee was, in fact, comparable to that of W. T. O'Brien on the Bonsack cigarette and W. A. Erwin's contribution in the textile industry.

Prior to these developments, Dr. W. Gill Wylie and his brother, Dr. Robert H. Wylie, had become interested in the late 1890's in developing hydroelectric power sites in South Carolina. In June, 1899, Dr. Gill Wylie sought, through B. N. Duke who had been his patient, to persuade the Dukes to come into the venture. Dr. Wylie performed an appendectomy on Ben Duke in August, 1899, and after thanking him for a "generous addition" to the bill for the operation, Wylie turned to the matter of the water power development in South Carolina. "Bob [Wylie] is straining at his work pretty hard & worrying some over our investment in the Catawba water power at Indian Bend," Dr. Wylie explained. "We have bought now & have the deeds to most of the lands necessary to give us a fall of full 18 ft. . . . We will have to raise about $20,000 sure to complete the purchase and if you don't come in with us or your company buy us out we will have to borrow the cash and go it alone. . . . Bob & I would rather go in with you and your brother as individuals than sell out to any one else. From our experience at Anderson [South Carolina] I am sure we have a good thing but it is too much for us to carry out alone. . . ."[7]

Although Ben Duke assisted Dr. Gill Wylie, the Duke brothers, still fully occupied with tobacco and textiles, were not ready at the turn of the century to become significantly involved in any power enterprise in South Carolina. The Wylies, therefore, proceeded with-

6. Erwin to Ben Duke, April 1, 1905, *ibid.*
7. W. G. Wylie to B. N. Duke, June 3, October 31, 1899, *ibid.*

out the Dukes but with whatever financial assistance they could secure. In May, 1902, Dr. Gill Wylie, admitting that he was embarrassed in light of all that Ben Duke had already done for him, declared that "the Charleston men who have taken up the financing of the Catawba Power Company urged that your name would be of great help to us in S.C. where we desire to have a good portion of our bonds & stock held. . . ." Wylie added that he and his brother had thus far expended about $300,000 for land, water rights, and machinery; the power house, 190 feet long and 75 feet wide, and dam were nearing completion. "This kind of letter is new to me," Wylie concluded, "and I have such a warm affection for your kind & gentle self that I really have for so few men that I ever met that I am afraid you may class me with many others that have approached you." Wylie did not appeal in vain, for Ben Duke subscribed for $25,000 worth of bonds of the Catawba Power Company.[8]

Scattershot development of power sites was not, however, what the Dukes had in mind. In 1903 they were still obtaining advice and technical information about hydroelectric power. One expert whom they consulted prepared a map of southern North Carolina and northern South Carolina, the territory to be served by the various prospective water power sites shown on the map.[9]

By the time James B. Duke developed erysipelas in his foot and had to take to his bed for treatment by Dr. Gill Wylie in the fall of 1904 and again in the spring of 1905, the Dukes, in a limited way to be sure, had been involved in matters relating to hydroelectric power for more than five years. Since J. B. Duke was never an easy person to pin down for an appointment and wrote as few letters as possible, Dr. Wylie no doubt did capitalize on the availability of his captive auditor to expound on the future of hydroelectric power in the Carolinas and on the brilliance of William S. Lee, who had joined the Catawba Power Company as chief engineer in 1902. After earlier experience in hydroelectric projects in the South, Lee had designed and supervised the construction of the Wylies' dam and power plant on the Catawba river some thirty-two miles north of Great Falls and about eighteen miles below Charlotte. One historian has suggested that by 1904 "Lee

8. Wylie to B. N. Duke, May 21, 1902, and Wallace Deane, president of the Southern Power Development Company, to B. N. Duke, July 29, September 3, 1902, *ibid.*

9. M. D. Barr, sales manager of Stanley Electric Manufacturing Company, to B. N. Duke, March 11, 1903, *ibid.*

was the most experienced hydroelectric engineer in the South." Only thirty-two years old in 1904 when he became associated with the Dukes, Lee was a native of Lancaster, South Carolina, and a graduate of the Charleston Military Academy (later the Citadel). He would eventually achieve an international reputation and become the first Southerner to be elected to the presidency of the American Institute of Electrical Engineers.[10]

Hard-working and experienced, as well as technically skilled, Lee was the sort of man with whom J. B. Duke most liked to deal. Accompanying Dr. Wylie to Duke's home, Lee later recalled that Duke, after carefully examining the diagrams and preliminary plans which Lee had prepared for extensive developments on the Catawba, asked about the cost. "I told him about $8,000,000," Lee noted. "I thought that was about the biggest amount I had ever heard of, but it seemed to attract him."[11]

Lee soon realized that hydro power for industrial uses was the aspect that most interested J. B. Duke. Because long distance transmission of electric power at high voltage was still in the early, experimental stages, many financiers were wary of the risks involved. Lee found Duke, because of his interest in promoting the industrialization of the Piedmont section of the Carolinas, willing to take the risk provided practical plans were prepared. On this point Lee was ready, for he had prepared a map showing transmission lines that tied together projected plants at Great Falls and at Mountain Island, which was on the Catawba to the northwest of Charlotte and more than fifty miles north of Great Falls. Lee aimed at continuity of electric service through linking the various plants together. There was also another site, soon to be known as Wateree, down the river some eighteen miles below Great Falls, which Lee envisioned as part of the system.

James B. Duke asked many sharp questions, which he always preferred to reading documents. "I know that in many cases he never had studied or heard of the things brought up," Lee recalled, but "readily grasping the idea, his mind passed on to the next step." Wary of conferences involving what J. B. Duke regarded as too much talk— "town meetings" he termed them—he quickly made up his mind and verbally issued many important instructions. "He had a wonderful power of making decisions," according to Lee. Sometimes they "seemed to be almost off-hand," but "they were as accurate as they

10. Brittain, "Electricity and the Development of the South, 1880–1920," pp. 4–5.
11. Jenkins, *J. B. Duke*, pp. 173–174.

182

were swift." Lee, whose admiration for J. B. Duke was obviously great, concluded: "Generally, he had gone into the matter thoroughly, had the points fixed in his mind and was sure of his ground. He merely thought faster, more accurately, and grasped the points of a situation more quickly than most men. And, once he had decided, he acted promptly."[12]

Thus, after several years of cautious preliminary investigation the Duke brothers were ready by 1905 to act on their power venture. The Southern Power Company was incorporated in New Jersey on June 22, 1905, with an authorized capital stock of $7,500,000. By March, 1906, $6,000,000 worth of stock had been issued in exchange for $1,097,794 in cash (mostly from B. N. and J. B. Duke), the entire $850,000 worth of the capital stock of the Catawba Power Company, a demand note from that company to the Southern Power Company for $118,579, and property, real estate, and water rights valued at $3,933,607 (mostly paid for by the Dukes.)[13]

Construction began at Great Falls in August, 1905, and the first operations there began in March, 1907, though the plant was not completed until later. As of January 1, 1908, Lee expected to be furnishing from the Catawba and Great Falls stations together between 38,000 and 40,000 horsepower, for all of which contracts had been signed. Lee hoped that the power plant at Rocky Creek on the Catawba, just below Great Falls, and the one at Ninety-nine Islands on the nearby Broad river could be completed expeditiously.[14]

Though the Dukes complained privately of the vast quantities of capital demanded by their power projects, they never failed to provide the money as it was needed. They disposed of various of their stock holdings in other enterprises, on some occasions, to plow more capital into the Southern Power Company and other related companies. A young Virginia-born lawyer who joined the company in its infancy, Norman A. Cocke, later recalled one occasion when he was talking about some needed extensions with J. B. Duke, who inquired where the capital was coming from. "We're going to get it from you," Cocke replied. "No, you ain't," Duke retorted, "I'm like the farmer who had a young steer that he wanted to break to a yoke,

12. *Ibid.*, pp. 176–177.

13. R. B. Arrington to B. N. Duke, March 7, 1906, B. N. Duke MSS. The Duke brothers each loaned Dr. Gill Wylie, who was named as president of the company, a bit more than $118,000 so that he might purchase additional stock. In October, 1906, the capital stock was increased to $10,000,000.

14. R. B. Arrington to B. N. Duke, June 21, 1907, *ibid.*

so he got a double yoke and he put his head through one side of it, and he put the young steer's head through the other. And the steer lit out and he ran all around the yard, and this fellow couldn't stop. He hollered to his son and said, 'Come here, Bill, and head us off, durn our fool skins!' That's what I want somebody to do for me," Duke laughingly concluded, "head me off."[15]

The panic of 1907 only temporarily slowed down and did not "head off" the steady growth of the Southern Power Company. The original idea was to sell power only to industries, and even that was no simple matter at the beginning. An engineer for the Southern Power Company tried to sell one president of a textile mill on the idea of electric power. After listening for some fifteen minutes, the textile man ended the discussion by asserting, "You must be drunk or a damned fool if you think I will bring electricity into my mill to kill my people."[16]

To overcome such fear and skepticism and to encourage the mill owners to buy electric power, the Dukes invested generously in a large number of textile mills in both Carolinas. Even before the Southern Power Company was launched, the Dukes had taken the lead, and put up the lion's share of the necessary capital, in establishing a large textile bleaching and finishing company in Greenville, South Carolina. After 1905, however, their investments in the textile mills of the area around Charlotte, Spartanburg, and Greenville began to increase dramatically. When James W. Cannon, the founder of what grew to be one of North Carolina's largest textile enterprises, approached J. B. Duke about investing in his mill, Duke sent word that if Cannon would "go to the site of one of our water power developments, say Great Falls for instance, and build a big plant, . . . he [Duke] would be glad to become interested, and largely interested, with you." Duke thought the plant "should be a very large one, operating not under 100,000 spindles, and possibly 200,000 to 250,000 spindles." The mill might well produce "plain sheetings" and do so in such large quantities as to become known in the whole country as "the largest and best in this line of production." A vast amount of capital

15. Transcript of interview with Norman A. Cocke by Frank Rounds, Charlotte, N.C., 1963, pp. 19–20. The Duke Endowment MSS, Duke University Library. Hereinafter cited as Rounds interview.

16. Rounds interview with John Fox, June 1963, p. 18. Fox also had earlier written an unpublished sketch of the history of the power company, a copy of which is in The Duke Endowment MSS. Among other things, he describes some of the pioneering technical innovations made by W. S. Lee and his associates.

would be required for building on such a scale, but Duke thought "the money could be provided without much difficulty."[17]

Although Cannon did not go to Great Falls, another large textile mill did go there, and the Dukes invested substantially in it. Later, James Cannon's son, Charles A. Cannon, asserted that Kannapolis, home of the extensive Cannon mills, could never have been built without the Southern Power Company, for no other power was available in that location. His mother had nervously inquired, "Now, are you sure that this electric power will be a success?" And his father had replied confidently, "Yes, Mr. Duke will make it a success."[18]

Concentrating on industrial users and wholesale selling of power, the Dukes had not originally envisioned supplying power to individuals in residential areas. There was, in other words, no master blueprint of the whole vast business that ultimately became, after 1924, the Duke Power Company. Yet even in the early years of the company, there were pressures toward the retailing of electric power to residential communities and small businesses. In some cases, mill owners were willing to switch to electricity only if their communities could also be provided with it. Gradually, the power company found itself more and more involved in retail distribution as well as in the operation of streetcar systems in Charlotte and many other communities in the Piedmont. As a result, the Southern Public Utilities Company was organized in 1913 as the retailing arm of the Duke-backed enterprise. There were no household electrical appliances to sell in the beginning years of the company, but one of the first to come along was the electric iron. One pioneer employee strapped some electric irons on the back of his bicycle and took them to new customers for a two-week trial.[19]

What with electric irons and streetcar systems, the Dukes' move into the power industry led to some surprising developments. Eager to utilize the electric power of the Piedmont to the fullest, J. B. Duke launched a search in 1908 for bauxite, the raw material from which aluminum is manufactured in a process requiring abundant, cheap power. Though that quest would continue, at different intervals, for more than a decade, Duke also purchased European patents for the

17. R. B. Arrington to J. W. Cannon, November 5, 10, 1908, J. B. Duke letterbook.
18. Rounds interview with Charles A. Cannon, July, 1963, p. 7.
19. Manuscript of speech by C. S. Reed, "Progress in the Piedmont Carolinas," 1954, in The Duke Endowment MSS.

fixation of nitrogen from the air and built a plant in 1910 near the Fishing Creek dam, a few miles north of Great Falls, to produce high-grade nitric acid. A few years later he and his associates launched another company near Mount Holly, North Carolina, for the extraction of phosphoric acid from rock. Though this latter plant proved to be unsuccessful and ceased operation soon after J. B. Duke's death, the idea behind these ventures was the utilization of hydroelectric power by the plants at times when there was an excess of power available.[20]

More important than the nitric- and phosphoric-acid plants for the economic development of the region and for jobs and the pay-checks of many people was the Piedmont and Northern Railway. Begun in 1910–11 as an electric interurban line for passengers as well as freight, the South Carolina branch finally consisted of about a hundred miles running between Greenwood, Greenville, Anderson, and Spartanburg. The North Carolina division ultimately had about fifty miles of track, with the main line running between Charlotte and Gastonia along with several shorter branch lines. Carrying train loads of cotton and soldiers by the time of World War I, the Piedmont and Northern, with its slogan of "A Mill to the Mile," became an important factor in the economic life of its region.

The Dukes, together with W. S. Lee and Edgar Thomason, a long-time official of the road, were the key figures in the building of the electric railway. One example of the role of the Dukes came during J. B. Duke's visit in 1913 to London, where he went regularly in connection with his chairmanship of the British-American Tobacco Company. B. N. Duke was left to cope with the financing of the Piedmont and Northern. The brothers had organized a syndicate in 1911 to raise the money and persuaded a number of their business associates in New York, such as Oliver H. Payne and Anthony N. Brady, to join in the venture. When Lee informed B. N. Duke in June, 1913, that the work on the railroad would require $250,000 in the next ten days, Duke advanced $100,000 and cabled his brother in London for $150,000. A few weeks later Ben Duke wrote his brother in great detail about their various enterprises, especially the Piedmont and Northern. Urgently requiring additional money, Lee spent almost a month in New York attempting to arrange a loan for the railway.

20. Fox, unpublished outline history of the power company, p. 13c. J. B. Duke's attempt to utilize some of the power company's lands in farming ventures also proved to be a losing proposition economically.

When he finally failed, B. N. Duke went to work on the original subscribers to the syndicate and got most of them to agree to increase their subscriptions. "I feel very much gratified that we could handle the matter in this way," Ben Duke declared, "rather than borrow so much money at a time like this. I figure that we will get in say, $1,250,000.00 from these increased subscriptions. . . ." Financial conditions in New York and elsewhere in the country "have been pretty 'rocky,' " he added. "I hope no new and unexpected thing will turn up that will require additional money for I am about worn threadbare." "I have had to pay out," he continued, "over a million dollars since January 1st for enterprises that I did not know the first of the year I would be called upon for. Over $600,000 of this, of course, went to the Southern Public Utilities Company. I have managed to get through it all and have some money left to my credit in the Banks. I hope the storm is now over and that we can take things more quietly."[21]

When the Piedmont and Northern's main lines were completed in 1914 and the railway began its long, profitable career, B. N. Duke could feel rewarded for his own endeavors in the building of the road. The last of North Carolina's electric railways to switch to diesel engines (in the 1950's), the Piedmont and Northern had a proud, efficient history of its own until it was merged into the much larger Seaboard Coast Line Railroad in July, 1969.[22]

Seeking ways, such as the Piedmont and Northern, to utilize the hydroelectric power that then seemed so inexhaustible, James B. Duke after 1905 found himself increasingly drawn back to his native region, particularly to Charlotte and the surrounding area. He and his brother usually rented a private Pullman car to take them and various of their associates from New York to the Carolinas, where they visited construction sites and inspected various installations of the power company. J. B. Duke acquired early in 1917 his own private railway car, which he named the "Doris" and used thereafter for most of his travel in this country. Ben Duke, after the onset of his long intermittent illness, made fewer and fewer trips with his brother, but J. B. Duke kept a vigilant eye on the power company's operations. He had no office of his own in Charlotte but when there he would sit by the hour in the offices of the power company and study the "operating log," which showed the water level at the various dams, the load on

21. B. N. Duke to J. B. Duke, July 2, 1913, B. N. Duke letterbook.
22. Michael J. Dunn, "Farewell, Piedmont & Northern," *The State*, XXXVII (December 1, 1969), pp. 14–15.

each plant, the total system load, and other such data. Daily reports went from Charlotte to his New York office giving comparable statistics, and if J. B. Duke were at his home near Somerville, the information was telephoned there or cabled to London if necessary.

One young engineer newly employed by the company met J. B. Duke with trepidation and near silence, for the word had been passed around that "Mr. Duke was a dangerous man to talk to, that he remembered everything you told him, and he might bring it out two or three years [later] in an embarrassing way." Some time after the introduction, Duke invited the young man to ride out with him for an inspection of a new coal-burning steam plant that the company had recently built. After the inwardly alarmed engineer managed to arrange for someone to telephone the word ahead to the plant, he and J. B. Duke set out in the latter's old chauffeur-driven Rolls-Royce. As the car topped a hill near the plant and the engineer saw that both stacks were clear with no black smoke coming out, he felt one spasm of relief. But as Duke's actual inspection of the plant began, the engineer's tension mounted. After going through turbine, pump, and boiler rooms, questioning all along, Duke walked outside and, to the engineer's great consternation, proceeded to walk into an opening at the base of a chimney, where soot was gathered with a small electric machine. The area turned out to be perfectly clean. Returning to the car and sharing sandwiches and a thermos of coffee with the engineer, Duke looked straight at him and said, "You have a fine plant here. I like the way you run it." As the young engineer began to glow, Duke added, "Why don't you run the others like this?"[23]

Along with his pleasure in waterfalls, gardens, and trees, Duke enjoyed seeing construction in process, particularly of stone and masonry. While the dam and power plant at Wateree were being built between 1917 and 1919, he visited there frequently, often staying in the home of A. Carl Lee, younger brother of W. S. Lee and also an engineer. Smoking the small, mild cigars that he liked, Duke sat in a large rocking chair after dinner, occasionally held the Lee's baby daughter, and talked about his own daughter, Doris. Duke explained to Mrs. Lee that on one occasion he had been emphasizing to Doris that he had always been a Methodist, her grandfather had been a Methodist, and that he hoped she would be one. When Doris looked up at him and asked, "Daddy, what's the difference between a Methodist and a

23. Rounds interview with Edward Williams, April, 1963, pp. 19–24.

Presbyterian?" Duke had to do some quick thinking. "Doris, it's time to go to bed," he asserted. "You go to bed and tomorrow we'll settle all that." The next day Duke sought out a Presbyterian minister in Charlotte, got informed on a few of the fine points of theological and church history, and then tried to explain as best he could to his inquisitive young daughter.[24]

James B. Duke grew to feel comfortably at home with various of his associates in the power company and their families. Prior to the outbreak of the First World War in August, 1914, however, he committed more of his money than of his time to the Carolina Piedmont. As chairman of the world-girdling British-American Tobacco Company, with its home office in London, he naturally made regular, extensive visits there. Though he apparently never dreamed of giving up American citizenship to reside in England permanently, as the newspaper rumors had it around 1914, he did consider buying a house in England. For wealthy men such as he, who owned more than one residence, life in prewar England, with its greater formality and marked privileges according to wealth and class, had certain attractions. In 1914 he leased Crewe House, one of the great mansions of Mayfair in London's fashionable West End, with an option to purchase. The outbreak of the war later in that year, however, ended any notions Duke may have had of owning a house in England and sent him scurrying back to America.

As to what Mrs. James B. Duke may have thought of a part-time residence in England, there is no evidence. While she liked her mansion on Fifth Avenue, she may well have appreciated many aspects of stylish life in London. Wearing "white and gold brocade with pearls and diamonds embroidered upon the corsage," a court mantle or cape of "geranium red velvet lined with gold tissue," and ropes of pearls, she made a striking picture when presented at the Court of St. James.[25] Not even to please his lovely wife, however, would J. B. Duke don the purple silk knee breeches and other such vestments that were prescribed for his appearance at the royal presentation. He swore that with his thin legs and large stomach, the outfit would make him look like a "caricature of a brownie," and he arranged for the American ambassador to send somebody else to escort Mrs. Duke.[26]

Despite his aversion to costumed pomp, J. B. Duke returned to

24. Rounds interview with A. Carl Lee, April and July, 1963, p. 49.
25. Undated clipping in the "J. B. Duke" scrapbook, Southgate Jones MSS.
26. Rounds interview with Norman Cocke, p. 84.

America in 1914 convinced that the United States should sooner or later enter the war on the side of the Allies. Yet his unhappiness about many features of the Progressive Era, which had climaxed in the Democratic administration of Woodrow Wilson, led him for the first time in his life, with the undoubted help of an unknown friend or two, to publish an article. "It is not a pleasant contemplation, but it is the simple truth," Duke asserted in the *North American Review*, "that since 1904 the whole course of national political affairs, so far as it has been influential at all, has been—with one solitary exception—toward the depression of business, the hindering of business prosperity, the curtailment of the income of the capitalist and the laborer alike." The exception which Duke noted was the Federal Reserve Banking Act, but his guarded approval of that was far outdistanced by his denunciation of the Wilson administration's lowering of the protective tariff rates and by what Duke saw as the continuation of the war against large businesses which he traced back to 1904 and the beginning of President Theodore Roosevelt's antitrust fight.[27]

After the United States entered the war in 1917, Duke continued to attack the wartime fiscal and economic policies of the Wilson administration from the standpoint of a staunch Old Guard Republican. He argued, with the unshaken faith of an old-fashioned capitalist, that the railroads would perform more efficiently if left in private hands rather than being run by the federal agency set up to control them in the wartime emergency and that "enormous and unparalleled inheritance taxes and surtaxes" were raising comparatively little revenue while they hurt "all of our enterprises and the individuals who are engaged in and dependent upon them." The United States government, Duke charged, was "pulling down the pillars of our business temples."

The income tax, made constitutional by the ratification of the Sixteenth Amendment in 1913 and made telling in its impact by the higher rates that accompanied American military preparations and then entry into the war, came in for special attack from many of the country's wealthy people. J. B. Duke was no exception, and he argued that the government could not hope to sell its bonds to "those whose incomes are too largely taken by taxation." The draft law Duke applauded, though he asserted that it should go further and include "for

27. James B. Duke, "Politics and Prosperity," *North American Review*, CCI (April 9, 1915), 521–529.

purposes of labor, every man, woman and child over sixteen years of age and mentally and physically fit."[28]

J. B. Duke's great and creative talent for industrial enterprises clearly did not carry over into government and public policy. Having spoken his piece, without any discernible impact on the course of events in wartime America, he quickly returned to and remained in his more natural sphere. There were, at any rate, more than enough large, challenging projects to occupy his energies.

As the family's great electric system grew in the Carolinas, J. B. Duke also became involved in a Canadian venture that was of great importance in the economic history of that nation as well as forming the basis for a substantial part of the Dukes' wealth. Making a trip to the Pacific Northwest in 1912, J. B. Duke, B. N. Duke, W. S. Lee, George G. Allen, and Dr. Samuel Eyde, a prominent scientist from Norway, were intent upon inspecting power sites that might be developed for the manufacture of the nitrogenous compounds which had attracted the attention of J. B. Duke. Arthur Vining Davis, president of the Aluminum Company of America, had gone along to show the Duke party some power sites in which his company was interested but left the group as the private car proceeded into Canada.

Thomas L. ("Carbide") Willson, a pioneer in the electrochemical field, persuaded the Dukes to change their itinerary and visit the Saguenay river, a tributary of the St. Lawrence about a hundred miles north of the city of Quebec. Leaving their private car upon arrival in the town of Chicoutimi, the party eventually took to a "duck boat" to go up the river as far as they could; then they had to walk up trails along the bank of the river for two miles or so. Fed by Lake St. John, which covered an area of some four hundred square miles, the Saguenay dropped over three hundred feet in the approximately thirty-seven miles from the lake to Chicoutimi. As J. B. Duke clambered over the rough terrain and gazed on only a portion of the mighty river as it broke and fell through the gorges, he declared, "Lee, I'm going to buy this."[29]

Buy it he did, though the process of acquiring the two major power resources on the Saguenay—the upper site near the outlet of Lake St. John at Isle Maligne and the lower one twenty-one miles down the river at Chute-à-Caron—required over two years. Then for more than three years W. R. Perkins and other lawyers and agents struggled to

28. Jenkins, *J. B. Duke*, pp. 220–230.
29. *Ibid.*, p. 188.

purchase for the Dukes the vast areas of land required for the water rights of the enormous projects that were envisioned.

There was also a vital question about what industries would consume the enormous amounts of power that would be generated, for the area was then largely given over to farming. J. B. Duke ultimately joined forces with Sir William Price, an important figure in the Canadian newsprint industry, who agreed late in 1922 to take for his paper company a portion of the 540,000 horsepower that would ultimately be produced at Isle Maligne. Price also took a minority interest in the Duke-Price Power Company which built in 1923–24 the dam and power plant at the upper development that one historian has described as "the world's largest hydrostation" at that time.[30]

With much power still to be sold from the Isle Maligne plant and with an even greater development slated for Chute-à-Caron, Duke returned to his old interest in finding bauxite and began to explore the possibility of producing aluminum on the Saguenay. Assisting Duke in the search for bauxite were various officials, scientists, and technicians in the American Cyanamid Company. He acquired substantial stock in that company in 1916 in exchange for his holdings in a corporation which owned phosphate mines in Florida and a plant in New Jersey where ammonium-phosphate, a highly concentrated fertilizer, was produced. Duke also picked William Brown Bell, a lawyer who had been in W. R. Perkins' office, to become president of American Cyanamid in 1922.[31] The upshot of complicated and longdrawn negotiations, about which there was litigation for some years after Duke's death, was that he and Arthur Vining Davis struck an agreement in 1925 whereby Duke's power site at Chute-à-Caron would be merged into a reorganized Aluminum Company of America in which Duke would be given one-ninth of the stock, that is, $17,000,000 worth of the total $125,000,000 capital value of Alcoa at that time. Alcoa also contracted to take a large block of power from the Duke-Price Company.[32]

30. Paul Clark, "James Buchanan Duke and the Saguenay Region of Canada," p. 160, privately printed booklet presented to the Manuscript Department, Duke University Library, by T. L. Brock of the Aluminum Company of Canada in 1968. After J. B. Duke's death, Alcoa acquired his majority stock in the Duke-Price Power Company, which was renamed the Saguenay Power Company in 1935.

31. Kenneth C. Towe, "William Brown Bell . . . ," an address to the Newcomen Society, New York, 1953, a printed copy of which is in The Duke Endowment MSS.

32. Ibid., pp. 169–170. The story of J. B. Duke's Canadian venture will be dealt with by the author in a subsequent study.

Despite the enormous scope and economic significance of the Canadian properties of the Dukes, J. B. Duke's own personal interest and involvement as far as the development of hydroelectric power was concerned remained primarily in the Carolinas. From 1915 on he had begun to spend more and more time in and around Charlotte, a hustling city which aspired to rival Atlanta and which J. B. Duke obviously liked.

For all his growing satisfaction about Southern water powers, the production of electricity by harnessing the rivers of the Southern Piedmont brought serious problems. W. A. Erwin had long before warned that the erratic rise and fall of so many of the region's rivers limited the usefulness of water powers on them during different times of the year. A mighty torrent in one season of the year, the same Southern river could shrink to a pitiful stream after the prolonged heat and drought of a long, sun-baked summer. In July, 1916, not drought but pounding rains and severe flooding played havoc with the Dukes' power system. A young employee who had just been hired in the New York office reported that a stenographer emerged from W. R. Perkins' office with a dazed look and declared that they had best look for new jobs because the "rains have been so heavy down there . . . at the Catawba river, that the company's washed the hell down the river."[33]

The rains came so fast and furiously, in fact, and the rivers rose so alarmingly that some old-timers on the Catawba river began to talk of "the greatest flood since Noah." With railway and highway bridges destroyed and lines of communication down, the power stations were crippled too. The Catawba plant, oldest in the system, went out on the morning of July 16, 1916, and could not resume service until December. A number of other plants were knocked out for periods ranging from six days to two months, and at Great Falls service was interrupted from July 16 until July 26.[34]

Although there were inevitably some serious interruptions in the delivery of power, W. S. Lee and his associates had pioneered several years earlier in linking their system with other electric systems in the region, and in the six weeks or so after the 1916 flood the Georgia Power Company alone supplied some 8,000,000 kilowatt hours of power to the stricken Southern Power system. Through that aid and

33. Rounds interview with Clarence E. Buchanan, August, 1963, p. 12.
34. Fox, outline history of the power company, p. 9.

the carrying of dangerous overloads in the plants of its own that were able to operate, the company struggled back to its feet.[35]

Although James B. Duke knew he could hardly check the rains from the sky, he rushed south, alarmed as well as angry about the large losses. Bringing his niece, Mary, and her husband, Anthony Biddle, with him, he travelled around inspecting the damage, no doubt making frequent use of his favorite expletive, "I'll be dinged." Edward Carrington Marshall, an executive of the power company and a friend in whose home Duke frequently stayed while in Charlotte, finally confessed: "Mr. Duke, I don't blame you for being mad. If that were my money floating down the river, I would be mad too. . . . We just don't know how to cope with the river and the flood." Duke grunted his assent to the explanation but added that he meant to find out how to cope with such problems and that he expected the others in the company to apply themselves to the same task.[36]

One way of coping when hydro power stations were rendered inoperative through floods or droughts was the utilization of coal-burning steam plants to produce electric power. Regarded as strictly auxiliary to the hydro stations, four relatively small steam plants had been built by the Duke-owned companies before the 1916 flood—at Greenville, South Carolina, and at Greensboro, Mount Holly, and Durham in North Carolina. The last named was completed in 1915 and marked the approximate eastern limits of the Southern Power system. Duke had never dreamed that steam plants might become the principal producers of power, with hydro stations reduced to the auxiliary role, but such in fact was destined to be the case. A catastrophic drought in the summer of 1925, as disruptive to the company and its service as the flood of 1916, though in a slower way, forced him to confront the necessity of additional huge investments in steam plants. Pragmatic and flexible even as he was dying, he made his last decision concerning the power company in favor of a vast, coal-burning steam plant. That decision, however, lay in the future.

Engrossed in the work of the power company and sufficiently enamored of Charlotte to want to reside in it a part of each year, Duke purchased a house there in 1919. It was in the new suburban section known as Myers Park and close to the homes of the E. C. Marshalls

35. *Ibid.*

36. Rounds interview with Mrs. E. C. Marshall, October, 1963, p. 18. Marshall, a great-grandson of Chief Justice John Marshall, held various high offices in the power company, eventually serving as president from 1949 until his death in 1953.

and other officials in the power company. Remodeling the house extensively and developing handsome grounds around it, Duke installed a fountain in front of his house that threw a stream more than eighty feet in the air. The house itself was spacious and comfortable, rather than pretentious, but the fountain was clearly Duke's special pride.

By the time he acquired his home in Charlotte he was sixty-three years old and obviously mellowing, even if in no way losing his zeal for work or his penetrating sense of business. Mrs. E. C. Marshall, who had been a girlhood friend of Mrs. Duke in Macon, Georgia, became a good friend also of J. B. Duke. The Duke she saw in Charlotte was a man who "loved to laugh and . . . to enjoy watching people's grass grow and he would go in and ask them how they grew their dahlias or chrysanthemums or violets or whatever. . . ." When Mrs. Marshall and Mrs. Duke met and proceeded to chat, as they frequently did, J. B. Duke laughingly declared, "You women go ahead and knock each other. I never have time to sit down and listen to women talk." He sat there laughing, however, and when a lull occurred in the women's conversation, he said, "Go ahead and say some more."[37]

Entertaining small groups of friends for dinner, Duke often had movies shown in the living room after dinner. There were home movies of young Doris and some of the silent spectacles then coming out of Hollywood too. On one occasion when there was conversation rather than movies, Mrs. Marshall made some laughing comment about J. B. Duke's shoes. All his life he had had trouble with his feet and his shoes, and the difficulty began with the rough, heavy brogans that he had had to wear as a boy. Needled by Mrs. Marshall's remark, Duke laughed and proceeded to remove a shoe, demonstrating the built-up support of his arch and explaining that the comfortable shoes were one of six pairs made in Italy some twenty years earlier. "I would not wear those awful looking shoes you have with that nice slender foot," Mrs. Marshall retorted. "I thought you had deformed feet."[38] Though the whole espisode was silly and provoked general laughter, Mrs. Duke, if she was present at the time, probably did not care for such undignified behavior as the removal of a shoe in public. She did, in fact, frequently accompany her husband to Charlotte, where Doris was enrolled for a while in a kindergarten conducted in

37. *Ibid.*
38. *Ibid.*, p. 19.

the rear of a neighborhood grocery store.[39] The Dukes occasionally attended Sunday morning services in some of the Methodist churches in Charlotte, to which he made large contributions.

Just as Washington Duke had heard Sam Jones preach a generation or so earlier, J. B. Duke in Charlotte went to hear Billy Sunday, a famous evangelist of the early twentieth century, and invited him home for a visit. When Duke asked Billy Sunday why he indulged in so many gymnastics in the pulpit, the evangelist replied, "Oh, Boss, you know how it is. If I'd get up there and just preach a dry sermon, I'd never get these people in there." Chuckling, Duke authorized one of his associates to give Sunday $1,000 from him.[40]

Many such aspects of life in Charlotte appealed to Duke, but New York and Newport were more to the taste of Mrs. Duke. After leasing different houses at Newport for several seasons, in 1922 Duke purchased a place there for his wife, who always insisted that she was "no picnic girl." She certainly did not have to "picnic" at Newport—the mansion Duke bought, "Rough Point," had been built by Frederick W. Vanderbuilt in 1886 and was one of the great houses of the famed resort. Just as Mrs. Duke often accompanied her husband to Charlotte, he dutifully put in appearances at Newport. But he growled some, too: "I like those old ladies in Newport, but I don't want to sit by them every night."

On one occasion when Mrs. Marshall visited the Dukes at "Rough Point," she and Mrs. Duke slipped away for a cigarette. Duke, who never liked to see women smoke, later confronted his wife with the accusation, "You've been smoking." Crossing her fingers no doubt, she quickly replied, "I can prove by Bertha Marshall that I haven't." To the relief of Mrs. Marshall, Duke dropped the subject.[41]

For all of Mrs. J. B. Duke's enjoyment of certain expensive things, she, like Mrs. Ben Duke, was quite capable of counting pennies and watching expenditures. Both women had grown up in a time and place where poverty was the general rule, and all the money in the world could hardly eradicate indelible childhood memories and attitudes. When Mrs. J. B. Duke complained privately to Mrs. Marshall about certain of J. B. Duke's expenditures connected with the Charlotte residence, the latter promptly retorted, "Now, you just let

39. The Charlotte *News*, October 24, 1963, had a story about the man who ran the store and who remembered the Dukes' coming there.
40. Rounds interview with Norman Cocke, p. 65.
41. Rounds interview with Mrs. Marshall, p. 42.

him alone. Look at all those beautiful diamonds he has given you This [residence in Charlotte] is his diamond bracelet. . . . Let him enjoy himself."[42]

Mrs. Marshall was only partly right: J. B. Duke's real "diamond bracelet," in the sense of affording him great pride and pleasure, was not so much the residence in Charlotte as it was the great dams with their giant cascades of water and the electric power system as a whole. Just precisely when he began to explore in his own mind the idea of using the power system as the basis for some large philanthropic project for the Carolinas no one can say for certain. But almost from the time that William R. Perkins became Duke's chief legal counselor in 1914, Perkins had in one of his desk drawers an early rough draft, made for Duke, of what eventually became, a decade later, the indenture creating The Duke Endowment.[43]

The beginning of Ben Duke's protracted illness around 1915 was another development that influenced J. B. Duke, for it forced a modification of the old division of labor between the two brothers. While J. B. Duke had taken the lead in the family's involvement first in tobacco and then in electric power, Ben Duke for about thirty years had specialized in the family's charitable concern for many institutions in North Carolina, particularly for the Methodist church and Methodist-related Trinity College. Starting in 1915, however, J. B. Duke directly assumed certain annual philanthropic responsibilities that were relatively new to him.

As for the power company itself and its relationship to philanthropic possibilities, many of J. B. Duke's closest associates in the enterprise were always struck by the fact that he took neither salary nor expenses from the company during the many years he was so closely involved in it. More significantly, Duke was not interested in his and and his family's receiving dividends from the vast blocks of stock they held in the various companies that made up the Southern Power system. A typical example of this came in 1911 when Ben Duke learned that no dividends would be paid on the preferred stock he held in the Southern Power and Great Falls Power companies. "We have more than earned the dividends," the Dukes' executive secretary and treasurer of the power companies explained, "but it seems to be the

42. *Ibid.*, pp. 43–45.
43. W. R. Perkins, "An Address on the Duke Endowment: Its Origin, Nature and Purposes," delivered before the Sphex Club at Lynchburg, Virginia, October 11, 1929. Printed pamphlet in Duke University Library.

same old story, namely that we have been spending so much money for extensions and new acquisitions that we have not sufficient money in the bank to pay the dividends without cramping ourselves. I took the matter up with Mr. J. B. Duke and his decision was that we should not attempt to pay the dividends on the 1st of April."[44]

Both J. B. Duke and B. N. Duke advanced the equivalent of the dividends to certain kinspeople or friends who held small quantities of the power company stock and who might have needed the income. The principal owners of the company, however, were not building the vast Southern Power system for the quick enrichment of themselves and their families. Rather, the Dukes exerted themselves to find the necessary capital for the enterprise. In the spring of 1917, Ben Duke, his wife, and his two children had loans out to the Southern Power Company and one other related company that totalled $1,020,000. By August, 1917, Angier Duke was selling the family's American Tobacco preferred stock as well as other stocks in order to gain additional cash for the power company.[45]

Harnessing the water power of rivers that flowed through the Piedmont and then turning a substantial portion of the profits that might be made over to the philanthropic service of the people who lived in the Carolinas, who used the electric power, and who really owned the rivers—such was the idea that James B. Duke, quietly and privately, seems to have begun to entertain around 1915. The all-important institutional instruments for the philanthropy were, however, completely undetermined. And James B. Duke so enjoyed building dams, in the Carolinas as well as in Canada, that there was always the question of whether, before the end of his days, he would actually stop long enough for a kind of creative endeavor that would be new to him.

44. R. B. Arrington to B. N. Duke, March 25, 1911, B. N. Duke letterbook.
45. Alex Sands to B. N. Duke, April 2, 1917, and to Mrs. B. N. Duke, August 31, 1917, *ibid.*

CHAPTER 10. THE PHILANTHROPIC CULMINATION: THE ESTABLISHMENT OF THE DUKE ENDOWMENT

The Duke Endowment, announced to a surprised public in December, 1924, was not a sudden or impulsive inspiration on the part of James B. Duke but the ripened fruit of a deeply rooted family tradition and pattern of giving that went back to the 1880's and 1890's. True, J. B. Duke, preoccupied by business affairs, had long been content to leave the family's charitable activities largely in the hands of his older brother. But Ben Duke, in turn, had always proceeded in close communication with J. B. Duke.

The Duke Endowment was destined to become one of the largest permanent foundations of its kind in the nation and to exert a major influence on the quality of life for millions of people in the two Carolinas. In its magnitude and boldness of purpose and vision, the Endowment clearly bore the stamp of J. B. Duke's mind. Creator first of a vast commercial empire in tobacco and then the prime mover behind the building of one of the nation's pioneering electric power systems, he finally turned his capacity for thinking and planning on a large scale to philanthropy for his native region. Despite the industrial progress of the two Carolinas beginning in the late nineteenth century and accelerating in the early twentieth, the material standard of living for the people of the two states—as measured in per capita income, average family income, and other indices—was still considerably below national norms. This fact helped James B. Duke decide to confine his gifts to educational, health-care, and other eleemosynary institutions in the two Carolinas.

Duke's movement towards his own philanthropic action was thoroughly entangled with the family's long-standing identification with Trinity College. A plan to have the executive committee of the trustees of the college actually administer the endowment was eliminated at the last minute. But Trinity College and its needs, as interpreted to J. B. Duke by Ben Duke and the president of the college, William P. Few, were, in a manner of speaking, the "starter dough" which, when added to some other ingredients, rose into the great loaf that became The Duke Endowment.

With John C. Kilgo's election to the Methodist episcopacy in 1910, Ben Duke's constant interest in Trinity College did not wane, as some people thought it might. On the contrary, William P. Few, the new president of the college, quickly won Ben Duke's endorsement as a "rousing good college president." A quiet peacemaker instead of a fiery controversialist like Kilgo, Few was an academic man's academic. That is, he was a quiet, well-trained scholar who, after graduating from Wofford College in Spartanburg, South Carolina, took his Ph.D. degree in English at Harvard University. Having come to Trinity in 1896, he soon became the college's first dean and Kilgo's indispensable aid in academic administration. Moreover, he was, to an unusual degree, totally and selflessly dedicated to the service of Trinity College. It was to be above all else, he declared in his inaugural speech, "a shining place where high-minded youth may catch aspirations to true character and genuine excellence. . . ."[1]

Perhaps because Ben Duke was also a quiet, idealistic man like Few, they enjoyed a rapport that grew closer with the years. Ben Duke continued to serve on the executive committee of the college's trustees, as he had since the early 1890's, and kept in the closest touch with the institution's problems and needs. During the first two years of Few's presidency, 1910–12, Ben Duke arranged for the college to acquire new buildings for administration and classrooms, known respectively as the East Duke and West Duke buildings, and two new dormitories, Jarvis and Aycock. "I have just had a conversation with my brother in reference to the new dormitory which he was to give the College," Ben Duke advised Few in a typical communication. "He authorizes me to say to you that you can proceed with the erection of the building at once."[2]

In addition to much-needed new buildings for the growing college, the Dukes made it possible for Trinity to waive tuition for many of its ambitious and able "poor boys," though that charge was still only fifty dollars per year. Ben Duke gave $20,000 a year for the operating budget of the college while his brother gave $7,500 for the same purpose. Careful never to interfere in the academic aspect of the college's

1. The best introduction to Few may be found in Robert H. Woody, ed., *The Papers and Addresses of William Preston Few* (Durham, 1951), which has an excellent "Biographical Appreciation."

2. B. N. Duke to W. P. Few, January 27, 1912, B. N. Duke letterbook. The two dormitories were named, with the Dukes' approval, Jarvis and Aycock, after two former Democratic governors of North Carolina whom the Dukes respected.

life, Ben Duke continued as he had from the first to take a particular interest in the grounds, the one area where he volunteered advice along with the money to implement it. "I am writing mainly now to say that I hope you will, if you have not already done so," he urged Few, "commence work on the grounds in front of this [administration] building and the sidewalk leading to the street, so that it will be in presentable shape by the coming commencement." Ben Duke thought the fund for the grounds that he had already provided would cover the expense but if it would not he would "see that the bill is paid."[3]

While Few, like so many country-born Southerners, genuinely loved trees and flowers, his constant attention to the appearance of Trinity's campus clearly had an element of sheer prudence in it. Bishop Kilgo, who continued to serve on the executive committee of the trustees, also recognized the importance of the matter and after visiting the Dukes in New York gave this advice to Few: "Concerning the landscape work at the College there must be exceeding care. It is the one place in which our friends are more than experts and are very much interested. We must not allow persons who are not well fitted to tamper with the grounds. Trees and flowers are delicate things and always tell their own tales. There is no way to hide misuse of them. But of this we can talk when we meet. . . ."[4]

As interested in the physical environment of Trinity College as the Dukes were, they well knew that the true reason-for-being of the institution lay in the education it gave to its students. And despite the ever-expanding generosity of the Dukes, Trinity aspired to do more than it possessed the means to do. With the number of undergraduates climbing from 334 in 1910 to 551 in 1916, Few and his faculty were aware that the small number of women students whom the college had been able to admit since 1896 should and could easily be increased, provided certain facilities for women, such as dormitories, were available. A coordinate college for women, talked of earlier, was a high-priority item on Trinity's agenda, as was expansion of the law school, which was limited in size but proud of its high standards. President Few, in fact, drummed away at the idea, which the Dukes also encouraged, that Trinity was more interested in quality than in quantity. "At the time when the attendance is larger than it has ever been," he advised an influential friend of the college in 1915, "we are in a posi-

3. *Ibid.*, March 19, 1912.
4. J. C. Kilgo to Few, June 13, 1916, W. P. Few MSS, Duke University Archives.

tion to resist strongly the craze for numbers and the pagan doctrine of mere bigness."[5]

In Ben Duke, Few found his strongest support for the aims of the college, and he expressed his thanks in many graceful letters. "During the past fifteen or twenty years I know that you have often felt the financial responsibility for the College to be very burdensome," Few declared in one letter in 1913. He continued: "I am glad to believe that it is at last in a position where you will not feel obliged periodically to come to its rescue, but where you and others of the family can give to it just as you feel inclined to give. Burdensome as I know this responsibility has sometimes been to you, I believe you will be more and more grateful for the good fortune that has brought you into the place of chief benefactor of this College. Most thoughtful men agree that despite all its defects, education is to be a main reliance of our civilization. You have the unique distinction of being in this region a pioneer builder of education on a vast scale, for it is already clear that Trinity is to rank among the very greatest colleges of our country."[6]

Ben Duke soon needed all the encouragement he could get from any source, for he was about to embark on a long and grim physical ordeal. His illness was intermittent, and though there were periods when he came close to resuming his normal life, he gradually slipped into semi-invalidism. Beginning around September, 1914, in fact, at age fifty-nine, Ben Duke suffered from such debilitating "nervousness" and a "dizziness in the head" that he had to give up going regularly to his office in New York. Though he and Dr. Gill Wylie traveled to Saratoga, New York, seeking a change of scene and a few weeks later he and his brother had Bishop Kilgo visit them at Duke's Farm near Somerville, New Jersey, Ben Duke increasingly found himself unable to cope with business affairs. In early 1917 he gave a power of attorney to his son, and he, his wife, and a nurse traveled on a private railway car to St. Petersburg, Florida, where he subsequently purchased a home.

By May, 1917, he had entered a hospital in Philadelphia for what turned out to be a stay of five months. His executive secretary in New York described it as a "rest cure." In a long, handwritten letter to his

5. Few to the Rev. H. M. Blair, editor of *The Christian Advocate*, September 7, 1915, Few MSS. Porter's chapter on "Few: Patience and Tenacity, 1910–1918," in *Trinity and Duke*, pp. 174–209, covers the major developments in the period as well as the Dukes' relationship to them.
6. Few to B. N. Duke, March 20, 1913, Few MSS.

secretary in Durham, Ben Duke reported that he felt that he was improving and that his doctor had said it was "only a matter of time" until he was "entirely well again." His old habits were obviously still with him, for he had numerous small chores for the secretary: she was to give twenty and ten dollars, respectively, to the nurse and secretary who had been kind to him in the doctor's office in Durham, and she was to telephone Dr. Few and explain that he, Ben Duke, had arranged to cover the tuition for two young women in Durham (one of them a daughter of a cousin for whom Ben Duke had built a house) to enter Trinity College. "Please give my love to George Watts, Jones Fuller [one of the family's lawyers], Miss Ross [a secretary], & keep a lot of it for yourself," Ben Duke concluded. Then he scribbled a postscript: "You can give my love to Jones Fuller's wife too. I guess Jones would not object to taking her the message or you can phone it."[7]

One of the things that cheered Ben Duke was the solicitude shown him by his family and especially by J. B. Duke. Long news-filled letters from Few also kept him informed on the college and various matters in Durham. Ben Duke had given the money for a granite wall to be built around the campus of Trinity, and he took keen interest in the progress of its construction. After reporting on the wall, the fine commencement Trinity had enjoyed, and the number of teachers who had been called to military service, Few added: "As you know, I am not much of a man to give expression to my personal feelings; but I want you to know how much I esteem and love you and that you have multitudes of friends here and everywhere who feel the same way."[8]

During his long hospitalization in 1917, Ben Duke requested copies of publications containing pictures of Trinity College that he could show to his friends in the hospital. "If you have pictures of the wall send them also," he added. Few, of course, complied and each week reported on things that he knew would interest Ben Duke: the vegetable garden that had been planted on the campus as part of the war effort was producing well; the hydrangeas were in full bloom and "very beautiful"; the rains had been plentiful, making the lawns around Duke's home in Durham and around Memorial Church lushly green. "We are getting used to khaki here as everywhere else," Few noted. "You can fairly see the flutter of the girls' hearts as nu-

7. B. N. Duke to Miss E. A. Child, no date [May, 1917?], B. N. Duke MSS. All of his adult life Ben Duke sent flowers to his friends on various occasions; he kept doing so even during his long illness.

8. Few to B. N. Duke, June 13, 1917, Few MSS.

merous commissioned officers (most of them our graduates) go about the streets in their glittering uniforms." In a more serious vein, Few explained that he and others from the college had travelled all over North Carolina "to rally our constituency for the service of the country in this trying time and through the education of the youth for the great task of reconstructing the world after the war." The response had been extraordinary, Few added, and he believed that "the College today is in more intimate and sympathetic relations with the people of the state and this section than it has ever been in its history. . . ."[9]

As much as Few's letters meant to Ben Duke, probably nothing touched him so much as a personal letter from J. B. Duke at a period when Ben Duke had to struggle especially hard to keep up his courage. As close as the two brothers were, they remained estranged from their older half-brother, Brodie Duke, after his spectacular marital misadventure late in 1904 on the eve of Washington Duke's death. Events connected with Brodie Duke may have partially inspired J. B. Duke's letter of February, 1919, to Ben Duke.

Brodie Duke never again broke into headlines as he had early in 1905. In June, 1910, however, at age sixty-three he married a striking young girl in Durham who was more than forty years younger than he, Miss Wylanta Rochelle, and the background of this episode may be told briefly. On occasional walks between his home and his office in downtown Durham, Brodie Duke passed the Rochelle residence. Southerners still spent as much of the year as they could on their front porches in that more sedate time, and Brodie Duke, a staunch Republican like his father, liked to stop by, sit on the porch, and argue about politics with the head of the Rochelle family, who was a Democrat. Soon Brodie Duke began to notice and finally to court the good-looking daughter whom he made his fourth wife.[10]

When Brodie Duke died on February 2, 1919, he and his half-brothers had never been reconciled, though even if they had been, Ben Duke would not have been able to attend the funeral. Few did attend it, and he wrote about it to James B. Duke: "The service was conducted at the residence and was well attended by citizens of Durham and kinspeople and friends from a distance. An appropriate talk was made by Dr. T. A. Smoot, pastor of a leading Methodist church in Richmond, Virginia. It developed from Dr. Smoot's talk that Mr.

9. B. N. Duke to Few, July 25, 1917, and Few to B. N. Duke, July 25, 31, August 2, 9, 16, 22, September 11, 1917, Few MSS.
10. Interview with Mrs. Wylanta Rochelle Duke . . . Holt, October 2, 1973.

Duke had helped him through Trinity College years ago. This gave Dr. Smoot an opportunity to bring out many of the good traits of character in the life of the deceased. There were many flowers and altogether the occasion was as appropriate as it could have been made." Few added that he was writing to B. N. Duke in St. Petersburg but would say nothing about the death. "If it will not disturb his mind and if you think wise," Few concluded, "you are at liberty to send this letter on to him."[11]

Whether J. B. Duke actually did forward Few's thoughtful letter to Ben Duke is not known, but he probably did. And J. B. Duke probably took the occasion, when a death had struck close to home, to make an unusual statement of brotherly affection. "I have received your two letters and was very glad to hear from you and to know that you continue to improve," J. B. Duke began his letter to Ben Duke. "You must not get impatient," for it had taken a long time "to get into this condition and will require time to get cured. At any time I can serve you don't fail to call upon me. I have your interest at heart and it has always been a pleasure to help you in any way I can. You are the dearest brother in the world, and my heart goes out to you in your many afflictions. I know that you have always been ready to serve my every interest and desire and I cannot write or even tell you of my love and deep appreciation of what you have been to me since we were little boys together." Next, J. B. Duke reported that with plenty of water for the hydro plants, the power company was doing well, and the construction work underway was moving along better than it had for some time. The country, even the world, was in a "very chaotic condition" and would probably remain so for a long period "before normal times will return." In closing, J. B. Duke asked to be excused for "all mistakes in this letter," but it was, he added, the first he had attempted by hand in ten years. "With a heart full of love and affection, I beg to remain, Your devoted brother. . . ."[12]

Such a letter meant a great deal to Ben Duke, who showed it proudly to a few of his closest friends. He also gained great satisfaction from his grandchildren. Angier and Cordelia Biddle Duke had two sons, Angier Buchanan Duke, Jr., who was born on November 30, 1915, and Anthony Newton Duke who was born on July 28, 1918.[13]

11. Few to J. B. Duke, February 4, 1919, Few MSS.
12. Copy of J. B. Duke to B. N. Duke, February, 1919, B. N. Duke MSS.
13. The former subsequently exchanged the "Buchanan" for "Biddle" as a middle name and the latter substituted "Drexel" for "Newton."

On the forty-third wedding anniversary of the Ben Dukes, February 21, 1920, their daughter gave birth to Mary Duke Biddle, II, and on September 1, 1921, Anthony J. Drexel Biddle, III, was born to Mary and Tony Biddle.[14]

With frequent visits by his grandchildren whether he was in New York, St. Petersburg, or Durham, Ben Duke took great comfort in the good looks and vitality of the four youngest members of his family. While the divorce of Angier B. Duke and his wife in 1921 greatly distressed the Ben Dukes, they maintained cordial relations with their former daughter-in-law and continued regularly to see and enjoy her two young sons.

As the Ben Dukes and Angier Duke's two sons basked in fine Florida weather in March, 1921, Ben Duke braced for a sadness that he saw in the offing. George Watts had been ill in the previous year, but now Ben Duke seemed to expect the worst as he wrote his secretary in Durham: "I am so distressed over Mr. Watts' condition—he is almost continually on my mind. He is a dear good fellow & I am so sorry I cannot see him & do something to cheer him up. We have been associated together in business for 42 years & not a single cross-word ever passed between us. I think that a pretty good record. . . . If you should see him give him my love & tell him that I wish it were possible for me to be with him in his suffering."[15] George W. Watts died on March 7, 1921, two days after Ben Duke's letter was written, and the long-standing, close relationship between him and the Dukes was finally ended.

But an even greater and more poignant loss soon befell the Ben Dukes. Their son, Angier Buchanan Duke, had accepted election to the board of trustees of Trinity College, his alma mater, in 1913 and moved to shoulder some of the responsibilities of his father after the latter's illness worsened. Ben Duke gradually divided up most of his fortune between his wife and his two children after 1916, and, accordingly, Angier Duke and Mary Duke Biddle began to make sizable contributions in their own names to Trinity College, the Memorial Church, and to other traditional recipients of the family's philanthropy. "Thinking that Trinity College will doubtless be in need of additional funds to meet its running expenses for the coming year," Angier Duke wrote Few in 1921, "I am enclosing herewith my check

14. The second child subsequently changed his legal name to Nicholas Benjamin Duke Biddle.

15. B. N. Duke to Miss E. A. Childs, March 5, 1921, B. N. Duke MSS.

for $10,000 to be used for such purposes as the College sees fit."[16] In the following year, Angier Duke and Mary Duke Biddle together contributed $25,000 toward the erection of a new gymnasium that was designated as a memorial to Trinity's alumni who had been killed in World War I. Ben Duke naturally rejoiced to see his children grow to accept the family's tradition and to share his own special interest in Trinity College. All the more, therefore, did the death of thirty-nine-year-old Angier Duke crush his parents.

Early in the morning hours of September 3, 1923, Angier Duke, two male companions, and three women arrived at a yacht club in Greenwich, Connecticut, after having visited one or two of the country clubs in the area. As the group got into a rowboat to go to Angier Duke's yacht, he accidentally stepped on the side of the boat and capsized it. In the darkness and confusion of the moment, as the others clambered back on to the dock, no one noticed at first that Angier Duke was missing. When the other members of the group did realize it, they began a frantic search, but his body, caught under a raft, was not found for some seven hours. Despite the fact that Angier Duke's right arm had been amputated at the elbow many years earlier, he was a powerful swimmer. Anthony Biddle, who took charge of the funeral arrangements, gave the likeliest explanation for his brother-in-law's death by drowning when he surmised that Angier Duke had struck his head, possibly on an oarlock, when he came up from the water for the first time. Thus stunned he was swept under the raft by the tidal current.[17] The Charlotte *Observer*, noting that Angier Duke in his will left a quarter of a million dollars to Trinity College, declared: "There is something much more than sentiment behind the flow of Duke money to Trinity College. The descendants of the first great friend of that institution [Washington Duke] have developed a passion for education."[18]

The Charlotte *Observer* was right, but the ironic fact was that the member of the family who finally gave the most money for education in the Carolinas was the most deliberate in acquiring the passion. Not until around 1915 did James B. Duke begin, tentatively and warily at first, to establish his own lines of communication with Trinity Col-

16. A. B. Duke to Few, September 7, 1921, Few MSS. Earlier Angier Duke and his sister had each contributed $10,000 to Trinity College in a Methodist educational campaign, while Ben Duke and his wife each gave $20,000 in the same campaign. See Few to C. W. Toms, May 31, 1921, *ibid.*

17. *New York Herald*, September 4, 1923.

18. As reprinted in the *Durham Morning Herald*, September 12, 1923.

lege. Many members of its faculty had never seen J. B. Duke, but in 1914 Few went to New York to confer with him and his brother and then wrote one of his first letters directed solely to J. B. Duke. "We want you to understand what we are doing and to approve of it," Few explained. "I do not want to feel that you have thrown us overboard. But I do want you to feel that we will live within our means; that we will incur no added financial responsibilities without the approval beforehand of your Brother and yourself; and that any further contributions are to be free will offerings made because you feel like making them and not because they are expected of you." In closing, Few struck a note that reappeared many times in his letters and later speeches: "And speaking for myself I am particularly anxious that you shall get enduring personal satisfaction and happiness out of what you have done for Trinity College, because you are able to feel that through it you have done some permanent good upon the earth."[19]

Doing "permanent good upon the earth" may or may not have been an idea that appealed to J. B. Duke, but with the onset of Ben Duke's illness the younger brother clearly was willing to put more of his own time and an increasing amount of his money into the family's philanthropic work. Bishop Kilgo as well as Ben Duke helped nudge J. B. Duke toward the acceptance of more charitable responsibilities. Kilgo, after visiting again with the Duke brothers in New York and at Duke's Farm in the summer of 1915, reported enthusiastically to Few: "I feel that I used the opportunity for its full value, and if there had been nothing except the companionship I should have written down the trip as one of life's highest points. But as things turned out, it became a mountain peak event in my life." Kilgo added, in unhappy words for the historian, that it was all too lengthy for him to try to relate in a letter.[20]

James B. Duke was soon assigning his own landscape architects to the preparation of plans for the Trinity campus, and he provided a special fund of $10,000 for the grounds. Starting in 1915 he commenced the practice of making an annual contribution to supplement the funds of the two Methodist conferences in North Carolina for their "worn-out preachers" and the widows and orphans of deceased preachers. He requested Trinity College annually to disburse $10,000 for that purpose, a chore that Few performed happily and gracefully just before Christmas each year and that brought in a large number

19. Few to J. B. Duke, March 31, 1914, Few MSS.
20. Kilgo to Few, July 13, 1915, Few MSS.

of heart-warming letters of thanks.[21] In additon, Duke began giving $25,000 annually to the Board of Church Extension of the Methodist Episcopal Church, South; $15,000 of the gift was earmarked for the building of rural churches and $10,000 for assistance with the current expenses of such churches. In 1920, J. B. Duke requested Trinity College to administer these funds also and explained to the Board of Church Extension that he made the change not through any dissatisfaction but simply because "I have always been very closely identified with Trinity College, and not only would like for them to handle it for me, but think it would help the college by its so doing."[22]

The identification with Trinity College that J. B. Duke mentioned was certainly not close enough to suit William P. Few. Extremely helpful to him in getting information to and from J. B. Duke was Clinton W. Toms, a trustee of the college and member of the executive committee. A former superintendent of the Durham schools, as were several other able young men whom the Dukes recruited for executive positions in the tobacco companies, Toms was quiet and always off-stage, but he served as a vital link between Trinity College and Few on the one hand and the Duke brothers on the other. In 1916, for example, Toms informed Few confidentially that the college would probably get $50,000 from each of the brothers for the new gymnasium, science building, and other improvements needed in the college's plant. "We must not under any circumstances," Tom warned, "put up on the Trinity campus any building which does not in every way meet our requirements and which does not conform in lines and dignity with the present buildings." There had already been, Toms asserted, possibly echoing J. B. Duke, "entirely too much tearing down and rebuilding, which, of course, is a great waste of money."[23]

Keeping J. B. Duke informed about developments at Trinity was a constant worry and challenge to Few. Having been asked by Duke about the aims of the college, Few wrote his annual report in 1917 with the elusive younger Duke brother especially in mind. The twenty-fifth anniversary of the institution's move to Durham also

21. J. B. Duke to Few, November 18, 1918, and Few to J. B. Duke, November 26, 1918, and *passim*, Few MSS.

22. J. B. Duke to Board of Church Extension and to Board of Trustees, Trinity College, April 22, 1920, J. B. Duke letterbook. Duke gave directly to Methodist churches in Durham and New York city and especially to the Methodist church in Somerville, New Jersey, which he sometimes attended when at Duke's Farm.

23. Toms to Few, October 16, 1916, Few MSS.

called for a retrospective look and recapitulation. Although the thirty-page document covered many points and was about three times longer than earlier reports, Few perhaps wished to emphasize that the college had been a "working, undoctrinaire institution, all the time dedicated to sound ideas and disciplined by sacrifice in behalf of great causes." He included a capsule history of the institution, with generous praise for Presidents Crowell and Kilgo and for the college's chief benefactors.

Few did not stop, however, with eulogistic hymns to past presidents and wealthy benefactors. After noting that the United States had specialized in becoming the richest nation in the world—as Elizabethan England had specialized in great poetic literature and the ancient Greeks in their artistic and physical prowess, Few asserted that America's wealth remained to be humanized. "The men who succeed in America are victims in turn of overpraise and bitter denunciation," Few declared. "Colleges and educated men ought to hold a steadier light and become a more constant inspiration to the proper employment of wealth as of all of every man's power of whatever kind."[24]

James B. Duke may have read Few's report, but even if he did not there was always Clinton Toms. "I think we ought to keep [J. B. Duke] informed as to what we are doing and proposing to do," Few confided to Toms. "I have the opportunity of seeing him at such rare intervals that the obligation would seem to fall on you." Later Few admitted that his conscience bothered him about such frequent calls upon Toms for help, "but if certain things are to go on as they ought to go on, I have no other recourse."[25]

Few was not being merely greedy or ambitious for Trinity College in his pursuit of J. B. Duke. It was partly a matter of Ben Duke's intermittent illness and the resulting loss upon occasion of that familiar and time-tested support. More importantly, Few's dilemma arose from a series of large, new problems thrown upon the college by America's entry into World War I, the ensuing loss of students and some faculty to military service, and then the war-induced inflation that ate away a significant part of the college's real income from endowment and caused the buying power of faculty salaries to shrink pitifully.

24. "Twenty-five years of Trinity College: Report of the President of Trinity College to the Board of Trustees, June, 1917," pp. 10–11, 29.
25. Few to Toms, February 18, May 20, 1918, Few MSS.

At Ben Duke's suggestion, James B. Duke agreed to become a trustee of Trinity College in 1918, but he did not attend meetings of the board. By the end of the war in November, 1918, Few was more and more harassed by the inflation as well as by the increasingly urgent need for adequate provisions for women students and for more up-to-date scientific facilities. In reporting to J. B. Duke about the disbursement of the annual fund for the superannuated preachers, Few wrote a particularly forceful letter late in 1918 in which he mentioned that the ever-improving conditions within the Methodist church in North Carolina were attributable to a significant degree to Trinity College, for it not only furnished most of the Methodist preachers in the state but was the "inspiration of North Carolina Methodism." Thus the strength of the church was inescapably tied to the ability of Trinity "to keep pace with the growing needs of a growing section of the country in a time of rapid change." Few concluded with a candid request: "I shall be grateful if you will allow me, as opportunity affords, to talk freely to you upon these questions and then leave action to your judgment and to your own good time. I am giving my life to these things that seem to me to be most worth while. That is all I can do, except to bring the needs and possibilities of these great causes to the attention of a man like you."[26]

Few finally had gotten through to J. B. Duke, for the two men conferred early in 1919. Duke had earlier, once in 1916 and on one or two other occasions, referred vaguely to his long-range philanthropic plans in conversations with Few, but in 1919 matters became more specific. In a tantalizingly short letter after the conference, Few wrote: "As I have thought of your plan, it grows in my mind. I think it is really a sounder idea than that around which any other large benevolence in this country with which I am familiar has been built. I have done a good deal of thinking concerning your suggestions, and I should be glad of an early opportunity to talk with you again."[27]

Later in the month Few submitted more detailed plans which he hoped might implement the ideas J. B. Duke had advanced. "If you and your lawyer find that the property cannot be administered under the charter of Trinity College," Few wrote, "I would suggest that you create a separate corporation, perhaps to be called the James B. Duke Foundation or Fund, as you might prefer." The trustees of the foundation might be self-perpetuating and be seven in number, the seven

26. Few to J. B. Duke, December 15 (?), 1918, Few MSS.
27. *Ibid.*, February 1, 1919.

members, in fact, of the executive committee of the Trinity Trustees. A vancancy on the latter body was coming up, and Few hoped Duke might consent to fill it. "To carry out your ideas as I understand them," Few continued, "I think the charter of the Foundation ought to provide that the income is to go to Trinity College, Durham, N.C., and to the building of rural Methodist churches and the supplementing of rural Methodist preachers in the states of North Carolina and South Carolina." The trustees should make an allotment each year of the amount to go to Trinity and the amount to the Methodist churches and preachers.[28]

James B. Duke had finally revealed to Few something of his plan for basing a philanthropic foundation for the Carolinas on a substantial portion of the stock of the Southern Power and affiliated companies. At that point, the scope of the projected foundation was apparently limited to Trinity College and to certain Methodist causes in North and South Carolina. Nothing had thus far been said, in other words, about Trinity College's fulfilling the dream that went back to President Crowell in the early 1890's of becoming a university; about grants to any other educational institutions; or about aid in the area of health care. As Few would discover, however, J. B. Duke was simply not ready to act in the matter, for one reason because the stock of the power companies was not paying what he regarded as adequate dividends and could not do so until the rates could be adjusted upwards. Another reason for the delay was Duke's continued absorption in the power company and its affairs as well as in his still undeveloped Canadian holdings.

Unaware that there was to be an inevitable delay, Few allowed his hopes to soar in the first half of 1919 only to face an immediate financial crisis in the college's affairs later in that year. Through the aid of Toms in New York and an architect in Charlotte who served both the college and J. B. Duke, Few managed to ascertain the whereabouts of Duke and waylay him for another talk in Charlotte in April, 1919. Duke entertained Few for luncheon at the newly purchased house in Charlotte and was no doubt cordial, but nothing tangible came from the conference.

In Ben Duke, Few still had his strongest ally, and long, news-filled letters not only cheered the sick man but kept him constantly informed about Trinity College. "Men as they are released from the

28. *Ibid.*, February 27, 1919.

Army continue to come back to us in a steady stream like martins to a gourd," Few wrote early in 1919. Later in the year Few declared that there was "a regular land-slide in our direction." The "policies of justice, fairness and open mindedness" for which Ben Duke had always wished the college to stand, Few avowed, "have been the very qualities in the College that have won for it its present place of leadership."[29]

Ben Duke felt well enough to attend commencement at Trinity in June, 1919, and to entertain some of the guests at "Four Acres." President Few informed Clinton Toms that "we never had altogether a more successful commencement," with "the tides of life running high," and that Ben Duke "seemed to be happier than I have seen him in a long time."[30]

As the summer passed and the crises of the next school year mounted, Few needed Ben Duke more than ever. More than a dozen of Trinity's faculty members, most of whom were able and experienced men who were strongly committed to the institution, had turned down offers at substantially higher salaries from other colleges; yet they literally could not live in the inflationary postwar period on their prewar salaries. As if that and the effort to obtain a new dormitory for women were not enough, Few had daily worries about the college's antiquated heating plant and the urgent need for new boilers, for which there was no money. After an illness and a short vacation, which was his first one in nine years, Few confessed wearily to Clinton Toms: "If we can within the next two or three years make adequate provision for six hundred men and for a relatively small number of women who will come here I shall be content to leave further developments to a windfall or to future generations."[31]

The tireless president of Trinity College soon recovered from his moment of fatigue and limited hopes. For the most pressing problem, that of faculty salaries, Ben Duke offered $12,000 for the "running expenses account" of the coming year. From Atlantic City, New Jersey, he also informed Few that he had talked over the situation at Trinity with his brother and convinced him also to give $12,000 a year for "the running expenses" of the institution. "I am very sorry he did not make it at least double this amount," Ben Duke confessed. He added the personal note that, though he was trying a new diet and

29. Few to B. N. Duke, February 28, August 30, 1919, Few MSS.
30. Few to C. W. Toms, June 5, 1919, Few MSS.
31. *Ibid.*, August 22, 1919.

"living up to it strictly," he feared that his was "a hard case" and that there was nothing that could do him any good.[32]

Thus temporarily bailed out, Few took heart also from the enthusiasm with which the townspeople of Durham launched a campaign to raise money for a women's dormitory at Trinity which would be a memorial to the recently deceased James H. Southgate, longtime chairman of Trinity's board of trustees and a widely respected citizen. "In all events, let's put down this peg," Few declared to Toms, "we must have a building for the women before college opens next year. You can scarcely realize the depths of the hole we find ourselves in. Perhaps you and I may have been dragooned into it, but I believe in Providence; and I think after all it is going to be for the best." A few weeks later, with the new boilers for the heating plant in sight and the addition of a fulltime secretary for alumni affairs, Few expressed his relief: "This is the first year since I have been president of the College that my head, financially speaking, has not been under the water a good part of the time."[33]

James B. Duke, for his part, probably felt annoyed that his brother, Few, Toms, and other friends of Trinity College would not leave him alone to proceed at his own pace in pursuit of his long-range philanthropic goals. As much as Few might sympathize with those goals, however, he could not afford the luxury of ignoring immediate problems in order to concentrate on some brightly envisioned future. In September, 1919, Toms advised Few that as best he could learn progress was "being made on the formation of the Trust to be administered by the College and that within a year it would yield a very substantial income to the College." Since the document might be submitted for suggestions to Senator Furnifold M. Simmons, an alumnus and trustee of Trinity, Few should see to it that Simmons became fully informed of the "needs of the College and the great work that it has done. . . ." Toms added that it was of "prime importance" that "this whole thing should be kept in the strictest confidence. . . ."[34]

Though Toms continued to be optimistic about the imminence of the proposed foundation, in December, 1919, J. B. Duke made it

32. B. N. Duke to Few, September 8, 1919, Few MSS. The archivist of Duke University, Dr. William E. King, helpfully provided this letter, which was rescued from a cardboard box stored in the basement of East Duke Building.

33. Few to Toms, September 19, October 9, 1919, Few MSS. With the people of Durham raising over $100,000 for Southgate Dormitory and Ben Duke giving an additional $100,000, it was occupied in the fall of 1921.

34. Toms to Few, September 17, 1919.

clear that while he was not ready to act on his foundation he would not ignore the requests of Ben Duke and others that Trinity's more pressing, immediate needs be met. After additional talks with the champions of the college in New York, J. B. Duke informed Few that he was giving $100,000, of which not more than $20,000 could be spent each year over a five-year period. Few promptly conveyed the institution's thanks for the "generous gift" that would "help relieve the strain put upon us by the rapid growth of the College at the very time the value of money has fallen to the lowest level this generation has known."[35]

Having bought more time in order to pursue larger plans for the future, James B. Duke in the winter of 1920–21 set out to win increased rates for the electric power company and thereby what he regarded as more adequate dividends on its stock. Although the fight was a hard one and success came only in slow stages, by early 1924 Duke had gained the change that he regarded as an essential preliminary to the creation of his foundation.

The legislature of North Carolina had put electric power companies under the regulation of the state's Corporation Commission in 1913, but the Southern Power Company subsequently denied the commission's jurisdiction over its rates or its operating rules and regulations. When the inevitable legal test reached the state's supreme court in 1919, it ruled that since the power company was a public service corporation enjoying the right of eminent domain in the state, the company could be compelled to furnish electric power to customers without unjust discrimination in rates or in other respects.[36]

Losing additional legal battles in 1920, J. B. Duke and his associates acquiesced in the matter of the Corporation Commission's right to regulate rates and in November, 1920, filed a petition with the commission accepting the principle of uniform rates but asking for an increase in the charges levied by the company against its customers, particularly the large industrial ones which were mostly textile mills.

35. Few to James B. Duke, January 3, 1920, and A. Sands to Few, January 6, 1920, Few MSS. Few also secured a pledge from the General Education Board of $300,000 provided the college raised an additional $700,000, with the entire million to be added to endowment. When the Methodist educational campaign, on which Few initially pinned his hopes, failed because of the depression that hit in 1921, Trinity's share was ultimately met by the Dukes, including especially J. B. Duke's gift of one million dollars in 1922. The story may be followed in the Few Papers, 1920–1922, or in Porter, *Trinity and Duke*, p. 211.

36. 179 N.C. 18, at 19–39; Raleigh *News and Observer*, December 21, 1919.

The power company maintained, though some of the mill owners questioned the figure, that it had $46,894,256 invested in North Carolina alone but realized only 3.81 percent earnings in 1919. Although there was a pressing need for additional power production in the Piedmont, the company spokesmen argued that the capital needed for further development could not be secured without a larger return on the investment.[37]

Opposition to the increased rates came largely from a number of textile mills that had made contracts of varying duration with the power company and that now charged it with bad faith in seeking the abrogation of the contracts. To this the company responded that it had made the contracts in good faith only to be told subsequently by the Corporation Commission and the state's highest court that it could not discriminate between customers.[38]

Not all of the textile manufacturers, by any means, opposed the increase. Through their attorneys, some took the position that the proposed rates were just. These manufacturers asserted that they were more interested in the Southern Power Company's proceeding with "further development, so that they could get more power for additional enterprises, than they were in the difference in rates for power now being used by them."[39] The fact that 41 percent of the new cotton mills constructed in the South in the preceding five years, and 72 percent of all the new mills in North Carolina in the same period, were built under the electric lines of the Southern Power Company impressed those who hoped for future economic growth in the region.

The textile men who did oppose the rate increase also retained able lawyers and soon found vocal allies in the state legislature. Quite a few of the legislators were always eager to join in battle against large corporations and especially against the so-called "power trust" that had been created by the former head of the once mighty "tobacco trust." Consequently a bill to take the matter out of the hands of the Corporation Commission and to compel public service corporations to abide by contracts soon found vigorous support in the legislature. As the matter approached a climax in late February, 1921, J. B. Duke, W. S. Lee, other officials and attorneys for the company, and W. P. Few along with other interested parties, went to Raleigh. Al-

37. *News and Observer*, November 23, 1920.
38. *Ibid.*
39. North Carolina Corporation Commision *Report*, 1921–1922, p. 47.

though Lee testified at length in various of the hearings, Duke sat quietly as a keenly involved spectator.

Some individuals and newspapers that had always strongly championed state regulation of utility companies suddenly found themselves calling for an exception to that principle. The *News and Observer*, for example, urged a recall of the power granted to the Corporation Commission "to the extent that it may under no circumstances be employed to permit the annulling of contracts by raising rates involving an additional expense of millions to consumers." Denying any need for worrying about the profits of the power companies, the *News and Observer* asserted that "they will usually come out of any sort of an emergency 'right side up.' "[40]

The Charlotte *Observer*, on the other hand, quoted at length from the decision of the state's supreme court demanding that all rates for power must be equal for customers receiving similar categories of service. Denouncing the strong movement in the legislature to bypass the Corporation Commission so that the textile mills could keep their existing contracts, the Charlotte newspaper declared that it viewed the matter not "as a fight on Duke and his power company, but as a fight against the industrial interests of this part of North Carolina." A few days later the Charlotte *Observer* suggested that if "personal prejudices and designs against Mr. Duke might be forgotten and the consequences of such legislation [as that proposed to limit the power of the Corporation Commission] are considered, the people would have reason to feel easier as to the final outcome."[41]

As the legislative session approached its end, the champions of those textile mills that fought for their old contracts lost out in heated last-minute voting. The Corporation Commission resumed its hearing in April, 1921, on the power company's petition, and the contending forces transferred their debate to that forum, with J. B. Duke again in attendance. According to one reporter "nothing disturbed the equanimity of J. B. Duke, . . . who, neither smiling nor frowning, neither particularly interested nor particularly disinterested, neither piqued nor bored, watched the proceedings through, sitting with hands folded across his lap, thumbs rubbing slowly together, while he consumed many cigars."[42]

40. February 25, 1921.
41. February 26, March 3, 1921.
42. *News and Observer*, April 13, 1921.

With Josephus Daniels himself freshly returned to Raleigh and his newspaper after eight years as secretary of the navy under President Wilson, the editorial attacks of the *News and Observer* on the Southern Power Company took on a new militance. "The people of North Carolina are threatened with a monopoly in power, in lights, in electric transportation, in gas by reason of the methods of the Southern Power Company," Daniels' newspaper charged. "It aims to dominate power and heat and transportation along the same lines that steel, oil, and tobacco have become monopolies." If the rate increase were granted, the *News and Observer* warned, "Duke would not be the 'Duke of Durham' but would soon be the Czar of North Carolina, and and we would all be his vassals, paying tribute to the alchemist who actually turned water into gold."[43]

Despite the dire threats of Daniels and others, the Corporation Commission in July, 1921, granted the power company an increase in its rates, though not the full amount that had been requested. The commission expressly provided, however, that the company could request a rehearing and revaluation of its total worth when certain properties which were under construction but not operating, and which the commission refused to include in evaluating the company's property, actually went into operation. Subsequent legal battles by various of the larger textile mills against the Corporation Commission's ruling failed. Increasing its generating capacity by 200,000 horsepower in the two and a half years after the original petition in November, 1920, the Southern Power Company accordingly requested in 1923 the full increase it had failed to get in 1921, the company's avowed aim being to obtain a 6.86 percent return on its investment. The *News and Observer* continued to train its biggest guns against the power company, charging on October 21, 1923, for example, that J. B. Duke, "having monopolized the tobacco raised by the farmers, had the vision of monopolizing the water that fell from heaven so he could dominate all industry in the Piedmont section of North Carolina and South Carolina." The Corporation Commission, nevertheless, granted the company the increased rates to become effective on February 1, 1924. As a consequence, James B. Duke, with the help of his associates and numerous sympathizers in North Carolina, had removed an important roadblock to the establishment of the philanthropic foundation about which he had been thinking for

43. *Ibid.*, April 14, 15, 1921.

a decade and of which only Few and a handful of others had any ink-ling at all.

While the rate fight proceeded through the early 1920's, there oc-curred another important development that affected both Trinity College and J. B. Duke's philanthropic plans: William Preston Few had what might be called a brainstorm. Hospitalized throughout the summer of 1920, Few's illness continued on and off through the winter of 1920–21. In his convalescence from pneumonia in the spring of 1921 he had much time for reflection, and a number of ideas, many of them foreshadowed by past efforts or proposals, finally fell into place in his mind. Few's initial blueprint for a "Duke University" that could be organized around Trinity College was no hastily conceived scheme designed to lure a large benefaction; it was, rather, the care-fully considered synthesis of a number of ideas that had long been evolving and of developments in Trinity College that were already underway.

In the first place, Few held an almost passionate belief in the no-tion, as he put it in 1919 and repeated many times throughout his career, that the best American universities "have at their heart a great college of arts and sciences. . . ."[44] Though a simple fact, it was an idea that some educational institutions, and even more research-obsessed academicians as well as much of the public, often minimized or failed to understand. Few not only saw the undergraduate college as the "heart" of any true university, but he placed effective teaching, es-pecially of freshmen, towards the top of his list of educational priorities.

Much of the strength that Trinity College had developed by the early 1920's derived from the fact that a large proportion of the faculty shared Few's faith in the college and in teaching. Yet beginning with the young faculty members who had to be recruited after the move to Durham in 1892, Trinity had emphasized for its faculty the relatively new research degree, the Ph.D. John Spencer Bassett, himself one of the ablest members of the faculty at Trinity College during his years there, had urged his colleagues to "make your stand for scholarship; it is what Trinity needs most and what the South needs most."[45]

A significant number of the Trinity faculty shared Bassett's belief, and by the early 1920's the college not only had a research committee,

44. Few to H. N. Snyder, September 4, 1919, Few MSS.
45. Bassett to W. K. Boyd, September 22, 1907, as cited in Porter, *Trinity and Duke*, p. 219.

with its own small fund for grants, but it also had underwritten a series of research monographs. The first volume to carry the imprint of "Trinity College Press" appeared in 1922. These and other developments evinced the ambition and industry of an able, albeit small faculty. President Few welcomed and assisted all these steps, yet he was obviously under all the more pressure to provide the money and the facilities that the academically ambitious institution required.

Efforts to strengthen Trinity's law school began early in the twentieth century, and the hope for a coordinate college for women had grown steadily stronger since Washington Duke had successfully urged the admission of women students in 1896. Though Few had acknowledged before World War I that Trinity was essentially a college for men, by 1920 he boasted to Ben Duke: "I like to think that it is characteristic of the progressive spirit of Trinity College that it took a forward step in the education of women a quarter of a century ago, a step that has only lately been taken by the University of North Carolina, this year by the conservative University of Virginia and by the ancient University of Oxford in England."[46] Despite Few's pride in the matter, he well knew that Trinity's commitment to the education of women was not matched by adequate facilities for them.

There were other developments that pointed in the direction of a significantly enlarged Trinity College. A medical school was one of them, and Few began tentative inquiries in that direction as early as 1916. Significant expansion in the training of preachers began in the early 1920's, and though a department of engineering had long existed at Trinity it too pushed for development. If Trinity were to be enlarged, why not keep the college as the "heart" and seek another name for a university that might be built around it?

The idea for naming the enlarged institution "Duke University" came from Few, who spoke for himself as well as for the leaders among the trustees and the faculty who had been privately consulted about the matter. Their principal reason for favoring the change was that there were already in the United States alone a Trinity University (in Texas) and several other Trinity Colleges. In the British Isles and elsewhere in the English-speaking world there were numerous other institutions named "Trinity."[47] Not wishing to share a name with so

46. Few to Ben Duke, March 27, 1920, Few MSS.
47. "Personal statement by President Few," Few MSS. In many of his published statements as well as in his letters, Few repeated the account of the naming of the university.

many other institutions, Few and his associates turned to the name that various people first began to suggest in the 1890's, but there is no evidence that any member of the Duke family had ever shown any interest in changing the institution's name.

Thus it was that Few, pulling together all his ideas including the naming of the university during his convalescence in the spring of 1921, for the first time visualized the university and its component parts. He then drew up the following statement that he hoped J. B. Duke would sign:

> I wish to see Trinity College, the law school & other schools expanded into a fully developed university organization. It has been suggested to me that this expanded institution be named Duke University as a memorial to my father whose gifts made possible the building of Trinity College in Durham, and I approve this suggestion. I desire this university to include Trinity College, a coordinate College for Women, a Law School, a School of Business Administration, a School of Engineering (emphasizing chemical & electrical engineering), a Graduate School of Arts & Sciences, and, when adequate funds are available, a Medical School. I desire this enlarged institution to be operated under the present charter with only such changes, if any changes at all, as this enlargement may require. To this university that is to be thus organized I will give —— millions of dollars. I agree to pay in within —— years —— millions in cash or good securities.[48]

As soon as Few was able to leave his sick bed, he took the plan to Ben Duke, who was residing in his Durham house at the time. Ben Duke read the document and promptly gave his approval to the whole idea. When Few shortly went to New York, however, J. B. Duke was not ready to commit himself so definitely and showed no inclination either to fill in the monetary blanks that Few had left or to sign the document.

But the idea of a university organized around Trinity College had at least been clearly planted by Few in the mind of J. B. Duke. Moreover, Duke obviously gave some sort of general approval for the scheme, for when the board of trustees of Trinity met in June, 1921,

48. In Few's unpublished and unfinished history, "The Beginnings of an American University," Few MSS, and also in *Duke University Alumni Register*, XVIII (Dec., 1932), pp. 341–342.

Few alluded briefly to a possible reorganization looking toward the status of university. To one or two close friends of the institution, he referred to "great plans which I think in due course will be completely realized" and to "our reorganization for the future." Long conferences on the subject between J. B. Duke and Few followed, one of them later in 1921, although the record reveals nothing about them except that they occurred.[49]

J. B. Duke apparently indicated to Few in 1921 or 1922 that he wished to include in his philanthropic plans some aid to an institution or institutions in the vicinity of Charlotte, which was the focal point of the Southern Power Company's system. Nothing had been worked out, however, and Few redoubled his efforts to convince J. B. Duke regardless of what else he might include in his philanthropy, of the wisdom of building a university around Trinity. Ben Duke was clearly Few's most influential ally in the effort, though Clinton Toms and others also helped.

Few's plan for the university included a medical school, "when adequate funds are available." The qualifying phrase was important, for Few had been learning about medical education and its extremely high costs from the most authoritative teacher on the subject in the country, Dr. Abraham Flexner. Author of a report for the Carnegie Foundation that helped revolutionize medical education in the United States after 1910, Flexner began advising Few as early as 1916. As Crowell in the 1890's and Kilgo in 1901 had advanced the idea of a medical school at Trinity, Few turned to the subject only to learn quickly that a vast sum of money would have to be obtained first. With no four-year medical school in the entire state, North Carolina's need for one was obvious.

After the distraction caused by the nation's involvement in the World War, Few returned to the matter of the medical school and interested George W. Watts in a plan to link the school with Watts Hospital and to have both the school and the hospital act in cooperation with the existing two-year medical school at the University of North Carolina. The General Education Board was eager to help a soundly conceived and well-financed medical school in the southeastern region. The death of George Watts in March, 1921, interrupted, but did not halt Few's plan, for Watts' widow and his son-in-law, John Sprunt Hill, were interested in the project. Negotiations be-

49. Few to J. H. Separk, May 28, 1921, and Few to C. W. Toms, July 23, 1921, Few MSS.

tween Few, the General Education Board, and the other key parties continued quietly, out of the fear that premature publicity would complicate if not kill the whole project.[50]

Assured by the General Education Board of half of the $6,000,000 needed if Trinity College found the other half, Few turned to his "right-hand man," as he called Clinton Toms. Mrs. Watts had pledged $1,000,000. "I think you ought to talk to J. B. D[uke]," Few urged Toms. "If he will say he will give us $1,000,000 within five years, I will undertake the task of raising the rest. If he will give us $2,000,000, success will be assured; and I of course wish he would give three or more."[51]

Before Few could pursue the matter further with J. B. Duke, the initiative in the matter of a four-year medical school for the state passed, in 1922, to the University of North Carolina. The question of the location of the school became a tangled political issue in the legislature, however, and the subject of a struggle between those who championed Chapel Hill, which was still quite small in population, and those who favored the much larger city of Charlotte. With matters thus delayed, Few, assured privately of J. B. Duke's support, made a bold effort for an unusual compromise.[52]

Having gained the support of Governor Cameron Morrison and of the president of the University of North Carolina, Harry W. Chase, Few proposed late in 1922 that Trinity College and the University of North Carolina cooperate to build a medical school in Durham that would be operated in conjunction with Watts Hospital. Wake Forest College and Davidson College would also be invited to take part in the venture, which would represent an unconventional but economical merging of effort by public and private institutions. When certain Baptists voiced fears about possible violation of the principle of the separation of church and state and the *News and Observer* and others raised various objections to the plan, Few realized that he had failed. He had written Ben Duke earlier, however, that even if his proposal should fail, "I feel sure that we can handle the matter in such a way as to leave the College stronger in the eyes of the Rockefeller people and other such great foundations." When it became clear early in

50. James F. Gifford, Jr., *The Evolution of a Medical Center: A History of Medicine at Duke University to 1941* (Durham, 1972), pp. 11–34, has the most detailed, recent study of these matters.

51. Few to Toms, December 10, 1921, Few MSS.

52. Gifford, *Evolution of a Medical Center*, pp. 28–34.

1923 that Few's idea was ahead of the times and would not be accepted by the state legislature, he reassured Ben Duke: "If our much cherished plan to combine Trinity and its professional schools into a university organization can be carried through without too much delay we may even yet get from outside sources [the General Education Board] a considerable amount of money for a medical school to belong wholly to us."[53]

One of the important by-products of Few's abortive efforts to gain a full-fledged medical school for the state was the educational effect the movement had on James B. Duke. Few already knew about the expensiveness of medical education, but J. B. Duke was now learning about it also. Furthermore, one of Few's strongest supporters in the matter was Dr. Watson S. Rankin, then the secretary of the State Board of Health. Rankin strongly favored a four-year medical school but warned that it alone would not alleviate the shortage of doctors in North Carolina, which was still predominantly rural. The main remedy for that shortage, according to Rankin, would be the establishment of local hospitals jointly financed by the state and the counties. Experience in the Canadian province of Saskatchewan, which he had especially studied, and elsewhere in the United States convinced Rankin that the local hospitals were the prime requisites for a better distribution of adequate health care.[54]

James B. Duke may certainly have thought of including hospitals in his philanthropic plans in the interval after his conversation with Few in 1919, when the subject was apparently not mentioned. Both B. N. Duke and J. B. Duke had a long-standing interest in Watts Hospital as well as in Lincoln Hospital, the institution they had given to Durham's black population in 1901. But Few's early efforts in seeking a medical school, and particularly Dr. Rankin's emphasis on the crucial importance of local hospitals in luring doctors away from the larger cities and into the rural districts, clearly exerted a profound influence on J. B. Duke's thinking and planning about his philanthropy.

The pace toward the creation of J. B. Duke's foundation quickened in 1923. Duke once told his friend Mrs. Marshall that the electric power business would never make anyone rich and that there simply was not as much money to be made in it as there had been in the

53. Few to B. N. Duke, December 3, 1922, January 22, 1923, Few MSS.
54. Raleigh *News and Observer*, December 28, 1922.

tobacco industry.[55] Yet with the adjustment of the rates that the power company could charge after 1923 and with what Duke regarded as a more adequate return on the investment, he was ready to proceed with his plans. Not until early in 1923 did Few even meet George G. Allen, a native of Warrenton, North Carolina, who was J. B. Duke's closest associate and adviser, but in June of that year Allen was elected to Trinity College's board of trustees.[56] Duke's executive secretary requested Few's assistance in getting a list of hospitals in North Carolina, with information about their costs and number of free-bed days, and also a list of the orphanages, their per capita cost, capacity, and other pertinent data. Few turned to Dr. Rankin on the matter of the hospitals, and Rankin, eagerly assisting as much as possible, gave this encouragement to Few: "Your idea of developing a large, adequate medical service for the State of North Carolina is one of the biggest conceptions of public service that I have heard of in many a day."[57]

When a newspaper story early in 1924 alluded to statements made by Rankin in what he had presumed to be an off-the-record gathering, he hastily apologized to Few. Rankin noted that when he had been asked why he did not push the idea of local hospitals in the state legislature, he had explained that "the problem was such a large one, one which eventually would require so much money, and one that as yet the public had not begun to think seriously about, that it seemed to me that it should be first undertaken by philanthropy rather than public funds, and that there was reason for believing that the idea might appeal to those who were financially able to begin the development." When J. B. Duke's name was mentioned by someone in the group, Rankin had declared that "if Mr. Duke would take the initiative in the development of such a system of hospitals . . . it would perhaps be best for the State to wait inasmuch as the right sort of program would require twenty-five years for its development."[58]

The hints about J. B. Duke's plans that found their way into the newspapers were too incomplete and scattered, however, for Rankin to have worried. Amidst all the various, confidential preparations, J. B. Duke was finding, as he told one friend, that it had been easier

55. Rounds interview with Mrs. E. C. Marshall, p. 51.
56. Few to Allen, January 20, June 19, 1923, Few MSS. William R. Perkins, Duke's principal legal advisor, was elected to the board late in 1924.
57. Alex. Sands to Few, October 27, 1923, and W. S. Rankin to Few, December 29, 1923, Few MSS.
58. Rankin to Few, January 4, 1924, *ibid.*

to make his money than it was to give it away wisely.[59] Nevertheless he proceeded as carefully and methodically in his approach toward philanthropy as he always had in his business affairs.

The prospect of extensive construction at Trinity College probably appealed personally to James B. Duke as much as anything else. He picked his architectural firm as early as 1923 when Horace Trumbauer, whose staff had designed J. B. Duke's mansion on Fifth Avenue as well as some of the greenhouses at Duke's Farm, began to correspond with Few about the overall plan of the college campus. In the spring of 1924, Few and Frank C. Brown, a professor of English who was a good friend of Ben Duke and a key aide to Few in matters pertaining to the grounds and plant, embarked on an extensive tour of a large number of colleges and universities in the North. Conferring first with Trumbauer in Philadelphia, Few and Brown carefully studied the stone buildings at Bryn Mawr College that were constructed in what was often referred to as the collegiate Gothic or Tudor Gothic style.[60]

At Princeton University where handsome dormitories in the Tudor Gothic style had been built before World War I, Few and Brown collected pictures, some blueprints, and detailed information about the buildings as well as such prosaic matters as arrangements for the kitchens and the mail delivery. Duke's Farm was not far from Princeton, and J. B. Duke himself had admired the newer stone buildings at Princeton. He could no more have explained all of his reasons for liking the buildings than Brodie Duke had been able to do when he first saw and was thrilled by the buildings at Oxford University in England in 1891. But perhaps the Duke brothers unconsciously shared the sentiment of Woodrow Wilson, who offered this explanation early in the century while he was still president of Princeton: "By the very simple device of constructing our new buildings in the Tudor Gothic style we seem to have added to Princeton the age of Oxford and of Cambridge; we have added a thousand years to the history of Princeton by merely putting those lines in our architecture which point every man's imagination to historic traditions of learning in the English-speaking race."[61]

59. Rounds interview with Bennette E. Geer, April, 1963, p. 23.
60. Few-Brown Scrapbook of March-April, 1924, in F. C. Brown MSS, Duke University Archives.
61. Arthur Link, *et al.*, eds., *The Papers of Woodrow Wilson*, XIV, *1902–1903* (Princeton, New Jersey, 1972), p. 269. Contrary to an often-repeated story, J. B. Duke could not have admired the chapel at Princeton, for it was built after his death.

Few and Brown thoroughly agreed with Woodrow Wilson about the Tudor Gothic style, and they proceeded to study it at Yale, Cornell, the City College of New York, Chicago, and on other campuses. At Harvard they particularly noted the Widener Memorial Library, which Trumbauer's firm had designed, and at Johns Hopkins and especially at the University of Virginia, as at some other institutions in Virginia, they were impressed by the felicitous use of red brick and white columns in collegiate buildings of Georgian or neo-classical design.[62]

At any rate, J. B. Duke and Trumbauer, after conferences with Few and Brown, had decided by September, 1924, still three months or so before the public knew anything about either Duke's philanthropic plans or Few's projected university, that the new buildings to be erected on the Trinity campus would be constructed of stone in the Tudor Gothic style. Few reported happily to Ben Duke that such was "distinctly my first choice." Increasingly elated by the prospect of the future, Few added: "It is but the sober truth to say that when these buildings as now planned are put on the grounds we will have here the most harmonious, imposing, and altogether beautiful educational plant in America."[63]

"Personally, I have no doubt that Mr Duke, when he once makes up his mind definitely to go ahead, will see that a most creditable job is done," George G. Allen avowed to Few.[64] Duke had finally concluded to "go ahead" with his project, and in late October, 1924, Robert L. Flowers, vice-president of the college and Few's close associate in administration, began sending to Few some interesting letters from New York marked "personal & confidential." Conferring at great length with Alex. Sands, executive secretary to the Duke brothers, as well as with Allen and Perkins, Flowers found that he faced a challenge in explaining various aspects of Trinity College to New York businessmen who were just becoming acquainted with it. "I think everything is going all right," he assured Few. "From what they all tell me, Mr. J. B. is right in behind the thing now. Mr. B. N. is greatly interested." Later in the same day Flowers dispatched an-

62. Few-Brown Scrapbook.
63. Few to B. N. Duke, September 9, 1924, Few MSS. A few days after this, the board of trustees named a building committee consisting of the chairman of the board, Joseph G. Brown, J. B. Duke and G. G. Allen and gave it full power to "remove or remodel existing buildings and to locate and erect new buildings." Few to G. G. Allen, September 13, 1924, *ibid.*
64. Allen to Few, September 18, 1924, *ibid.*

other bulletin: "Mr. J. B. is undecided how to have the trust fund administered." Up until that time and during about five years of preliminary planning, the idea had been to have the executive committee of Trinity's board of trustees administer the fund. Now Flowers reported a new wrinkle: "They have been to confer with the Rockefeller Foundation and at present they are very much inclined to have fifteen trustees of the fund." Flowers thought it might be unfortunate to have the trustees of the foundation and those of the reorganized college too widely separated. Still, the personnel of the foundation's board would be the important thing, and both Allen and Perkins were eager "to get in touch with the College."[65]

Andrew Carnegie had written extensively to advise wealthy men to disburse their fortunes wisely and carefully during their lifetimes, and Ben Duke, unlike J. B. Duke, probably had read this advice. Ben Duke constantly urged his brother, as he would have done regardless of Carnegie's advice, to proceed with the proposed philanthropy. Flowers found Ben Duke enjoying a spell of improved health and "in better shape than for a long time" and "in fine spirits." Ben Duke, according to Flowers, credited Allen with "spurring up Mr. J. B. not to wait longer to establish his trust" and at long last "Mr. J. B. is pushing things just as fast as he can."[66]

Flowers proved to be quite correct about J. B. Duke's "pushing things" rapidly, for early in December, 1924, Duke arrived in Charlotte with his wife, his daughter Doris, George Allen, W. R. Perkins, and Anthony Biddle. They were soon joined at Duke's house by Norman Cocke, Edward C. Marshall, and Charles I. Burkholder from the power company, by an attorney from Charlotte, E. T. Cansler, and for part of the time by Few, Flowers, and others. Duke announced that he had been working on his philanthropic plans for a number of years and that he now wanted the group to remain assembled until the job of polishing and completing the indenture that would create the perpetual trust was completed. Stopping only for meals, the group worked until around ten o'clock each evening for about four days and discussed, section by section, the draft of the indenture that had been originally prepared largely by W. R. Perkins. Norman Cocke later recalled no substantial alterations or additions that the group made. "Of course, Mr. Duke . . . was a positive man,"

65. Flowers to Few, October 29 (two letters), 30, 1924, *ibid.*
66. *Ibid.*, November 1, 1924.

Cocke added, "and when he made a positive assertion very few people controverted it."[67]

Although J. B. Duke did not formally sign the indenture creating The Duke Endowment until December 11, 1924, at his legal residence in New Jersey, news of the philanthropy leaked out in the newspapers two days earlier. While the nation at large paid ample heed to the announcement of Duke's philanthropy, the largest impact of the news was in the Carolinas where the beneficiaries were located. Securities worth approximately $40,000,000 were turned over to the trustees of the Endowment, and the annual income was to be distributed among educational institutions, hospitals, orphanages, and the Methodist church as specified in the indenture. First of all, however, the fifteen trustees, after dividing among themselves 3 percent of the annual income as compensation for their services, were instructed to set aside 20 percent of the annual income to be added to the principal until an additional $40,000,000 had been accumulated. The remaining 80 percent of the annual income would be distributed in the two Carolinas as follows: 46 percent to educational institutions, 32 percent to hospitals for both races, 12 percent for specified purposes of the Methodist church (in North Carolina only), and 10 percent for orphanages of both races.[68]

The lion's share, 32 percent, of the annual income earmarked for education was designated to go to "an institution of learning to be known as Duke University," and to establish it the trustees were authorized to expend $6,000,000 from the corpus of the trust. "However, should the name of Trinity College . . . be changed to Duke University" within a three-month period, then the $6,000,000 should go to that institution.

While Durham, the home of Trinity College, was at the eastern edge of the territory covered by the Duke Power system, the other three educational beneficiaries were located much closer to the hub of that system. Given the largely Protestant and biracial character of the population of the two Carolinas, the selection of the schools also reflected a gesture in the direction of ecumenism as well as racial liberalism. Davidson College, a Presbyterian institution in Davidson, North Carolina, and close to Charlotte, would receive 5 percent of the

67. Rounds interview with Norman Cocke, pp. 106–107.
68. The indenture creating The Duke Endowment is reprinted in an appendix; a clear, accessible summary may be found in Porter, *Trinity and Duke*, pp. 232–236.

annual income as would Furman University, a Baptist institution in Greenville, South Carolina. In Charlotte itself, Johnson C. Smith University, an institution for blacks, was to receive 4 percent.

The 32 percent of the net income that was earmarked for the area of health care provided, at the "uncontrolled discretion" of the trustees, for aid to hospitals, not operated for private gain, of both races in the Carolinas. At a time when Dr. Rankin and others figured that it cost three dollars per bed per day to provide hospitalization, the trustees were authorized to pay one dollar "per free bed day" provided by a hospital. Any residue of income left after the provision designed to assist in free care would be used for the erection and/or equipment of hospitals, preferably in the two Carolinas but possibly in states contiguous to them if surplus funds should be available.

For the Methodist church in North Carolina, the institution that originally inspired Washington Duke and then his sons to begin their charitable giving, 12 percent was designated. To help build and maintain rural Methodist churches in the state there would be 10 percent of the income, and the remaining 2 percent would supplement the church's payments to superannuated preachers and to their widows and orphans. For the institutions that served the white and black orphans of the two Carolinas there would be 10 percent of the annual income.

Far back in 1893, Ben Duke had acted for the family in disbursing about $13,500 for charitable purposes. In 1924, J. B. Duke apportioned the income from a forty-million-dollar perpetual trust that was destined to grow much larger; it would be more than doubled by the terms of Duke's will. The striking point, however, is not so much the difference in the two sums of money but the continuity in the purpose and nature of the giving. The creation of The Duke Endowment was certainly not an inevitable development, for many rich men have found countless other ways to dispose of their wealth. The Endowment was, nevertheless, the culmination of a deeply rooted and longstanding tradition and pattern of giving that Washington Duke had begun, Ben Duke had largely supervised for many years, and J. B. Duke institutionalized for posterity on a princely scale.

James B. Duke wanted the trustees of the Endowment to be a carefully picked, working group. He specified in the indenture that the trustees should "make a special effort to secure persons of character and ability" as their successors, that they should meet at least ten times each year, and, as stated, that they should be paid for their chores from a fixed percentage of the annual income. Because, as Duke explained in his indenture, he had long planned for much of the revenue from the power company to be used for the social welfare of "the communities which they serve," he recommended that the securities of the power company be "the prime investment for the funds of this trust," to be changed only in "response to the most urgent and extraordinary necessity." One reason for dropping the plan to make the executive committee of Trinity's trustees act as the trustees of the endowment, aside from a possible conflict of interest, was made clear by Duke's next phrase, for he requested that the Endowment's trustees "see to it that at all times these [power] companies be managed and operated by the men best qualified for such a service." He intended, in other words, for the trustees of the Endowment, which he thought would eventually hold a controlling share of the power company's stock, to maintain a close watch over the actual managers of the company. That was a task for which the trustees of a college or university might or might not be suited.

Toward the end of his indenture, J. B. Duke summarized his intentions: he had "endeavored to make provision in some measure for the needs of mankind along physical, mental and spiritual lines. . . ." He conceded that he might have extended aid to other causes and to other sections of the country but asserted his belief that "so doing probably would be productive of less good by reason of attempting too much." He urged the trustees "to seek to administer well the trust hereby committed to them," and he, who through much of his adult life preferred having documents read aloud to him rather than reading them himself, asked that "at least at one meeting each year this Indenture be read to the assembled trustees."

The twelve persons whom Duke selected as the original trustees of the endowment were, in the order of their signing the indenture, Nanaline H. [Mrs. J. B.] Duke, George G. Allen, William R. Perkins, William B. Bell, Anthony J. Drexel Biddle, Jr., Walter C. Parker, Alex. H. Sands, Jr., William S. Lee, Charles I. Burkholder, Norman A. Cocke, Edward C. Marshall, and Bennette E. Geer. They soon added J. B. Duke to their number, named Dr. Watson Rankin as a trustee and put him in charge of the hospital section of the Endowment, and specified that Doris Duke become a member of the board when she became twenty-one in 1933.

James B. Duke by no means regarded the establishment of the Endowment as a stopping point for himself. True, as congratulations and letters of thanks poured in he actually signed more letters than he probably had in the past ten years combined; but he was obviously warmed by the response to his philanthropy and wished to acknowledge the letters of those who troubled to write him. Vigorous and apparently in good health at age sixty-eight, he had dams to build in the Carolinas and in Canada and a whole new complex of buildings to erect and then give to Duke University. There was even talk of his building a home in Durham so that he might supervise at first hand the construction of the Tudor Gothic buildings. He was one Tarheel who had begun to come home again, only partly to be sure, when water powers lured him early in the century. Now it appeared that he might just come all the way home to Durham, from whence the Dukes and their tobacco business had gone far together.

CHAPTER 11. THE LAUNCHING OF DUKE UNIVERSITY AND THE DEATHS OF THE DUKE BROTHERS

At Christmas in 1924, no North Carolinian could have been happier than William P. Few. "Then after all, my dream and your dream is to be realized in full," he exulted to Ben Duke. "Isn't it glorious?"[1] Although Few had privately expressed his fears that some of the Trinity alumni might object to the creation of a new Duke University around the old college, he quickly gained overwhelming support from the great majority of the institution's alumni and friends. "Personally, when it comes to that point where Trinity can take the lead in educational circles of the entire South," one of the alumni wrote, "I am inclined to shout with Shakespeare: 'WHAT'S IN A NAME?' " Another prominent alumnus declared: "As you are aware, changing the name to Duke University had been my wish for some years, and it is with genuine satisfaction that I now see a realization of this about to take place."[2]

The trustees agreed with the majority of the alumni, and when the official board met on December 29, 1924, they voted unanimously to accept J. B. Duke's offer. Declaring that the new university was "to be developed according to plans that are perfectly in line with our hopes for the expansion of this historic College," the trustees explained that the "control of Duke University and all its relations to its constituency will remain identical with the control and relations to constituency that Trinity College has had."[3]

In the indenture creating The Duke Endowment, J. B. Duke explained that he had selected Duke University as one of the principal beneficiaries because he recognized that "education, when conducted along sane and practical, as opposed to dogmatic and theoretical lines, is next to religion, the greatest civilizing influence." Duke requested that "this institution secure for its officers, trustees and

1. Few to B. N. Duke, December 13, 1924, Few MSS.
2. Banks Arendall to Few, December 10, 1924, and P. H. Hanes, Jr., to Few, December 17, 1924, *ibid.*
3. Minutes, Board of Trustees, December 29, 1924, as cited in Porter, *Trinity and Duke*, pp. 234–235.

faculty men of such outstanding character, ability and vision as will insure its attaining and maintaining a place of real leadership in the educational world. . . ." For its students he urged that "great care and discrimination be exercised" to admit "only those whose previous record shows a character, determination and application evincing a wholesome and real ambition for life." He advised, finally, that "the courses at this institution be arranged, first, with special reference to the training of preachers, teachers, lawyers and physicians, because these are most in the public eye, and by precept and example can do most to uplift mankind, and, second, to instruction in chemistry, economics and history, expecially the lives of the great of [the] earth, because I believe that such subjects will most help to develop our resources, increase our wisdom and promote human happiness."

Perhaps in response to J. B. Duke's words, the college's trustees in their statement of acceptance declared that Duke University would "be concerned about excellence rather than size," and it would "aim at quality rather than numbers—quality of those who teach and quality of those who learn." Moreover, the university would be developed "with a view to serving conditions as they actually exist" and would be "for the use of all the people of the State and Section without regard to creed, class or party, and for those elsewhere who may seek to avail themselves of the opportunities it has to offer."[4]

Enthusiastically supported by the students then enrolled at Trinity-Duke, Few and Duke University also received an encouraging word from an important neighbor. Harry W. Chase, president of the University of North Carolina, was a generous, broad-visioned man like Few. Moreover, the state's university was itself undergoing a significant awakening and expansion in the 1920's. "Two universities, located as ours are," Chase prophetically declared, "growing up side by side, the one in response to private benefaction and the other under State control, should supplement each other, and each, I believe, will be a stimulus to the other's development." Chase maintained that J. B. Duke's gift to promote Duke University would "advance at the same time the whole level of thinking about higher education in the State and in the South."[5]

Despite the happy harmony between J. B. Duke, President Few, the trustees, and most of the alumni, all was not sweetness and light as Trinity moved to accept the largesse of J. B. Duke. A few alumni

4. *Ibid.*
5. Chase to Few, December 9, 1924, Few MSS.

objected to the new name for the institution. One objected not so much to the name as to the geographic location and to J. B. Duke's failure to consider Asheville in the western part of the state. "The Divinity which engineered the building of the Pyramids in the desert sands of Egypt probably understands why Duke University is going ahead in Durham County," this irate alumnus declared, "but His great plan does not comprehend that people outside of Durham should understand it." Few patiently explained that he had once discussed with J. B. Duke the possibility of "going to Asheville" but found him opposed to the idea. "When you go out to get $40,000,000 from a man," Few asserted, "you will find that he has some ideas of his own." When the stubborn champion of Asheville retorted by insisting that "nothing short of a *miracle* can ever establish a truly great university in a place like Durham," Few closed the correspondence on a confident note: "We have never thought of ourselves as miracle workers but we have not a shadow of doubt that we can work the miracle that may seem to be necessary to build a great university here."[6]

Much more serious than the grumbles of the small handful of disgruntled alumni was the widespread and long-persisting misunderstanding about the relationship of James B. Duke to the creation of Duke University around Trinity College. Norman Cocke, one of the original trustees of the Endowment, revealed that there had been few alterations made in the draft of the indenture during the intense discussion of it just prior to its formal signing. J. B. Duke would have been better served by more candid and critical associates, for there were regrettable and avoidable flaws in the indenture. The limiting of the investments to the securities of the power company would pose serious problems several decades later, although Duke and his friends could certainly not be expected to have had the foresight to look that far into the future and to imagine a totally changed set of circumstances. A flaw with more immediate repercussions was the section which provided that $6,000,000 should be used to establish "an institution of learning to be known as Duke University," but "should the name of Trinity College . . . be changed to Duke University" then it would receive the $6,000,000.

Some people quickly seized on this section and interpreted it, understandably enough, as a blatant case of "Buck Duke's buying himself

6. J. L. Jackson to Few, November 10, 28, 1925, and Few to Jackson, November 26, 30, 1925, *ibid.*

a university" or "bribing" a college in order to memorialize himself and his family. Since the idea of building a university around Trinity College and naming it Duke had originated with Few and his closest associates, the popular interpretation was hardly fair to J. B. Duke. Yet he and his lawyers were responsible for the clumsy, legalistic language that inspired the popular notion. Few issued explanatory statements to the public and privately confessed that he was "only sorry that the legal phrasing in the Indenture of Trust seemed to put Mr. Duke in a bad light."[7]

Truth often never catches up with error, especially when the falsehood may be turned to witty and amusing ends. H. L. Mencken's *American Mercury* specialized in sophomoric attacks on J. B. Duke and his presumption in thinking he could build himself a university allegedly from scratch.[8] Other journalists in newspapers and magazines would for many years ignore Few's patient efforts to set the record straight and keep alive the story of J. B. Duke's "buying" himself a university. An additional twist was soon added with the allegation that J. B. Duke had first tried to "buy" Princeton (or Yale or whatever university) but having failed there, turned to a small college in the South that was unknown to so many in the East. Strangely enough, students at Duke University itself have for decades passed along the tale about J. B. Duke and Princeton, a 1973 version in the student newspaper putting it this way: "Many years ago, before the expansion of Trinity College, James Duke tried to 'buy' Princeton so that he would have a little school to which to give his name." A variation appeared in another publication: J. B. Duke "is reputed to have first urged his money (and his name) on Yale. Rebuffed by Yale, he decided to rival it in prestige and physical beauty. Thus was Duke University grandly formed from Duke's millions."[9]

The examples could be multiplied endlessly, but most of the silly and groundless myth-making arose out of ignorance not only about President Few's part in the origin of the university's name but more especially about Trinity College itself and the Duke family's long and close relationship to the institution. At any rate, it is doubtful that J. B. Duke himself gave a moment's thought to the matter, if he ever

7. Few to J. H. Reynolds, December 29, 1924, *ibid.*

8. A bitter attack on J. B. Duke and his philanthropy by a newspaperman to whom he had earlier given one of his rare interviews may be found in Ben Dixon MacNeill, "Duke," *American Mercury*, XVII (August, 1929), pp. 430–438.

9. Chris Scheck in *The Duke Chronicle*, March 13, 1973; Lawrence Wright, "A Slow Dance with Progress," *Race Relations Reporter* (March, 1973), p. 14.

became aware of it. He had long before developed a tough hide, possibly too tough for his own good, when it came to what newspapers and other journals had to say. He believed, whether rightly or wrongly, that he had more important things to do than worry about misunderstandings on the part of the public.

Starting in 1924, almost a year before the Endowment was officially established, Duke and Horace Trumbauer, or some of the latter's associates, visited the Trinity campus from time to time in connection with the contemplated expansion. Early in 1924 Few informed Duke that he had given much thought to the "relaying out of our campus along the general lines you suggested to me in Charlotte the other day." Sending four preliminary sketches, Few pronounced his eagerness to cooperate in the planning.[10]

An essential preliminary for the expansion was the acquisition of additional land, for despite the fact that Trinity's campus was already spacious, it was not big enough for the new buildings that J. B. Duke had in mind. Land to the north of the campus, particularly in the area of Watts Hospital, would be needed for the possible medical school. By the spring of 1924 Few's agents had been quietly securing options for land around the college for more than a year. When informed in May, 1924, that the price of the various parcels of land under option totalled $161,000, J. B. Duke sent word to Few that "it would be all right to go that far but not to pay any more than that, and to be sure that you get all of it."[11]

Getting "all of it" at reasonable prices, however, proved to be increasingly difficult as rumors spread through Durham about Trinity's expansion, and land prices rose accordingly. By October, 1924, Few was still optimistic about acquiring the desired land but admitted that "it will require some time."[12] Impatient with the delays and increasingly angered by what he regarded as the price-gouging of landowners in the vicinity of Trinity's campus, J. B. Duke in the fall of 1924 made threatening noises about giving up in Durham and trying to build a university in Charlotte. One kinswoman to whom he allegedly said something along those lines reported that she made this reply: "Uncle Buck, that would be awful. This is the place you all were born; your father started that college and he lived here and had great faith in Trinity College and all, and [going to Charlotte] would

10. Few to J. B. Duke, January 31, 1924, Few MSS.
11. Alex. Sands to Few, May 5, 1924, *ibid.*
12. Few to J. B. Duke, October 28, 1924, *ibid.*

look awful silly and foolish." When Duke responded that the university was going to be a large one and that Charlotte might be able to handle it better, the staunch partisan of Durham and Trinity retorted, "Well, you do it, but I don't think it is a true memorial to the Duke family or to your father if you move it to Charlotte."[13]

If J. B. Duke was merely trying to light a fire under Few and the other college officials with the talk of Charlotte, and he probably was attempting just that, he succeeded admirably. Walking with his sons through a lovely wooded area a mile or so to the west of the Trinity campus, where he had often ridden horseback as a younger man, Few hit upon the idea of expanding in that direction rather than north towards Watts Hospital. The ground rolled gently, there were pine forests as well as some oaks and other hardwood trees, and no one, including the landowners, had even dreamed of Trinity's going that far afield. "It was for me a thrilling moment when I stood on a hill," Few later wrote, ". . . and realized that here at last is the land we have been looking for."[14]

James B. Duke assented to an effort to acquire land in the new direction, and while some limited buying continued north of the campus, Robert L. Flowers, operating with the utmost discretion and quietness, went to work. Securing the first option on November 7, 1924, Flowers had, by the spring of 1925, succeeded in acquiring at reasonable prices much more land than was immediately needed. In fact, purchases to round out the holdings continued for many years, and Duke University eventually wound up owning approximately 8,000 acres, most of it in a forest preserve, and would never face the problem of land scarcity that plagues many educational institutions. "The acquisition of the land," Flowers assured his old friend Ben Duke, "has been to me one of the most absorbing things I have ever been connected with." All who saw the new land, Flowers declared, were "carried away with the prospect." Nor had there ever been "any greater mystery in Durham than the land transaction."[15] For several months while the new land was being acquired, however, no one knew whether it would actually be used or just how it might be used. James B. Duke had the final word on that and not until late March, 1925, was his decision made.

13. Rounds interview with Mrs. John Williams, January and July, 1964. Mrs. Williams is the widow of J. B. Duke's nephew, Buchanan Lyon.

14. Few's unfinished manuscript, "The Beginnings of An American University," pp. 6–7.

15. Flowers to B. N. Duke, May 8, 1925, R. L. Flowers MSS, Duke University

With any luck at all, spring in the North Carolina Piedmont, with its abundant wild dogwood and redbud trees and other native flowering shrubs, can be a splendid time. Such it was when J. B. Duke finally inspected the new land and, in consultation with Few and others, quickly decided: the Tudor Gothic buildings, with a soaring chapel at their center, would be built on the new land on a crest or plateau overlooking a deep ravine that J. B. Duke envisioned as a lake; there would be a large fountain in the central quadrangle, and the water would cascade over falls that emptied into the lake; the long-desired coordinate college for women, instead of being crowded into the northwest corner of the old campus, would occupy that entire campus, and while several of the existing buildings would be retained, some would have to go in order to make room for eleven new buildings to be constructed of red brick and white marble in the Georgian style.

A prosaic work-diary or notebook of Horace Trumbauer's superintendent, B. M. Hall, is the best source—as well as one of the few documentary sources—for all of the important decisions concerning Duke University that J. B. Duke, Few, and their associates made late in March, 1925. The trustees of The Duke Endowment were meeting in Durham at the time, at Ben Duke's home in fact. Many years later two things about that meeting remained vivid in the memory of one of the trustees who was present: the first was that during one of the trustees' sessions young Doris Duke entered the room, climbed on to her father's knee, and remained there quietly for the remainder of the meeting; the other was that J. B. Duke invited the trustees to inspect the new land with him. "We walked all over those grounds," Dr. Watson Rankin stated, "jumping ditches and crossing wagon roads and going through shrubbery and all that kind of thing, with Mr. Duke always in the lead. Again I was impressed with the man's vigor."[16]

Trumbauer's construction superintendent merely noted: "Met Mr. Duke today and went over the ground for the new University." Then the following day the superintendent recorded that he had met Trumbauer and another of the architects, who had arrived on the train in Raleigh, and "explained the new location of the layout on top of the hill moving the chapel forward so it will come on the high ground." The superintendent noted also that the library was "to be moved over

---

Archives. The total cost of the new land that had been purchased up to the spring of 1929 came to $1,762,617 according to a memorandum from A. Sands to Flowers, April 12, 1929, *ibid.*

16. Rounds interview with Dr. Rankin, pp. 57–58.

to a high spot to the right of where shown on plans, this being Mr. Duke's idea of how the layout should be." Further on, after mentioning various other activities, the superintendent wrote: "Went over to the new location and Mr. Duke approved of the general layout but ordered another fountain on the opposite hill to flow down into the lake that will be down in the ravine in front of the chapel." On the third day of all the intense activity, Few, Flowers, and Frank Brown attended a "full meeting" where a reduction of over 900,000 cubic feet was worked out in the plans, but at a subsequent session "a goodly portion of our saving was put back by Mr. Duke and Mr. Allen. . . ." Trumbauer and his associates headed back to Philadelphia with instructions to proceed with working drawings, first for the new buildings on the Trinity campus, soon to become known as the East Campus, and then for the Gothic structures that would be erected on the new land, the West Campus. A great deal of the planning for the two campuses of Duke University had been accomplished in three busy spring days.[17]

Concurrently with the matter of the new land, J. B. Duke helped to decide another problem that keenly interested him; this concerned the kind of stone to be used in the Tudor Gothic buildings of Duke University. He originally thought that the stone for the buildings should come from one of the well-known quarries in the North, in Pennsylvania, New Jersey, Indiana, or Massachusetts. Accordingly, he arranged for car-loads of various samples of the stone to be shipped to Durham and for test walls to be built on the Trinity campus. Frank C. Brown, in the meantime, checked out the possibility of North Carolina stone and found in the possession of the state geologist some specimens of volcanic stone from an abandoned quarry near Hillsborough, North Carolina, only a few miles from Durham. By March, 1925, on the eve of J. B. Duke's inspection of the new land, Brown informed Trumbauer that a sample wall of the local stone had been built; it was not only "much more attractive than the Princeton wall" and "much warmer and softer in coloring," but he estimated that it could be quarried and delivered on the ground at not more than $3.50 per ton whereas he estimated that the Princeton stone would cost approximately $21.00 per ton. When Flowers informed George Allen about the exciting possibilities of the local stone and how cheaply the "entire ridge" with "an almost unlimited supply" of stone could

17. B. M. Hall's work-diary, March 29–31, 1925, in the Frank C. Brown MSS.

be purchased, J. B. Duke ordered the acquisition of the quarry and further testing of the stone.[18]

Pleased by the wide range of colors in the stone—various shades of brown, yellow, black, blue, green, and gray—as well as reassured of its durability by tests conducted both in the state geologist's office and in the Bureau of Standards in Washington, J. B. Duke in late March, 1925, proudly led the trustees of the Endowment to the sample walls where balloting indicated an overwhelming preference for the native stone. Duke wanted additional walls built, however, with "less of the yellow and gold colors." Accordingly, Frank Brown suggested a wall showing "as predominating colors the dark blue, the light blue, the light green, the light gray and the dark blue with face mottled with dark brown." All those colors, Brown believed, could be obtained from the Hillsborough quarry "in unlimited quantities."[19] The buildings of Duke University's West Campus were inspired by a venerable style of English architecture but the warmly colored stone would come from a neighboring hillside in Piedmont North Carolina.

James B. Duke, no less than his brother, loved landscaping, and to lay out the grounds of the new campus as well as to redesign the ones of the old Trinity campus he selected one of the leading firms in the country, Olmstead Brothers of Boston, a firm founded by Frederick Law Olmstead, the creator of Central Park in New York and of many other famous parks. Even before J. B. Duke had seen the new land, he requested that contour maps of its central portion show all the large trees, for he clearly intended to build the new campus in such a fashion as to save as many of the significant trees as possible.

Apart from a few pioneers, the American public in the 1920's was not spending much time worrying about "the environment" or "ecology." Not until the latter half of the century, in fact, would a significant segment of the nation become concerned about those matters. The Duke brothers were, however, rather ahead of their times in their concern for the physical setting, the environment, in which educational activities were to proceed. John Spencer Bassett, still a devoted friend of Trinity-Duke though he had moved on to another institution some years earlier, perhaps put it best when he suggested to

18. Brown to Trumbauer, March 20, 1925, F. C. Brown MSS, and Flowers to Allen, March 21, 1925, R. L. Flowers MSS. William Blackburn, "Summary of Information about Duke Stone, July 10, 1935," in the Flowers MSS, is helpful as is Blackburn's *The Architecture of Duke University* (Durham, 1939).

19. Brown to B. M. Hall, April 18, 1925, F. C. Brown MSS.

Few that educated men of the South needed "to turn to this aesthetic problem." College men should "make standards of living," Bassett thought, and Trinity College could "afford to spend money liberally for beautiful grounds and artistically designed buildings well placed." They were "educational in just the way we need education just now."[20]

James B. Duke would probably not have used Bassett's words, but he instinctively understood their meaning and acted accordingly. Other than agreeing with Few about the new university's pursuit of excellence rather than numbers and its national as well as regional service and orientation, J. B. Duke was content to leave the academic planning, the faculty recruitment, and similar problems in professional hands. He intended to provide the buildings, the grounds, and as much of the monetary means as he could and leave the rest to Few, Flowers, Dean W. H. Wannamaker, and their associates on the faculty. Large problems, such as the location of the projected chapel, and small ones, such as the width of the hallways in the girls' dormitories (J. B. Duke wanted, and got, wider ones) and the arrangements of the rooms within those buildings—all were of keen interest to the industrialist who had turned philanthropist.[21]

Greatly interested as J. B. Duke was in the building of Duke University, there were yet other large projects of vital concern to him. In July, 1925, he, together with George Allen, W. S. Lee, and various officials of the Aluminum Company of America visited the Saguenay river in Canada to inspect the power site there for which Duke had earlier received a one-ninth interest in the aluminum company. He and his party travelled on his private railway car, the "Doris," and Arthur Vining Davis, Secretary of the Treasury Andrew Mellon, his brother R. B. Mellon, Roy A. Hunt, who later became president of Alcoa, and other officials of the aluminum company went on another private car. Having already lost some weight, J. B. Duke was dieting and, according to Roy Hunt, grumbled about having only "three damned prunes" for breakfast. He carried a walking cane, as he had for some years, but so did Lee and Allen.

There was much visiting back and forth between the private railway cars during the several days the group remained in Canada.

20. Bassett to Few, May 20, 1920, Few MSS.
21. J. B. Duke's involvement in the planning of what became the East Campus of Duke University may be traced in the Few, Flowers, and F. C. Brown MSS. Brown served as the liason between Few and his associates in Durham, on the one hand, and Trumbauer and his staff in Philadelphia on the other. Relations were notably amicable, but various matters were referred to J. B. Duke for final decision.

When Andrew Mellon advocated investing money in art works, Duke reportedly replied that that was all right, but he was more interested in "putting it in Duke University and in the schools and helping out the people there in North and South Carolina and doing that as far as investment is concerned." Later the conversation turned to the subject of Henry Ford and cheap transportation for the ordinary man, and Duke argued that he had helped give "the poor man a lot of pleasure in cheap cigarettes." Amidst the laughter of the group, he asked, "Where can a man get as much fun out of fifteen cents as buying a package of cigarettes and enjoying them?"

Duke impressed Roy Hunt as alert and possessed of a sharp mind. Physically he kept up with the group in several days of fairly strenuous moving about in what was then a relatively undeveloped region. Altogether, Hunt sized him up as a "soft-spoken" person, a "courteous Southern gentleman" who seemed "very friendly and very keen."[22]

Matters went well for J. B. Duke in Canada, but in the Carolinas during the summer of 1925 the Duke Power system had fallen upon a bad time. Prolonged drought in the Piedmont region left many rivers and reservoirs perilously low, so low that the company's coal-burning steam plants, which had been built for auxiliary or standby use only, had to be operated around the clock, seven days a week. By August the company had to call for curtailment of power consumption, first only for those customers in particular zones and then for all customers. The crisis had not come with the dramatic speed of the 1916 floods, but it was none the less acute.[23]

James B. Duke had grown increasingly aware of the need for more steam plants even before the drought. His wife told Mrs. Marshall that "for two years he has talked of nothing but steam plants," a subject that Mrs. Duke claimed not to understand. He went to Charlotte, before going to Canada in fact, and for several days conferred with his associates in the power company and toured various plants. Because his wife and daughter were at Newport, Duke was lonely one evening and invited Norman Cocke to come over. Duke looked well, Cocke thought, but was in an unusually reminiscent mood and talked at length about the early tobacco business, his unsuccessful farming venture at Great Falls, and various other topics. The drought had not reached its critical stage by the time of Duke's visit, however,

22. Rounds interview with Roy A. Hunt in Pittsburgh, October and December, 1963.

23. John W. Fox, outline history of the Duke Power Company, p. 11.

and nothing was decided about an additional large steam plant.[24]

Having touched base at Duke University, Charlotte, and on the Saguenay, J. B. Duke joined his family at Newport in the latter part of July, 1925. He continued to confer there with his associates who came up to deliver important papers or to gain a final decision on some question. Robert L. Flowers visited him at Newport about university affairs; George Allen and Alex. Sands may have made more than one trip, but in September Allen sent word from Newport that J. B. Duke had decided to use the "pinkish granite" rather than the less expensive gray granite in certain parts of the new Georgian buildings on the East Campus and that marble rather than limestone would be used even though the former cost $350,000 more.[25]

Despite J. B. Duke's continuing involvement in various affairs, he became ill at Newport the latter part of July, 1925. As late as the end of August, his wife felt optimistic, for she wrote W. P. Few that "though Mr. Duke's improvement has been slow, it still continues, from day to day." She thought it would be "at least two or three months, however, before he is back to his normal health again."[26] When Duke's illness only seemed to grow worse, he was carried on his private railway car to New York and there his doctors discovered in September that he suffered from what they diagnosed as pernicious anemia. A disconsolate Ben Duke finally admitted that his brother would never recover.[27] In fact, on October 10, 1925, three days after Ben Duke confronted the sad truth, James B. Duke died in his mansion on Fifth Avenue. He would have been sixty-nine years old on December 23.

Death seems to have caught J. B. Duke by surprise. Vigorous, especially for a man of his age, he had suffered few serious health problems for the fifteen or twenty years preceding his death. He was happily involved in building Duke University and in the problems of the power company and had mentioned to several of his associates that he hoped to live long enough to see some of his favorite projects completed.

Even after his return to New York, he conferred with Norman Cocke and E. C. Marshall about the drought in the Carolinas. When

24. Rounds interview with Mrs. Marshall, p. 35, and with Cocke, p. 121.

25. A. Sands to Flowers, September 9, 14, 1925; copy of Allen to Trumbauer, September 24, 1925, Flowers MSS.

26. Nanaline Duke at "Rough Point," Newport, R.I., to W. P. Few, August 30, 1925, Few MSS.

27. B. N. Duke to R. L. Flowers, October 7, 1925, Flowers MSS.

Duke's private nurse had noticed his restlessness at one point and inquired if he wanted something, Duke responded, "Please don't disturb me. I'm building a steam plant down South." Sure enough, after studying blueprints and estimates, he authorized Cocke and Marshall, when they visited him in New York, to proceed with the construction of a large steam plant on the Yadkin river near Salisbury, North Carolina. With a proposed capacity of 70,000 kilowatts, it would be the first central-station-type steam plant in the Duke Power system, one of the first power plants in the country to utilize the new technology and equipment that allowed the burning of pulverized coal, and a significant benchmark in the transition of the Duke Power system from water to steam as its primary source of power.[28]

Having made on his death-bed a crucially important decision concerning the power company, J. B. Duke also kept Duke University and its problems and needs much on his mind. Earlier in the year he had added $2,000,000 to the original building fund of $6,000,000. Few had hammered away at J. B. Duke about the great expensiveness of medical education, and in the indenture creating the endowment Duke had incorporated Few's own careful phrasing about the university's including a medical school "as and when funds are available." Carefully refraining from committing the university until funds were clearly in sight, Few dutifully persisted in reminding J. B. Duke about the need to make special provision for a medical school if he really wanted to see one built at Duke University. In his will that had been signed in December, 1924, when the Endowment was established, Duke specified that an additional $10,000,000 be given to The Duke Endowment and that $4,000,000 of that sum should be used for the construction of a medical school, hospital, and nurses' home at Duke University, with the income from the remainder to go to Duke University. Another provision of the will left the remainder of his estate after all other bequests, or more than the equivalent of the original $40,000,000, to The Duke Endowment.[29]

Not content with those provisions that were not made public until after his death, J. B. Duke worried much about the adequacy of the funds for building the university. Consequently he summoned George Allen, and on October 1, 1925, signed a codicil to his will leaving an

28. Jenkins, *J. B. Duke*, p. 259; Rounds interviews with Norman Cocke, p. 63, and with C. T. Wanzer in Charlotte, July, 1963, p. 36.

29. "Last Will and Testament of James B. Duke," J. B. Duke MSS; Jenkins, *J. B. Duke*, pp. 299–302.

245

additional $7,000,000 for "building and equipping" Duke University. Altogether then, and apart from the annual income that the university was to derive from its share of The Duke Endowment, J. B. Duke provided $19,000,000 for the building of Duke University on its two campuses.[30]

Perhaps some ease came into J. B. Duke's mind after he made the additional provision for the institution that his father and brother had first befriended and that he had more recently come to cherish also. At any rate, soon after signing the codicil he developed pneumonia and breathing became difficult. Recognizing the butler shortly before lapsing into a coma, J. B. Duke said, "I'm in pretty bad shape, Edward." When the butler assured him that he looked "pretty good," Duke retorted, "But you can't go by looks." Because the windows were all open to let in the brisk autumn air, Nanaline Duke, a small trim woman, sat beside her husband's bed huddled in a fur cape.[31]

After a simple, private service without eulogy or sermon in the New York residence, J. B. Duke's body was carried by train to Durham. There on October 13, 1925, after services in Duke Memorial Methodist Church, he was buried beside his father in the family mausoleum. His wife, who continued to live in New York, died at age ninety on April 12, 1962.

Generous to his wife during his lifetime and by the terms of his will, J. B. Duke was so munificent in his provisions for his daughter that she would long be plagued by unwelcome publicity about one whom the tabloids liked to call the "richest girl in the world." Duke had established trusts for the future benefit of his daughter before she was even eight years old. In 1924, when he created The Duke Endowment and signed his will, he also established the Doris Duke Trust. Two-thirds of the income of the trust was to go to Doris Duke and one-third to J. B. Duke's nieces, nephews, and their descendants. Although Duke placed only $35,000 in cash and two thousand shares of the Duke Power Company's stock in the trust at the time of its creation, by

30. *Ibid.*; Gifford, *Evolution of a Medical Center*, pp. 43–44, describes the successful effort of Few and others to protect The Duke Endowment from loss of income under Federal revenue laws.

31. Rounds interview with Edward Hansen in New York, September and December, 1963, May 1964, pp. 88-89. After J. B. Duke's death, Dr. George R. Minot, a specialist in Boston who had advised Duke's doctors in New York, studied samples of Duke's blood and later advised Dr. F. M. Hanes, March 21, 1945, that he did not believe Duke died of pernicious anemia but from "one of those fundamental disorders of blood formation that have commonly been called aregeneratory anemias. . . ." Copy in The Duke Endowment MSS.

his will he left it all the shares that he still possessed in the power company. Since that was 125,904 shares, the Doris Duke Trust, at least for a time, held slightly more stock in the power company than did The Duke Endowment. Duke also provided that one-third of his residuary estate, after certain deductions had been made for the university and other specified purposes, should go to his daughter in various portions at three different ages up to thirty. An intelligent, shy thirteen-year-old girl, who seemed to share a number of her father's traits, had been left with the dubious blessing of extraordinarily immense wealth.[32]

Just as money could hardly console a girl just entering her teenage years for the loss of her doting father, so Ben Duke was bereft and probably missed his brother as much as anyone did. An old friend from Durham who had earlier played a key role in the American Tobacco Company, W. W. Fuller, wrote to Ben Duke that he knew "Buck's going will bear most heavily on you." Fuller added: "I have never known of such deep, unvarying affection between men as has existed all your lives between you and him. I have, in the years of intimate association with him, known his love for you at all times and his unquestioning trust and confidence in you, and how you returned his love and trust." Ben Duke himself, writing to Robert Flowers about contributions to various new Methodist churches that were being built in Durham, confessed in a hand-written letter, "I am feeling wretched & of course filled with grief over the passing of my dear brother."[33]

In 1924, a year or so before J. B. Duke's death, Ben Duke enjoyed an interlude of improved health. For the use of his brother as well as himself, he set out to compile lists of all the living descendants of his aunts and uncles, that is, lists of his own cousins. Since the families had been large on both paternal and maternal sides, however, Ben Duke's task was not easy. That he enjoyed it is shown by his statement early in 1925 that he had in the previous six months given to cousins between $500,000 and $550,000, and Ben Duke added, "I have never done anything that has given me more satisfaction and pleasure."[34]

Ben Duke's joy in distributing money to cousins and other distant

32. Jenkins, *J. B. Duke*, pp. 298–301.

33. Copy of Fuller to B. N. Duke, October 11, 1925, Few MSS; B. N. Duke to Flowers, October 22, 1925, Flowers MSS.

34. B. N. Duke to Edna Vaughan, January 26, February 10, 1925, and to E. L. Vaughan, February 10, 25, 1925, J. B. Duke MSS.

relatives began to pall as complications arose even before his brother's death. After that, however, he became especially disgusted when hundreds of honest but confused claimants, plus a few plainly dishonest ones, began to scramble for a share of the $2,000,000 that J. B. Duke left to the descendants of his uncles and aunts, whom he did not, however, specify by name in his will.[35]

Returning to the kind of institutional philanthropy in which he had been engaged for more than thirty-five years, Ben Duke made one of his most significant gifts to Duke University. To commemorate his dead son, he established the Angier B. Duke Memorial, Incorporated, which immediately became and remained a principal source of scholarships and loan funds in the university. Institutionalizing on a large scale something that he, his father, and others in the family had been doing since the early 1890's, Ben Duke could hardly have picked a more useful way to erect a special kind of monument to his son.[36]

After J. B. Duke's death, Ben Duke found two principal sources of pleasures in life—his grandchildren and giving away money to colleges and churches scattered throughout the southeastern region of the country. Utilizing Alex. Sands, R. L. Flowers, W. P. Few, and one or two others as his principal advisers, Ben Duke, who was increasingly confined to his home and even had to begin using a wheelchair, contributed to an amazing number of institutions. In 1925 he distributed $1,382,837, with the largest single sum, $270,131, going to the Angier B. Duke Memorial, which grew much larger through subsequent gifts from Ben Duke and his family.[37]

The second largest sum, $203,000, went to Kittrell College, an institution for blacks that the Dukes had begun to assist in the 1890's. Kittrell, in fact, acquired an unusual architectural link with Trinity College: Ben Duke arranged to have Trinity's handsome library, which J. B. Duke had given early in the century and which had to be removed because of the building program on the East Campus, carefully dismantled and rebuilt on the Kittrell campus by the same architect who had originally designed it. A couple more of the Trinity buildings were removed to Kittrell College, and Flowers, Frank C.

35. This matter is the subject of the author's "Troubled Legacy: James B. Duke's Bequest to His Cousins," *North Carolina Historical Review*, L (October, 1973), pp. 394–415.

36. Forrest Hyde to W. P. Few, August 20, 1925, and Few to Hyde, August 24, 1925, Few MSS.

37. These figures and those that follow are from a tabulation made by Alex. Sands showing B. N. Duke's gifts from 1925 through 1928, B. N. Duke MSS, 1966 addition.

Brown, and others at Duke University assisted in the redesigning of the Kittrell campus.[38]

In Durham itself Ben Duke played an important role in assisting the North Carolina College for Negroes (later to become North Carolina Central University) at a crucial time in its history. Aside from the $50,000 that Duke supplied the college in 1925, when the state was barely beginning to provide meager support, R. L. Flowers, serving as chairman of the institution's board of trustees, involved himself deeply in its affairs, to a large degree because of Ben Duke's interest in the college. When Lincoln Hospital, which the Duke brothers had originally given to Durham's black community in 1901, needed a new building in the early 1920's, the Dukes put up half of the cost ($75,-000), with the balance being raised in Durham. Then in 1925 Ben Duke provided an additional $30,000 for a nurses' home and other improvements at the hospital. There were also gifts in 1925 of $30,250 to the Colored Orphanage in Oxford, North Carolina; of $15,000 to an orthopedic hospital in Gastonia, North Carolina, for crippled black children; and of another $15,000 for a school for blacks in Mississippi.

Clearly in order to help soothe the feelings of the friends of various institutions that were not included in J. B. Duke's Endowment, Ben Duke in 1925 made gifts of $100,000 to Wake Forest College and $50,000 to Meredith College, two Baptist schools in North Carolina. Several educational institutions in North Carolina that had long-standing ties with the Duke family also were helped by Ben Duke to accept their exclusion from The Duke Endowment's support: Louisburg College and Greensboro College, two Methodist schools, each received $101,500, and Guilford College, the Quaker school that Mary Duke and her two brothers had attended briefly in the early 1870's, was given $51,125. Ben Duke gave $60,000 to Davenport College in Lenoir, North Carolina, $25,750 to St. Mary's School in Raleigh, and $31,000 to Elon College.

B. N. Duke took a special interest in helping schools and colleges that catered to the less affluent. For example, Pineland School for Girls in Salemburg, North Carolina, appealed to him so effectively that he gave it $52,500 in 1925 and an additional $17,500 the following year. The Berry School in the hills of Georgia and Berea Col-

38. B. N. Duke to J. R. Hawkins, May 27, 1925, *ibid.*; Alex. Sands to R. L. Flowers, December 11, 1925, Flowers MSS. Ben Duke gave Kittrell College an additional $100,000 in 1926.

lege in the mountains of Kentucky received in 1926 $27,000 and $25,000, respectively. Perhaps his favorite institution of this type, however, turned out to be Lincoln Memorial University in Harrowgate, Tennessee. Because of its chartered pledge "to make education possible for the Humble Common People of America" as well as because of the investigations of the school conducted by Alex. Sands, Ben Duke provided it with $4,250 in 1925, $50,000 in 1926, $100,000 in 1927, and $5,000 in 1928. Unlike some of his gifts that went unpublicized at his request, the grants to Lincoln Memorial University were announced by the institution, and another well-known philanthropist, George Foster Peabody, hailed Ben Duke's action: "Our Southland still calls to me of its great needs," Peabody wrote, "and I rejoice in the knowledge of what your brother did and what you are doing and yet will do."[39]

Closer to home, Ben Duke also took a special interest in a large Baptist academy at Buie's Creek, North Carolina, that became Campbell College in 1926. Pleased by what he had learned of the school and by letters that he received concerning it after an initial gift of $25,000, Ben Duke sent an additional check for $10,000 and scribbled these instructions to Alex. Sands: "Write the Buie's Creek school a nice letter when you send this check & tell them I have heard so many nice things about what a wonderful school they have built up that I feel disposed to help them with the enclosed check. . . ."[40]

During 1926 Ben Duke's gifts totalled $1,111,358 or some $270,000 less than in 1925. Ben Duke granted $100,000 to Wofford College in Spartanburg, South Carolina, to the great delight of W. P. Few, who was an alumnus of the institution, as were Kilgo and Dean Wannamaker. Wesleyan College in Macon, Georgia, received a similar amount as did George Foster Peabody College for Teachers in Nashville, Tennessee. In South Carolina he gave $50,000 each to Columbia College and Lander College and $25,000 to Limestone College. In North Carolina, Rutherford College received $50,000, and to Catawba College, Chowan College, Livingstone College, and Peace Institute he gave $25,000 each.

By 1927 Ben Duke had not only disposed of about all that he wanted

39. G. F. Peabody to B. N. Duke, June 12, 1928, B. N. Duke MSS, 1966 addition. Ben Duke's grants to Lincoln Memorial University as well as to many of the other institutions were on a matching or challenging basis. For many of the schools that either had no endowment or else quite small endowments, his gifts were significant.

40. B. N. Duke to Sands, August 23, 1926, *ibid*. He gave the school an additional $15,000 in 1927.

to give away—in the last four years of his life his contributions totalled nearly $3,000,000—but the steady deterioration of his health made it increasingly difficult for him to operate as a one-man foundation for the support of colleges, churches, orphanages, and other such institutions, mostly but not exclusively in the Carolinas. Late in 1925 he informed a friend that he had not been to his office since April and that he only got out "for a little drive around the park when the weather is good." By the spring of 1926 he confessed to his cousin and his wife's sister-in-law, Lida Duke Angier, who was also an old and close friend, just how serious his plight was. "I am in such a fix," Ben Duke wrote, "I have to be helped up and down by someone and cannot dress myself or carve my food at the table. I can, as you see, still write fairly well; each morning I am a little worse than I was the previous morning. I hope I may not have to bear this terrible pain I am suffering much longer."[41]

One who kept Ben Duke much in mind was William P. Few. As he had been doing for many years, Few wrote long regular letters reporting on the progress of construction at Duke University and many other matters that he knew would interest Ben Duke. The new buildings on the East Campus were occupied in the fall of 1927 and work had already begun by then on the Gothic buildings of the West Campus, which would not be used by students until the fall of 1930. "You would get extreme pleasure out of it, I am sure," Few declared to Ben Duke, "if you could see here with your own eyes the wonderful developments that have come from the small beginnings that you nourished in the big formative years of the past quarter-century." Earlier, on Ben Duke's birthday, Few had written that he spoke to the students in a chapel assembly about "what you have meant to this institution in all its strivings these thirty years past." Few added: "I told them if they or their successors in the long future ever allowed themselves to forget all this then they would be unworthy of their great heritage. But they will never forget in this or in any other generation."[42]

Methodist affairs, both local and national, were of mutual interest to Few and Ben Duke. Both men strongly favored the reunification of the Southern wing of the church with the larger, national Methodist body. Few took an active part in the struggle to heal the schism that

41. B. N. Duke to Miss A. O'Donnell, December 4, 1925, and to Mrs. J. C. Angier, April 27, 1926, *ibid.*

42. Few to B. N. Duke, September 23, 1926, April 27, 1926, Few MSS.

went back to the antebellum sectional quarrel about slavery, and Ben Duke encouraged and supported him in the fight as best he could. "I do not think much of these Methodist preachers, especially the bishops," Ben Duke declared, "who are going around trying to destroy [prevent] the unification of the Northern and Southern churches."[43]

One matter that Few did not discuss with Ben Duke, or with anyone else for that matter, save Clinton Toms and a few other intimates, was an embarrassing situation that had to do with Duke University and its needs. On the one hand, the new university being built around an old college was spectacularly blessed and richly endowed. The South had never known its like, and the whole nation was taking notice of the good fortune of Duke University. But, on the other hand, Few had first suggested in his proposal of 1921, and J. B. Duke had included in the indenture creating the Endowment, a large number of tasks for Duke University. By comparison, Princeton University, another relatively small institution in size and only about one generation older than Duke as a university, had a much larger and richer body of alumni. Moreover, despite its wealth, Princeton had no medical school, law school, divinity school, or one or two other schools that Duke University included. In other words, J. B. Duke, at W. P. Few's suggestion, had called for a most ambitious undertaking at Duke University. If J. B. Duke had lived, matters probably would have been different, and Few would not have felt the embarrassing constraints that he knew to be a painful fact but could hardly explain to a public dazzled by Duke University's good fortune.

Few could only confess his dilemma privately, as he did, for example, to Dr. W. S. Rankin: "I am frankly worried. It was just as clear to me the day Mr. Duke died as it is now that we do not have either in hand or in sight sufficient resources to develop the other departments of the University as Mr. Duke expected us to develop them and also support the sort of medical school and hospital that the public expects of us and that all of us want to see here." Few admitted that he did not yet see a solution but, eternal optimist that he was, insisted that his faith had "always been that what ought to be done can be done." To another friend of both Duke Universtiy and the Duke family, James A. Thomas, Few explained that J. B. Duke had "done one of the greatest things in the whole history of America; still

43. B. N. Duke to Few, July 14, 1925, *ibid.* The movement for reunification failed in the 1920's but succeeded a decade later.

he died before he had finished his work." Few continued: "To do promptly all the things he expected us to do involves an overwhelming financial burden unless the burden can be rather widely distributed. The good friends who help now help twice because they help quickly."[44]

Adding enormously to Few's problem was the widespread misunderstanding about the resources that were actually available to Duke University. Despite careful efforts on the part of Few, Allen, Perkins, and others to prepare and issue exact statements for the public, many newspapers and magazines garbled the story and informed readers that the entire income of The Duke Endowment went to Duke University. The New York *Evening Post*, for example, declared in wildly inaccurate fashion that "for three years Duke University had been thinking over the best ways to use its $80,000,000 endowment."[45] A variation of the theme and even more erroneous was the widely repeated assertion that Duke University was the "richest endowed university in the world."[46]

Few gave liberally of his time to visiting journalists and the university's own news bureau attempted to set the record straight. But it was uphill work. "It will be wise I am sure," Few cautioned one concerned alumnus, "for all our graduates and entire constituency during the next few years to exercise a good deal of patience." Everybody was going to write about Duke University, Few continued, and he had recently spent a number of hours with representatives from the Baltimore *Sun*, *New York Times*, New York *World*, and various other newspapers. Nevertheless, Few insisted that "it will be quite unfair to hold any of us responsible for what is written about us in the way of interpreting either the past, present or future." Few concluded in characteristic fashion: "I am trying my best to keep it all straight, and I am trying my best to see that nothing goes into the building of this new institution that will not be true and abiding in its power for good."[47] A few years later, a wearier but still indefatigable Few confessed to the same alumnus, "While I am something of a reformer, I have given up all hope of keeping straight the facts in newspapers even as they affect Duke University." And to another friend of the institution,

44. Few to Rankin, September 16, 1927, and Few to Thomas, April 4, 1928, *ibid.*
45. December 13, 1927.
46. New York *Sunday News*, August 4, 1935.
47. Few to Bruce Craven, November 17, 1925, Few MSS.

Few declared, "Nobody in America should become excited by anything in a newspaper until he first makes sure that he has the bottom facts."[48]

Despite the general public's exaggeration of Duke University's wealth, Few, Flowers, Allen and Perkins grappled with a painfully tight budget and cut down on various plans in order to stay within available income. The lake that J. B. Duke had envisioned on West Campus, and that the preliminary plans had shown, was eliminated as were the two great fountains that he had wanted on the West Campus—one on the quadrangle in front of the chapel and one in the circle at the top of the drives that were to lead to the chapel. On the East Campus a fountain that J. B. Duke planned for the large circle between the handsome Georgian library and the matching union building had to be omitted. More importantly, various amenities in the Gothic dormitories, such as commons or assembly rooms, had to be eliminated from the plans and the cubic space of various buildings reduced.[49]

News of none of these stringencies and curtailments reached Ben Duke, for Few felt two primary obligations to that increasingly frail man. On the immediate and personal level, Few attempted through his letters to cheer and support his old friend and longtime ally as best he could. As for the larger obligation and the future, Few desperately wished to have within Duke University some fitting memorial to the older brother whose long years of service and generosity to Trinity-Duke had been overshadowed by the younger brother's spectacular philanthropy. "Speaking for myself," Few wrote to one friend of Ben Duke's, "may I say to you that there is not one thing about this whole big development here which concerns me more than the building up here of an appropriate and adequate memorial to Mr. B. N. Duke? And I so much wish that we could get this done in his life time."[50]

As of yore, Clinton Toms stood by in New York to assist Few and also expressed keen interest in the matter of honoring Ben Duke. Toms and Few first hit on a specially designated Benjamin Newton Duke Endowment Fund, with the securities that had been given by Duke

48. Few to Bruce Craven, October 1, 1929, and Few to Dr. Albert Anderson, March 24, 1927, *ibid.*

49. These developments may be traced in the Flowers MSS and Frank C. Brown MSS.

50. Few to E. B. Halstead, September 16, 1927, Few MSS.

himself as the nucleus. Since he had, however, contributed annually for so many years to the operating budget of the institution and given various buildings and other improvements on the Trinity campus, the amount of endowment attributable directly to B. N. Duke was not extensive, being only about $400,000.[51]

Few persisted in his search for some sizable and significant memorial to B. N. Duke and in 1928 came up with the idea of a "Benjamin Newton Duke Institute for the Advancement of Knowledge" to be established within Duke University. Essentially Few had in mind a graduate school, a research council to assist in scholarly enterprises, and a few other features designed to enhance the advanced research and teaching in the university. On Ben Duke's seventy-third birthday, April 27, 1928, a marble bust of him was unveiled in the library at Duke University, and Robert L. Flowers spoke about B. N. Duke's role in the institution's life and about the proposed institute. If B. N. Duke had not been born, Flowers declared, "Trinity College would never have been in Durham . . . and Duke University would never have existed."[52]

To Ben Duke himself, Few wrote a warm tribute: "You are in my mind every day. While Duke University itself is a wonderful monument to you as well as to your Brother, your Father, and the Duke family, still much of the life that remains to me I am going to devote to an effort to build up for you here in Duke University a personal memorial of magnitude and permanent significance enough to be in all generations a reminder of the greatness of your spirit and the greatness of your deeds. This undertaking will grip my heart as nothing else here grips it for the rest of the way." To this pledge Ben Duke responded in a note, probably written by a nurse but signed shakily by himself, that Few's was "decidedly the nicest letter I ever received in my life." His friends in New York to whom he had shown the letter agreed. "May God bless you and your family," Ben Duke concluded, "I love you . . . ."[53]

Ben Duke died in his house in New York on January 8, 1929. His wife kept a diary during the last two years of his life, and while most of the entries are about goings and comings and small family matters,

51. Few to Toms, May 14, 19, 1927; Toms to Few, May 24, 1927; Few to Mrs. A. J. D. Biddle, June 23, 1928; and Mrs. Biddle to Few, July 16, 1928.

52. Raleigh *News and Observer*, April 28, 1928. Few also published his plan for the institute in the *Alumni Register of Duke University*, XV (February, 1929), pp. 50–52.

53. Few to B. N. Duke, May 31, 1928, and B. N. Duke to Few, June 10, 1928, Few MSS.

one gets an interesting glimpse of Ben Duke's final years. Mrs. Duke spent many of her mornings with her invalid husband, to whom she always referred, even in her diary, as "Mr. Duke." A typical entry noted that "Mr. Duke's condition is about the same," or "Mr. Duke had a terrible spell" and the doctor had to remain for the night. On one occasion Mrs. Duke recorded that "Mr. Duke consented for me to go to Durham"—but four days later she noted that "Mr. Duke said come home." Mrs. Duke was particularly fond of hearing sermons preached by Dr. Ralph W. Sockman, a leading Methodist minister in New York, and she made frequent entries like this one: "Went to church with little Mary [her granddaughter, Mary Duke Biddle] and Beth [Miss Elizabeth Gotham, a governess]. They came to dinner and we had a lovely time with Catechism lessons after lunch." Or, on another Sunday: "Little Mary, Beth, and I went to church. Came by to see 'Pa.' . . . Later went to Park." On January 8, 1929, Mrs. Duke made her next-to-last entry in the diary: "An awful sad sad day. My best friend and loved one gone."[54]

Mrs. Ben Duke herself lived until September 2, 1936. Two years prior to her death, Dr. Frederick M. Hanes, head of the Department of Medicine in Duke Hospital, interested her in an iris garden in a part of the university campus where J. B. Duke's lake would have gone if more money had been available. As matters turned out, it was just as well that there was no lake, for Mrs. Mary Duke Biddle in 1938 completed the project that her mother had earlier helped start. The magnificent Sarah P. Duke Gardens became a source of year-round pleasure of the university community as well as for thousands of out-of-town visitors each year. In words of Dr. Sockman's that were gracefully rearranged by Few, a bronze plaque in a wisteria-covered gazebo at the head of the gardens attests that they honor one "in whose life were blended the strength of the soil and the beauty of flowers."[55]

Few never succeeded in obtaining a special memorial to B. N. Duke. Immediately after Ben Duke's death, Few renewed the call for the

54. Diary of Mrs. B. N. (Sarah P.) Duke, 1927–1929, B. N. Duke MSS, 1966 addition. After her husband's death, Mrs. Duke came to believe that he had suffered from Ménière's disease or syndrome, which is characterized by attacks of vertigo, tinnitus (ringing in the ears), prostration and gradually developing deafness. Robert H. Durham, *Enclyopedia of Medical Syndromes* (New York, 1960), pp. 354–355.

55. Copy of Sarah P. Duke to Dr. F. M. Hanes, May 31, 1934, Flowers MSS; folder on the Sarah P. Duke Gardens in Mary L. D. Biddle portion of Semans Family MSS.

institute that he thought would be a fitting memorial as well as contribute vitally to the scholarly mission of the university. Friends of the Duke family, however, and particularly James A. Thomas, who was joined by George Allen and W. R. Perkins, proposed the creation and incorporation of "The Duke Memorial," an organization which would attempt to raise money for a suitable memorial to all three of the major philanthropists in the family—Washington, B. N., and J. B. Duke. Thomas appealed widely to the students and staffs of the various educational institutions that had been assisted by the Dukes and also to the employees of the power company and of the tobacco companies, the well-to-do associates of the Dukes in New York and elsewhere, and even the school children and other groups in the Carolinas.[56]

Few had strong backing, nonetheless, for his earlier proposal for a scholarly institute. William K. Boyd, chairman of the History Department at Duke University and longtime fighter for worthy academic causes, wrote an especially interesting letter to his friend, James A. Thomas. "It seems to me that the Dukes represent as no other group of persons," Boyd declared, "the latent productive power of men which was unloosed by the Civil War." He saw the family as typifying "the creative forces in Southern society of the modern period." The most appropriate memorial would therefore be, Boyd argued, one which "stimulates and serves creative power," especially "the creative power of mind." Boyd continued: "And this is just what the South needs, particularly it is what Duke University needs more than anything else." As chairman of the Library Council as well as of the Committee on Research, Boyd claimed intimate knowledge of the university's resources for advanced scholarly work. He had concluded that "those resources must be multiplied by three before Duke University can take rank with the *real* universities of this country—and then it will rank only with small real universities, such as Stanford, Princeton and some of the western state universities." Boyd insisted that his comparison was also true with respect to the other Southern universities, for he asserted that "not one of them is on a par in equipment with such institutions as I have just named." He advocated, in conclusion, the establishment of a "Duke Foundation for the Advancement of Knowledge," with the income to be used to increase the intellectual resources of the university. Art should be included within

56. Duke Memorial MSS, Duke University Archives.

the scope of "knowledge," Boyd added, especially since no Southern institution then had a "high-grade curriculum and equipment" in the area of the fine arts.[57]

Other influential persons on the faculty supported Few's proposed memorial. Paul M. Gross, an able young chemist who had cast his lot with Trinity College in 1919, studied J. B. Duke's indenture creating the Endowment and concluded that, above all, J. B. Duke had been interested in the service which Duke University could render its section of the country. "The proper rendering of this service by the University will call for ever increasing expenditures for research and investigation in the social and natural sciences," Gross maintained, "both for the acquirement of new knowledge and for the application of knowledge already in existence."[58]

But all the arguments of Few and his academic allies were in vain, for James A. Thomas, Allen, and others in New York had early decided that the chapel, or some part of the chapel, to be erected on the West Campus would be the most appropriate form for the memorial to take. Construction of the chapel, the centerpiece of the Gothic campus as originally envisioned by J. B. Duke, had not begun when B. N. Duke died and was not scheduled to begin until 1930. Few accepted with good grace the defeat or indefinite deferment of his own plan. "It is a big matter you are engaged in," he assured Thomas, "and it is being laid down along lines that not only assure immediate success but even larger ultimate good to Duke University." Few conceded that the "B. N. Duke Foundation for the Advancement of Knowledge . . . will have to wait perhaps," but he hoped that in the long run the efforts of Thomas and his associates might also help that cause.[59]

With President Few's blessings, therefore, Thomas and his associates set out to raise money for the memorial to Washington Duke and two of his sons. Anthony Biddle expressed great interest in the project and suggested the need of a good publicity agent. "Men in this country, irrespective of their qualities and financial standing,"

57. W. K. Boyd to J. A. Thomas, March 26, 1929, *ibid.*

58. P. M. Gross to J. A. Thomas, June 19, 1929, *ibid.* Although J. Fred Rippy, another historian, and others supported the type of memorial that Few had first suggested, one member of the faculty suggested a Greek amphitheater on the campus. One citizen of Durham advocated an art gallery on the campus because there was "not a city south of Washington City that has a first class painting, a piece of sculpture or other worthy piece of art." W. L. Foushee to Alex. Sands, June 8, 1929, *ibid.*

59. Few to Thomas, February 26, 1929, *ibid.*

Biddle argued, "are just as much subject to what is known as well conceived propaganda, which in the vernacular of today has become ballyhoo, as any member of the mob."[60]

James A. Thomas followed Biddle's advice and was able to obtain ample publicity for the memorial campaign. He had once hoped to raise more than a million dollars, but the crash of the stock market in the fall of 1929 ended that dream. With the approximately $135,000 that actually was raised, the Duke Memorial, Inc., contributed primarily to three things: the creation of the small Memorial Chapel to the left of the chancel in the chapel of Duke University; the three marble sarcophagi in the Memorial Chapel where rest the remains of Washington Duke, Benjamin Newton Duke, and James Buchanan Duke; and the bronze statue of James B. Duke which stands on the quadrangle in front of the chapel.[61]

Few could accept with equanimity the frustration of his hopes for some significant memorial to Ben Duke because, to a greater degree than most men, William Preston Few lived in the realm of the mind and the spirit. As much as he loved the architecture and the handsome grounds of Duke University, no one needed to tell him that those were hardly of central importance. A great college or university, Few once suggested, was essentially an "assembling of great personalities." Deeply conscious always of the long future as well as of the past, Few believed that "an institution like this [Trinity-Duke] lives on and will live as long as American civilization endures, and it cherishes the memory of those who have served it."[62]

The assemblage of "great personalities" at Trinity and Duke included in a special way, as W. P. Few reiterated, Washington Duke, Benjamin N. Duke, and James B. Duke. By 1930, as the chapel began to climb upward among the towering pine trees, Few felt easier about the institution with which the names of the three men were most closely identified. "The routine at times may be dull and gray," Few confessed, "but the vision of the future is always golden and infinitely inspiring." Having thanked George G. Allen and William R. Perkins for their personal gift of the carillon for the chapel, Few declared, "I

60. A. J. D. Biddle, Jr., to J. A. Thomas, April 11, 1929, *ibid.* Biddle ended his association with the project, as well as his trusteeship on The Duke Endowment, when he and Mrs. Mary Duke Biddle were separated in 1930 and divorced in the following year.

61. Alex. Sands to J. A. Thomas, April 15, 1936, *ibid.*

62. Few to his nephew, Benjamin Few, October 26, 1917, and Few to Mrs. John C. Kilgo, October 9, 1922, Few MSS.

feel that we have now hit the open sea and that a long journey is ahead of Duke University."[63]

Three who would inevitably be a part of that "long journey" had come from a small farm in the North Carolina Piedmont, worked hard, grown wealthy, and given a substantial part of that wealth to the people of the Carolinas. Washington Duke led his family onto the pathways of industry and philanthropy. His sons, Benjamin N. Duke and James B. Duke, travelled farther down both roads than the penniless Confederate veteran of 1865 could ever have dreamed.

63. Few to G. G. Allen, May 3, July 3, 1930, Few MSS.

A NOTE ON THE SOURCES

Scattered throughout the footnotes of this volume are references to important monographic studies, such as Nannie May Tilley, *The Bright-Tobacco Industry, 1860–1929* (Chapel Hill: University of North Carolina Press, 1948), or Earl W. Porter, *Trinity and Duke, 1892–1924: Foundations of Duke University* (Durham: Duke University Press, 1964). They and a few others like them shed valuable light on the economic and philanthropic careers of the Dukes and have been indispensable in the writing of this book. By and large, however, the Dukes have not been lucky in their treatment, or lack of treatment, by historians.

James B. Duke, in particular, has long deserved more serious and scholarly interpretation than he got from his two biographers. The first of them, John Wilber Jenkins, was a Tarheel-born newspaperman whom George G. Allen recruited to write a biography of Duke. Passionately averse to personal publicity (as distinct from the advertising of his products during the days of his career in tobacco), James B. Duke granted few interviews to journalists and went far out of his way to try to keep his name and his picture out of newspapers and magazines. Yet after the establishment of The Duke Endowment, Allen, aided possibly by others, persuaded Duke in 1925 to allow Jenkins to write a biography. Although Duke died before the project had been really launched, Jenkins published *James B. Duke: Master Builder* (New York: George H. Doran Company) in 1927. The book is much too reverential and eulogistic in its treatment of its subject and tends to minimize significant contributions that many others, such as William S. Lee, William P. Few, and even Ben Duke, made to the career of J. B. Duke. Yet Jenkins at least had the advantage of talking with Allen, William R. Perkins, Lee, Few, and others who were intimately associated with J. B. Duke. Therefore certain portions of the book, if used carefully and critically, are still of value. The lack of an index is merely the most obvious of the book's limitations.

In *Tobacco Tycoon: The Story of James Buchanan Duke* (New York: Random House, 1942), John K. Winkler wrote a melodramatic, muckraking study that derives whatever substance it has mostly from Jenkins' book, although there is no documentation in either book. Winkler, author of popularized biographies of a number of tycoons such as John D. Rockefeller and J. P. Morgan, includes long, rather silly sections on J. B. Duke's disastrous first marriage, and he attempts, without much success, to make something of a pathetic, if not tragic, figure out of Mrs. Lillian McCredy Duke. The result is like nothing so much as certain "Sunday supplements" that appeared in many newspapers in the 1930's.

That Benjamin Newton Duke barely appears in either of the above biographies is not surprising. He became ill a decade before his younger brother died, and many of the people associated with James B. Duke during the last period of his life knew Ben Duke only as a semi-invalid, one who after about 1915 was increasingly more concerned about dividing his wealth among the members of his family and various charitable causes than he was about making money. Ben Duke in his later years probably was, in short, something of a thorn in the flesh for some of J. B. Duke's hard-working and dedicated associates in business.

Since the printed works used in this study have been fully listed in the footnotes, this essay will focus on the manuscript sources, first those that came from various members of the family and then others in alphabetical order. All of the collections are in the Manuscript Department or the University Archives in the William R. Perkins Library, Duke University.

BENJAMIN NEWTON DUKE PAPERS

This is a massive collection of nearly 40,000 items and some 96 volumes (mostly letterbooks and albums). While there are a vast number of inconsequential letters, both incoming ones and outgoing copies in the letterbooks, there are also many valuable letters, enough certainly to make this the documentary backbone for any study of the family. Important materials on the tobacco, textile, and electric power industries are scattered throughout the collection, and the family's continuing philanthropic activities are richly documented. The papers begin around 1890, although there are a few items from the earlier period. After 1915, the collection grows progressively thinner, although the "1966 addition" to the papers has much valuable material on Ben Duke's philanthropy in the closing years of his life. Some of the best of the old photographs of the family are in this collection also.

JAMES BUCHANAN DUKE PAPERS

The largest part of this collection consists of materials relating to the estate of J. B. Duke and particularly to the long, drawnout legal processes involved in settling Item VI of his will, whereby he left $2,000,000 to be divided among the descendants of his uncles and aunts, of whom there had been twenty altogether—although the courts finally had to settle that fact.

Until the recent discovery of the ten letterbooks of J. B. Duke, as described in footnote one of chapter 3, there were remarkably few letters written by J. B. Duke in the collection. For many years prior to the unveiling, or, more accurately, the uncrating, of the letterbooks, historians and others had believed that Alex. H. Sands, Jr., in clearing out old files some years after the death of J. B. Duke had destroyed Duke's papers, not because they were revealing but, on the contrary, because in the opinion of Sands and any others whom he might have asked the papers were too insignificant and useless as business records to be worth keeping.

Sands, as he informed Dr. Mattie Russell, the curator of the Manuscript Department at Duke, did destroy some papers, but it is unlikely that there were very many for the simple reason that James B. Duke wrote relatively few letters after 1890. He even kept his own business correspondence to a minimum. The answers to many of the incoming letters in the J. B. Duke MSS, particularly those letters of a nonbusiness nature, were sent by B. N. Duke; and executive or confidential secretaries, first Richard B. Arrington and then Alex. H. Sands, Jr., wrote and signed their own names to many letters that employed such phrases as "Mr. J. B. Duke instructs me to say . . ." or "Mr. Duke wishes. . . ."

As indicated in chapter 3, the three letterbooks that cover the period from 1884 to 1890 are a veritable treasure-house of information about the cigarette industry in the years immediately preceding the formation of the American Tobacco Company. Those were the years about which least has been known about the industry, too, since the investigations of the Federal government's Bureau of Corporations and then of the Justice Department in the antitrust case fully illuminated the activities of the American Tobacco Company between 1890 and 1911, when the giant combination was broken up. Those three letterbooks also shed more light on the business personality and technique of young J. B. Duke than any other single source does. The remaining seven letterbooks are much less valuable and contain only a few significant items about the tobacco industry and other economic activities of the Dukes. There is a gap in the letterbooks from 1911 to 1920, and the last letterbook, covering the period from February, 1920, to January, 1923, is thin and fragmentary. Although letterbooks for the period from 1911 to 1920 may miraculously turn up some day, it is more likely that they may have been among the records destroyed by Alex. Sands.

The earliest and most revealing personal letter written by James B. Duke that is now known to exist was the one of August 18, 1880, to "Dear Ben and Sallie," his brother and sister-in-law. It is quoted in part on pp. 16–17 of this book and reprinted in full in the *Duke Alumni Register* (March, 1974).

WASHINGTON DUKE PAPERS

Consisting of only around 3,000 items, mostly incoming, this is the thinnest of the family's collections. Washington Duke more or less retired from an active role in business affairs about 1880 when he was sixty years old. A most reserved and dignified person anyhow, he apparently revealed himself only to his family and to certain close and old friends in Durham. His dry sense of humor does not come through in the few letters of his that survive, and most of the extant answers to his incoming mail are to be found in the B. N. Duke letterbooks.

SEMANS FAMILY PAPERS

Only the early portion of this vast collection, the portion that deals with Mrs. Mary Lillian Duke Biddle, was pertinent to this study, but there are certain useful materials therein for the family's history. Her daughter, Mary Duke Biddle, married Dr. Josiah C. Trent, and they had four daughters. After Dr. Trent's death, his widow married Dr. James H. Semans and they have three children. The family is, therefore, a large one, as is the collection of papers. There are also several boxes of fine old photographs and snapshots of the family, from Washington Duke to his great-great-great grandchildren, that is the grandchildren of Mrs. James H. (Mary Duke Biddle Trent) Semans.

ANGIER BIDDLE DUKE PAPERS

This large, valuable collection covers a period beyond the scope of this study and focuses on the many-faceted diplomatic career of Angier B. Duke; but it does include many scrapbooks and photograph albums, the older ones of which have items that are relevant for the closing phase of this book.

JOHN FRANKLIN CROWELL PAPERS

The beginnings of the Duke family's association with Trinity College may be documented from this collection, but it is neither extensive nor a particularly rewarding one. Crowell's memoir, *Personal Collections of Trinity College, North Carolina, 1887–1894* (Durham: Duke University Press, 1939), is more useful than the collection.

THE DUKE ENDOWMENT PAPERS

In 1963 the officials of The Duke Endowment in New York arranged through the Oral History Project of Columbia University to have the late Frank W. Rounds, Jr., a journalist and author, interview various persons who had known James B. Duke or who had been associated with the activities of the Duke family. The interviews were conducted in New York, Durham, Charlotte, and one or two other places in 1963 and 1964. The results were most uneven in quality, and the transcripts of the interviews should be used only with great caution, since many of them contain misinformation as well as much hearsay. Yet some of the interviews, particularly the ones in Charlotte concerning the power company, are invaluable. There is less documentary material concerning that phase of J. B. Duke's career than any other, and Rounds, especially in interviews with Norman Cocke and Mrs. Edward C. Marshall, captured certain reliable information about James B. Duke that is available nowhere else. There are also photographs and some printed material gathered by Rounds in the collection. Only copies of the typed transcripts are at Duke, the originals as well as the tapes themselves being at Columbia.

THE DUKE MEMORIAL, INCORPORATED, PAPERS

This collection is in the University Archives, as are the papers of the three presidents of Trinity College who figure in this book—Crowell, Kilgo, and Few. The Duke Memorial papers are important only for the light they shed on the efforts of James A. Thomas and others to raise money beginning in 1929 to memorialize Washington, B. N., and J. B. Duke on the campus of Duke University.

FRANK CLYDE BROWN PAPERS

Since this collection in the University Archives was only recently unpacked from cardboard boxes, it has not been widely known. Because of Brown's friendship with B. N. Duke and his close association with Few and Horace Trumbauer in the planning and building of Duke University, the collection is an important one for that phase of the story. As mentioned in the text, the work-diary of Trumbauer's superintendent at Duke University, B. M. Hall, is in the Brown MSS and is one of the few documentary sources for James B. Duke's dramatic decisions, made late in March, 1925, about the physical plans for Duke University.

WILLIAM PRESTON FEW PAPERS

A vast and rich storehouse of material about a number of subjects, this collection sheds much light on both B. N. Duke and J. B. Duke as well as on Few himself. Although Few lived until 1940, the collection was used for this book only until about 1930. When the research for this study was done, some of the letters were arranged alphabetically in folders and some were divided under subject headings; the Archivist has now had them arranged chronologically, which will facilitate their use.

ROBERT LEE FLOWERS PAPERS

Although Flowers joined the Mathematics Department of Trinity College in 1891, a year before the college moved to Durham, this collection only begins around 1924. While nowhere nearly as important or useful as the Few MSS, the papers of Flowers are helpful for following the creation of Duke University and for the roles of both Duke brothers, who were friends of Flowers.

JOHN CARLISLE KILGO PAPERS

Thinner even than the Crowell papers, this collection hardly represents the brilliant and controversial character of Kilgo's leadership. An orator more than a writer, which was the reverse of the situation with Few, Kilgo played a key role in binding the Duke family to Trinity College even though these papers do not adequately demonstrate that fact.

EDWARD JAMES PARRISH PAPERS

A veteran tobacco man from Durham, Parrish went to Japan to represent the American Tobacco Company in 1899 and remained there until mid-1904. His letterbooks and other papers offer a fascinating glimpse of American businessmen and capital in a turn-of-the-century Japanese context. In constant communication with James B. Duke and the home office, first of the American Tobacco Company and then after 1902 of the British-American Tobacco Company, Parrish apparently enjoyed and succeeded admirably in his exotic job. Although he had occasional business contacts with the Dukes and George Watts after returning from Japan and getting out of the tobacco business, the important part of the collection covers the Japanese period.

EDWARD FEATHERSTON SMALL PAPERS

Although Small later grew to have an exaggerated idea of his importance as a salesman in the 1880's for W. Duke, Sons and Company, this little collection is important for the light it sheds on the aggressive advertising tactics of the Dukes before the American Tobacco Company was formed. Indeed, until the letterbooks of James B. Duke recently became available, the Small papers were one of the few manuscript sources for that early period of W. Duke, Sons and Company.

JAMES AUGUSTUS THOMAS PAPERS

In light of Thomas' long association with James B. Duke, particularly after the formation of the British-American Tobacco Company, these papers are surprisingly disappointing. While they do have some interesting material on various political and economic developments in China during the first two decades or so of this century, they contain very little about J. B. Duke and his global interests in the tobacco industry. Thomas' memoir, *A Pioneer Tobacco Merchant in the Orient* (Durham: Duke University Press, 1928), was much more useful than his papers for this study.

RICHARD HARVEY WRIGHT PAPERS

This collection is so large—over 232,000 items and some 178 volumes—that the researcher pales upon confronting it. Yet for various facets of the tobacco industry and especially for technological aspects, it is excellent. The letter-books cover from the mid-1880's to the late 1920's, though they and the incoming letters were used for this study only down to about 1900. Unfortunately, many of the early letterpress copies are illegible because of fading as well as the difficulty of reading the handwriting in the letters. A cantankerous man in some ways, Wright was also a prodigious saver of documents, for which his name should be praised.

APPENDIX

James B. Duke
To
Nanaline H. Duke and Others, Trustees

Indenture and Deed of Trust of Personalty
Establishing
The Duke Endowment
December 11, 1924

THIS INDENTURE made in quadruplicate this 11th day of December, 1924, by and between JAMES B. DUKE, residing at Duke Farms, near Somerville, in the County of Somerset, and State of New Jersey, United States of America, party of the first part, and NANALINE H. DUKE, of Somerville, N. J., GEORGE G. ALLEN, of Hartsdale, N.Y., WILLIAM R. PERKINS, of Montclair, N.J., WILLIAM B. BELL, of New York City, N.Y., ANTHONY J. DREXEL BIDDLE, JR., of New York City, N.Y., WALTER C. PARKER, of New Rochelle, N.Y., ALEX. H. SANDS, JR., of Montclair, N.J., WILLIAM S. LEE, of Charlotte, N.C., CHARLES I. BURKHOLDER, of Charlotte, N.C., NORMAN A. COCKE, of Charlotte, N.C., EDWARD C. MARSHALL, of Charlotte, N.C. and BENNETTE E. GEER, of Greenville, S.C. as trustees and their successors as trustees under and in accordance with the terms of this Indenture, to be known as the Board of Trustees of the Endowment, parties of the second part,

WITNESSETH:

That in order to effectuate the trusts hereby created, the first party has given, assigned, transferred and delivered, and by these presents does give, assign, transfer and deliver, the following property, to wit:

122,647 Shares of Stock of Duke Power Company, a corporation organized and existing under the laws of the State of New Jersey.

100,000 Ordinary Shares of the Stock of British-American Tobacco Company, Limited, a corporation organized and existing under the laws of Great Britain.

75,000 Shares of the Common "B" Stock of R. J. Reynolds Tobacco Company, a corporation organized and existing under the laws of said State of New Jersey.

5,000 Shares of the Common Stock of George W. Helme Company, a corporation organized and existing under the laws of said State of New Jersey.

12,325 Shares of the Stock of Republic Cotton Mills, a corporation organized and existing under the laws of the State of South Carolina.

7,935-3/10 Shares of the Common Stock of Judson Mills, a corporation organized and existing under the laws of said State of South Carolina.

unto said trustees and their successors as trustees hereunder, in trust, to be held, used, managed, administered and disposed of, as well as all additions and accretions thereto and all incomes, revenues and profits thereof and therefrom, forever for the charitable purposes, in the manner and upon the terms herein expressly provided, and not otherwise, namely:

FIRST.

The trust established by this Indenture is hereby denominated The Duke Endowment, and shall have perpetual existence.

SECOND.

Each trustee herein named, as well as each trustee selected hereunder, shall be and remain a trustee so long as such trustee shall live and continue mentally and physically capable of performing the duties of a trustee hereunder, subject to resignation and to removal as hereinafter stated. The number of trustees within two years from the date of this Indenture shall be increased to, and thereafter remain at, fifteen, such increase being made by vote of the trustees at any meeting. He suggests, but does not require, that, so far as practicable, no one may be selected trustee if thereby at such time a majority of the trustees be not natives and / or residents of the States of Carolina and / or South Carolina. It is the wish of the party of the first part, and he so directs, that his daughter, Doris Duke, upon attaining the age of twenty-one years, shall be made a trustee hereunder, for that purpose being elected to fill any vacancy then existing, or, if there be no such vacancy, added to the trustees thereby making the number of trustees sixteen until the next occurring of a vacancy, whereupon the number of trustees shall again become and remain fifteen.

Subject to the terms of this Indenture, the trustees may adopt and change at any time rules and regulations which shall govern in the management and administration of the trust and trust property.

Meetings of the trustees shall be held at least ten times in each calendar year at such time and place and upon such notice as the rules and regulations may provide. Other meetings of the trustees may be held upon the call in writing of the chairman or a vice-chairman or any three trustees given in accordance with the rules and regulations, at such place and time and for such purpose as may be specified in the call. A majority of the then trustees shall constitute a quorum at any such meeting, but less than a majority may adjourn any such meeting from time to time and from place to place until a quorum shall be present. The affirmative vote of the majority of a quorum shall be necessary and sufficient at any such meeting to authorize or ratify any action by the trustees hereunder, except as herein otherwise expressly provided. Written records, setting forth all action taken at said meetings and the voting thereon, shall be kept in a permanent minute book of the trustees, and shall be signed by each trustee present at the meeting.

The trustees shall select annually from their number a chairman and two vice-chairmen, and a secretary and a treasurer, who need not be trustees. Such officers shall hold office for one year and thereafter until their respective successors shall be selected. The compensation of the secretary and treasurer shall be that fixed by the trustees.

The trustees shall establish an office, which may be changed from time to time, which shall be known as the principal office of this trust, and at it shall be kept the books and papers other than securities relating to this trust.

By the affirmative vote of a majority of the then trustees any officer, and by the affirmative vote of three-fourths of the then trustees any trustee, may be removed for any cause whatever at any meeting of the trustees called for the purpose in accordance with the rules and regulations.

Vacancies occurring among the trustees from any cause whatever (for which purpose an increase in the number of trustees shall be deemed to cause vacancies to the extent of such increase in number of trustees) may be filled by the remaining trustees at any meeting of the trustees, and must be so filled within six months after the vacancy occurs; provided that no person (except said Doris Duke) shall remain or become a trustee hereunder who shall not be or at once become a trustee under the trust this day being created by the party of the first part by Indenture which will bear even date herewith for his said daughter and his kin and their descendants, so long as said latter trust shall be in existence.

Each trustee shall be paid at the end of each calendar year one equal fifteenth part of three percent of the incomes, revenues and profits received by the trustees upon the trust properties and estate during such year, provided that if any trustee by reason of death, resignation, or any other cause, shall have served during only a part of such year, there shall be paid to such trustee, if alive, or if such trustee be dead then to the personal representatives of such trustee, such a part of said one-fifteenth as the time during which said trustee served during such year shall bear to the whole of such year, such payment to be in full for all services as trustee hereunder and for all expenses of the trustees. In the event that any trustee shall serve in any additional capacity (other than as chairman or vice-president) the trustees may add to the foregoing compensation such additional compensation as the trustees may think such trustee should receive by reason of serving in such additional capacity.

No act done by any one or more of the trustees shall be valid or binding unless it shall have been authorized or until it shall be ratified as required by this Indenture.

The trustees are urged to make a special effort to secure persons of character and ability, not only as trustees, but as officials and employees.

THIRD.

For the purpose of managing and administering the trust, and the properties and funds in the trust, hereby created, said trustees shall have and may exercise the following powers, namely:

To manage and administer in all respects the trust hereby created and the properties and funds held and arising hereunder, in accordance with the terms hereof, obtaining and securing for such purpose such assistants, office space, force, equipment and supplies, and any other aid and facilities, upon such terms, as the trustees may deem necessary from time to time.

To hold, use, manage, administer and dispose of each and every of the properties which at any time, and from time to time, may be held in this trust, and to collect and receive the incomes, revenues and profits arising therefrom and accruing thereto, provided that said trustees shall not have power to dispose of the whole or any part of the share capital (or rights of subscription thereto) of Duke Power Company, a New Jersey corporation, or of any subsidiary thereof, except upon and by the affirmative vote of the total authorized number of trustees at a meeting called for the purpose, the minutes of which shall state the reasons for and terms of such sale.

To invest any funds from time to time arising or accruing through the receipt and collection of incomes, revenues and profits, sale of properties, or otherwise, provided the said trustees may not lend the whole or any part of such funds except to said Duke Power Company, nor may said trustees invest the whole or any part of such funds in any property of any kind except in securities of said Duke Power Company, or of a subsidiary therof, or in bonds validly issued by the United States of America, or by a State thereof, or by a district, county, town or city which has a population in excess of fifty thousand people according to the then last Federal census, which is located in the United States of America, which has not since 1900 defaulted in the payment of any principal or interest upon or with respect to any of its obligations, and the bonded indebtedness of which does not exceed ten per cent of its assessed values. Provided further that whenever the said trustees shall desire to invest any such funds the same shall be either lent to said Duke Power or invested in the securities of said Duke Power Company or of a subsidiary thereof, if and to the extent that such a loan or such securities are available upon terms and conditions satisfactory to said trustees.

To utilize each year in accordance with the terms of this Indenture the incomes, revenues and profits arising and accruing from the trust estate for such year in defraying the cost, expenses and charges incurred in the management and administration of this trust and its funds and properties, and in applying and distributing the net amount of such incomes, revenues and profits thereafter remaining to and for the objects and purposes of this trust.

As respects any year or years and any purpose or purposes for which this trust is created (except the payments hereinafter directed to be made to Duke University) the trustees in their uncontrolled discretion may withold the whole or any part of said incomes, revenues and profits which would otherwise be distributed under the "FIFTH" division hereof, and either (1) accumulate the whole or any part of the amounts so withheld for expenditures (which the trustees are hereby authorized to make thereof) for the same purpose in any future year or years, or (2) add the whole or any part of the amounts so withheld to the corpus of the trust, or (3) pay, apply and distribute the whole or any part of said amounts to and for the benefit of any one or more of the other purposes of this trust, or (4) pay, apply and distribute the whole or any part of said amounts to or for the benefit of any such like charitable, religious or educational purpose within the State of North Carolina and / or the State of South Carolina and / or any such like charitable hospital purpose which shall be selected therefor by the affirmative vote of three-fourths of the then trustees at any meeting of the trustees called for the purpose, complete authority and discretion in and for such selection and utilization being hereby given the trustees in the premises.

By the consent of three-fourths of the then trustees expressed in a writing signed by them, which shall state the reasons therefor and be recorded in the minutes of the trustees, and not otherwise, the trustees may (1) cause to be formed under the laws of such state or states as may be selected by the trustees for that purpose a corporation or corporations so incorporated and empowered as that the said corporation or corporations can and will assume and carry out in whole or in part the trust hereby created, with the then officers and trustees hereof officers and directors thereof, with like powers and duties, and (2) convey, transfer and deliver to said corporation or corporations the whole or any part of the properties then held in this trust, to be held, used, managed, administered and disposed of by said corporation or corporations for any one or more of the charitable purposes expressed in this Indenture and upon all the terms and with all the terms, powers and duties expressed in this Indenture with respect to the same, provided that such conveyances, transfers and deliveries shall be upon such terms and conditions as that in case any such corporation or corporations shall cease to exist for any cause the property so transferred shall forthwith revert and belong to the trustees of this trust and become a part of the corpus of this trust for all the purposes thereof.

Said trustees shall have and may exercise, subject to the provisions of this Indenture, any and all other powers which are necessary or desirable in order to manage and administer the trust and the properties and funds thereof and carry out and perform in all respects the terms of this Indenture according to the true intent thereof.

Any assignment, transfer, bill of sale, deed, conveyance, receipt, check, draft, note, or any other document or paper whatever, executed by or on behalf of the trustees, shall be sufficiently executed when signed by the person or persons authorized so to do by a resolution of the trustees duly adopted at any meeting and in accordance with the terms of such resolution.

FOURTH.

The trustees hereunder are hereby authorized and directed to expend as soon as reasonably may be not exceeding Six Million Dollars of the corpus of this trust in establishing at a location to be selected by them within the State of North Carolina an institution of learning to be known as Duke University, for such purpose to acquire such lands and erect and equip thereon such buildings according to such plans as the trustees may in their judgment deem necessary and adopt and approve for the purpose, to cause to be formed under the laws of such state as the trustees may select for the purpose a corporation adequately empowered to own and operate such properties under the name Duke University as an institution of learning according to the true intent hereof, and to convey to such corporation when formed the said lands, buildings and equipment upon such terms and conditions as that such corporation may use the same only for such purposes of such university and upon the same ceasing to be so used then the same shall forthwith revert and belong to the trustees of this trust as and become a part of the corpus of this trust for all of the purposes thereof.

However, should the name of Trinity College, located at Durham, North Carolina, a body politic and incorporate, within three months from the date hereof (or such further time as the trustees hereof may allow) be changed to

Duke University, then, in lieu of the foregoing provisions of this division "FOURTH" of this Indenture, as a memorial to his father, Washington Duke, who spent his life in Durham and whose gifts, together with those of Benjamin N. Duke, the brother of the party of the first part, and of other members of the Duke family, have so largely contributed toward making possible Trinity College at that place, he directs that the trustees shall expend of the corpus of this trust as soon as reasonably may be a sum not exceeding Six Million Dollars in expanding and extending said University, and improving such lands, and erecting, removing, remodeling and equipping such buildings, according to such plans, as the trustees may adopt and approve for such purpose to the end that said Duke University may eventually include Trinity College as its undergraduate department for men, a School of Religious Training, a School for Training Teachers, a School of Chemistry, a Law School, a Co-ordinate College for Women, a School of Business Administration, a Graduate School of Arts and Sciences, a Medical School and an Engineering School, as and when funds are available.

FIFTH.

The trustees hereof shall pay, apply, divide and distribute the net amount of said incomes, revenues and profits each calendar year as follows, to wit:

Twenty per cent of said net amount shall be retained by said trustees and added to the corpus of this trust as a part thereof for the purpose of increasing the principal of the trust estate until the total aggregate of such additions to the corpus of the trust shall be as much as Forty Million Dollars.

Thirty-two per cent of said net amount not retained as aforesaid for addition to the corpus of this trust shall be paid to that Duke University for which expenditures of the corpus of the trust shall have been made by the trustees under the "FOURTH" division of this Indenture so long as its name shall be Duke University and it shall not be operated for private gain, to be utilized by its Board of Trustees in defraying its administration and operating expenses, increasing and improving its facilities and equipment, the erection and enlargement of buildings and the acquisition of additional acreage for it, adding to its endowment, or in such other manner for it as the Board of Trustees of said institution may from time to time deem to be to its best interests, provided that in case such institution shall incur any expense or liability beyond provision already in sight to meet same, or in the judgment of the trustees under this Indenture be not operated in a manner calculated to achieve the results intended hereby, the trustees under this Indenture may withhold the whole or any part of such percentage from said institution so long as such character of expense or liabilities or operations shall continue, such amounts so withheld to be in whole or in part either accumulated and applied to the purposes of such University in any future year or years, or utilized for the other objects of this Indenture, or added to the corpus of this trust for the purpose of increasing the principal of the trust estate, as the trustees may determine.

Thirty-two percent of said net amount not retained as aforesaid for addition to the corpus of this trust shall be utilized for maintaining and securing such hospitals, not operated for private gain, as the said trustees, in their uncontrolled discretion, may from time to time select for the purpose and are located within the States of North Carolina and / or South Carolina, such utilization to be exercised in the following manner, namely: (a) By paying to each and every such hospital, whether for white or colored, and not operated for private gain, such sum (not exceeding One Dollar) per free bed per day for each and every day that said free bed may have been occupied during the period covered by such payment free of charge by patients unable to pay as the amount available for this purpose hereunder will pay on a pro rata basis; and (b) in the event that said amount in any year shall be more than sufficient for the foregoing purpose, the whole or any part of the residue thereof may be expended by said trustees in assisting in the erection and / or equipment within either or both of said States of any such hospital not operated for private gain, payment for this purpose in each case to be in such amount and on such terms and conditions as the trustees hereof may determine. In the event that said amount in any year be more than sufficient for both of the aforesaid purposes, the trustees in their uncontrolled discretion may pay and expend the whole or any part of the residue thereof in like manner for maintaining and securing hospitals not operated for private gain in any other State or States, giving preference, however, to those States contiguous to the States of North Carolina and South Carolina. And said trustees as respects any year may exclude from participation hereunder any hospital or hospitals which the trustees in their uncontrolled discretion may think so financed as not to need, or so maintained and operated as not to deserve, inclusion hereunder.

Five per cent of said net amount not retained as aforesaid for addition to the corpus of the trust shall be paid to Davidson College (by whatever name it may be known) now located at Davidson, in the State of North Carolina, so long as it shall not be operated for private gain, to be utilized by said institution for any and all of the purposes thereof.

Five per cent of said net amount not retained as aforesaid for addition to the corpus of the trust shall be paid to Furman University (by whatever name it may be known) now located at Greenville, in the State of South Carolina, so long as it shall not be operated for private gain, to be utilized by said institution for any and all of the purposes thereof.

Four per cent of said net amount not retained as aforesaid for addition to the corpus of the trust shall be paid to the Johnson C. Smith University (by whatever name it may be known), an institution of learning for colored people, now located at Charlotte, in said State of North Carolina, so long as it shall not be operated for private gain, to be utilized by said insitutiton for any and all of the purposes therof.

Ten per cent of said net amount not retained as aforesaid for addition to the corpus of this trust shall be paid and distributed to and among such of those organizations, institutions, agencies and / or societies, whether public or private, by whatsoever name they may be known, not operated for private gain, which during such year in the judgment of said trustees have been properly operated as organizations, institutions, agencies and / or societies for the benefit of white or colored whole or half orphans within the States of North Carolina and / or South Carolina, and in such amounts as between and among such organizations, institutions, agencies and / or societies as may be selected and determined as respects each year by said trustees in their uncontrolled discretion, all such payments and distributions to be used by such organizations, institutions, agencies and / or societies exclusively for the benefit of such orphans.

Two per cent of said net amount not retained as aforesaid for addition to the corpus of the trust shall be paid and expended by the trustees for the care and maintenance of needy and deserving superannuated preachers and needy and deserving widows and orphans of deceased preachers who shall have served in a Conference of the Methodist Episcopal Church, South (by whatever name it may be known) located in the State of North Carolina.

Six per cent of said net amount not retained as aforesaid for addition to the corpus of the trust shall be paid and expended by the trustees in assisting (that is, in giving or lending in no case more than fifty per cent of what may be required for the purpose) to build Methodist churches under and connected with a Conference of the Methodist Episcopal Church South (by whatever name it may be known) located in the State of North Carolina, but only those churches located in the sparsely settled rural districts of the State of North Carolina and not in any city, town or hamlet, incorporated or unincorporated, having a population in excess of fifteen hundred people according to the then last Federal census.

Four percent of said net amount not retained as aforesaid for addition to the corpus of the trust shall be paid and expended by the trustees in assisting (that is, in giving or lending in no case more than fifty per cent of what may be required for the purpose) to maintain and operate the Methodist churches of such a Conference which are located within the sparsely settled rural districts of the State of North Carolina, and not in any city, town or hamlet, incorporated or unincorporated, having a population in excess of fifteen hundred people according to the then last Federal census.

Expenditures and payments made hereunder for maintaining such superannuated preachers, and such widows and orphans, as well as for assisting to build, maintain and operate such Methodist churches, shall be in the uncontrolled discretion of the trustees as respects the time, terms, place, amounts and beneficiaries thereof and therefor; and he suggests that such expenditures and payments be made through the use of said Duke University as an agency for that purpose so long as such method is satisfactory to the trustees hereof.

SIXTH.

Subject to the other provisions of this Indenture, said trustees may pay, apply, divide and distribute such incomes, revenues and profits at such time or times as may in their discretion be found best suited to the due administration and management of this trust, but only for the purposes allowed by this Indenture.

In the event that any stock dividend or rights shall be declared upon any of the stock held under this instrument, the said stock and rights distributed pursuant thereto shall for all purposes be treated and deemed to be principal though the said stock dividend and / or rights shall represent earnings.

No trustee hereby appointed and no trustee selected in pursuance of any powers herein contained shall be required to give any bond or other security for the performance of his, her or its duties as such trustee, nor shall any trustee be required to reserve any part of the income of any investment or security for the purpose of creating a sinking fund to retire or absorb the premium in the case of bonds or any other securities whatever taken over, purchased or acquired by the trustees at a premium.

The term "subsidiary" as herein used shall mean any company at least fifty-one per cent of the voting share capital of which is owned by said Duke Power Company.

The party of the first part hereby expressly reserves the right to add to the corpus of the trust hereby established by way of last will and testament and / or otherwise, and in making such additions to stipulate and declare that such additions and the incomes, revenues and profits accruing from such additions shall be used and disposed of by the trustees for any of the foregoing and / or any other charitable purposes, with like effect as if said additions, as well as the terms concerning same and the incomes, revenues and profits thereof, had been originally incorporated herein. In the absence of any such stipulation or declaration each and every such addition shall constitute a part of the corpus of this trust for all of the purposes of this Indenture.

SEVENTH.

The party of the first part hereby declares for the guidance of the trustees hereunder:

For many years I have been engaged in the development of water powers in certain sections of the States of North Carolina and South Carolina. In my study of this subject I have observed how such utilization of a natural resource, which otherwise would run in waste to the sea and not remain and increase as a forest, both gives impetus to industrial life and provides a safe and enduring investment for capital. My ambition is that the revenues of such development shall administer to the social welfare, as the operation of such developments is administering to the economic welfare, of the communities which they serve. With these views in mind I recommend the securities of the Southern Power System (the Duke Power Company and its subsidiary companies) as the prime investment for the funds of this trust; and I advise the trustees that they do not change any such investment except in response to the most urgent and extraordinary necessity; and I request the trustees to see to it that at all times these companies be managed and operated by the men best qualified for such a service.

I have selected Duke University as one of the principal objects of this trust because I recognize that education, when conducted along sane and practical, as opposed to dogmatic and theoretical, lines, is, next to religion, the greatest civilizing influence. I request that this institution secure for its officers, trustees and faculty men of such outstanding character, ability and vision as will insure its attaining and maintaining a place of real leadership in the educational world, and that great care and discrimination be exercised in admitting as students only those whose previous record shows a character, determination and application evincing a wholesome and real ambition for life. And I advise that the courses at this institution be arranged, first, with special reference to the training of preachers, teachers, lawyers and physicians, because these are most in the public eye, and by precept and example can do most to uplift mankind, and, second, to instruction in chemistry, economics and history, especially the lives of the great of earth, because I believe that such subjects will most help to develop our resources, increase our wisdom and promote human happiness.

I have selected hospitals as another of the principal objects of this trust because I recognize that they have become indispensable institutions, not only by way of ministering to the comfort of the sick but in increasing the efficiency of mankind and prolonging human life. The advance in the science of medicine growing out of discoveries, such as in the field of bacteriology, chemistry and physics, and growing out of inventions such as the X-ray apparatus, make hospital facilities essential for obtaining the best results in the practice of medicine and surgery. So worthy do I deem the cause and so great do I deem the need that I very much hope that the people will see to it that adequate and convenient hospitals are assured in their respective communities, with especial reference to those who are unable to defray such expenses of their own.

I have included orphans in an effort to help those who are most unable to help themselves, a worthy cause, productive of truly beneficial results in which all good citizens should have an abiding interest. While in my opinion nothing can take the place of a home and its influences, every effort should be made to safeguard and develop these wards of society.

And, lastly, I have made provision for what I consider a very fertile and much neglected field for useful help in religious life, namely, assisting by way of support and maintenance in those cases where the head of the family through devoting his life to the religious service of his fellow men has been unable to accumulate for his declining years and for his widow and children, and assisting in the building and maintenance of churches in rural districts where the people are not able to do this properly for themselves, believing that such a pension system is a just call which will secure a better grade of service and that the men and women of these rural districts will amply respond to such assistance to them, not to mention our own Christian duty regardless of such results. Indeed my observation and the broad expanse of our territory make me believe it is to these rural districts that we are to look in large measure for the bone and sinew of our country.

From the foregoing it will be seen that I have endeavored to make provision in some measure for the needs of mankind along physical, mental and spiritual lines, largely confining the benefactions to those sections served by these water power developments. I might have extended this aid to other charitable objects and to other sections, but my opinion is that so doing probably would be productive of less good by reason of attempting too much. I therefore urge the trustees to seek to administer well the trust hereby committed to them within the limits set, and to this end that at least at one meeting each year this Indenture be read to the assembled trustees.

EIGHTH.

This Indenture is executed by a resident of the State of New Jersey in said State, is intended to be made, administered and given effect under and in accordance with the present existing laws and statutes of said State, notwithstanding it may be administered and the beneficiaries hereof may be located in whole or in part in other states, and the validity and construction thereof shall be determined and governed in all respects by such laws and statutes.

It being the purpose and intention of this Indenture that no part of the corpus or income of the trust estate hereby created shall ever for any cause revert to the party of the first part, or to his heirs, personal representatives or assigns, it is hereby declared that: (a) Each object and purpose of this trust shall be deemed and treated as separate and distinct from each and every other object and purpose thereof to the end that no provision of this trust shall be deemed or declared illegal, invalid or unenforceable by reason of any other provision or provisions of this trust being adjudged or declared illegal, invalid or unenforceable; and that in the event of any one or more of the provisions of this trust being declared or adjudged illegal, invalid or un-enforceable that each and every other provision of this trust shall take effect as if the provision or provisions so declared or adjudged to be illegal, invald or unenforceable had never been contained in this Indenture; and any and all properties and funds which would have been utilized under and pursuant to any provision so declared or adjudged illegal, invalid or unenforceable shall be utilized under and in accordance with the other provisions of this Indenture which shall not be declared or adjudged illegal, invalid or unen-forceable; and (b) in the event any beneficiary for which provision is herein made shall cease to exist for any cause whatever, then so much of the funds and properties of this trust as otherwise would be utilized for the same shall be thereafter utilized for the remaining objects and purposes of this trust.

IN WITNESS WHEREOF, the said JAMES B. DUKE, at his residence at Duke Farms in the State of New Jersey, has subscribed his name and af-fixed his seal to this Indenture, consisting with this page and the preceding and following pages of twenty-one pages, each page of which, except the following page, he has identified by signing his name on the margin thereof, all on the day and year first above written.

JAMES B. DUKE (L.S.)

INDEX

Barnes, Caroline, 8n

Bassett, John Spencer: on Washington Duke's political affiliation, 6; supports the library, 112; and the crisis of academic freedom at Trinity, 114–120; emphasizes importance of scholarship, 219; endorses the idea of beautiful grounds and buildings, 241–242; mentioned, 153

"Battle Ax," 64–65

Bell, William Brown: is picked by J. B. Duke to head American Cyanamid, 192; is named a trustee of The Endowment, 231

Belmont, August, Jr., 174

"Benjamin Newton Duke Institute for the Advancement of Knowledge," 255–258

Berea College, 249

Berry School, 249

Biddle, Anthony J. Drexel, Jr.: meets and marries Mary L. Duke, 175; explains Angier Duke's death, 207; in Charlotte for final conference about the indenture and is named a trustee of The Endowment, 228, 231; urges good publicity for the Duke memorial, 258–259; is divorced, 259n

Biddle, Anthony J. Drexel, III: is born in 1921, 206

Biddle, Cordelia. See Duke, Mrs. Angier B.

Biddle, Mrs. Mary Duke: is born, 87; graduates from Trinity in 1907, 113; enjoys theater and opera in New York, 171–172; begins to make gifts to Trinity, 206–207; completes gardens as memorial to her mother, 256; is divorced, 259n; mentioned, 60

Biddle, Mary Duke, II: is born in 1920, 206; pays frequent visits to her grandfather, 256

"Biltmore," 87

Blackwell Park, 92

Blackwell, William T.: as pioneer tobacco manufacturer, 17–18; 31; is converted and in economic distress, 84

Bonsack cigarette machine: plays key role in origins of American Tobacco Company, 26–55; 57

Bonsack, James A.: invents cigarette machine, 25; 41, 68

Bonsack Machine Company, 26–55, 65

Boone, Rev. T. A., 124

Boyd, William K.: on the naming of Erwin Mills, 129; supports Few's plan for memorial to B. N. Duke, 257

Brady, Anthony N., 68, 186

Branson, W. H., 124, 133

British-American Tobacco Company: and its creation in 1902, 77–80, 142, 167, 168, 186, 189

Brown, Frank C.: as professor of English, friend of Ben Duke's, and key associate of Few in matters concerning building and grounds, 226; helps plan the new buildings and find the stone for them, 240–241, 248, 250

Buffalo Lithia Springs, Virginia, 88

"Bull Durham," 17–18

Bureau of Corporations, 26, 70n

Burkholder, Charles I.: as executive in the power company and trustee of The Duke Endowment, 228, 231

Caldwell, Morrison H., 146

"Cameo," 23, 39, 40

Campbell College, 250

Camp Holmes, 9

Crowell, John F. (*continued*)
new faculty members, 95; defends academic freedom and resigns, 96; and his relations with B. N. Duke, 107; 119, 212

Daniels, Josephus: attacks President Crowell, 96; champions "white supremacy," 101; 114; leads campaign to oust Bassett, 117–118; attacks the American Tobacco Company, 159; assails J. B. Duke and power company in rate fight, 218
Davenport College, 249
Davidson College, 223; is named a beneficiary of The Duke Endowment, 229
Davis, Arthur Vining, 191, 192, 242
Day, John, 26n
Democratic party: champions "white supremacy," 101, 115–118; is blamed by Washington Duke for secession and war, 154
Department of Justice, 26, 165
The Doris Duke Trust, 246–247
"Dragoon," 66
Drummond Company, 64, 65
Drummond, Harry, 67
Duke, Angier Buchanan: is born, 87; graduates from Trinity in 1905, 113; writes his grandfather, 156; enjoys the affluent life, 173–174; meets and marries Cordelia Biddle, 175; becomes a father and is divorced, 205–206; is elected as a trustee of Trinity and makes large gifts to it, 206–207; dies in boating accident, 207; mentioned, 198
Duke, Mrs. Angier B.: meets and marries Angier B. Duke, 175; becomes a mother and is divorced, 205–206
Duke, Angier Buchanan, Jr.: is born in 1915, 205
Duke, Anthony Newton: is born in 1918, 205
Duke, Benjamin Newton: birth of, 4; on his father's politics, 6–7; attends school, 14; copes with cash shortage, 24; reports on cigarette machine, 33, 39; sends good news to his father, 68–69; becomes family's chief agent for philanthropy, 82–96; marries Sarah P. Angier and becomes a father, 87; writes his brother about the family's charities, 97–98; becomes interested in Oxford Orphanage, 98–100; as a Republican and friend of blacks, 100–104; gives Lincoln Hospital, 104; supports various colleges, 105–106; refuses pleas from Methodist bishops, 106–107; and his relations with Crowell and Kilgo, 107–109; increases his financial support of Trinity, 109–114; in "the Bassett Affair," 114–120; as staunch supporter of President Few, 120–121; loses money farming, 126–127; leads family into textile manufacturing and works closely with Erwin, 128–145; helps black capitalists start a cotton mill, 145–147; cooperates with Watts in banking and railway ventures, 148–149; buys a house in New York, 157; moves on to Fifth Avenue, 168–169, 171; introduces J. B. Duke to Mrs. Inman, 170; enjoys theater and opera in New York, 171–172; and his lifestyle in New York and Durham, 172–173; reports on birth of Doris Duke, 173; enjoys the wedding of his daughter, Mary, 175; and the electric power industry, 177–181, 186–187; as the chief benefactor and friend of Trinity College, 199–202; enters on long illness, 202–203; receives unusual letter from J. B. Duke, 205; enjoys grandchildren, 205–206; expresses affection for George Watts, 206; is saddened by son's death, 207; helps nudge J. B. Duke towards larger philanthropy, 208; is cheered by Few's letters, 212–213; aids Trinity in postwar crisis, 213–214; endorses Few's proposed University, 221; mourns J. B. Duke's death, 247; gives money to family, 247; creates memorial to his son, 248; acts as one-man foundation for colleges in the Southeast, 248–250;

is comforted by Few, 251, 255; and his last days and death, 255–256; mentioned, 16, 18, 19, 24, 28, 56, 59, 67, 72, 81, 156, 191, 197–198, 233, 260

Duke, James Buchanan (*continued*)

Durham County, North Carolina: created in 1881, 101n

Durham County Republican, 11

Durham, Dr. Bartlett, 11

Durham Home Savings Bank, 148

Durham Loan and Trust Company, 148

Durham, North Carolina: is built around a railway station, 11–12; grows rapidly, 15; goes through boom-and-bust cycle, 84–85; and its industrial development, 122–128; and the growth of its banks and railways, 148–151

Durham *Recorder*, 101, 125, 127

Durham *Tobacco Plant*, 38, 101, 123, 125, 127

Dwight, Illinois, 85–86

East Duke Building, 200

East Durham: grows around textile mills, 134

Eastman Business College, 14

Elon College, 249

Emery cigarette machine, 37, 43

E. M. Holt Plaid Mills, 129

Emory College, 116

Erwin Cotton Mills: origins and early history of, 128–145

Erwin, J. Harper: works with W. A. Erwin in textile enterprises, 133

Erwin, North Carolina: is so named in 1925, 138. *See also* Duke, North Carolina

Erwin William A.: comes to Durham, 28; works with Ben Duke in launching Erwin Mills, 129–131; sells textiles, 132; plays key role in growth of company, 133; and labor, 133–136; helps locate new mills, 137–138; has ups and downs in profits, 139–142; and the Federal tariff, 143–144; gains salary increase, 144; helps the Dukes find water-power sites, 151, 179–180

Eyde, Dr. Samuel, 191

Fairbrother, Al, 130

"Fairview," 152

Farmers' Alliance, 125

Few, William Preston: joins Trinity faculty in 1896, 111; becomes president of Trinity, 120–121; requests renaming of town of Duke, 138; and his relationship with B. N. and J. B. Duke leading toward the creation of The Duke Endowment and Duke University, 199–232; and the launching of Duke University, 233–242, 245; as friend and advisor to Ben Duke, 247–252; is embarrassed by the university's financial worries, 252; struggles against erroneous publicity, 253; strives in vain to secure an appropriate memorial to Ben Duke, 254–260; mentioned, 114, 153

Fidelity Bank, 148

Fifth Avenue: and the Dukes' move on to "Millionaires' Row," 168–171

First Presbyterian Church, 84

Fitzgerald, R. B., 157

Flexner, Dr. Abraham: advises Few concerning a medical school, 222

Flowers, Robert Lee: joins Trinity faculty, 113; reports from New York on conferences about J. B. Duke's plans, 227–228; quietly buys the "new land," 238; visits J. B. Duke at Newport, 244; helps B. N. Duke distribute money to colleges, 248–250; pays tribute to Ben Duke's role in life of Trinity-Duke, 255; mentioned, 153, 247

Ford, Henry, 243

Fort Sumter, 7

Holt, Nanaline. *See* Duke, Mrs. J. B.
Hunt, Roy A.: accompanies J. B. Duke to Canada in 1925 and describes him, 242–243
Huntoon, Frank T., 164–165

Imperial Tobacco Company, 78–79, 167
Indian Chief, 9
Industrialization: in Durham and the New South, 122–151; as related to the power
    industry, 177–194
Inman, Mrs. Walker P. *See* Duke, Mrs. J. B.
Iwaya Company, 75

Jackson, Andrew, 6
Jarvis Dormitory, 200
Jenkins, John Wilber, 165
"Jim Crow system," 100
Johns Hopkins University, 91, 95, 227
Johnson C. Smith University: is named a beneficiary of The Duke Endowment, 230
Johnson, Edward A., 147
Johnston, General Joseph E., 12
Jones, Samuel Porter, 84

Keeley, Dr. Leslie E., 86
Keeley Institute: and B. L. Duke's attendance at, 85–86; and the establishment of
    one at Greensboro, 86
Keene, James R., 67
"Kilgo-Gattis controversy," 115
Kilgo, John Carlisle: becomes president of Trinity College, 107; gains strong support
    from the Dukes, 108–114; as supporter of Bassett and academic freedom, 114–
    120; talks with Washington Duke about death, 162; is elected to episcopacy but
    keeps close ties with the Dukes, 200–202; mentioned, 120, 153, 208
Kimball and Company, 29, 37, 43, 58
Kinney Brothers (also mentioned as F. S. Kinney Company), 29, 36, 43, 57, 69
Kittrell College: as school for blacks supported by the Dukes, 97; 100; 163; receives
    large gifts and Trinity buildings from B. N. Duke, 248–249
Knights of Labor, 135
Krise, P. A., 28

Lake Toxaway, North Carolina, 170
Lander College, 250
Lee, A. Carl: entertains J. B. Duke in his home, 188
Lee, General Robert E., 10, 117
Lee, William States: plays central engineering role in development of the Dukes'
    power companies, 180–183, 186; and the Dukes' Canadian ventures, 191–192; as a
    pioneer in power industry, 193; is named a trustee of The Endowment, 231; ac-
    companies J. B. Duke to Canada, 242; mentioned, 216
Liggett and Myers Company, 15, 64, 65, 68, 69, 168
Limestone College, 250
Lincoln, Abraham, 7
Lincoln Hospital: is given to Durham's black community by Ben Duke and J. B. Duke,
    104, 224; later gifts of B. N. Duke to, 249
Lincoln Memorial University, 250
Livingstone College, 250

Lone Jack Cigarette Company: is led by Richard Wright into competition with the Dukes, 35–36, 39–40; and J. B. Duke's scorn for, 44; sues Bonsack Machine Company, 48–49

Lorillard Company, 64, 67, 168

Lorillard, Pierre, 67

Louisburg Female College, 105, 249

Lyon, Benjamin, 87

Lyon, Bertha, 87

Lyon, Edwin ("Buck"), 87

Lyon, George, 87

Lyon, Mary, 87

Lyon, Robert E.: as husband of Mary E. Duke, 87

Lyon, Mrs. Robert E.: birth of, 4; sews tobacco bags, 13–14; attends school, 14; marries Robert E. Lyon, has five children and her death, 87; and her interest in Trinity College, 95–97; is commemorated at Guilford College, 105; mentioned, 152

Lynchburg, Virginia, 35

Lynchburg *Virginian*, 125

McCredy, Mrs. Lillian Fletcher: becomes friend of J. B. Duke, 60; marries and is divorced by J. B. Duke, 161, 164–165

McKinley, President William, 80, 102, 155

McMannen, Martha: as B. L. Duke's first wife, 85

Main Street Methodist Church: begins in the Duke factory and as the special concern of the Duke family, 83, 88; and Washington Duke's deep interest in, 153–154; becomes Duke Memorial Church, 163; mentioned, 98, 152

Marshall, Edward Carrington: as business associate and friend of J. B. Duke, 194; attends conference about the indenture and is named a trustee of The Endowment, 228, 231; confers with J. B. Duke during his final illness, 244–245

Marshall, Mrs. Edward C.: as personal friend of J. B. Duke and Mrs. Duke, 194–197, 224, 243

Matsubara, S. H., 74

Mebane, B. F., 138

Mebane, Dr. G. A., 138

Mellon, Andrew: debates types of philanthropy with J. B. Duke, 242–243

Mellon, R. B., 242

Mencken, H. L., 236

Meredith College, 249

Merrick, John, 157

Methodist Episcopal Church, South: and Washington Duke's early affiliation with, 4–5; and the economic plight of its preachers and rural members, 88–90; 106; and J. B. Duke's attachment to, 188; gains annual support from J. B. Duke starting in 1915, 208–209; and Few's emphasis on Trinity's relationship with, 211; and Few's and Ben Duke's hopes for reunification of, 251–252

Metropolitan Opera, 172

Milan, Tennessee, 16

Mims, Professor Edwin, 111, 113

Moore, Dr. Aaron M., 104

Moore and Schley, 72

Morgan, J. Pierpoint, 80, 165, 172, 178

Morgan, Samuel Tate, 13

Peace Institute, 250
Pearl Cotton Mill, 133, 139
Perkins, William R.: helps arrange for biography of J. B. Duke, 165; and the Dukes'
    Canadian ventures, 191; has early draft of philanthropic plan in 1915, 197; is
    elected as trustee of Trinity, 225n; is in Charlotte for final conference about the
    indenture and is made a trustee of The Endowment, 228, 231; supports the Duke
    Memorial and gives carillon, 257–259
Philanthropy: and how the Dukes began practicing it, 82–96; and J. B. Duke's ven-
    ture into, 199, 207–246; and B. N. Duke's practice of, 200–202, 248–251
Phillips, Samuel F., 154
Piedmont and Northern Railway, 186–187
Pineland School for Girls, 249
"Pin Head," 20, 21, 23
Pittsburgh Reduction Company, 178
"Plug war" in tobacco industry, 63–69
Populist (or People's) party, 96, 101–102
Porter, Earl, 109
Price, Sir William: joins forces with J. B. Duke in Canada, 192
Princeton University, 174, 226, 236, 252
"Pro Bono Publico," 13
Progressive Era, 190

Ragland, A. T., 164
Raleigh *News and Observer*: as leader in "white supremacy" campaign, 102; attacks
    Bassett, 117–118; 159; opposes increased rates for the power company, 217–218;
    223
Raleigh, North Carolina, 3, 11, 92
Raleigh *State Chronicle*, 96, 101, 159
Randolph County, North Carolina, 91
Randolph-Macon Woman's College, 110
Rankin, Dr. Watson S.: supports building of medical school and urges establishment
    of local hospitals, 224; is named a trustee of The Endowment, 231; 252
Reidsville, North Carolina, 82
Republican party: gains political allegiance of the Dukes as well as of most blacks,
    100–104; and Washington Duke's devotion to, 154–155
Reynolds, Richard J.: proposes to sell his tobacco business, 70–71
Rhea, Madame, 21
R. J. Reynolds Tobacco Company, 70, 168
Richmond, Virginia, 20
Riverside (Dan River) Mills, 139n
Rochelle, Miss Wylanta: marries Brodie L. Duke in 1910, 204
Rockefeller Foundation, 228
Rockefeller, John D., 36, 57
Rockefeller, John D., Jr., 172
Roney, Ann, 4, 152
Roney, Artelia: as Washington Duke's second wife, 4
Roney, Elizabeth, 4
Roosevelt, President Theodore: speaks at Trinity, 120; 190; mentioned, 56, 80–81, 117
"Rough Point," 196
Russell, Daniel L.: as Republican governor and friend of the Dukes, 102
Rutherford College, 250
Ryan, Thomas Fortune, 68, 69

St. Joseph's African Methodist Church, 104n
St. Louis, Missouri, 16
St. Mary's School, 249
Salem, Virginia, 27
Salisbury, North Carolina, 9
Sands, Alex. H., Jr.: becomes executive secretary of the Duke brothers, 174n; 227;
    is named a trustee of The Endowment, 231; visits J. B. Duke at Newport, 244;
    helps B. N. Duke distribute money to colleges, 248–250
Sarah P. Duke Gardens, 256
Saskatchewan, 224
Savannah, Georgia, 21
Semmes, Rear Admiral Raphael, 10
"Semper Idem," 15
Shakespeare Club, 114
Sherman Anti-Trust Act, 56, 80, 165
Sherman, General William T., 12
Simmons, Furnifold M.: leads in Democratic "white supremacy" campaign, 102;
    as trustee of Trinity and opponent of Bassett's retention, 119; 214
Sixteenth Amendment, 190
Slade brothers, 12
Slavery, 7–8
Small, Edward Featherston: as a star salesman for W. Duke, Sons and Company, 20–
    22
Smoot, Dr. T. A., 204
Sockman, Dr. Ralph W., 256
Somerville, New Jersey, 60
South Atlantic Quarterly, 117
Southern Association of Colleges and Preparatory Schools, 113
Southern Cotton Manufacturers Association, 143
Southern Power Company: its origin and expansion, 181–184; becomes Duke Power
    Company, 185; gains increased rates, 215–218; and J. B. Duke's final plans for,
    243–245
Southern Public Utilities Company, 185
Southgate, James H.: as chairman of Trinity's trustees, 119; speaks to visiting dele-
    gation, 124; is commemorated by a dormitory, 214
Spanish-American War, 73
Springfield, Mass., *Republican*, 120
Spuches, John, 26n
Stagg, James Edward: as kinsman and executive secretary of the Dukes, 150; sends
    message for Washington Duke, 153–154; 160, 161
Standard Oil Company, 36, 57, 67
Strouse, D. B.: negotiates with Dukes as president of Bonsack Machine Company, 27–
    39; is pressed by Richard Wright, 39; plays key role in negotiations leading to
    creation of American Tobacco Company, 41–55
Sullivan and Cromwell, 50, 52
Sunday, Billy: is heard and entertained by J. B. Duke, 196
Supreme Court of the United States, 167

Terrell, H. D., 69
Thomas, James A.: represents American Tobacco Company in Orient and describes
    first meeting with J. B. Duke, 76–77; confers with Erwin, 142; heads an organiza-
    tion to memorialize Washington, B. N., and J. B. Duke, 257–259; mentioned, 252

Thomason, Edgar, 186
Tobacco, 52
Tobacco Board of Trade, 124
Toms, Clinton W.: as close friend and business associate of the Dukes, 100; plays vital
    role as liason between Few and the Dukes, 209–210, 213–214; is described as
    "righthand man" by Few, 223; assists Few in effort to honor Ben Duke, 254
Town Topics, 170
Trinity College: attracts support from Ben Duke and then Washington Duke, 90–92;
    moves to Durham, 92–94; rescued from collapse by B. N. Duke, 94–98; Kilgo
    becomes president of, 107; gains renewed support of Washington Duke, 107–109;
    gains increased support from Ben Duke, 109–114; admits women, 110–111; chal-
    lenges orthodoxies and aspires to higher standards, 112–113; and the "Bassett
    Affair," 114–120; Few becomes president of, 120–121; is increasingly supported by
    Ben Duke, 199–204; is aided by Angier Duke and Mary Duke Biddle, 206–207;
    gains increasing support from J. B. Duke, 207–215; and Few's plan to build a
    university around, 219–232; mentioned, 130, 138. *See also* Duke University
Trinity College Press, 220
Trinity Methodist Church, 83
Trinity University (in Texas), 220
Trumbauer, Horace: designs J. B. Duke's mansion on Fifth Avenue, 171; is selected
    by J. B. Duke as architect for new university, 226–227; confers with J. B. Duke on
    plans, 237, 239–242
Tyer, Andrew P.: suggests that Trinity become "Duke College," 110

Union Institute, 91
Union Tobacco Company, 68–69
United Cigar Stores Company, 71, 167
University of North Carolina, 111n, 220, 223, 234
University of Virginia, 220, 227

Valentine, Edward V., 164
van Buren, Martin, 6
Vanderbilt, Frederick W., 196
Vanderbilt, George W., 87
Vanderbilt University, 106

Wake Forest College, 223, 249
Walker, T. A., 164
Walker, William E., 8
Wannamaker, Dean W. H., 242, 250
Washington, Booker T., 103, 116, 117
Watts, Annie: marries J. S. Hill, 148
Watts, George Washington: becomes partner of the Dukes, 18–19; admonishes the
    Bonsack Machine Company, 37–39; writes important letter, 49–50; becomes dedi-
    cated Presbyterian, 84; gives Watts Hospital, 104; joins Dukes in textile enter-
    prise, 128–129; urges larger capital for Erwin Mill, 131; helps launch his son-in-
    law in business, 148; thanks J. B. Duke for loan, 149; dies in 1921, 206; supports
    Few's proposed medical school, 222; mentioned, 24, 28, 54, 56, 60, 69, 72, 86,
    133, 138, 144, 164, 202
Watts Hospital: is given by George Watts, 104; 222, 224, 237
W. Duke, Sons and Company: and the origins of, 11–18; employs immigrant cigarette-